MAPPING LIVES

The Uses of Biography

Andrew Linn
Sheffield 2002

MAPPING LIVES

The Uses of Biography

Edited by
PETER FRANCE
WILLIAM ST CLAIR

Published for THE BRITISH ACADEMY
by OXFORD UNIVERSITY PRESS

Oxford University Press, Great Clarendon Street, Oxford OX2 6DP

Oxford New York

Athens Auckland Bangkok Bogotá Buenos Aires Cape Town
Chennai Dar es Salaam Delhi Florence Hong Kong Istanbul Karachi
Kolkata Kuala Lumpur Madrid Melbourne Mexico City Mumbai Nairobi
Paris São Paulo Shanghai Singapore Taipei Tokyo Toronto Warsaw

with associated companies in Berlin Ibadan

Published in the United States
by Oxford University Press Inc., New York

British Library Cataloguing in Publication Data
Data available

ISBN 0–19–726269–4

Phototypeset by Intype London Ltd
Printed in Great Britain
on acid-free paper by
Antony Rowe Limited
Chippenham, Wiltshire

Contents

vi

Notes on Contributors

SERGEI S. AVERINTSEV is a professor at the Universities of Moscow and Vienna and a member of the Russian Academy of Sciences, the Academia Europea (London), and the Pontifical Academy of Social Sciences (Rome). His many publications include *Plutarch and Greek and Roman Biography* (Moscow, 1973; in Russian), *L'anima e lo specchio: L'universo della poetica bizantina* (Milan, 1988), *Atene e Gerusalemme* (Rome, 1994), and *The Rhetorical Sources of European Literature* (Moscow, 1996; in Russian).

MALCOLM BOWIE is Marshal Foch Professor of French Literature at the University of Oxford and director of the European Humanities Research Centre. His publications include *Henri Michaux: A Study of his Literary Works* (1973), *Mallarmé and the Art of Being Difficult* (1976), *Freud, Proust and Lacan: Theory as Fiction* (1987), *Lacan* (1991), *Psychoanalysis and the Future of Theory* (1993), and *Proust among the Stars* (1998).

IAN CHRISTIE has researched and presented many aspects of Russian and British cinema and the work of such film-makers as Sergei Eisenstein, Michael Powell, and Martin Scorsese. His particular interest in early cinema and its antecedents led to a BBC TV series and book, *The Last Machine*, in 1995. He is a regular broadcaster, an Associate Editor of the *New Dictionary of National Biography*, and Professor of Film and Media History at Birkbeck College, London.

IAN DONALDSON is Grace I Professor of English and Director of the Centre for Arts, Social Sciences and Humanities at the University of Cambridge. He is a Consultant Editor for the *New Dictionary of National Biography* (Literature 1500–1780) and is currently completing a life of Ben Jonson for the Clarendon Press.

KAY FERRES teaches cultural history and applied ethics at Griffith University, Brisbane. She has written widely on biography and autobiography, most recently as co-author (with Jane Crisp and Gillian Swanson) of *Deciphering Culture: Ordinary Curiosities and Subjective Narratives* (2000). Her current projects include a history of private life in modern Australia and a study of media environments and public reasoning.

PETER FRANCE is Professor Emeritus of French at the University of Edinburgh. He has published numerous studies of French and Russian literature and translations from Russian and French and is the editor of the *New Oxford Companion to Literature in French* (1995), the *Oxford Guide to Literature in English Translation* (2000), and (with Stuart Gillespie) the forthcoming *Oxford History of Literary Translation in English*.

RICHARD HOLMES has written lives of Shelley, Coleridge, and the young Dr Johnson, and two works of speculative biography, *Footsteps* (1985) and *Sidetracks* (2000). His books have won the Somerset Maugham Award, the James Tate Black Memorial Prize, and the Whitbread Prize. In 1997 he delivered the Johan Huizinga Memorial Lecture, University of Leiden on 'Biography and Death'. In 2001 he was appointed the first Professor of Biographical Studies at the University of East Anglia.

CHRISTINA HOWELLS is Professor of French at the University of Oxford and Fellow of Wadham College. She is author of *Sartre's Theory of Literature* (1979) and *Sartre: The Necessity of Freedom* (1988) and editor of *The Cambridge Companion to Sartre* (1992) and of a collection of essays on Sartre's literature (1995). Her most recent publication is *Derrida: Deconstruction from Phenomenology to Ethics* (1998), and she is currently working on contemporary French women philosophers.

ANN JEFFERSON is Fellow and Tutor in French at New College, Oxford. She has written on the French *nouveau roman* and on Stendhal. Her most recent publication is *Nathalie Sarraute, Fictional Theory: Questions of Difference* (2000), and she is currently working on a study of the role of biography in defining the literary.

MARK KINKEAD-WEEKES is Professor Emeritus of the University of Kent at Canterbury and has published critical books on Richardson and Golding. He edited D. H. Lawrence's *The Rainbow* in the Cambridge Edition (1989) and is the author of Volume 2 of the Cambridge Biography of Lawrence, *Triumph to Exile (1912–1922)*, published in 1996. He has written numerous articles on English, American, African, and West Indian fiction.

MARTIN McLAUGHLIN is Fiat-Serena Professor of Italian Studies and Fellow of Magdalen College, Oxford. His publications include *Literary Imitation in the Italian Renaissance* (1995), *Italo Calvino* (1998), and (as editor) *Britain and Italy from Romanticism to Modernism* (2000). He is General Editor of the *Modern Language Review*, and has translated a number of works by Italo Calvino, including *Why Read the Classics?* (1999).

LAURA MARCUS is Reader in English at the University of Sussex. Her publications include *Auto/biographical Discourses: Theory, Criticism, Practice* (1994) and *Virginia Woolf* (1997). She is currently working on a study of cinema and modernism, and is co-editing the *Cambridge History of Twentieth-Century English Literature*.

ROGER PAULIN is Schröder Professor of German at the University of Cambridge. He is the author of *Ludwig Tieck: A Literary Biography* (1985) and is completing a study of the reception of Shakespeare in Germany.

AVRIL PYMAN is Reader (Emeritus) in Russian at the University of Durham. She has published a *History of Russian Symbolism* (1994; Russian translation 1998), a biography of Alexander Blok (1979–80; Russian translation in progress) and numerous studies and translations concerning Russian art and literature.

WILLIAM ST CLAIR is Senior Research Fellow of Trinity College, Cambridge. His books include *Lord Elgin and the Marbles* (third rev. edn, 1998), *That Greece Might Still be Free* (1972), *Trelawny, the Incurable Romancer* (1978) and *The Godwins and the Shelleys: The Biography of a Family* (1989).

MIRANDA SEYMOUR is a biographer, novelist, and critic. She is Visiting Professor at Nottingham Trent University.

ELINOR S. SHAFFER is Senior Fellow of the School of Advanced Study, University of London, Director of the Research Project on the Reception of British Authors in Europe, and Deputy Director of the Centre for the Reception of German Literature and Thought (Institute of Germanic Studies, University of London). She is the author of *'Kubla Khan' and The Fall of Jerusalem: the Mythological School of Biblical Criticism and Secular Literature, 1770–1880* (1975) and editor of the annual *Comparative Criticism*.

JAMES WALTER is Professor of Australian Studies at Griffith University, Brisbane, where he was formerly director of the Institute for Modern Biography. His books include *The Leader: A Political Biography of Gough Whitlam* (1980), *Reading Life Histories* (1981), *The Ministers' Minders: Personal Advisers in National Government* (1986), *Intellectual Movements and Australian Society* (1988, with Brian Head), and *Tunnel Vision: The Failure of Political Imagination* (1996).

Editors' Note

Quotations in foreign languages are normally given in English translation. Titles of foreign works may be given in the original language, in English translation, or in both, depending on such factors as familiarity, the existence of well-known translations, and the ease with which the title can be understood by English-speaking readers. Transliterations of Russian names follow the non-academic British convention in the text (e.g. Yury Tynyanov), but in the notes an academic transliteration is used (e.g. Iurii Tynianov).

Copyright Acknowledgement

Introduction

Is biography possible? Jean-Paul Sartre's early fictional hero Roquentin is driven in *La Nausée* to the conclusion that he cannot seriously undertake to write the life of another person. Biography is for him an impossibility, a work of 'pure imagination', emanating from the biographer, and bearing no verifiable resemblance to the supposed subject. Biography is fiction, but without the freedom that the novel bestows on the writer. As Christina Howells argues in Chapter 15, one might equally well accept and welcome the subjective, hypothetical quality that biography shares with all other intellectual work; Sartre's own career as biographer gives ample proof that Roquentin's position was not his own. Even so, the reader of *La Nausée* is unlikely to come away with a comfortable view of biography.

In the early days of life-writing, when the aim was to celebrate exemplary existences and offer them as models for imitation (see Chapters 2, 3, and 5), Roquentin's worries would perhaps have seemed unfounded. The essential thing was to tell a story, following externally attested facts and meeting the general requirements of psychological plausibility, as outlined for instance in Aristotle's *Rhetoric*—a hero behaves like a hero, a saint behaves like a saint. But in an age, beginning traditionally with Rousseau's *Confessions*, where it is the inner truth (*intus et in cute*) that counts, the biographer's task looks difficult indeed. In a preamble to the *Confessions* that remained unpublished in his lifetime, Rousseau justified his own enterprise of self-revelation by saying that even those who claim to know human nature tend to know only themselves, and constantly misinterpret other people in the light of their own experience, creating 'ingenious novels' in their attempts to write truthful lives. An autobiography, on the other hand, is based in his view on real inside knowledge and will therefore offer readers a piece of reliable evidence that will help them better to know themselves and others: 'No-one can write a man's life but himself'.[1]

It might indeed seem plausible that we know ourselves better than we know other people, or better than they know us. Even so, the *Confessions*, like the myriad autobiographies they have indirectly engendered, make it

[1] See Jean-Jacques Rousseau, *Oeuvres complètes*, ed. M. Raymond and B. Gagnebin (Paris, 1969–), I, 1148–55.

only too obvious that self-knowledge can be as problematic as knowledge of others. David Hume wrote of Rousseau that nobody knew themselves less well than he did—whom should we believe, the sceptically reasonable outsider or the passionate insider? But if we cannot know ourselves, how can we hope to know and understand other people, even those closest to us, even those for whom we have the fullest documentary record? Nowadays the biographer is offered various aids to understanding—psychoanalysis being perhaps the most insistent—but none of these comes with any guarantee of reliability. And at the same time, other modern or postmodern theories of various kinds insist on the complex, fragmented nature of the 'self', very different from the coherent individuality which much traditional biography aimed to uncover.

For the sceptical reader, then, biography must be a suspect enterprise. But this of course is what gives it its perennial interest, for both writers and readers, encouraging the production of ever new biographies of the famous (and very occasionally the obscure), none of which can ever be, as they say, definitive. And it is this difficulty, among other things, which has justified the succession of twentieth-century attempts to found a 'new biography'.[2]

To write the life of another may appear a quixotic enterprise, but when that other is a writer (as is so often the case, including most of the cases studied in the present volume), equally sceptical voices may be raised to call into question the relevance of the exercise. Is it not better to go straight to the copious records they have so often left, their published novels, poems, essays, memoirs, or letters? For many readers the answer is clearly no. Often biographies of poets prove more attractive than the poems themselves, and it is against this all-too-human tendency to prefer life to letters that so much twentieth-century literary theory, from the Russian Formalists on, rejected the 'biographical fallacy'. Over half a century ago, René Wellek and Austin Warren argued that while biography may have its value for the student of literature, for instance in explaining allusions, 'the biographical approach actually obscures a proper comprehension of the literary process, since it breaks up the order of literary tradition to substitute the life cycle of an individual'.[3]

Or if we prefer to listen to the writer rather than the academic, we may heed the warnings of Marcel Proust, himself the victim of massive

---

[2] Early twentieth-century concepts of the 'new biography' are discussed here in Chapter 11. For one recent example among many, see Jo Burr Margadant, ed., *The New Biography: Performing Femininity in Nineteenth-Century France* (Berkeley, Los Angeles, and London, 2000), where the 'new biography' is placed at the service of women's history.

[3] René Wellek and Austin Warren, *Theory of Literature* (Harmondsworth, 3rd edn, 1963), Chapter 7, 'Literature and Biography', pp. 75–80.

biographies, against the illusion that a knowledge of the writer's social self reveals anything about the *moi profond*, the self that writes. It is true that since Roland Barthes and Michel Foucault proclaimed the Death of the Author back in the 1960s, the author has obstinately refused to lie down (Foucault himself being the subject of several narratives), but it remains difficult for literary scholars (and their colleagues in cognate disciplines) to approach biography without some misgiving. In the final chapter of the present volume, James Walter outlines some recent attempts to deal with such worries.

Nevertheless, for all that can be said against biography, it remains irresistibly attractive to writers and readers alike. Thus Avril Pyman, in Chapter 9, shows how the severity of the Russian Formalists' anti-biographical principles was tempered by the actual practice of a Tynyanov. If even those opposed to literary biography succumb to it, this must be partly because they are aware that this genre, more than criticism or theory, reaches out to a broad public, indeed that it is a form of literature in its own right, comparable (for better or worse) with the master-genre of modern times, the novel, and perhaps seen by the more naïve as possessing the added advantage of being 'real'.

Putting it more strongly, Yeats once declared that 'we may come to think that nothing exists but a stream of souls, that all knowledge is biography'. Certainly life-writing has played a vital role in the history of European culture (to speak only of Europe), from Antiquity to the present. Some of the reasons for this are explored below: providing inspiring examples to be imitated, celebrating the great men and women of a nation, exalting the self-image of a profession, showing how an individual life takes a meaningful shape, illuminating the true meaning of poetry, laying bare an existential project, allowing a new understanding of gender roles in society, and so on. Above all, though, biography gives *pleasure* by satisfying curiosity and by telling good stories. Or, as Dr Johnson, at once a great biographer and biographee,[4] put it in his essay on the subject in *The Rambler* no.60 (1750), 'no species of writing seems more worthy of cultivation than biography, since none can be more delightful or more useful, none can more certainly enchain the heart by irresistible interest, or more widely diffuse instruction to every diversity of condition'. In our own times, in the English-speaking world at least, we have only to look at the shelves of bookshops or the book pages in the newspapers to become aware of the extraordinary and apparently growing popularity of biography.

It is this vitally important cultural phenomenon which we are seeking to

---

[4] On Johnson as biographer, see Richard Holmes, *Dr Johnson & Mr Savage* (London, 1983).

investigate in the present volume, produced for the centenary of the British Academy. Taking its origins in the work of the Section of the Academy concerned with 'languages, literatures, and other media', it seems appropriate that this collective publication should offer a historical, theoretical, and critical perspective on biography, and particularly, though not exclusively, on the biography of writers, philosophers, and other cultural creators. Our concern is not simply with the writing of biography, its changing form and recurrent problems, but with the functions which it can serve and has served in different societies, its *uses*.

There have been a fair number of books, conferences, and the like devoted to biography in recent years, many of them, like the present one, bringing together a number of contributors. One quite common formula is to invite eminent practitioners to discuss their craft, the problems they encountered, the approaches they adopted. This element is present here too; several of our contributors have written major biographies, and in some cases they use their own experience to pose more general problems or to argue for particular ways of proceeding. The main focus of the book, however, is critical and historical—not so much 'How I wrote my biography' as 'What has biography been, what role has it played, in a given social setting?'

Some of the chapters that follow are predominantly theoretical or critical, posing such questions as the possibility of biography as an academic course (Chapter 1), the relevance of biography to literary criticism (Chapter 8), the contribution of psychoanalysis to the practice of biography (Chapter 10), the reliability of archival evidence (Chapter 12), the problem of chronology (Chapter 13), the ethics of biography—what to reveal, what to hide (Chapter 14), the new possibilities offered by cinema (Chapter 16), and the demands placed on biography by feminist and gender history (Chapter 17). But theory is illuminated by practice. All of these chapters tend to focus on particular cases, biographers, and biographies: Chapter 8 is entirely devoted to Sainte-Beuve; Chapter 10 almost entirely to Freud. By the same token, the particular case studies of Tynyanov (Chapter 9) and Sartre (Chapter 15) immediately raise theoretical and critical problems, as do those chapters (2, 3, 4, 5, 6, 7, 11) which could be broadly described as historical.

History and cultural geography are essential elements here. Our assumption is that biography is not the same, and does not perform the same tasks, at different times and in different places. Nor can we assume some sort of progressive movement away from primitive and outmoded forms towards the ideal biography of the future. Various kinds of 'new biography', implying a refusal of the 'old biography', emerged during the twentieth century—and it is probable that we shall not easily return to hagiography and the exemplary celebration of the great. Even so, one may doubt if old impulses die out entirely; some element of celebration is present in those biographies which see themselves as most scientific, critical, or aware of the complexities and contradictions of life. And in any case, it is important not to forget how genres change, how the same name can hide many different practices. This book is not, of course, a full-scale history of biography, but it does offer some sense of the often radical shifts in the life of the subject. So we have included here essays on Antiquity, the Italian Renaissance, seventeenth-century England and eighteenth-century France before coming on to the area of our principal concern, the nineteenth and twentieth centuries. And we have looked abroad, to Germany, Russia, and France, aware that there is a temptation, in writing about biography in English, to forget that it may take on different forms and perform different functions in other cultures.

Mindful, then, of all that can be urged against biography, we offer this volume as a critical homage to a genre which has certainly not yet said its last word. It remains only to thank our contributors for providing such positive and thought-provoking responses to our invitation to take part in this celebration.

Peter France and William St Clair
June 2001

1

The Proper Study?

RICHARD HOLMES

As he set out to wreak havoc on his four Eminent Victorians in 1918, Lytton Strachey tenderly suggested that English biography might eventually rediscover its true calling as 'the most delicate and most humane of all the branches of the art of writing'. Some three generations later, the form has certainly expanded out of all recognition, gained a broad new readership, and achieved considerable (though not unchallenged) intellectual authority. At its best, I think, biography can indeed now call itself a true 'art of writing', and also perhaps a humanist discipline. It is 'the proper study of mankind'. But is it an art and a discipline that can also be taught? Is it a proper subject for an *academic* course?

This may seem an odd, even an indiscreet, place to ask such a question. But as Strachey himself said, discretion is not the better part of biography; and it raises some rather interesting issues about the *value*, as well as the nature, of the form. For a start, it has always seemed to me that the essential spirit of biography—of English biography at least—has been a maverick and unacademic one. (The French, German, and American traditions are different for interesting reasons which appear elsewhere in this book.) For some three hundred years, from John Aubrey via Lytton Strachey to Peter Ackroyd, its most exciting and innovative work has been done outside the established institutes of learning, and beyond the groves of academe. It has retained an uncloistered and anarchic spirit. As Somerset Maugham once remarked: 'There are three rules for writing biography, but fortunately no one knows what they are'.

Academia, in its turn, has not been very keen to recognize biography, especially of a literary kind. It has regularly assaulted the form as trivial, revisionist, exploitative, fictive, a corrupter of pure texts and probably also of scholarly morals. Most fatal objection of all, biography has no serious poetics, no set of post-Aristotelian regulations, and is therefore irredeemably subjective.

A whole essay, and indeed a very lively one, could be given over entirely to the history of these academic attacks, with some added firepower from the novelists. (John Updike remarked recently in the *New York Review of Books* of 4 February 1999 that most biographies 'are just novels with indexes'.) But one typical example may serve, from a study of Percy Bysshe Shelley's vegetarianism. This opens with the kind of witty broadside against all previous biographical follies that has become almost *de rigueur* in university English departments.

> Assuming that any biography is an imaginative reconstruction of events to suit certain needs of the biographer [. . .], a balanced assessment of Shelley's vegetarianism must negotiate between the medically unfit moral puritan, the *chic* radical, the humanitarian grazer, the introspective self-healer, the secular radical and the near-New Ager, presented in the various accounts of his life.' (Timothy Morton, *Shelley and the Revolution in Taste*, 1994, p. 80)

This kind of stand-off between gown and town (as it were) has been going on for a long time. In his letter of June 1680, Aubrey mischievously teased the Oxford historian Anthony à Wood with the improper and extracurricular nature of the biographical researches for *Brief Lives*. 'I here lay downe to you (out of the conjunct friendship between us) the Trueth, the naked and plain trueth [. . .] which is here exposed so bare, that the very *pudenda* are not covered'. Wood donnishly retaliated by calling Aubrey 'a shiftless person, roving and maggotie-headed, and sometimes little better than crazed'.

Yet even Aubrey regretted not being able to continue studying at Oxford. This is one of the themes of his own perceptive, third-person entry in *Brief Lives*. 'When a boy, he did ever love to converse with old men, as Living Histories'. Here he quotes Horace on what he had missed by being forced to leave the university: *Atque inter sylvas Academi quarere verum/ Dura sed amovere loco me tempora grato* (And so among the groves of Academe to seek the Truth/But harsh times drove me from that pleasant spot).

So the question I want to ask is whether the moment has come for biography formally to return to 'that pleasant spot', the Academy? And if so, on what terms? For me, this question has a peculiar autobiographical twist. If I were writing my own Brief Life, I would record that for thirty-five years I have worked outside academia. But in autumn 2000, out of the blue, I was invited to help pioneer and teach a postgraduate course in 'Life-Writing'. Would I consider taking on a new Chair of Biographical Studies at the University of East Anglia?

At the time of writing these reflections, I still do not know if I should accept the invitation. But for weeks I have been asking myself (and my long-suffering biographical colleagues) whether it is possible, or even desirable, to attempt such a course within the framework of an academic discipline. Can Biography really be turned into a university subject, based on an organized series of booklists, seminars, lectures, and of course a *body of theory*?

What would be its content, what would be its aims, what would be its benefits to the student? What would be its ultimate purpose? Is one being asked to do something quite humble, like teaching the basic methods of sound biographical research—working with archives, public records, letter collections, and carefully constructing life chronologies, character portraits and social contexts? Or something more ambitious, as in a Creative Writing course (famous at East Anglia), to launch a new generation of young biographical practitioners, who are really committed to biography as an 'art of writing'? Or something quite monumental—the founding of a Norwich School of Biography, perhaps?

So initially, on what grounds could one claim Biography as—at least potentially—a genuine humanist discipline? It is certainly a recognizable literary genre, although that is not quite the same thing. Yet its intellectual independence was proclaimed at least as early as Plutarch, writing in Greece around AD 110, and thus at roughly the same period as the later Gospel writers (who had very different ambitions). In the opening of his Life of Alexander, Plutarch distinguished Biography convincingly from History, and gave it both an ethical and a psychological dimension:

> It must be borne in mind that my design is not to write Histories, but Lives. And the most glorious exploits do not always furnish us with the clearest discoveries of virtue or vice in men; sometimes a matter of less moment, an expression or a jest, informs us better of the characters and inclinations, than the most famous sieges, the greatest armaments, or the bloodiest battles whatsoever. Therefore as portrait-painters are more exact in the lines and features of the face, in which character is seen, than in the other parts of the body, so I must be allowed to give my more particular attention to the marks and indications of the souls of men, and while I endeavour by these to portray their lives, may be free to leave more weighty matters and great battles to be treated by others. (*Plutarch's Life of Alexander*, Dryden translation, ed. A. H. Clough, 1864)

Roger North, that subtle eighteenth-century memoir writer (not to be confused with Plutarch's Tudor translator, Thomas North), crisply summarized the argument as follows: 'What signifies it to us, how many battles Alexander fought. It were more to the purpose to say how often he was drunk' (see *Biography as an Art: Selected Criticism 1560–1960*, ed. James

L. Clifford, 1962). Plutarch's chilling description of Alexander's drunken
rages, or equally of his post-battle gallantry and good humour, fully bears
out this claim to peer behind the mask of public behaviour and events, into
an individual 'soul'. Who can forget the wonderfully funny and unexpected
description of Alexander (after the bloody defeat of his great Persian enemy)
sardonically examining the luxury fittings of Darius's bathroom, with its
ornate and ridiculous 'waterpots, pans and ointment boxes, all of gold
curiously wrought'. And then how Plutarch clinches the scene, with Alexander's stinging jest: 'So this, it seems, is royalty!'

John Dryden, while preparing his edition of Plutarch (1683), defined
the genre similarly as 'Biographia, or the histories of Particular Lives'. But
he chose to emphasize even further its unique quality of human intimacy.

> There [in works of History] you are conducted only into the Rooms of State;
> but here you are led into the private lodgings of the hero: you see him in his
> undress, and are made familiar with his most private actions and conver-
> sations. You may behold a Scipio and a Lelius gathering cockle-shells on the
> shore, Augustus playing at bounding-stones with boys; and Agesilaus riding
> on a hobby-horse among his children. The pageantry of life is taken away;
> you see the poor reasonable animal, as naked as ever Nature made him; are
> made acquainted with his passions and his follies, and find the demy-God a
> man.

This touching vision of 'the poor reasonable animal', shorn not only of
divine but even of heroic status, ushered in the first great age of English
biography. Intimacy is subversive of grandeur and ceremonial, though not
necessarily of greatness or, indeed, goodness. This notion of a popular, even
a subversive discipline, which celebrates and studies a *common* human
nature (shared by criminals as well as kings), would seem to me crucial. It
is central to the claim that the English form has become progressively
greater than hagiography, formal obituary, modish gossip, or historical
propaganda. It suggests a profound humanist ambition, which could indeed
provide the basis for true study.

Samuel Johnson gave this theoretical weight and intense personal conviction in his remarkable *Rambler* no. 60, 'On Biography' (1750). Here,
arguably, is the first deliberate statement of a biographical poetics.

> No species of writing seems more worthy of cultivation than biography, since
> none can be more delightful or more useful, none can more certainly enchain
> the heart by irresistible interest, or more widely diffuse instruction to every
> diversity of condition [. . .]. I have often thought that there has rarely passed
> a Life of which a judicious and faithful narrative would not be useful. For,
> not only every man has, in the mighty mass of the world, great numbers in
> the same condition with himself, to whom mistakes and miscarriages, escapes
> and expedients, would be of immediate and apparent use; but there is such
> an uniformity in the state of man, considered apart from adventitious and

separable decorations and disguises, that there is scarce any possibility of good or ill, but is common to human kind [. . .]. We are all prompted by the same motives, all deceived by the same fallacies, all animated by hope, obstructed by danger, entangled by desire, and seduced by pleasure.

It is no coincidence that, in practice, the first short eighteenth-century masterpieces of English biography were about marginal and disreputable figures, not kings or kaisers. These were Daniel Defoe's two biographical studies of the housebreaker and incorrigible escape-artist Jack Sheppard (1724) and Johnson's own brilliant *Life of Mr Richard Savage* (1744), an account of the indigent poet and convicted murderer. All three works turn conventional moral judgements—and traditional social hierarchies—upside down, by insisting on the value and interest of common humanity, the universal 'possibilities of good or ill', wherever they are to be found. Johnson wrote: 'Those are no proper judges of his conduct who have slumber'd away their time on the down of plenty, nor will a wise man presume to say, "Had I been in Savage's condition, I should have lived, or written, better than Savage" '.

Boswell's own *Life of Johnson* (1791) gave this notion of common humanity the proportions of an epic—Johnson as Everyman. And the powerful idea of the marginal figure who is still representative of 'human kind' (in this case specifically 'woman kind') recurs in William Godwin's strikingly dramatic and candid life of his wife Mary Wollstonecraft, the *Memoirs of the Author of a Vindication of the Rights of Woman* (1798).

By the early nineteenth century, the cultural significance of biography's growing popularity was broadly recognized, and was already receiving some study, though not necessarily favourable. Coleridge wrote about it in his journal *The Friend* (1810), calling it the product of 'emphatically an Age of Personality'; and Wordsworth attacked the use of ungentlemanly revelations in a contemporary *Life of Burns* (1828). But in fact Romanticism embraced both the idea of 'personality' and of personal 'revelations' . In 1813 Robert Southey clinched his appointment as Poet Laureate by writing a short and wonderfully vivid biography of Nelson, which eventually became by far the most successful work he ever published. It enshrined the dead wartime leader as a new kind of national hero, a people's hero with the common touch, flawed (Emma Hamilton) but open-hearted and irresistibly courageous and *familiar*. 'The death of Nelson was felt in England as something more than a public calamity; men started at the intelligence, and turned pale, as if they had heard of the loss of a dear friend' (*Nelson*, 1813, Chapter 9).

Similarly, in 1817 Mary Shelley chose to educate Frankenstein's Monster in the complex ways of human civilization by making him read biography ('a volume of Plutarch's *Lives*') as well as Goethe's fashionable novel *The*

Sorrows of Young Werther and Milton's epic poem *Paradise Lost*. While fiction seems to emphasize the Creature's isolation and sense of exclusion, biography consoles him. Hidden in his woodshed, the Monster reflects: 'I learned from Werther's imagination's despondency and gloom: but Plutarch taught me high thoughts; he elevated me beyond the wretched sphere of my own reflections, to admire and love the heroes of past ages' (*Frankenstein*, 1818 edn, Chapter 7).

One cannot help wondering which exemplary biography Mary Shelley would have chosen to give the Monster today. Currently some 3,500 new titles are published in Britain a year. (However, this figure includes autobiography, ghosted books, and many pictorial show business biographies which are surely closer to the older forms of hagiography or demonology.) Virtually all bookshops have a Biography section which is larger than any other genre except Fiction, and is quite separate from History. Waterstone's have even recently renamed this section as a new category, calling it simply and demotically: 'People'. This seems to emphasize the continuing notion of a popular Pantheon, a kind of intimate collective memory of 'common human kind', which offers ever-expanding possibilities for serious study.

Yet commercially the genre of biography is still regarded as an ephemeral and utilitarian, rather than as a permanent art form. It is strongly content-orientated, and it is shelved alphabetically by subject, not by author. Even Boswell is shelved under J for Johnson. This seems to imply that most biographies are defined crucially by their subject matter, and don't really have a significant authorial status for the reading public. Essentially biographies are understood to write themselves, self-generated (like methane clouds) by their dead subjects. This popular misconception still affects much newspaper reviewing of new biography, which consists of a critical précis of the life, with perhaps two brief mentions of the actual author somewhere in the third and in the penultimate paragraph.

Yet, if biography is to provide a genuine academic course, it must surely concern itself primarily with the outstanding biographers, as literary artists, and their place in the changing history of the form. This would imply an agreed canon of classic works, and of classic biographical authors, as it does in the novel. But has such a canon ever been put forward or generally accepted? Does biography have a widely acknowledged Great Tradition, in the same way that the novel does?

There has been a considerable growth in modern biographical theory, especially since Leon Edel's *Writing Lives: Principia Biographica* (1984). But surprisingly little has been written about the specific question of a canon, between Harold Nicolson's *The Development of English Biography* of 1927 and Paula Backscheider's *Reflections on Biography* of 1999. Indeed Backscheider concludes that the need to establish and teach a canon is a paramount requirement for the future evolution of the genre as a whole: 'If biography is to come closer to reaching its potential either as an art or a cultural force, then readers must demand art, collect the books, think in terms of canons and schools, and biographers must have the daring to accept the calling' (*Reflections*, p. 234).

But what about the daring to propose a canon? Leaving aside Classical and Renaissance precursors, and concentrating on the early modern English tradition only, there are perhaps less than half a dozen names which would immediately spring to mind. These might be Johnson's *Lives of the Poets*, Boswell's *Johnson*, Mrs Gaskell's *Charlotte Brontë*, and Strachey's *Eminent Victorians*—though technical objections can be made to all of them as 'impure' biography. Johnson, it could be argued, was writing critical essays; Boswell a dramatized memoir; Mrs Gaskell a romantic novel; and Strachey a social satire.

However, let me propose for argument's sake a possible canon of twenty-five classic English works written between 1670 and 1970, which might form the basis for postgraduate study. (I give abbreviated working titles, though the full original versions are often revealing, as when Godwin omits to mention his wife's name but describes her only as 'the Author' of her most controversial book):

Izaak Walton: *Lives of John Donne* and *George Herbert* (1640, rev.1670)

John Aubrey: *Brief Lives* (1670–88, first published selection 1813)

John Dryden: *Plutarch's Parallel Lives* (translations edited 1683–6)

Daniel Defoe: *The History of John Sheppard* and *A Narrative of John Sheppard* (attributed, 1724)

Samuel Johnson: *The Life of Mr Richard Savage* (1744)

James Boswell: *The Life of Samuel Johnson LL.D.* (1791)

William Godwin: *Memoirs of the Author of a Vindication of the Rights of Woman* (1798)

Robert Southey: *Life of Nelson* (1813)

William Hazlitt: *The Spirit of the Age* (1825)

Thomas Moore: *Life and Letters of Lord Byron* (1830)

John Gibson Lockhart, *The Life of Sir Walter Scott* (1837–8)

Thomas Carlyle: *Life of John Sterling* (1851)

Elizabeth Gaskell: *Life of Charlotte Brontë* (1857)

G. H. Lewes: *Life of Goethe* (1855, rev. 1863)

Alexander and Anne Gilchrist: *Life of William Blake* (1863)

John Forster: *The Life of Charles Dickens* (1872–4)

David Brewster: *Life of Sir Isaac Newton* (1855, rev. 1880)

J. A. Froude: *Life of Thomas Carlyle* (1882–4)

Lytton Strachey: *Eminent Victorians* (1918)

Geoffrey Scott: *Portrait of Zélide* (1925)

A. J. A. Symons: *The Quest For Corvo* (1934)

Cecil Woodham-Smith: *Florence Nightingale* (1950)

Leon Edel: *Henry James* (1953–72)

Richard Ellmann: *James Joyce* (1959, rev. 1982)

Michael Holroyd: *Lytton Strachey* (1967–8, rev. 1994)

All these books could be justified on grounds of literary quality, the historic pictures they achieve of their subjects, and their significance within the development of the form. Yet one is immediately aware of several objections to their place in a canon for study. First there is the simple problem of elephantine length, upon which Virginia Woolf once expatiated with such eloquent irony in *Orlando*: 'documents, both private and historical, have made it possible to fulfil the first duty of a biographer, which is to plod, without looking to right or left, in the indelible footprints of truth; unenticed by flowers; regardless of shade; on and on methodically till we fall plump into the grave and write *finis* on the tombstone above our heads' (*Orlando*, 1928, Chapter 2).

This is particularly evident in the nineteenth-century convention of inflating a chronological narrative with enormous excerpts from original letters and diaries, which by modern scholarly convention would now be published separately. For example, Froude's *Carlyle* (though one of the greatest studies of Victorian marriage) is in four volumes; Lockhart's *Scott* is in seven. How are these dinosaurs to be recovered? Perhaps by editing?

Next, there are certain obvious biases within the selection. There is the large predominance of literary biography, over scientific, political, or military. Equally, there is the overwhelming predominance of men over women, either as biographers or as subjects. This seems historically unavoidable. Aubrey included only three women in his *Brief Lives*, though one was the remarkable Countess of Pembroke; Johnson wrote nothing about his large circle of brilliant blue-stocking friends; Hazlitt included none in *The Spirit of the Age*. It was only with the late recognition of the mid-Victorian heroine—Charlotte Brontë, Florence Nightingale, Mary Somerville, Caroline Herschel—that the biography of women began to emerge, and only with modern feminism that it began to have serious impact on the form after 1970.

But there is a wholly different level of objection. How can the term 'classic' (in the sense of unique and enduring) be applied to even the greatest of these biographies, when their facts and interpretations will always be altered by later research? This crucial question of the outdating of any biography raises several issues. At the simplest level, it is a question of factual accuracy. This is an obvious problem in the case of Thomas Moore, who altered and spliced so many of Byron's letters and journal entries; or Boswell, who could not fully come to terms with Johnson's early, unsettled years in London; or Mrs Gaskell, who suppressed much of Charlotte Brontë's amorous life and correspondence with Monsieur Heger. (These letters, largely unsent, were published after her death; for their use in *Villette*, see Chapter 7 below.)

This leads on to a much larger, almost philosophical question about the apparently ephemeral nature of biographical knowledge itself. If no biography is ever 'definitive', if every life-story can be endlessly retold and reinterpreted (there are now more than ten lives of Mary Wollstonecraft, thirty lives of Johnson, two hundred lives of Byron, four hundred lives of Hitler), how can any one life ever hope to avoid the relentless process of being superseded, outmoded, and eventually forgotten: a form of auto-destruction which has no equivalent in the novel?

This would also seem to imply that as 'factual content' grows out of date, the artistic structure is fatally weakened from within. When we learn of the young actress Ellen Ternan and her place in Dickens's life, from the modern biographies by Peter Ackroyd (1990) and then Claire Tomalin (1991), doesn't this fatally superannuate John Forster's *Life*? (Forster mentioned Ellen Ternan only once—in his index, with reference to Dickens's will). Or when we discover from Richard Westfall's magisterial *Never at Rest* (1980, abridged as *The Life of Isaac Newton*, 1993) the real extent of Newton's astrological interests, and their impact on his concept of universal gravity, doesn't this weaken the authority of Sir David Brewster's great two-volume *Life, Writings, and Discoveries of Sir Isaac Newton* (1855)?

In fact, one might suggest that precisely here lies one of the greatest arguments in favour of the disciplined, rigorous academic study of biography as a developing form. It is exactly in these shifts and differences—factual, formal, stylistic, ideological, aesthetic—between early and later biographies that students could find such an endless source of interest and historical information. They would discover how reputations developed, how fashions changed, how social and moral attitudes moved, how standards of judgement altered, as each generation, one after another, continuously reconsidered and idealized or condemned its forebears in the writing and rewriting of biography.

Here one is considering virtually a new discipline, which might be called comparative biography. It is based on the premise that every biography is the interpretation of a life, and that many different interpretations are always possible. (If there can be innumerable different interpretations of a fictional character—Hamlet, Moll Flanders, Mr Pickwick, Tess—then surely there can be as many of an historical one.) So in comparative biography the student examines the handling of one subject by a number of different biographers, and over several different historical periods. In the case of Shelley, for example, one might compare the biographies by his contemporaries Hogg and Peacock (1858) with the late Victorian one by Professor Edward Dowden (1886), the jazz age one by André Maurois (1924), and the American New Deal biography by Newman Ivey White (1940). The 'Shelley' that we have inherited has grown out of all these versions, and he in turn reflects back a particular picture of each generation which has, alternately, been inspired or bored or scandalized by him.

Some comparative work has already begun. Sylva Norman has written about the strange shifts in Shelley's posthumous reputation in *Flight of the Skylark* (1954); Ian Hamilton about the cumulative influence of literary executors in *Keepers of the Flame* (1992); Geoffrey Cantor about changing 'public images' of scientific heroism in the Victorian biographies of Michael Faraday (see *Telling Lives in Science*, edited by Michael Shortland and Richard Yeo, 1996); or very recently Lucasta Miller in her study of the increasingly exotic literary cult of Haworth Parsonage in *The Brontë Myth* (2001).

The notion of comparative biography also raises the question of the perceived limits of the traditional form. Ever since Edmund Gosse wrote a second child's-eye version of his father's biography (1890), as *Father and Son* (1907), and Virginia Woolf transformed a biography of Vita Sackville-West into the historical romance *Orlando* (1928), the boundaries between fact and fiction have become controversial and perilous. These experimental novel-biographies also form part of the tradition that might be usefully taught and studied. No critical account of modern ideas about biographical narrative could ignore Julian Barnes's *Flaubert's Parrot* (1984) or A. S. Byatt's *Possession* (1990).

The subtle question of the nature of non-fiction narrative, and how it differs from fiction, offers one of the most fascinating and fruitful of all possible fields for students. It is, I think, different from the conventional discipline of historiography. All good biographers struggle with a particular tension between the scholarly drive to assemble facts as dispassionately as possible and the novelistic urge to find shape and meaning within the apparently random circumstances of a life. Both instincts are vital, and a biography is dead without either of them. We make sense of life by establishing 'significant' facts, and by telling 'revealing' stories with them.

But the two processes are rarely in perfect balance or harmony. Indeed with some recent postmodern biography the two primal identities of the biographer—the scholar and the storyteller—may seem to split completely apart, and fragment into two or more voices. This happens at unexpected, diverting moments in Peter Ackroyd's *Dickens* (1990), or in a rich, continuous polyphonic way with Anne Wroe's *Pilate: The Biography of an Invented Man* (1999), or in a deliberately sinister, insidious, disconcerting manner with Andrew Motion's *Wainewright the Poisoner* (2000). Yet this too is part of an older tradition already explored in Woolf's *Flush* (1933), the playful biography of Elizabeth Barrett Browning's dog (with its genuine scholarly notes). Indeed, I believe it goes back through certain texts as far as the eighteenth century, and I have tried to investigate the roots of these bi-polar forces (which may also be described as 'judging versus loving') in *Dr Johnson & Mr Savage* (1993). It is, of course, tricky terrain, the impossible meeting of what Woolf herself called 'granite and rainbow'. But for that very reason, and because it requires a growing degree of critical self-knowledge, it could be rewarding for students to explore further.

Equally, the close textual study of biography could throw much more light on the unsuspected role of rhetorical devices such as 'suspense', 'premonition', 'anecdote', and 'ventriloquism' in the apparently transparent narrative forms of life-writing. And this in turn could reflect on the way that we are all, continuously, reinterpreting our own lives with story-based notions such as 'success', 'failure', 'chance', 'opportunity' and 'achievement'. So biography could have a moral role, though not exactly the naïve exemplary one assigned to it by the Victorians. It may never teach us how to behave, how to self-help, how to find role models. But it might teach us simply how to understand other people better. And hence, through 'the other', ourselves. This, too, is part of the potential humanist discipline.

So, finally, I return to the fundamental question: what would students be studying biography *for*? To discover and appreciate a great literary tradition: certainly. To learn both the values and the limitations of accuracy and historical understanding: without doubt. To grasp something of the complications of human truth-telling, and to write well about them: yes, with any luck. But above all, *to exercise empathy*, to enter imaginatively into another place, another time, another life. And whether that can be taught, I still have no idea at all.

Clearly, such neo-romantic aspirations for biography require an ironic postscript. So here are my Ten Commandments for any other practising biographers who are already bravely teaching in the postgraduate seminar rooms of life-writing (or of Life).

1   Thou shalt honour Biography as living, experimental, and multifarious in all its Forms.

2   Thou shalt not covet thy neighbour's Novel, for there are as many rooms in the Mansion of Non-Fiction as there are in the House of Fiction.

3   Thou shalt recognize that Biography is always at best a Celebration of Human Nature, and all its glorious Contradictions.

4   Thou shalt demand that it be greater than Gossip, because it is concerned with historical Justice and Human Understanding.

5   Thou shalt require that it chronicles an outward story (the Facts) only to reveal an inward life (a Comprehensive Truth).

6   Thou shalt see that this Truth can be told, and re-examined, again and again unto each Generation.

7   Thou shalt greet it as a Life-giving form, as it is concerned with Human struggle and the Creative spirit, which we all share.

8   Thou shalt relish it as a Holiday for the Human Imagination—for it takes us away to another place, another time, and another Identity—where we can begin quietly to reflect on our own Lives and come back refreshed.

9   Thou shalt be immodestly Proud of it, as it is something that the English have given to the World, like cricket, and parliament, and the Full Cooked Breakfast.

10   And, lastly, thou shalt be Humble about it, for it demonstrates that we can never know, or write, the Last Word about the Human Heart.

2

From Biography to Hagiography: Some Stable Patterns in the Greek and Latin Tradition of Lives, including Lives of the Saints

SERGEI S. AVERINTSEV

Let us begin with some lexical reflections on the words used in my title. We speak of 'biography' and 'hagiography'—but although both of these terms have Greek roots, neither of them would be familiar in its modern meaning to any Greek-speaking person of Classical, early Christian or medieval times. The ponderous composite noun *biographia* was created, as far as we know, not earlier than the sixth century AD, but even then it occurs as a *hapax legomenon*, a very special invention not for common usage. As for the words *hagiographos, hagiographia*, etc., they are used often enough in early Christian literature, but have nothing to do with the Lives of the Saints, denoting rather a theological assessment of some author or text as belonging to holy writ or God-inspired scripture (the word *hagiographa* was the accepted translation of the Hebrew *kethubim* as used to denote the third part of the Old Testament, coming after the first and second parts, the Thora and the Prophets). In the usage of the Greek-speaking and Latin-speaking peoples the designation for both genres, the 'biographical' and the 'hagiographical', was the same: *bios* or *vita*, that is, 'Life'.

What then does 'Life' mean as the designation of a literary genre? Greek, unlike English, Latin, and many other languages, has not one, but

two different words for life: *bios*, but also *zoe*. The latter denotes vital
energy, either natural and physical or—in Christian authors—spiritual and
divine, that is, the quality of being alive; as for *bios*, it means rather mode
of life, manner of living, often what we name 'conduct' or 'behaviour'. A
Byzantine lexical work, *Etymologicon Magnum*, belonging to the twelfth
century but representing a compilation of much earlier sources, defines *bios*
in a significant manner as *eidos zoes*, that is, 'way [literally shape] of life'.
Very revealing in this respect is the use of the noun *bios* in the philosophical
satire of Lucian of Samosata entitled *Bion prasis*, that is, 'Ways of Life for
Sale'; Lucian shows us, for example, how the Pythagorean ethos and other
rules and prescriptions for individual behaviour competed for the attention
of the customers on the 'market' established by the different philosophical
schools of Hellas. (In the classic German translation of Christoph Martin
Wieland the title is properly rendered as *Versteigerung der Lebensformen*,
the very specific German word *Lebensform* being the lexical equivalent of
'way of life'). To be precise, we must add that this binary distinction
of meanings—*zoe* being life itself and *bios* a mode of the former—is not
equally evident in different concrete cases, and there are instances of *bios*
being used in the modern sense of the 'story of a life'; but on the whole it
really does work.

　　If then the word *bios*, exclusively used for 'biography' as well as for
'hagiography', is to be interpreted as 'way of life', what does this imply
for the inner form of the oldest biographical and hagiographical literature?
For us the 'life' of a person is first of all a process, a flux, a chronological
succession of events, and consequently a biography must be a narrative, a
chronicle of the subject's life. But if the *bios* is to be considered primarily
as *eidos*, a form, a pattern, a mode, then description seems to be more
appropriate a procedure than narrative. And we rather frequently find facts
that fit exactly this descriptive paradigm. For example, Suetonius, author
of the *De vita Caesarum* and *De viris illustribus*, declares explicitly that he
will order his account not *per tempora*, that is in chronological sequence,
but *per species*, point by point, according to logical criteria (*Life of Augustus*,
9). As a synonymous designation for this *per species* order he uses
also an adverb *summatim* (*Life of Caesar*, 44), which does not mean here
'in sum' but 'in logical order', a translation of the Greek *kephalaiodos*,
which is typical enough of the phraseology of Hellenistic literary theory.
Suetonius also writes in his biography of Caligula (22), after demonstrating
some positive or at least neutral features of his hero and before passing
over to his decidedly revolting traits: 'Up to now this was a tale about a
sovereign, and now it will be about a monster'. In a very similar way the
logical order is accentuated in his biography of another 'monster' (*Life of
Nero*, 19): 'these deeds of his deserve considerable praise; I have gathered

them all together to separate them from his vices and crimes which will be my theme from now on'. Not by chance the chapters and sections in Suetonius' *Lives* often start with key-words, designating the point of each section and functioning rather like subtitles or subheadings. Here are the beginnings of some chapters in the *Life of Caesar*, taken at random from among many similar examples: 'As for wine [*Vini*], even his enemies do not deny him to be very temperate' (53); 'As for eloquence and the art of war [*Eloquentia militarique re*], his glory was either equal or superior to the most illustrious examples' (55); 'As for the use of arms and the art of cavalry (*Armorum et equitandi . . .*), he had the greatest proficiency in them' (57).[1]

To be sure, it would be an exaggeration to suggest that all Greek and Roman biographers practised this way of structuring their works no less deliberately and consistently than did Suetonius; had the *per species* organization been taken for granted as a mere matter of course, the explicit declarations of the Roman author would be entirely superfluous. Plutarch of Chaeronaea, with Suetonius doubtless the best-known representative of Classical biography, deploys very different devices: he has far less rigid rules of composition than Suetonius, and free association of ideas plays a greater part in his work, so that sometimes associations and *a-propos* serve as the main criterion of order, as is normal for the Greek moralistic and essayistic genre of diatribe; after all, Plutarch was not only a biographer but the author of many such essays (the so-called *Moralia*). Yet, seen against the background of the 'normal' biographical literature of Greece and Rome, it is Suetonius who appears as a more standard phenomenon, Plutarch being, rather, an interesting and fruitful exception made possible precisely because of the unique combination in one person of the literary habits of moral essayist and biographer. The rhetorically elaborated encomiastic biographies, presenting conventional praise, *enkomion* (or more rarely conventional denunciation, *psogos*) of their heroes, are both determined much more by the descriptive than by the narrative attitude. As examples we may cite a great variety of biographical writing, such as the *Agesilaus* of Isocrates or the *Agricola* of Tacitus, the biographical pasquinades of Lucian, or the tentative biographies of poets and philosophers, which in other respects bear no resemblance to one another.

The grounds for this state of affairs are manifold. Some of them can be traced quite simply to the way life is lived; our concept of biography as a chronicle of the subject's life is obviously conditioned by the fact that the life of a person in the modern world (at least in the West) is more or less abundantly delineated in documents available in archives, etc. It is imposs-

---

[1] Unless otherwise stated, all translations are my own.

ible for us to forget the major dates of our own personal existence, but this is caused not so much by some general rule about our 'nature' as by the fact that we are obliged to give them again and again in every *curriculum vitae* and in every questionnaire. Under different cultural conditions things can be very different. I have met in my early years in Russia some illiterate or poorly literate persons of the premodern rural type, who, without being in any sense idiots, were not at all sure about the chronology of their own lives. As for the Greek and Roman world, and maybe even more for the early medieval epoch, the privilege of having one's date of birth registered in a precise way was mostly reserved for persons of quite exceptional status, for instance those born to the purple. So the idea of biography as a 'chronicle of a life' could not have been such an obvious one for them as it is for us.

This, however, was by no means the sole reason for the preponderance of biography occupied with the description of a character over the coherently chronological narrative; indeed it was not even the most important one. There are other reasons, connected with the primordial conception of the meaning and purpose of the biographical genre as such. The biography of the Greek and Roman epoch, non-existent in the period predating post-Socratic philosophy and originally connected with the school of Aristotle, was one of the results of the advance of Aristotelian rationalism: and this, like any elaborated rationalism before the great change of paradigm articulated by Francis Bacon and other early modern partisans of induction, was dominated essentially by deductive patterns of thinking, proceeding mostly from general conceptions to particular judgements and not vice versa. The great achievement of Aristotle's formal logic was the technique of the syllogism, a method of deducing a particular statement from a general one with the help of a minor premise. The Universals seemed to enjoy every kind of priority, in the ontological order as well as in that of the hierarchy of values, but above all as cognitive method, being more instructive and at the same time more accessible than any other. As Aristotle himself put it, 'Each definition and each scientific cognition (*episteme*) deals with general notions' (*Metaphysics*, XI, 1, 1059b25). The classic manifestations of this principle of deductive rationalism were such central and lasting achievements of the Greek and Roman genius as Euclidean geometry (deducing theorems from axioms) and Roman Law (deducing special cases from the Legal Code).

When applied to the study of ethics and psychology, the same principle underlies for example the *Ethical Characters*[2] of Aristotle's follower Theo-

---

[2] The title is given in this form (*Ethikoi Characteres*) by Diogenes Laertius 5, 47, otherwise simply *Characteres*. About the true meaning of these Greek words, see n. 3.

phrastus of Eresos, who succeeded his master as the head of the Peripatetic School and, on the whole, continued the main trends of Aristotle's research. The work presents studies of thirty types, such as the flatterer, the chatterer, the rude fellow, or the superstitious person. Or, to be more accurate, each designates not so much a personal type as a character trait[3]—that is, not 'Flatterer' but 'Trait of Flattery' ([*charakter*] *kolakeias*), not 'Chatterer' but 'Trait of Idle Chatter' (*adoleschias*), not 'Boor' but 'Trait of Boorishness' (*agroikias*), not 'Superstitious Person' but 'Trait of Superstition' (*deisidaimonias*), even 'Trait of Authoritarianism' (*oligarchias*), and so on.

Again and again, these studies follow the same pattern: the whole begins with a general definition of a type, which is subsequently worked out, embellished with details and made clear by a series of examples. So the sketch of obsequiousness (*areskeia*, not to be confused with flattery, which is *kolakeia*) begins as follows:

> Obsequiousness, to put it in a definition, is a manner of behavior that aims at pleasing, but not with the best intentions. You can be sure that the obsequious man is the sort who greets you from a distance, then, after [. . .] expressing great respect, detains you by grabbing you with both hands, walks along a little farther, asks when he will see you again, and calls out compliments as he leaves. (tr. J. Rusten, p. 69)

Indeed, the general notion of *example* as one of the most important tools of discourse was created and largely elaborated by Classical rhetoric and only inherited by Christian homiletics. For our purposes, the continuity from one to the other is very significant (see below). Here once more, at the sources of theoretical reflection on the example, we meet the great figure of Aristotle (*Rhetoric*, A2 and B20–24). For the modern reader, however, the figure of the old-fashioned preacher garnishing his sermon with *exempla* (some from the life of his parish!) according to the rules of homiletics—an image which has not yet completely faded from European

---

[3] The Greek word used by Theophrastus for his title means exactly 'Traits'. See J. Rusten, Theophrastus, *Characters*, Loeb Classical Library (London and New York, 1993), Introduction, pp. 11–12: 'The meaning of ancient Greek *charakter* is derived from an original sense of an inscribing (*charassein*) onto a surface: the *imprint* on a coin, the *form* of a letter, often the *style* of an author for rhetorical analysis. "Character" in the modern sense is *not* one of its meanings—the Greek word for "character" is usually *ethos*—and if it were not firmly established, Theophrastus' title might better be rendered "traits". Basic to his whole enterprise is the notion that individual good or bad traits of character may be isolated and studied separately, a notion formulated most memorably by his teacher Aristotle in the *Nicomachean Ethics*, Book II: for each range of emotion (fear, anger) or sphere of action (wealth, honor), Aristotle defines moral virtue and vice (*arete kai kakia ethike*, literally "excellence and badness of character")'.

memory—may be more immediate that any reference to Classical
Antiquity.[4]

Just as typical of the intellectual arsenal of Classical Antiquity as Euclidean geometry and Roman law (even if much less impressive to the modern
mind) was the discipline of moral casuistry—not in the derogatory but in
the technical sense of the word, that is, the reflection on *cases of conscience*,
which was especially important for the ethical doctrines of Stoicism, but
also unavoidable in any other trend of post-Socratic moral philosophy.
Beginning with the ethical works of Aristotle, the Classical style of reflection
on the inner life presupposes the possibility of cataloguing virtues, vices,
and characters, sometimes with great subtleties of sophisticated definition,
division, and subdivision. For example, Aristotle, discussing the virtue of
justice in Book Five of his *Nicomachean Ethics*, having proposed a general
definition, distinguishes between 'universal' justice as a spiritual attitude of
obedience to the law and 'particular' justice as skill in applying the law;
particular justice is divided into distributive justice and remedial justice, this
latter being subdivided into civil law dealing with voluntary transactions,
criminal law dealing with involuntary transactions, and in addition com-
mutative (commercial) justice (*Eth. Nic.* 1129 ff.). He also develops a
theory about each virtue being a mean between two opposite vices, that of
excess and that of deficiency, thus giving rise again and again to symmetrical
triple systems of classification, correlating such central virtues as those of
courage (*andreia*) or liberality (*eleutheriotes*) with such pairs of vicious
extremes as, respectively, rashness/cowardice (the characters of *thrasys* and
deilos) and prodigality/illiberality (*asotia* and *aneleutheria*). Analogous lists
and descriptions of virtues and vices are to be found also in earlier philosophical literature in connection with the phenomenology of forms of
government, as in Plato (*Republic* VIII), or with ethnico-climatological
determination, as in Hippocrates' writings. As for the practice of virtue, it
is interesting that Aristotle describes moral choice as a kind of syllogism,
i.e. deducing the act from the notion of the end, which is the major premise,
and calculating means, which is the minor (*Eth. Nic.* 1141b ff.).

Now biography was understood by its most intelligent and ambitious
practitioners as a sort of psychologico-ethical essay, analysing each public
or private deed, word, or gesture as a display of this or that virtuous or
vicious trait of character (which meant subordinating narrative to
description). In the preface to his *Alexander*, Plutarch explains his under-

---

[4] See A. Lumpe, 'Exemplum', *RLAC*, VI (1966), 1229–57; J. Martin, 'Antike Rhetorik:
Technik und Methode', *Handbuch der Altertumswissenschaften*, II.3 (Munich, 1974), pp.
119–24. For the later Christian development of the Classical heritage, see K. Demoen, 'Pagan
and Biblical Exempla in Gregory Nazianzen: A Study in Rhetoric and Hermeneutics', *Corpus
Christianorum, Lingua Patrum*, II (Turnhout, 1996).

standing of the tasks of the biographical genre as opposed to historical narration: 'It is not Histories that I am writing, but Lives; and in the most illustrious deeds there is not always a manifestation [*delosis*] of virtue or vice, nay, a slight thing like a phrase or a jest often makes a greater revelation of character [*emphasin ethous*] than battles where thousands fall, or the greatest armaments, or sieges of cities.' This sentence is frequently cited as a justification for focusing on the private life, typical of the biographical approach, but it also indicates the prevalence of the descriptive attitude over the narrative; the latter functions rather as an instrument of description. Not by chance does Plutarch, in the very next sentence, compare biographical work to portrait-painting: 'just as painters get the likenesses in their portraits from the face and the expression of the eyes, wherein the character shows itself, but make very little account of the other parts of the body, so I must be permitted to devote myself rather to the signs of the soul in men [*ta tes psyches semeia*], and by means of these to portray the life of each [*eidopoiein ton hekastou bion*]'.[5] Each time it is a particular *bios*, i.e. way of life, that is 'portrayed', and by this procedure, as presented by Plutarch, any detail is obliged to serve as a symptom, a 'sign', a 'manifestation' and 'revelation' of some combination of traits; the combination is in itself individual and may be unique, but each trait as such is general—no less than the traits depicted by Theophrastus.

To proceed each time from the assumption that it is the general premise which co-ordinates particular facts was, for the biographical genre in the Greek and Roman cultural context, an intrinsic necessity. The exposition is carried on point by point, paragraph after paragraph, proceeding from theses formulated in general terms, from general assertions that the hero was magnanimous, arrogant, benevolent or ambitious, to particular episodic narratives functioning, as it were, as didactic visual aids to illuminate these assertions. Because of this auxiliary function, such narratives are frequently presented not in chronological but in logical order, not *per tempora* but *per species*. No less typical is the abundance of epithets of appraisal and in general of all sorts of explicit value judgements; these serve as a didactic device for delineating the moral characteristics of the hero, his virtues and his vices; his deeds are thus explicitly or at least implicitly subordinated to the general categories of ethical and psychological thought.

To be sure, not all Greek and Roman biographers were as committed to moral admonition as was Plutarch; had that been so, the Roman biographer Cornelius Nepos would scarcely have been justified in his formulaic

---

[5] *Plutarch's Lives*, tr. Bernadotte Perrin, 11 vols, Loeb Classical Library (London and New York, 1914–9), VII, 225.

expression of the supposedly widespread reputation of biography as a
'literary genre [which is thought to be] frivolous and not dignified enough'.
Indeed, there was a considerable body of Hellenistic and Roman biographical literature dedicated to persons of merely sensational interest, as
for example the notorious misanthrope Timon, who, long before the fulfilment of his glorious literary destiny as the hero of Shakespeare's tragedy,
was the subject of a biographical work by the Hellenistic author Neanthes
of Cyzicus. Odd individuals, indeed scandalous persons of different classes,
including famous whores (the subject of a lost work by Suetonius), not to
mention tyrants or eccentric poets and philosophers, were all among the
favourite heroes of the biographical genre. Yet, in spite of all the differences
between didactic and purely sensational purpose, the intellectual attitude
and the logical pattern remain the same: instructive or not, individual
characters were seen and pictured essentially as *exempla*.

At the same time a specific didactic purpose, explicit as in Plutarch or
implicit as in Suetonius' *Caesars*, was an efficient stimulus for heightened
interest in ethical universals. The 'parallel' classification of the heroes in
Plutarch was but one method of integrating the individual and unique into
such generalizing systems: each pair joins a Greek and a Roman reckoned
to be of the same class of character. So Lycurgus and Numa are depicted
as representatives of the class of 'Legislators of the Olden Times', Alexander
and Caesar as representatives of the class of 'Great Autocrats', and so
on. A comparative epilogue, the so-called *synkrisis*, completes the task of
generalization, making its points explicit. It is symptomatic that modern
taste, focused on the concrete, the unique, the particular, considers these
ekphraseis (portrayals) of Plutarch to be intolerably naïve and pedantic,
whereas Montaigne once admired them as 'the noblest part of Plutarch's
work' (*Essays*, II, 32). To be sure, they are schematic—but then, the main
task of Greek and Roman biography consisted precisely in the generalization of the particular, and this procedure can be carried out only in a
schematic manner. It is interesting that, in this part of his work, Plutarch
again and again chooses the same strategy as the more rational and dry
Suetonius: he often begins a section with a key phrase establishing the
comparision to follow, e.g.: 'in their [Demosthenes' and Cicero's] writings,
it is possible to see . . .' (VII, 213); 'in haranguing and guiding the people
both had equal power' (VII, 215).

And if, among authors whose texts have come down to us, only one
author, Plutarch, established the *synkrisis* as a special literary procedure of
explicit formal parallelism (albeit this procedure is known to have been
imitated later by a certain Amintianus, whose work is lost), in the ancient
world the tendency to treat heroes as potential objects of implicit comparisons was almost universal among biographers who saw biography as a

way of illustrating general moral principles. Only in the ambience of Classical rhetoric did this tendency become less rigid and yield to other formal considerations.

It is striking and very important that we do not find anything strictly analogous to all this in the Gospels, which represent the other 'literary' source for the medieval saints' lives. Whether or not we are entitled to consider the Gospels as belonging to the biographical genre has been much debated. The answer proposed by Rudolf Bultmann and his school was a negative one; it was based firstly on the 'kerygmatic' character of the Gospel narrative, as determined by the preaching activity of the Apostles that made it incompatible with any 'historical' genre, including biography; secondly, on the fact that two of the four canonical Gospels give no information about the early years of Jesus; thirdly, on the prevalence of such non-narrative material as the *logia* (Jesus's sayings and sermons) over narrative; and so on.

These arguments are unconvincing, because they assume an absolutely anachronistic conception of biography and do not take into account the concrete traits of the biographical genre as it really existed in the context of Late Antiquity. First of all, the orientation of the Gospels on the *kerygma*, the proclamation of the Good News, and the correlation of this with early Christian missionary work, scarcely proves anything in this case. I shall not insist here on my opinion that the absolute opposition of *kerygma* and history as such receives its plausibility from the philosophical climate of existentialism, which largely determined the mind-set of Bultmann and would not have been intelligible to previous generations of Christians (including those in whose midst and for the sake of whom the Gospels were written). Let us instead glance at non-Christian, pagan literature: such works as the lives of Pythagoras from Aristoxenos in the fourth century BC to Iamblichos in the third century AD, or the lives of the Neoplatonic masters and thaumaturges, such as Porphyry's *Life of Plotinus* or Damascius' *Life of Isidore*, clearly belong to the sphere of mystical and philosophical *kerygma*, that is, to teaching and preaching. Preaching and wonder-working are also prevalent topics in Philostratus' *Life of Apollonius of Tyana*, which was specially intended to propose a sort of pagan *kerygma* as an alternative to the Christian one on the open market of competing creeds. They were, to be sure, essentially different on the doctrinal, theological level, but not therefore necessarily so different in all facets of their literary elaboration. To return to Christian topics, all hagiographers—in the modern sense of writers of the lives of saints—sought to communicate to readers the values of faith and were thus both 'kerygmatic' and biographical; we shall see how hagiography was a homogeneous branch on the tree of Classical biography.

Secondly, the fact that such a large portion of the Gospels, especially in Mark and Luke, is devoted not to the narrative episodes of the life of Jesus, but to the *logia*, that is, to his sermons, parables, apophthegms, and aphorisms, is in itself no argument against the concept of the Gospels as biography. We have seen that the idea of biography being 'a chronicle of the subject's life' is essentially modern. Even Plutarch's lives of Lycurgus and Numa consist in the main of discussions about the laws of both legislators; much earlier, in the Hellenistic epoch, the lives of poets and philosophers were little more than catalogues of their works and expositions of their doctrines. After Plutarch, in the well-known *Life of Demonax* by Lucian, the ratio of apophthegms and *dicta* is higher than in the Gospels, because the life of this Cynic master, who lived to be nearly 100, gave his biographer no occasion for anything like the Passion story, which in the Gospels is the most weighty narrative component.

Consequently, neither the didactic or doctrinal tendency, nor the predominance of apophthegm over narrative, nor the absence of information concerning some stages of life are in themselves incompatible with the biographical genre as it was understood and practised in the Hellenistic cultural context. But even if Bultmann's arguments are highly questionable, the thesis they seek to prove remains basically sound.

Let us approach the problem the other way round. We can begin with a statement that may at first seem rather paradoxical: the canonic Gospels are as remote as they could possibly be from the didactic hagiographical manner, and precisely because of that they are remote also from the patterns and types of Greek and Roman biography. Whereas biographical, and *a fortiori* hagiographical, works offer narrations together with more or less explicit commentary of an ethical and psychological nature (which in the case of hagiography also touches on the theological, spiritual, and mystical) in such a way that the text may be said to include its own commentary, the Gospels do nothing of the kind. Even epithets of appraisal are absent: it is impossible for John the Baptist to be named 'God-beloved' or 'God-inspired', or for Herod or Caiaphas to be called 'God-hated' in the Gospel context. Only St Luke's Gospel, which deliberately describes itself in its words as a *diegesis ton* [. . .] *pragmaton* ('narrative of the events', first a formula reminding us of such Greek technical terms as the *historia pragmatike* of Polybius), is thus relatively closer to Hellenistic historiography (and in an indirect way also to biography). For example, Zacharias and Elisabeth were 'righteous before God, walking in all the commandments and ordinances of the Lord blameless' (1, 6), and Jesus at twelve years 'increased in wisdom and stature, and in favour with God and man' (2, 52). Even here, such value judgements (being of themselves closer to the Old Testament than to Classical patterns—cf. for example Job 1, 1: 'that man was perfect and upright, and one that feared God, and eschewed evil')—appear only as exceptions, that is, very rarely and at the margin of the narrative, becoming impossible somewhat nearer to its centre. What was said of the parents of John the Baptist cannot be said of John the Baptist himself; what is suitable for narrative about the early years of Jesus does not befit what follows. In the other Synoptic Gospels we do not find anything similar; as for the enigmatic and completely isolated remark in the Gospel of St John describing Judas Iscariot as a *kleptes* (a thief ?), it can hardly be called a value judgement in any normal sense of the word.

It seems that in the Gospels only one judge has authority to bring in verdicts:—the Master himself. The narrator has no such authority. Precisely because of that, the elucidation of the psychological motives for any action, so important for any serious biographical and especially hagiographical narrative, is here also absent, indeed unthinkable; 'the thoughts of many hearts' (Luke 2, 35) are to be revealed by the action of God within the history of salvation, but not by any human elucidation. Many things are thus bound to remain enigmatic and impenetrable, such as the causes that motivated Judas to betray Jesus (the above-mentioned remark in St John's Gospel does not explain anything, but rather requires explanation itself). Nearly every episode and every detail is presented in the Gospels as an enigma waiting for interpretation and comment; providing the material for future exegesis and preaching, for hymnography and iconography, for the entire universe of Christian cultures. Quite apart from their unique significance for the believer and the theologian, on the level of the history of culture the Gospels constitute the basic text of any Christian culture, more or less as Homer and Hesiod served as the basic text of Classical culture, provoking innumerable commentaries, interpretations, expositions. The task of interpretation of this primary text, never to be accomplished once and for all, gives to each culture its paradigm.

It is precisely because of this that no text that includes its own self-commentary or self-explanation, as do Classical biographies and Christian Lives of Saints, can function as the basic text of a culture. The basic text must be different: not a finite, self-sufficient sum of elucidations, but an open word addressing new generations. The answer to the much-discussed question, why do the Gospels not belong to the genre of Hellenistic biography, seems to be the following: because Jesus Christ, the Only-Begotten (*monogenes*), according to the faith of the Evangelists and later Christian generations, remains essentially incomparable and cannot be classified or incorporated in any system of generalization. His 'character', his 'ethos', are mysteries not to be in any definitive way elucidated by psychological, characterological or ethical reasoning, but to be again and again demonstrated through the paradoxes of Christian theology and even more through the Christian practice of 'following' Christ (cf. I Cor. 11, 1), that is, through the deeds of saints (which are the proper subject of hagiography).

This assumption of the uniqueness of the Gospels is not perhaps entirely based on 'academic' materials. Yet it does express a factual truth about the Gospels that can be traced back to the most concrete details of their literary elaboration. Where the content of a Classical biography is expounded *per species*, point by point, any attempt to divide the continuum of the Gospel narrative according to this rationalistic, 'syllogistic' paradigm will prove inadequate, indeed in the long term unrealizable. To be sure, such attempts have been undertaken again and again, sometimes through critical analysis of the Gospels' content, but especially by the practice of publishing translations for the more general public. In such translations, each part usually receives a subtitle; some incongruities arising from this practice are very instructive because of their symptomatic value. Let us look at the first chapter of St Matthew's Gospel. Verses 1–17 are introduced as the 'Book of Genealogy', and verses 18–25 as the 'Birth of Jesus'. But the case is not so simple. The Greek words rendered as 'Book of Genealogy' are *biblos geneseos*—a polysemic locution with a number of possible meanings and connotations, identical with the Greek title of the first book of the Pentateuch. This in its turn compels one to think of the Hebrew expression *sefer toledot* or simply of the noun *toledot* ('begettings; generations; genealogy; origin; history'), which is not used in the Synagogal tradition as the title of the book, but occurs many times in the text of Genesis (5, 1; 10, 1 and 32; 11, 10 and 27; 25, 12–13 and 19; 36, 1 and 9), functioning more or less as a subtitle. The Greek key-word *genesis* (with one *n*, that is, 'origin' rather than 'birth') significantly occurs again at 1, 18,[6] just at the beginning of the second section: *tou de Iesou Christou he genesis houtos en*, 'as for the origin of Jesus Christ, it has taken place this way' (this translation is as word for word as possible and tries to reproduce some nuances created in the original by the sequence of words and by the use of the particle *de*). As a matter of fact, the section introduced by this sentence tells not about the birth of Jesus, but literally about his 'origin', that is, about the Immaculate Conception (verses 18–25); as for birth as such, it is mentioned in a very succinct manner only in verse 25 ('and knew her not till she had brought forth her firstborn son: and he called his name Jesus'). True,

---

[6] *Textus receptus* gives *gennesis*, and this textual variant has conditioned the old translations (for example, that of the King James Bible: 'Now the birth of Jesus Christ was on this wise'). But there are strong reasons for preferring the variant *genesis*, which is adopted by modern New Testament textology (cf. B. M. Metzger, *A Textual Commentary on the Greek New Testament*, United Bible Societies, Corr. Ed., 1975, p. 8).

this miraculous 'origin' (*genesis*) does not cancel the legalistic-dynastic genealogy—in the context presupposed by St Matthew's Gospel it is very important that Jesus, being adopted by Joseph, becomes a legitimate heir to the Davidic dynasty—but the words are chosen to signal a very specific tension between different ontological levels, the mystical *genesis* being even verbally juxtaposed with the merely dynastical *genesis*, and this point seems to be expressed through the semiotically overloaded repetition of the same lexeme. For Classical biography such topics as 'origin' ('kin' or 'clan', *genos*), on the one hand, and 'birth' (*gennesis*), on the other, were clearly distinguishable and indeed of fundamental, functional significance. But the identity of Jesus as depicted in the Gospels exceeds all accepted biographical topics. 'Then said they unto him: "Who art thou?" ' (John 8, 25). This identity is first of all unclassifiable, and consequently as unbiographical as it is possible to be.

For later Christian hagiography, concerned not with the figure of Jesus himself, but with the gleam of his traits reflected in the persons of the saints, these difficulties in adopting the Classical biographical method did not exist. Each revered person was to be classified according to given ethical and characterological categories, but also according to the new concepts elaborated by specifically Christian theological, ascetic, and spiritual thought. The intellectual concern with the deductive method of thinking, proceeding from universals and generalities, patterns and commonplaces (*loci communes*), which was so typical of the deductive rationalism of Classical Antiquity, is not diminished, but has acquired a new formal rigidity, just as the mind-set of Scholasticism in general is more rigid than its Aristotelian or Neoplatonic sources. As a result, there are fewer exceptions to the canon, and the didactic element comes through more strongly. Epithets of appraisal and value judgements of all kinds fulfil a specific function in the Lives of the Saints as highly practical signposts indicating directions towards Heaven and Hell; they inform the reader, thoroughly and in detail, which persons and deeds are to be named God-fearing, indeed God-beloved and God-inspired, and which, on the contrary, are to be named God-hated or something similar.

It is typical of this genre that the inner motivation of each act accomplished by the saint, or by his or her antagonists, conceived in ethical and psychological, but also theological and spiritual terms, has even more importance that the act itself. Before God, *in the eyes of God*, it is not the external action that possesses decisive significance, but the inner disposition of the heart expressing and revealing itself in the deeds. This disposition of the heart, strictly speaking, can be known only to God, but seems to be somehow revealed to the author. Each concrete event receives its commentary, its explanation and elucidation through a generalizing correlation with abstract and universal notions and concepts. With each remaking of the earlier Lives of the Saints in such late hagiographical collections as the work of Symeon Metaphrastes in Byzantium or the famous *Golden Legend* of Jacobus de Voragine in the Latin West, this tendency towards generalization is unvariably on the increase. It was precisely in and through such generalization that the didactic function, which was the aim and end of all hagiographical creativity, was implemented.

Thus paradigmatic thinking became even more obligatory for early Christian and medieval thinking than it had been for Classical Platonism and Aristotelianism. As early as in the writings of the Apostolic Fathers and the Apologists, at every step there are allusions to biblical characters as archetypal models;[7] later the Classical pagan *exempla* were, in subordinate functions, amalgamated with the biblical ones in a great supersystem of didactic paradigms. It was no accident that a technical term of fundamental importance for Christian theology and iconography acquired a new lease of life in the theory of symbolism: it is the word 'typology'. All things are seen by medieval theology in some typological perspective. The primary reality is named in Greek *prototypos*, any likeness of it *antitypos*. In modern times Goethe proclaimed, at the end of *Faust*, that 'everything transient is merely a likeness'. A medieval thinker would say that everything transient is merely a type, a prefiguration, as Old Testament persons and events were believed to be prefigurations of those in the New Testament and the virtues of Christ to be prototypes of the traits of his saints.

Omnis mundi creatura / Quasi liber et pictura ('Each creature of this world is like a book and an image'), writes a Scholastic poet of the twelfth century. The ability of each person and event to serve as a sign and representation of things more general was considered their most important quality. The saints revered by the church and glorified in hagiography are divided into general groups, beginning with the Patriarchs and Prophets, including the Apostles, the Martyrs, the Confessors, the Virgins, etc.; these ranks of the hierarchy of saints, imagined as something like corporations and guilds of Heaven, as collective, supra-personal entities, are often, especially in the Byzantine and Russian Orthodox tradition, given the name of *choirs*, analogous to the nine choirs of the angelic hierarchy according to the Pseudo-Areopagites, beginning with Angels and Archangels and ascending to Thrones, Cherubim and Seraphim. (The Choirs of Saints are one of the important iconographical themes of medieval sacred art.) All these celestial corporations were incorporated into the all-embracing supra-

---

[7] See, for instance, Pope Clement I, *The First Epistle of Clement to the Corinthians*, ed. and tr. W. K. Lowther Clarke (London, 1937), pp. 74–5 (para. 46.1).

personal corporation named *Corpus Christi Mysticum*: the Mystical Body of Christ, the Church Triumphant. The saints carry out tasks of individual holiness; they live, die, and rise in heavenly glory not otherwise than 'in' Christ, *in Christo*: this expression, so strange to modern ears, is to be understood in a very strong sense. A great body consisting of an innumerable quantity of smaller bodies—this metaphor undergoes a curious visualization in Dante's *Paradiso* (the bodies of the Eagle and of the Mystical Rose, comprising within them the multitudes of saints).

All the paradigmatic traits and characteristics of Christ (which remained unnamed and uncatalogued in the Gospels, but which were later extrapolated with great zeal from the Gospel narratives and arranged anew in a system) constituted the supreme 'metatext' of Christian didactics, including hagiography. The virtues of the saints, especially of those belonging to the same category, estate, and class, to the same *choir* as the person looking for standards and models for his or her own behaviour, functioned as accessible paradigms. We find again and again in the life of this or that later saint traits which have obviously been brought nearer to the traits of some illustrious predecessor; but this literary convention became possible, indeed inevitable, only because such looking back for models was a universally accepted practice in the real life of medieval Christians.

An important early hagiographical text, which proved exceedingly influential in the evolution of the genre, is the *Life of St Antony of Egypt* by Athanasius of Alexandria, one of the greatest Greek Fathers.[8] (To be sure, the influence of this text exceeded by far the bounds of literary history: it stimulated the diffusion of monasticism, not to mention the widespread iconography of the Temptations of St Antony). The life begins, as was usual in Classical biography, with an account of the descent (*genos*) and the childhood of the saint; we obtain an image of a very unsociable psychological type, who seems predestined for the life of the hermit. As in the *Caesars* of Suetonius and in the comparative epilogues of Plutarch's *Parallel Lives*, in the *Life of St Antony* (especially the second half, which gives more space to reflections and meditation) the sections often begin with key-phrases, which function almost as rubrics: the result is something like a parade of ascetic virtues, anticipating innumerable passages of the medieval Lives of Saints. Here are the first sentences of some chapters: 'He possessed also the spiritual gift [*charisma*] set forth below' (66); 'Moreover, he was as for his character [*ethos*], long-suffering [*anexikakos*], and as for his soul, humble-minded [*tapeinophron*]' (67); 'As for his faith, he was a great believer [*pistei . . . pany thaumastos*] and a very pious person' (68); 'More-

---

[8] See Saint Athanasius, *The Life of Saint Antony*, tr. Robert T. Meyer (Westminster, MD, and London, 1950). Translations given below are my own.

over he was astonishingly intelligent [*phronimos*], and one could wonder
how it was possible that he, an unlettered man, was such a sharp [*anchi-
nous*] and clever [*synetos*] person' (72). These words introduce each time
a new theme to be developed and visualized in a little series of episodes.

While the medieval Lives of Saints were being written, so were the lives
of secular persons, such as emperors; these mostly had especially close
connections with the 'pagan' tradition of biography, because the political
ideology of medieval Empire, not by chance named *Sacrum Imperium
Romanum*, was based on Classical patterns. For example, the biography
of Charlemagne by Einhard[9] is frankly modelled on Suetonius' *Caesars*, so
that the description of Charlemagne's outward appearance (Ch. 22), beginning with the key-word *corpore*, represents largely a collage or mosaic
of quotations. The following chapters, offering descriptive accounts of
Charlemagne's temperance at banquets (Ch. 24) and skill in rhetoric (Ch.
25), begin in the same way: 'As for meals and wine, he was temperate';
'As for his eloquence, he spoke fluently'.

The thirteenth century, the century of Thomas Aquinas, was for Europe
a century of vast syntheses. A great enterprise analogical to the Scholastic
genre of the *summa* was undertaken by an Italian friar of the same Domin-
ican order as Aquinas; his name was Jacobus de Voragine, and his work,
called by a grateful posterity *The Golden Legend*,[10] not only provides a
compendium of available hagiographical material for the whole cycle of
the church year, but specifically imbues this material with abstract notions
for homiletic and meditative use. It is a typical proceeding that each hero
or heroine of *The Golden Legend* is introduced by an appraisal naming
his or her most important virtues. Sometimes this is shaped as a meditation
on the saint's name (supposed to be especially significant), for example:

> Lucia is named from the light; now, light makes beauty visible, indeed,
> according to St Ambrose, it belongs to the nature of light that all things are
> grace in the presence of light. The latter can be diffused without being
> profaned; it is not profaned even being diffused over impure things. It goes
> directly without curvature and passes over great distances without delays and
> decelerations. Through this image one can see that the blessed virgin Lucia
> possesses the glory of virginity without any corruption, the diffusion of
> compassionate love without any impure passion, direct aspiration towards
> God without any delay caused by negligence. In other words, Lucia signifies
> Way of Light.

Jacobus thus begins from the most abstract sense of the (often arbitrarily

---

[9] Einhard, *The Life of Charlemagne*, in *Two Lives of Charlemagne*, tr. Lewis Thorpe
(Harmondsworth, 1969). The translations given are my own.
[10] Jacobus de Voragine, *The Golden Legend*, tr. W. G. Ryan, 2 vols (Princeton, NJ, 1993); for
Lucia, see vol. I, ch. 4. The translation here is my own.

interpreted) personal name, which appears to us—but most emphatically did not appear to the author or to his expected reader—the most conventional, superficial, and shallow of personal attributes. Behind this Scholastic exercise stood not only the belief or superstition expressed in the Latin formula *nomen est omen*, but also the persistent intellectual demand for some generalizing pattern: the name of a saint stands here for a 'universal' in the medieval sense of the word.

In the modern epoch the descriptive approach to the hero's ethos, to his character, his traits, his type, has, like the tendency to generalize, become more and more unfashionable. The prestige of *universalia* declines in the face of the new preference for the concrete and the factual, and the glorification of the unique and the personal. Such time-honoured terms as rhetoric, casuistry, and Scholasticism have become words of abuse. As for biography, it shows itself eager to take a narrative, indeed epic form, stimulated by the possibility of ordering and verifying the chronology of events, but also by the influence of the novel as it gains ever greater ascendancy in the realms of literature.

Of course, this is to simplify. The actual process was in fact more complex, not reducible to any formula. British nineteenth-century literature, for instance, bucked the prevailing trend by offering an interesting phenomenon that can be considered as a proper epilogue to the long historical process which includes Plutarch and Suetonius as well as *The Golden Legend*. I have in mind Thomas Carlyle's *On Heroes, Hero-Worship, and the Heroic in History* (1841, based on lectures presented in 1840). Not belonging to the biographical genre in any strict sense of the word, whether Classical or modern, these essays are arguably much closer to the essence and *raison d'être* of Classical biography than anything else in the literature of modern Europe. The Carlylean key-word 'Hero' goes back to Classical pagan hero-cults, appropriated and transformed, to be sure, by the post-Renaissance and especially the Romantic mentality. Carlyle himself formulates his task in the following words: 'We have undertaken to discourse here for a little on Great Men, their manner of appearance in our world's business, how they have shaped themselves in the world's history, what ideas men formed of them'. So begins Lecture I, which serves as an introduction to the whole. Just as Greek and Roman biographers were looking for general types and categories and sought to represent any individual phenomen as an *exemplum*, just as medieval hagiographers classified the saints according to rank as *virgo, martyr, confessor*, etc., so Carlyle subdivided his theme of the 'heroic in history' into chapters with titles beginning 'The Hero as ...': for example, Luther and Knox appear under the heading 'The Hero as Priest', and Cromwell and Napoleon under the heading 'The

Hero as King' (a pattern reminiscent of Plutarch's *Parallel Lives*!). Each particular episode, indeed each particular *heroic* personality, functions as a visualization of some general paradigm. Behind all this stands the rhetorical attitude, expressing itself not only in more or less decorative ornamentation (which abounds in Carlyle), but in the intellectual perspective dominated by deduction, by *universalia*, again in the medieval sense of the word. So in an epoch comparatively close to our own time, we can observe at close quarters a kind of belated celebration of a tradition as old as the *Characters* of Theophrastus and the most ancient biographical eulogies: *sicut erat in principio*, a sort of *rondo* presented by the history of European culture.

Some Dates

Xenophon, *c.* 427–*c.* 354 BC
Agesilaos, *c.* 360 BC
Isocrates, 436–338 BC
Euagoras, before 360 BC
Theophrastus, *c.* 372–287 BC (*Characters*, after 319 BC)
P. Cornelius Tacitus, AD *c.* 55—after 115 (*De vita et moribus Julii Agricolae*, AD 98)
Plutarch, after AD 45–after 120 (*Parallel Lives*, AD *c.*105–115)
C. Suetonius Tranquillus, AD *c.*70–*c.*140 (*De vita Caesarum*, AD *c.*120)
Gospel of St Mark, AD *c.* 69–70
Athanasius of Alexandria, AD 295–373 (*Life of St Antony*, AD 357)
Symeon Metaphrastus, *fl. c.* 1000 (*The Lives of Saints*, late tenth century)
Jacobus de Voragine, *c.* 1230–98 (*Legenda Aurea*, 1263–73)

3

Biography and Autobiography in the Italian Renaissance

MARTIN McLAUGHLIN

Whether one accepts or rejects Burckhardt's controversial thesis of 'the rise of the individual' in the Italian Renaissance, the fact remains that biography and autobiography certainly flourished, or were 'reborn', in Italy in the period 1300–1600, both in Latin and Italian.[1] Of course, writing bio-graphies, particularly of rulers or writers, had never quite died out in the Middle Ages: Einhard's life of Charlemagne was indebted to Suetonius' biographies of the Roman Emperors, particularly his organization of the material by topics (*per species*) rather than chronologically,[2] while the lives of Virgil by Servius and Donatus were extremely influential both in estab-lishing the importance of this genre and in determining its constituent parts. The opening words of Servius' commentary, which singled out the life of the author as the first component in any commentary on an *auctor*, became canonical throughout the Middle Ages.[3] However, apart from the quali-tative differences discussed in this chapter, the sheer quantity of biographies written between 1300 and 1600 also constitutes part of the fault-line that separates the Middle Ages from the Renaissance in Italy.

---

[1] See Jacob Burckhardt, *The Civilization of the Renaissance in Italy* (1860), tr. S. G. C. Middlemore, ed. Irene Gordon (New York, 1960), Part II ('The Development of the Individual'), pp.121–44, and Part IV ('The Discovery of the World and of Man'), section on biography, pp. 240–47.

[2] G. B. Townend, 'Suetonius and his Influence', in *Latin Biography*, ed. T. A. Dorey (London, 1967), pp. 79–111. See also Chapter 2 above.

[3] 'In expounding authors the following are to be considered: the poet's life, the title of the work, the genre of poetry, the writer's intention, the number of books into which the work is divided, their order, then the commentary', *Servianorum in Vergilii Carmina Commentariorum Editio Harvardiana*, ed. E. K. Rand et al., 3 vols (Cambridge, MA, 1946–), II, 1.

A typology of the many biographical works written in this period suggests three main strands:

1   Collections of lives, the *De viris illustribus* tradition, first revived in Petrarch's work of the same name (begun around 1338), and inspired by Classical lives of famous rulers by Suetonius as well as by medieval *Viri illustres* collections, by St Jerome and others, which also included lives of famous writers and/or artists.

2   Individual biographies, again either of a single ruler or of an individual artist/writer, and once more derived from Classical models, such as Plutarch for the life of the ruler, and Late Antique lives of poets such as Virgil for biographies of the single writer or artist— Boccaccio's *De vita et moribus Francisci Petracchi* (1348–9) and his *Trattatello in laude di Dante* (1351–3, rewritten *c.* 1363) were the first secular biographies in Latin and the Italian vernacular respectively.

3   Autobiography: here again, as in so many other areas, Petrarch was the pioneer, composing a purportedly secret dialogue, the *Secretum* (1347–53), in which the first autobiographer, St Augustine, appears as a character, and an unfinished autobiography in epistolary form, his Letter to Posterity (*c.*1350, rev. *c.* 1370). In the Quattrocento artists too, as well as humanists, turned their hand to autobiography: of special interest here was Alberti's autobiographical *Vita* (written in the 1460s), which in some ways anticipates the 'Renaissance man' autobiography epitomized by Cellini's *Vita* (1558–66). Almost exactly contemporary with Cellini's Italian *Vita* was Girolamo Cardano's Latin work *De propria vita* (1575), an autobiography that was to influence Rousseau strongly.

This chapter, which will concentrate on the more distinctive examples of each strand, but particularly on the biographies and autobiographies of writers, charts the rise and principal developments of these genres, mainly in the period 1350–1550, since at one end Petrarch and at the other Cardano, Cellini, and Vasari have been well covered in secondary literature, and especially as the secondary works on autobiography have little to say about this period, jumping as they often do from Augustine and Abelard to Montaigne and Rousseau.

Collections of Lives

Petrarch (1304–74) epitomizes the humanist urge to revive the genres of Classical literature: apart from Latin epic (the *Africa*), he also revitalized verse and prose epistles, pastoral poetry, prose dialogues, and biography. His *De viris illustribus* was begun around 1338, and may have been inspired by the decision of his friend Giovanni Colonna to write a mammoth work with the same title, covering 350 illustrious men. Around the same time, Guglielmo da Pastrengo (1290–1362) also wrote a *De viris illustribus*, but this was more Scholastic in orientation, taking the form of an alphabetical list of brief entries from Anaximander to (San) Zeno.[4] Petrarch's aims were more ambitious, more literary and more coherent than either of these two, aiming at substantial biographies of a select group of ancient heroes, not the miscellany of famous men of all times included in Colonna's or Guglielmo's compilations. He initially intended to write a series of Roman biographies from Romulus to Titus.[5] But as with so many of his works, he soon interrupted then resumed the project, writing the twenty-three lives we now have in 1341–3, from Romulus to Cato the Censor (this last is unfinished).[6] Between 1351 and 1353 he wrote another twelve lives, giving the collection a more Christian slant: Adam, Noah, Nimrod, Ninus, Semiramis, Abraham, Isaac, Jacob, Joseph, Moses, Jason, Hercules (unfinished). In the late 1360s he was asked by his patron, Francesco il Vecchio da Carrara, to bring the number of Roman lives up to thirty-six to act as the verbal equivalent of the thirty-six portraits of Roman heroes that were to adorn his Sala dei Giganti in Padua. Although Petrarch never completed this project, the link between verbal and pictorial portraits runs throughout the Renaissance period and culminates two centuries later in Paolo Giovio's *Elogia* (1546), composed for his famed museum of portraits of 'viri illustres' on the shores of Lake Como.

Petrarch's title, *De viris illustribus*, may have come from the many medieval works entitled thus, by St Jerome and others (Petrarch probably did not know Cornelius Nepos' collection of lives of famous men), but the opening phrases about gathering together scattered historical details indicate that another model was a popular Late Antique collection, Valerius Maximus' *Factorum et dictorum memorabilium liber*. Petrarch's claim in the proem that he will follow only those sources that were more realistic or had greater authority and his subsequent remark that the lives will suggest models of behaviour to imitate or reject, a standard historiographical topos, confirm that in this work biography is subsumed under

---

[4] Guglielmo da Pastrengo, *De viris illustribus et De originibus*, ed. Guglielmo Bottari (Padua, 1991).

[5] In *Secretum*, III Augustinus says to Franciscus: 'you have begun a historical work beginning with king Romulus and ending with Titus Caesar' (Petrarch, *Opere latine*, ed. Antonietta Bufano, 2 vols, Turin, 1975, I, 234).

[6] This is the version in *De viris illustribus*, ed. Guido Martellotti (Florence, 1964), from which any quotations are taken.

the genre of history. As with historiography proper, its aim is to provide information, though here the emphasis is also on 'brevity and information' (p. 4). However, brevity is not an overriding quality, since Petrarch admits that 'I was often distracted from my original intent, and found it pleasant to remind others of the morals, domestic life, witty and weighty sayings, bodily stature, family background and manner of death of these famous men' (p. 4). These six topics suggest that Suetonius' *Caesars* also exercised a major influence on the *De viris*—and we know that Petrarch was a keen reader of Suetonius, owning at least four (possibly five) manuscripts of the Roman biographer, and numbering the *Caesars* among his favourite books.[7] On the other hand, when he enlarges the *De viris* in the 1350s, in order to include the lives of the biblical patriarchs, he also expands the proem and defines his concept of biography more precisely: he does not approve of writing the lives of those who cannot ever be illustrious, such as the kings of the Parthians, Macedonians, Goths, Huns, or Vandals, in other words those who were the historical enemies of Ancient Rome. Nor does he believe that biographies should include trivial details about which slaves or pet animals a ruler had, what cloaks he wore, the names of his wives or slaves, or details of his chariots or diet.[8] Here he seems to be attacking some of the more trifling details in Suetonius' *Caesars*, but particularly the biographers of the later emperors in the *Historia Augusta*, as well as Einhard's biography of Charlemagne, which has whole chapters on his dress and diet.

There were two lives in particular which grew out of this project and began to take on autonomous dimensions: the life of Scipio Africanus, Petrarch's favourite Roman hero and protagonist of his epic poem *Africa*, a life which went through three separate substantial versions, the last one of around 20,000 words; and the life of Julius Caesar (*De gestis Cesaris*), on which he was working at his death and which by then amounted to around 70,000 words. Both these major biographies anticipated the tendency of the single life to detach itself from the *De viris illustribus* collections and to develop its own autonomy. But whether a single life or a set of collected lives, for Petrarch, as is clear from the historiographical topoi and discussion of sources in the *De viris illustribus* prefaces, biography is very much a subsection of historiography.

Petrarch's expanded collection of lives suggested a synthesis of the

---

[7] Pierre De Nolhac, *Pétrarque et l'humanisme*, 2 vols (Paris, 1907), II, 33–4. On Petrarch's manuscripts, particularly the most heavily annotated one (now in Exeter College, Oxford), see Giuseppe Billanovich, 'Nella biblioteca del Petrarca. II: Un altro Svetonio del Petrarca (Oxford, Exeter College, 186)', *Italia medievale e umanistica*, III (1960), 28–58.

[8] This longer preface is in Francesco Petrarca, *Prose*, ed. Guido Martellotti et al. (Milan and Naples, 1955), pp. 218–26 (224).

Classical and Christian traditions, but still looking back towards an illustrious and now largely irrecoverable past (whether Romulus or Adam). However, his followers in the practice of writing collections of lives rejected this antiquarian stance, preferring instead to look towards the recent past and even to deal with the lives of their contemporaries. The first to do so was a humanist of the generation after Petrarch, Filippo Villani (*c.* 1325–1405), who in his *De origine civitatis Florentie et de eiusdem famosis civibus* (*c.* 1395) is spurred by patriotic Florentine instincts to offer brief biographies of Florence's most famous citizens.[9] He groups them into three broad categories: poets (though this also includes theologians, jurists, physicians, and rhetoricians), 'semipoete' (among whom are minor writers, mathematicians, musicians, and painters), and finally military leaders. Filippo justifies the inclusion of artists in his list by saying he is following the example of ancient historians (presumably the elder Pliny) who had included painters and sculptors among their 'famosis viris' (p. 411), by the analogy of the painter's main activity ('pingere') with the poet's ('fingere') and by the fact that the most famous painter mentioned, Giotto, was extremely learned. In an earlier version of the collection (completed *c.* 1382) he had originally included a fourth category, of famous comic actors, placed just after the artists, but this Villani later eliminated. Painters and comedy were closely linked in the Italian *novella* tradition, but it is indicative of the beginning of the rise in the artist's status that in his final redaction Villani retains not the comic actors but the painters, despite fears of criticism.[10] The emphasis in Villani's collection is thus mostly on the recent past and the present, and on men of intellectual and artistic culture rather than on rulers, princes, or soldiers.

Nearly a century later, in Lorenzo de' Medici's Florence, we find Cristoforo Landino (1424–98) drawing largely on Villani's list for his series of famous Florentines to be included in the proem to his influential commented edition of Dante's *Divine Comedy* (1481): apart from a lengthy life of Dante, Landino provides brief mentions of Florentines famous for their learning, their eloquence, in music, painting and sculpture, in civil law, and even in 'Mercatura'. Instead of Villani's three categories Landino offers us six, though in fact only the members of his last category, merchants, were not present in some form in Villani's earlier list. In the century between the two works the most striking difference is the elevation in status of the visual artist: no longer thrown in with the 'semipoete', they have a separate

---

[9] References in what follows are to Filippo Villani, *De origine civitatis Florentie et de eiusdem famosis civibus*, ed. Giuliano Tanturli (Padua, 1997).

[10] See Giuliano Tanturli, 'Le biografie d'artista prima del Vasari', in *Il Vasari storiografo e artista: Atti del Convegno internazionale nel IV centenario della morte, Arezzo–Firenze, 2–8 settembre 1974* (Florence, 1976), pp. 275–98.

category to themselves, and now include sculptors, who were not significant enough to merit attention in Villani's volume. In the case of both Villani and Landino, then, the *De viris illustribus* tradition is placed at the service of Florentine municipal patriotism, in a series of short sketches, and represents a celebration of recent and contemporary figures, unlike Petrarch's substantial lives, his historiographical concerns and his humanist adulation of the ancient past that was not linked to any contemporary city or state.

In fact already by the end of the fourteenth century Petrarch's *De viris illustribus* was being singled out for criticism by the humanist avant-garde of the generation after Villani for being too much like a scholastic scrapbook ('un zibaldone da quaresima').[11] In the course of the Quattrocento this shift of interest towards the present becomes more pronounced: Enea Silvio Piccolomini (Pius II) wrote a *De viris illustribus* (*c.* 1450) containing about forty brief biographies of major contemporary rulers or prelates (the only literary life is that of Leonardo Bruni);[12] and Bartolomeo Facio dedicated his continuation of Pius's work, also entitled *De viris illustribus* (1456), to the pope himself, a continuation which covers seven categories: poets, orators, jurists, medical men, artists, private citizens, and captains or princes. The main emphasis in Facio's preface is on the fact that he deliberately chose to write about his contemporaries because their illustrious examples provide morally sound stimuli, and because the ancients, who have been written about extensively, are now as remote as the ancient gods.[13] All of Facio's subjects come from the first half of the Quattrocento, including some of the earliest brief lives of artists such as Gentile da Fabriano, Pisanello, Rogier van der Weyden, Ghiberti, and Donatello. The status of artists is still somewhat problematic, as Facio says he ought to have placed them immediately after the poets since the two groups have so much 'affinitas' (p. 43). He explains that both rely on *inventio* and *dispositio*, both must possess knowledge of other disciplines, both often need to portray the same emotions. Both groups also produce works that fulfil the Horatian pairing of *utile* and *dulce*, and Horace's other pairing of painting and poetry ('ut pictura poesis') also justifies the entry of the life of the artist into the tradition of lives of the poets. However, despite this theoretical

---

[11] See Antonio Lanza, *Polemiche e berte letterarie nella Firenze del primo Quattrocento* (Rome, 1971), pp. 261–7 (263–4), and George Holmes, *The Florentine Enlightenment 1400–1450* (Oxford, 1969), pp. 1–6.

[12] For the edition, see Enee Silvii Piccolomini postea Pii II, *De viris illustribus*, ed. Adrianus van Heck (Città del Vaticano, 1991); see also Paolo Viti, 'Osservazioni sul *De viris aetate sua claris* di Enea Silvio Piccolomini', in *Pio II e la cultura del suo tempo*, ed. Luisa Rotondi Secchi Tarugi (Milan, 1991), pp. 199–214.

[13] Bartolomeus Facius, *De viris illustribus*, ed. Lorenzo Mehus (Florence, 1745), p. 2.

justification, the artists in fact appear between the medical men and private citizens.

Facio's arch-rival, Lorenzo Valla (1407–57), also attempted a biography of a contemporary ruler, his *Gesta Ferdinandi Regis Aragonum* (1445–6). Despite its title, this was not so much a single biography as the first part of a planned (but never completed) historical diptych about Ferdinand and Alfonso of Aragon. Despite, or perhaps because of, its occasionally critical approach, Valla's work remained an isolated and controversial example of a more realistic mixture of biography and history; but the polemics that surrounded it threw up important theoretical questions about humanist historiography and biography.[14]

In this as in all his other works Valla was an innovator. His enemy Facio, who obtained the commission to write the official biography of Alfonso, attacked the *Gesta* in his *Invective* (1446) on two counts: unclassical Latin (as Facio believed, but Valla was to prove him wrong) and impropriety of content. On this latter count he cites, among other episodes, Valla's narration of old King Martin's attempts at siring an heir (because of his obesity he had to be suspended from the ceiling before being lowered onto the nuptial bed): this for Facio was against both the *decorum* and the *brevitas* required by the humanist rules for writing history (*Invective*, p. 97). Valla defends the episode first by claiming that it served to illustrate how desperate the king was to have an heir, then by pointing out that decorum was not breached since the king and queen were a married couple; and finally he argues: 'Historians have never shrunk from relating this kind of detail. Leaving aside Greek historians, what about the details of the Caesars' lives found in Suetonius? Or Tacitus? Or later historians?'[15] Suetonius thus becomes a justification for inserting coarser details in biography and history, and is associated with veracity rather than elegance. When Facio claims that to portray King Martin snoring during an embassy goes against the 'verisimile', 'decorum' and 'dignitas' of history, Valla warns of the dangers for the historian of downgrading what is 'verum' for what is 'verisimile' (pp. 253–4). However, despite Valla's theoretical expertise and wider appreciation of ancient history and biography, his attempt at a critical, objective historiography had no followers, and in the South of Italy

[14] For the edition, see Lorenzo Valla, *Gesta Ferdinandi Regis Aragonum*, ed. Ottavio Besomi (Padua, 1973); for the polemics, see Valla, *Antidotum in Facium*, ed. Mariangela Regoliosi (Padua, 1981) and Bartolomeo Facio, *Invective in Laurentium Vallam*, ed. E. I. Rao (Naples, 1979); see also Giacomo Ferraù, 'La concezione storiografica del Valla: I *Gesta Ferdinandi Regis Aragonum*', in *Lorenzo Valla e l'umanesimo italiano: Atti del Convegno internazionale di studi umanistici, Parma, 18–19 ottobre 1984*, ed. Besomi and Regoliosi (Padua, 1986), pp. 265–310.

[15] Valla, *Antidotum in Facium*, p. 256. The final reference is probably to the historians of the *Historia Augusta*, mentioned elsewhere by Valla as justifying other details (e.g. p. 77).

his work was replaced by the 'agiografie laiche' of Facio's and Panormita's lives of Alfonso.[16]

Valla's praise of Suetonius as legitimating a more intimate and forthright kind of history is taken up later by Poliziano towards the end of the century in his *Praefatio in Suetonium* (1490). There he argues that biography is superior to broader histories since it allows models of behaviour for imitation or rejection to be discerned more clearly, and that consequently Plutarch and Suetonius are in no way inferior to Herodotus and Sallust.[17] Suetonius' wider popularity in the Quattrocento is well documented: in Italy there was an 'explosion' of manuscripts of the *Caesars*, and there were no fewer than fifteen printed editions between 1470 and 1500 alone,[18] not to mention commentaries written by scholars of the stature of Poliziano, Merula, and Beroaldo. However, Suetonius was never able to eclipse the major historiographical models, Livy and Sallust.[19]

The displacement of the past in favour of the present continues into the sixteenth century: Paolo Giovio's many biographies are mostly of powerful princes and popes, either contemporaries (Leo X, Hadrian VI, Bajazet) or from the recent past (the whole run of Visconti rulers of Milan from the thirteenth century to the fifteenth). Some of these lives could be critical of their subjects (notably those on the two popes), an approach which Giovio signals in the opening words of his dedicatory letter to Cosimo de' Medici (1548): 'I have written the lives of a number of outstanding men in imitation of Plutarch, that most weighty philosopher, though using a freer style. [. . .] For you know [. . .] with what intellectual candour, what zeal and open determination to tell the truth I have handed down to posterity the events I have seen.'[20] Even before this, Giovio showed that he was aware of the critical responsibilities of the biographer: when Girolamo Scannapeco claimed that his *Life of Pietro Gravina* (1532) had criticized its subject too harshly, the biographer's reply to Scannapeco (1534/5) defended his right to criticize his subjects, pointing out that biography is history, not eulogy; but he maintains that his criticisms have a light, reticent touch, not like Suetonius who painted his subjects' vices in large letters on Roman triumphal arches, as it were.[21]

---

[16] Ferraù, 'La concezione storiografica', pp. 306–9.

[17] Angeli Politiani, *Opera omnia* (Basle, 1553), p. 503.

[18] L. D. Reynolds, *Texts and Transmission: A Survey of the Latin Classics* (Oxford, 1983), p. 404.

[19] Pontano's *Actius* (1507), one of the few theoretical treatments of historiography in the century, deals only cursorily with biography in the last two pages of a forty-page discussion which concentrates on Livy and Sallust: see Giovanni Pontano, *I dialoghi*, ed. Carmelo Previtera (Florence, 1943), pp. 230–31.

[20] Pauli Iovii, *Vitae illustrium virorum* (Basle, 1578), fo. 5r.

[21] In Pauli Iovii, *Opera*, I: *1514–1544*, ed. G. G. Ferrero (Rome, 1956), pp. 74–9.

Giovio's most famous biographical enterprise was the collection of brief (usually one-page) *Elogia* of both writers and rulers, which was to be the literary equivalent of his collection of portraits in his celebrated museum on Lake Como.[22] The *Elogia*, meaning 'inscriptions' not eulogies, are more acerbic than Facio's laudatory accounts: the writers covered start from Albertus Magnus and Aquinas, include the main Italian Quattrocento humanists as well as some contemporary European ones (Budé, Erasmus, More, Vivès), and also include vernacular writers, from Dante, Petrarch, and Boccaccio to Ariosto, Castiglione, and Machiavelli. The whole project appears to have been modelled on the ancient writer Varro's lost *Imagines* of about seven hundred Greco-Roman subjects. Once more biography and portraiture go hand in hand.

Yet for all their popularity, Giovio's Latin biographies are really the end of the *De viris illustribus* genre in Italy, since after him Latin works in this tradition are rare, and belong solely to the academic world, into which humanism retreated. All the collections mentioned so far (apart from Landino's) were written in Latin, but as the *volgare* rose in status in the course of the Quattrocento, the biographical tradition began to emerge in the vernacular: in the late fifteenth century Vespasiano da Bisticci wrote a collection of lives of famous recent and contemporary prelates, rulers, and men of culture (1480–98).[23] By the time Giorgio Vasari compiles his famous collection of lives of artists alone (1550, 2nd edn 1568), beginning in the thirteenth century but bringing the sequence of artists to an end in his own times, the 'vita d'artista' has now separated to form an autonomous tradition, no longer dependent on the Horatian justification that artists are similar to poets. Vasari's initial title for the collection had been *Commentarii* (following the example of Ghiberti's fifteenth-century work on art), then *Storia*, before becoming, on the advice of Giovio himself, the *Vite de' più eccellenti pittori, scultori e architettori*, which with that adjective *eccellenti* thus reattached itself to the *De viris illustribus* tradition.[24] The fact that in the original edition Vasari accompanied each life with a portrait of each artist absolved him from the need to describe the subject's physique in detail, and reinforced that association of biographies with portraits that

[22] Giovio initially wrote the verbal 'portraits' of 146 (dead) writers (1546), and later added an accompanying volume of 133 famous rulers and captains (1551). His plan was to write two further volumes, on living writers, and on artists and famous wits (the link between artists and comedy again), but the former was never started, while the latter was eventually written, with Giovio's encouragement, by Giorgio Vasari: see T. C. Price Zimmermann, *Paolo Giovio: The Historian and the Crisis of Sixteenth-Century Italy* (Princeton, NJ, 1995), pp. 206–15.

[23] See Vespasiano da Bisticci, *Le vite*, ed. Aulo Greco, 2 vols (Florence, 1970–76).

[24] Zygmunt Wazbinski, 'L'idée de l'histoire dans la première et la seconde édition des *Vies* de Vasari', in *Il Vasari storiografo e artista*, pp. 1–25.

had characterized the collections of Petrarch and Giovio. Collections of lives in this period thus gradually come to emphasize more the present and recent past, and in tandem with this shift they are now mostly written in the vernacular rather than Latin.

Individual Lives: Biographies of Petrarch and Dante

Boccaccio's brief Latin sketch of Petrarch is the first secular biography of a contemporary by an Italian writer, just as Petrarch's Letter to Posterity is the first short autobiography by an Italian. But since those two texts are, as we shall see, very closely intertwined, it is more appropriate to consider them together in the next section. Boccaccio also wrote the first biography, or rather biographies, of Dante. Known until recently as his *Vita di Dante*, it was in fact called by the author merely *Trattatello in laude di Dante*: a more modest title but also a more accurate one, since this work belongs as much to encomium as to biography. The first version (I) was probably written between 1351 and 1355; a second, much briefer, redaction (IIA) was composed some time between 1361 and 1363: while version I amounts to 59 pages in the most recent edition, IIA is just over half that length (around 35 pages); and a third version (IIB), expanding slightly on the second one (around 39 pages), was written shortly afterwards.[25] However, it is the first two redactions and their differences that are most significant: the main alterations show that Boccaccio, after his meeting with Petrarch in the 1350s and particularly after the latter's critical letter of 1359 about Dante (*Familiares*, 21.15), toned down particularly his praise of Dante's Latin works and his links with medieval scholastic culture.[26] The fact that he wrote three full redactions of the *Trattatello* also demonstrates the importance this biography held in Boccaccio's eyes.

The content and structure of the life, in all versions, is of course modelled on the only examples of the genre available to Boccaccio: the medieval lives of the poets, notably the widely diffused life of Virgil attributed to Donatus, which Boccaccio had transcribed for himself. Donatus' Life has a basic chronological structure beginning with the poet's birth, then pro-

---

[25] References in what follows are to the edition of the three redactions of the *Trattatello*, ed. P. G. Ricci, in *Tutte le opere di Giovanni Boccaccio*, ed. Vittore Branca, 7 vols (Milan, 1964–92), III, 437–538 [5 further vols planned].

[26] See Carlo Paolazzi, 'Petrarca, Boccaccio e il *Trattatello in laude di Dante*', *Studi danteschi*, LV (1983), 165–249; reprinted in his *Dante e la "Comedia" nel Trecento: Dall'Epistola a Cangrande all'età di Petrarca* (Milan, 1989), pp.131–221. See also Martin L. McLaughlin, *Literary Imitation in the Italian Renaissance: The Theory and Practice of Literary Imitation in Italy from Dante to Bembo* (Oxford, 1995), pp. 53–8.

viding a physical and moral portrait, a list of works, mention of his death and his epitaph, and ending with his critical fortune. Boccaccio's biography of Dante is a longer, more articulated if more rhetorical piece, with a full introduction and conclusion, and a sense of structure which allows the life to end, as it began, with the interpretation of Dante's mother's prophetic dream. These and the other additions not in the lives of Virgil—the introduction, the invective against Florence, the defence of poetry, and the interpretation of the dream—all concern the question of literary fame and form a coherent programme of homage to Dante, who had been denied the Florentine laurel because of his exile. The whole work is thus a kind of literary laurel for Dante, and fulfils that rewarding of virtue that Solon had said was necessary to the well-being of any state, a maxim cited in Boccaccio's opening words.

There are, of course, many similarities between the two lives, but also significant differences. The medieval life of Virgil followed a straight chronological sequence from birth to death to posthumous fame and criticism, with the poet's physical and moral character inserted between his early studies and his maturity. Boccaccio's biography takes us from birth to death in the first half, the end of this sequence being signalled by the quotation of Dante's epitaph. This is then followed by a defence of poetry, an analysis of the poet's character, and a list of works: Dante's moral flaws (lust, anger, pride) are in this way protectively inserted between the humanist defence of poetry and the impressive roll-call of works. In any case, these were not excessive flaws in a poet, since Donatus too had noted that Virgil was prone to (homosexual) lust, and involved in civic strife and enforced exile from Mantua. But on the whole Virgil had been very chaste, so Dante's love for Beatrice is described as 'onestissimo' (I.37, II.29). Each life is shot through with quotations from the subject's works, and a prominent place is assigned to the poet's epitaph. However, the lengthy dream interpretation, at the end of Boccaccio's first redaction, with its celebration of the literary greatness and immortality of the *Comedy*, has no parallel in the lives of Virgil, which mention the dream briefly at the opening but offer no exegesis. His praise for Dante's powers of speech ('he was a most eloquent and smooth speaker, endowed with excellent fluency', I.117) and for his tendency only to speak when asked, and even then only to answer relevantly, is taken formulaically both from the Virgilian tradition ('he spoke with great smoothness and astonishing eloquence') and from Boccaccio's own earlier sketch of Petrarch.[27]

One final strand that is entwined in Boccaccio's biography of Dante is

---

[27] See Giuseppe Velli, 'Il *De vita et moribus Francisci Petracchi de Florentia* del Boccaccio e la biografia del Petrarca', *Modern Language Notes*, CLL (1987), 32–8.

his own innate talent for narrative. The life is enriched by 'romantic' vignettes of the poet's early meetings with Beatrice, by a bravura passage of medieval misogyny in the portrait of his married life with his wife Gemma, and by a series of anecdotes related to his travels: in Siena Dante becomes so absorbed in reading a book in an apothecary's shop that he fails to notice the noisy, day-long Palio procession taking place in the street outside; while in Paris he astounds the Sorbonne professors with his ability to recall the arguments for and against in fourteen theological *quaestiones* (obviously this also echoes Christ astonishing the Doctors in the Temple). In the later versions, Boccaccio eliminates the Siena and most of the Paris anecdote, not just in the interest of narrative economy, as has been suggested, nor for the sake of biographical 'truth', but for reasons of literary ideology, isolating Dante from his medieval scholastic context (with its guilds of 'speziali', to which Dante himself belonged, and its theological *quaestiones de quodlibet*). For this reason also Boccaccio systematically omits in the later version allusions to Dante's interest in natural philosophy (I.23, 214), logic, and the medieval technique of 'divisioni' in the *Vita nuova* (I.175): these were all targets of Petrarch's humanistic invectives. The two major versions of the *Trattatello*, then, are a locus of revision for Boccaccio: the second redaction, while leaving the structure and sequence of events undisturbed, registers a systematic series of modifications which were designed to make Dante an acceptable literary model for the new humanist age inaugurated by Petrarch, and to show how much the biographer had changed from the naïve Dante-admirer of his earlier days. However, even the modified later redactions failed to satisfy the next generation of humanists, those who came to maturity around 1400, particularly as with their knowledge of Greek they were now able to look to models other than the Latin lives of the poets.

Leonardo Bruni (1370/75–1444) was the greatest humanist of his generation and the epitome of what has become known as Florentine 'civic humanism'. This civic inflection of the humanist movement was characterized by its exaltation of the active over the contemplative existence, by its promotion of a republican ideology, and by its revaluation of the vernacular works of Dante, Petrarch, and Boccaccio, despite the fact that Latin was the dominant intellectual medium of the new humanist age.[28] Bruni was also the outstanding Greek scholar of his generation, and it is relevant for our purposes that most of his early scholarly activity was devoted to translating

---

[28] See Hans Baron, *The Crisis of the Early Italian Renaissance* (Princeton, NJ, rev. edn 1966), and his 'Leonardo Bruni: Professional Rhetorician or Civic Humanist?', *Past and Present*, XXXVI (1967), 21–37. For a critique of Baron's views, see *Renaissance Civic Humanism*, ed. James Hankins (Cambridge, 2000).

several of Plutarch's *Lives* into Latin.[29] In fact throughout Italy in the first half of the Quattrocento all the major Italian humanists were engaged in translating Plutarch from Greek into Latin, as an exercise in honing their Latin style, and the many manuscripts that survive attest to their popularity.[30] However, when one considers the Plutarch lives that Bruni elected to translate, their significance becomes more ideological than pedagogical or literary: *Mark Antony* (1405, dedicated to Salutati), *Cato the Younger* (begun 1405 in Florence, polished later), *The Gracchi, Aemilius Paulus* (1410), *Sertorius, Pyrrhus* (1408–12), *Demosthenes* (1412). Almost every one of these was either a great hero of the Roman Republic or its deadly enemy. No matter which side they had been on, it is clear that one of Bruni's aims in this project was to champion the Roman republican heroes against Plutarch's tendency in his comparisons to prefer the Greek exemplar. The only subject not a hero or enemy of Rome was Demosthenes, whom Plutarch coupled with and deemed superior to Cicero, but even this translation of *Demosthenes* was highly significant for Bruni: it eventually led him to compose another pro-republican work, his own biography of Cicero —the *Cicero novus* (1415)—when he discovered how critical Plutarch was of the Roman orator, and when he realized how poorly the *Cicero* had been translated by his older contemporary, Iacopo Angeli da Scarperia.[31]

At the outset of the *Cicero novus* Bruni declares that his aim is to rewrite Cicero's 'private life, character and public life' (p. 418) with fuller historical information and greater balance, stressing that there is nothing in this new biography which cannot be documented from reliable sources. Unlike Plutarch, he cites several other sources for the life, mostly Cicero's own works, especially the letters (including at one point a whole letter from Caesar to Cicero, p. 462), but also other authors such as Cornelius Nepos (p. 420) and Sallust (p. 432). But despite this 'objective' sensitivity to sources, Bruni's biography does have an ideological thrust: the key phrases that dominate his account are 'res publica' and 'libertas', the twin ideals of republicanism and liberty that underpinned his political stance. Bruni stresses that Cicero was the first to be called 'pater patriae', and that this happened during the Republic, long before Roman emperors usurped the title (p. 430). At the end, Cicero's motive for seeking out Antony's enmity is given as 'pro re publica' (p. 490), and even his orders to Brutus

[29] Gary Ianziti, 'The Plutarchan Option: Leonardo Bruni's Early Career in History, 1405–1414', *I Tatti Studies: Essays in the Renaissance*, VIII (1999), 11–35.
[30] See Gianvito Resta, *Le epitomi del Plutarco nel Quattrocento* (Padua, 1962). For manuscripts containing the lives, see, for example, Bodleian Library, Oxford, Canonici Class. Lat. MSS 172, 173, 270, 294.
[31] References in what follows are to the edition in Leonardo Bruni, *Opere letterarie e politiche*, ed. Paolo Viti (Turin, 1996), pp. 400–99.

to kill Antony are seen as being issued 'for the preservation of the freedom and safety of the Roman people' (p. 490), while the proscription of Cicero and others is considered by Bruni as having the sole aim of killing off the good men and defenders of liberty in the state (p. 494).

There is also considerable attention devoted to the claims of the active and contemplative lives: during his early philosophical training in Greece Antiochus urges the young Cicero 'with strong arguments, to take up political life' (p. 422), so when Cicero's time in Sicily makes him the forgotten man of Roman politics, he resolves to live henceforth 'before the eyes of the Roman people' (p. 428). Bruni's ideal of a balance between the active and contemplative lives is actualized by Cicero (and later Dante): the Roman orator is described as 'not abandoning scholarship and literature no matter how busy' (p. 446);[32] Cicero devotes himself entirely to literary activity only when power has fallen into the hands of one man, and the senate has no more authority (p. 468), so his title of 'pater patriae', given for his political services, is ideally matched by the tribute of 'pater eloquii et litterarum nostrarum' paid to him by scholars. As with his republicanism, so here again the main motivation for this emphasis on the active and contemplative existences was autobiographical. Bruni, like Cicero, turned to active political life only after he had read thoroughly and widely in philosophy (p. 470), and the biographical identification of the biographer with his subject is made explicit at the end of the list of works: Bruni points out that he too has translated from Greek into Latin the speeches for and against Ctesiphon by Demosthenes and Aeschines, since Cicero's Latin versions of them have perished (p. 472).[33]

Bruni's account is more laudatory than Plutarch's: although he does share some of the Greek biographer's criticisms of Cicero, namely his egoistic insistence on the importance of his consulship, he adds that this was necessary against his detractors, and that in any case nobody outdid Cicero in his praise of other writers (pp. 478–80). However, the humanist barely mentions his other main weaknesses, his cowardice in battle and his untimely jokes and sarcasm, to which Plutarch devotes several chapters (Plutarch, *Cicero*, 7, 9, 25–7). All he concedes is that Cicero was 'almost excessive' (p. 482) in his use of jibes and witticisms. In fact it seems that Bruni systematically suppressed all of Plutarch's (and other writers')

---

[32] Compare what Bruni says of Dante: 'After this battle Dante returned home and devoted himself more fervently than ever to study, and yet he never abandoned any aspect of his public life with his fellow citizens' (*Opere*, ed. Viti, p. 541).

[33] Similarly when Bruni, for these translations, asks Niccolò Niccoli to send him a copy of Cicero's own introduction to the lost versions, he wants this, he says, 'so that I can get as close as I am able to the great man' (Bruni, *Epistolarum Libri VIII*, ed. Lorenzo Mehus, 2 vols, Florence, 1741, I, 98).

criticisms of Cicero.[34] In his tripartite biography, containing his subject's 'res gestae', then his 'vita moresque', Bruni relocates moral questions to the latter two sections, his private life and his character, thus almost anticipating Machiavelli in severing the moral dimension from public life: this has been seen as 'a revolution in biography, since it frees the telling of the career from any surrounding judgments about the moral character of the man himself' (Ianziti, 'A Life in Politics', p. 55). So Bruni's biography of Cicero contains polemical claims against Plutarch at the outset, and certainly draws on more documentary evidence than his predecessor's, but is much less critical of his subject, and is permeated with republican ideology: Cicero is a hero of the Republic, but he is also the embodiment of that ideal union of literary and political activity that inspired the Florentine humanist's own existence.

Bruni's interest in biography continued into the 1420s with a new life of Aristotle (1429–30). This work evinces the same techniques as Bruni's other lives: use of documentary sources, including the subject's will (a closing motif favoured by Diogenes Laertius), the tripartite division of the biography into public life, character, and private life, and the insertion of significant digressions into the life (one on the harmony of Platonism and Aristotelianism; and another on Aristotle's eloquence).

Bruni's decision to write the biographies of Dante and Petrarch was conditioned by the political context of the time. Once more in 1435–6, as in the early years of the century when he had written his Latin panegyric of Florence, the *Laudatio Florentine urbis* (1403–4), Florence was being threatened by the expansionist aims of the Visconti rulers of Milan. This time Bruni chooses not the city itself but its two most famous writers as his subject. He writes in the *volgare* because, as he says in the life of Dante, poetry or literature can be written in any language, Latin or vernacular, Greek or Latin (Bruni, ed. Viti, p. 550). As with the *Cicero novus*, the stimulus for the biography is Bruni's critique of a work that he has just been reading: this time not a poor translation of Plutarch, but Boccaccio's life of Dante, in its later redaction. Bruni's life follows roughly the same order as Boccaccio's *Trattatello*, but with significant alterations which show that even Boccaccio's modified version of the Dante life no longer satisfied the new generation of humanists. Bruni makes no mention of Dante's mother's dream, nor even any allusion to Beatrice: instead the stress is on the civic Dante, the city politician and participant in the battle of Campaldino; and the major digression is in defence of the active life and marriage,

[34] Gary Ianziti, 'A Life in Politics: Leonardo Bruni's *Cicero*', *Journal of the History of Ideas*, LXI (2000), 39–58.

countering Boccaccio's now outdated misogyny and critique of the married existence.

As with his Cicero and Aristotle biographies, Bruni explicitly divides the life into the three broad sections of public life, private life and character, and relies more than his predecessors on documentary evidence. In the very first paragraph he states that Dante's claim that his forebears were descended from the early Roman founders of Florence is mere conjecture, as there is no external evidence for it (p. 539). Conversely, the young poet's feelings of apprehension at the battle of Campaldino are mentioned only because Bruni has seen the letter (now lost) in which he wrote about this (p. 540), and he cites other lost letters (or perhaps the same one) in the course of the biography: one in which Dante bemoans the fact that his woes all stemmed from his time as Priore (p. 542), and one which begins 'Popule mee, quid feci tibi?' (p. 546). However, experienced historian as he is, he does not trust all sources: he has seen an original letter in the Palazzo della Signoria, purporting to be proof that Dante's White Guelph Party was trying to collude with Charles of Valois, but he is so suspicious of it he is convinced it is a forgery (p. 545). When it comes to the standard section on the poet's appearance, Bruni again shows more documentary expertise than his predecessors, verifying his description of the poet by comparing it with his portrait in Santa Croce, and telling the reader precisely where it is: 'almost in the middle of the church, on the left as you head towards the high altar' (p. 548). He is even able to describe Dante's handwriting from autograph letters he has seen (p. 548), can cite an inscription from the Palazzo della Signoria (p. 541) to explain a detail of the battle, and is able to document Dante's possessions from the city archives (p. 547).

Bruni is obviously more of a historian than Boccaccio, but, not surprisingly in view of the anti-Milanese context, he is at times more eulogistic than his predecessor. He does mention Dante's 'animo altero' (p. 547), but passes over the other two flaws admitted to in Boccaccio's biography, his angry political partisanship and his lust; there is no mention at all of Beatrice, and his youthful passions stem, according to Bruni, merely from his association with other 'giovani innamorati' and his poetic cult of 'gentilezza di cuore', not from 'libidine' (p. 548). Unlike Boccaccio, however, he is prepared to admit that the reason Dante abandoned Latin for the vernacular to write the *Comedy* was that his Latin was inferior to his *volgare*, and he explicitly criticizes Dante's Latin prose and verse, which is not even half-decent ('mezzanamente'): other poets have written much better eclogues than Dante's (p. 550), for Dante was a product of his age, writing Latin poorly, 'in the monkish, scholastic fashion' (p. 551), the *Monarchia* itself being written 'in the monkish manner, with no elegance of style' (p.

552). Although he admits the *Comedy* is a masterpiece, Bruni does not mention its title (perhaps because it underlined Dante's misconception of what ancient comedy really was). Bruni's criticisms, then, are directed at the poet's literary shortcomings, not to character flaws, while he also exculpates Florence.

Dante, like Cicero, epitomizes the ideal union of the active and contemplative existences to which Bruni himself aspired: despite his intellectual appetite, he did not close himself off 'in leisure, nor did he hide away from the real world, but living as he did in the company of other young men of his age, he showed that he was civilized, prudent, and skilled at every activity' (p. 540). This enthusiasm for the active existence culminated in Dante's participation in the battle of Campaldino, his involvement in politics, and his marriage to Gemma Donati. Bruni wishes that his predecessor had written more about Dante's 'virtú' than about his falling in love with Beatrice at nine years of age and other 'leggerezze'. Boccaccio's medieval exaltation of the contemplative existence is another object of Bruni's attack: where the former had devoted a whole misogynistic section to the dreariness of Dante's married life which distracted him from his literary occupations, Bruni counters with a short digression against those 'ignoranti' who believe that only those who live 'in solitudine et in otio' (p. 541) can become true scholars. Instead Bruni points out that the great writers and thinkers—Socrates, Aristotle, Cicero, Cato—were all married, had children, and took part in running the 'republica' (p. 542); and the digression ends with Bruni claiming that marriage is the primary unit on which every city is built (p. 542). The whole work concludes with a sentence about Fortune's wheel constantly turning (p. 552), a *sententia* deployed by Plutarch in some of the lives translated by Bruni.

By contrast, Bruni's life of Petrarch is less than half the length of the Dante biography (5 pages against 14 in Viti's edition), surely indicating the biographer's closer identification with the exponent of the active and literary life than with the champion of the 'vita solitaria'. The structure is predictable, starting with his birth in Arezzo, and centring on his revival of humanism, his crowning with the laurel and his lionization by major rulers, before ending with a mention of Boccaccio as his literary successor. As in the life of Dante, Bruni again rejects legends, and relies on documentary evidence. The digression articulating Bruni's republican theory of literature—corresponding to his digressions on the active life and the nature of poetry in the life of Dante—is deliberately placed in the middle of the biography and clearly states that once the Republic gave way to Empire, Latin literature declined (pp. 554–55). Perhaps this digression is inserted into the life of Petrarch as an oblique criticism of his subject, who had been too closely associated with single rulers and princes such as the

Carrara of Padua and Florence's historical enemy, the Visconti of Milan. But explicit criticism is limited, as in the life of Dante, to a critique of Petrarch's literary rather than moral flaws: 'although his style was *not perfect*, nevertheless he alone divined and opened up the way towards the present stylistic peak, by discovering works by Cicero and appreciating and understanding them; and he adapted his style to that highest peak of eloquence, *as much as his abilities would allow him to*' (p. 556; my emphases). Bruni does not list Petrarch's works, because they are too well known, and the life ends with a brief sentence about the succession of the Florentine Muses passing from Petrarch to Boccaccio.

The historian's concern for sources even comes out in Bruni's refusal to write the life of Boccaccio: the reason is that he does not know the details of his birth, private condition, and public life, without which no biography should be written (p. 558). Consequently, instead of writing a third vernacular biography, Bruni writes a Plutarchan comparison between Dante and Petrarch. Here he strives after a balanced synthesis: Dante was superior to Petrarch in three areas: 'nella vita activa et civile', in writing great works in the midst of adversity, and in his knowledge of philosophy and mathematical sciences (p. 559). However he balances these with three other points which counter them respectively: Petrarch was more prudent in electing to live the life of leisure, and in retaining the favour of rulers; it is just as difficult to write literature amidst the temptations of leisure as in adversity; and Petrarch was superior in his knowledge of literature, particularly of Latin. Bruni then does a final balance sheet: in all his Latin works Dante is inferior to Petrarch; in the vernacular they are both equal in writing canzoni, but Petrarch is better at sonnets; yet he ends by stating that in his major work Dante outdoes every work by Petrarch. The comparison concludes as the two biographies did, with a brief sentence once more about fortune and its opposite, virtue: that Petrarch was crowned with the laurel and not Dante is irrelevant, Bruni claims, since while the crown of fortune goes sometimes to deserving, sometimes to undeserving cases, only 'la virtù è certa' (p. 560).

Bruni is a key figure in Renaissance Italian biography: he is the first to be interested in the free-standing life, as opposed to collections of lives, and the first to adapt the Plutarchan comparison to the vernacular. But unlike Plutarch he is more interested in 'res gestae' than character.[35] He is also keen on using major digressions (on the unity of Platonism and Aristotelianism, on the active life, on the nature of poetic inspiration, on republican ideology and literature) in the middle of the work to convey his

---

[35] Ianziti, 'A Life in Politics', pp. 55–8.

own ideals.[36] Indeed these digressions form the backbone of Bruni's ideology: the importance of philosophy, the balance between the active and contemplative lives, the links between republicanism and culture. His humanist training certainly made Bruni 'scientific' in his use of sources, but his systematically uncritical approach to his subjects shows that his ideological convictions carried considerable weight and that his biographies are not really 'objective'.

After Bruni, Renaissance biographies of writers become even more hagiographic: there is now not even any criticism of the works, never mind the character, of the subject. Giannozzo Manetti (1396–1459) wrote his lives of Dante, Petrarch, and Boccaccio around 1440.[37] His main motives for writing were: (1) to provide a Latin equivalent of Boccaccio's and Bruni's vernacular lives, for a learned, humanist audience; (2) to write the lives of all three writers, since Boccaccio wrote only about Dante, Bruni only about Dante and Petrarch; and (3) although Filippo Villani did write Latin lives of all three, he mixed them in with so many other jurists, theologians, and artists that he seems to have squeezed these poets into a small corner of his work, dealing with them 'in a slight and brief manner' ('ieiune et exiliter)' (p. 111): all three lives represent a scaled-down version of the *De viris illustribus* tradition, harnessed to the municipal patriotism of Quattrocento Florence.

By the end of the fifteenth century hardly any critical notes can be detected in free-standing biographies. Girolamo Squarciafico's life of Petrarch was often the first item in the early printed editions of the poet.[38] The biographer could distinguish enough to see that Petrarch's Latin was more like Seneca's than like Cicero's, but the other elements of his biography are thoroughly uncritical: Petrarch is now physically unsurpassed and even his need for glasses, admitted to prominently in the Posterity Letter, is now denied (p. 356). Similarly his eloquence is said to have been such that he could use it for whatever subject he had to write about, and Squarciafico even denies the poet's lust, although he does mention his illegitimate daughter and her tomb in Treviso. The life is also enriched with fanciful anecdotes: the pope of the time would have permitted the poet to marry Laura, especially because the pope himself was in love with Petrarch's sister and wanted to bribe him with a cardinalship in order to have access to her,

---

[36] On digressions as a canonical element in Renaissance biographies, see Tanturli, in *Il Vasari storiografo e artista*, pp. 275–98 (esp. 283–5).

[37] This is the date suggested by C. A. Madrignani, 'Di alcune biografie umanistiche di Dante e Petrarca', *Belfagor*, XVIII (1963), 29–48. All references are to the text in *Le vite di Dante, Petrarca e Boccaccio*, ed. Angelo Solerti (Milan, 1904), pp. 108–51.

[38] I quote from the edition in *Le vite di Dante, Petrarca e Boccaccio*, ed. Solerti, pp. 347–59.

but Petrarch refused partly on moral grounds, but also because marriage to Laura would have terminated his poetic inspiration (p. 353).

The life of Petrarch attributed to Bernardo da Ilicino and regularly found at the start of early printed editions of the *Trionfi* is equally fanciful. Here Petrarch is portrayed in almost Christ-like terms, when as a child in Avignon he is described as 'growing up in upright character and with great subtlety of intellect'.[39] In it we also find the first mention of places of literary pilgrimage in France: in Vaucluse, he says, 'a little house and small garden still show his traces to this day' (ibid.); similarly just outside Milan 'the extremely modest house which he built is still visible today' (p. 2v). The life attributed to Antonio da Tempo and usually printed with the *Canzoniere* is also entirely encomiastic, and as in Squarciafico there is not even any mention of failing eyesight.[40] The free-standing biography ends up regularly as the first item in the new printed editions of poets and writers (as Servius said it should), but by this stage, the early sixteenth century, the critical spirit of a century before has gone, the poet is praised both in human and in artistic terms, as print culture aims to sell the work, not to put off potential buyers.

Autobiography

It is because of his enthusiasm for writing the biographies of famous men that at the end of his autobiographical dialogue, the *Secretum* (*c.* 1347–53), Petrarch has Augustinus tell Franciscus to stop dwelling on the past, on the lives of the illustrious Romans, and to write something about his own life.[41] This turn from the life of others to the self, though it may owe something to Abelard,[42] mainly derives from Augustine's own *Confessions*, which is also the narrative of a rejection of pagan culture. In the rest of the *Secretum* Augustinus dialogues with Franciscus about how he is living his life, grilling him in particular in the last of the three books about his two major weaknesses, his love for Laura and his pursuit of literary immortality through his humanist writings. The second book is also significant in that there Franciscus pleads guilty to four of the seven deadly sins: pride, anger,

---

[39] Francesco Petrarca, *Opera* (Venice, 1515), fo. 2r.

[40] The biography was probably written by the Milanese humanist Decembrio: see Gabriella Mezzanotte, 'Pier Candido Decembrio e la *Vita* del Petrarca attribuito a Antonio da Tempo', *Studi petrarcheschi*, n.s. 1 (1984), 211–24.

[41] Petrarch, *Opere latine*, ed. Bufano, I, 234.

[42] Petrarch possessed and annotated the main manuscript of the *Historia Calamitatum*: see De Nolhac, *Pétrarque et L'humanisme*, II, 217–24, 287–92.

lust, and sloth, but not to the others (envy, avarice, and gluttony).[43] Of course, the *Secretum* is not an autobiography proper: the overarching Christian framework means that character traits are considered not in secular terms but through the grid of the seven deadly sins, and there is no consideration of the development of a personality and no narrative of a life. This fictional dialogue between two sides of Petrarch's psyche simply registers a point of stasis.

Much shorter than the *Secretum*, but more explicitly an autobiographical narrative, is Petrarch's Letter to Posterity, begun around 1351, but added to at least as late as the 1370s, which was to have constituted the final, eighteenth book of his Letters of Old Age (*Seniles*).[44] The Letter is also inspired by a biography, Boccaccio's earlier Latin sketch of Petrarch's life, *De vita et moribus Francisci Petracchi de Florentia* (1348–9), and a comparison of the Letter with the Life, the autobiography with the biography, is instructive.

The title of Boccaccio's brief biography hints at two of the three main sections of the work, which consists of: (1) an outline of Petrarch's life up to the moment when he moves to Parma in 1343; (2) an account of his physical appearance and mores; (3) a list of his major works. The account is more eulogy than biography, Petrarch being hailed in formulaic terms as a second Virgil in poetry, another Cicero in prose, and a latter-day Seneca in moral philosophy. His physical features and powers of speech are portrayed in equally superlative terms.[45] However, in spite of the overwhelmingly encomiastic tone, Boccaccio does admit that the great poet had two character flaws, beset as he sometimes was by two of the seven deadly sins, anger (on occasions) and lust—though even this last flaw elicits attenuation from the biographer, who insists that the Laura of Petrarch's vernacular verse was not a real woman but simply an allegory of poetic fame (Fabbri, ed. Branca, p. 908). But the excessively eulogistic nature of Boccaccio's account causes Petrarch to modify it significantly in his Letter to Posterity.

The most obvious differences are the factual errors in Boccaccio's biography: Petrarch points out that he had studied first in Montpellier then Bologna, not vice versa, and where Boccaccio had claimed that his family had been 'wealthy' ('copiosa fortuna') (p. 898), the autobiographer changes

---

[43] *Opere latine*, ed. Bufano, I, 114–42.

[44] References in what follows are to the edition in *Modelling the Individual: Biography and Portrait in the Renaissance. With a Critical Edition of Petrarch's "Letter to Posterity"*, ed. Karl Enenkel, Betsy de Jong-Crane, and Peter Liebregts (Amsterdam and Atlanta, GA, 1998), pp. 243–81. English translations are my own.

[45] See the edition by Renata Fabbri in *Tutte le opere di Giovanni Boccaccio*, ed. Branca, V.1 (Milan, 1992), pp. 881–911.

this to 'of average wealth, and to tell the truth, more bordering on poverty' (Enenkel, p. 256). There are also major structural changes: in the Letter Petrarch inverts the order of Boccaccio's first two sections, starting first with a self-portrait of his physical, moral, and intellectual make-up, then giving an account of his life, which also includes mention of his works. The physical self-portrait is interesting because it is clearly a more accurate account than Boccaccio's: where the latter had singled out the poet's 'attractive physique', and 'eyes full of gravitas, a pleasant look and keen sight' (Fabbri, p. 906), Petrarch qualifies both remarks, insisting instead on the effects of age: 'I do not boast an excellent physique, but one which was pleasing in my younger years. [. . .] after my sixtieth year I reluctantly had to resort to glasses' (Enenkel, p. 258). He uses a similar formula to tone down his intellectual gifts. Where Boccaccio had used nothing but superlatives, including a lengthy description of his captivating conversation and prodigious memory (Fabbri, p. 908), Petrarch insists: 'My intellect was well-balanced rather than keen, able to turn to every good, sound discipline, but particularly inclined towards moral philosophy and poetry' (Enenkel, p. 262). He immediately adds, echoing Augustine's rejection of the *Aeneid* for the Bible, that with the passing of time he soon turned from poetry too, in order to devote himself to sacred literature. Similarly on his eloquence, he notes: 'According to some people, my eloquence was brilliant and powerful; in my view it was rather fragile and obscure. [. . .] When the subject matter or occasion or audience seemed to demand it, I strove for something higher, though I am not sure how successful I was; let those who heard me be the judge of that. As far as I am concerned, as long as I have lived well, it does not really matter to me whether I can speak well. To seek fame solely from verbal brilliance is empty glory' (p. 262). Here the final *sententia*, on which many of the paragraphs of the Letter end, shows that any sense that Petrarch is being more accurate than Boccaccio about his physical or intellectual qualities is counterbalanced by what is an obvious attempt to fashion a suitable self-image of the Christian, Stoic sage.

When it comes to moral qualities, Petrarch admits to the same two flaws cited by Boccaccio (lust and anger), but strategically surrounds these with declarations that he was unaffected by the other deadly sins (avarice, gluttony, pride, envy). This moral portrait then is carefully constructed and more circumspect than the physical description. Even when admitting to lust, Petrarch offers more excuses than Boccaccio, in the end seeming to protest too much: 'I was plagued by a fierce passion, but it was just one, in my adolescence, and it was totally chaste; and I would have suffered longer from it had not [Laura's] early but beneficial death totally quenched the fires that were already growing cold. [. . .] Eventually as I approached my fortieth year, while I still was capable of strong passions, I abjured not only that obscene act but also any memory of it, as though I had never cast eyes on a woman' (Enenkel, pp. 258–60). Such words, along with the overall attempt to present himself as turning from pagan poetry to sacred scripture, are clearly modelled on Augustine's conversion from lust and pagan literature to Christian morality and Scripture.

However, a number of allusions suggest that beside the Christian saint there is another figure who inspires the Italian poet to write about his own life: the pagan Emperor Augustus. Octavian Augustus occupied a major position in Christian historiography, particularly as it was under his rule that, in medieval eyes, the single greatest event of human history occurred, the Incarnation of Christ. In secular terms he was also the most famous emperor because he presided over the greatest flowering of Latin literature ever seen, notably the 'Augustan' poets Virgil, Horace, Ovid, Propertius. Petrarch was a keen reader of Suetonius' lives of the Caesars, and a quick glance at the indexes to his collected letters, both the *Familiares* and the *Seniles*, reveals that the life of Augustus, who also wrote an autobiography, was his favourite life from Suetonius' *Twelve Caesars*.[46]

It is not surprising, then, to find in the Letter to Posterity explicit allusions to passages from Suetonius, most significantly one from near the beginning and one from the end of the *Augustus*. At the very outset Petrarch states: 'I was one of your race, posterity, a mere mortal man, not sprung from a great nor yet from a lowly background, but from an ancient family, as Augustus says of himself' (p. 256). The allusion here is to Suetonius, *Augustus*, 2.3: 'Augustus himself writes that he was sprung from a family that was no higher than the equestrian class, but it was an old and wealthy family'. Petrarch thus identifies with Augustus in the antiquity of his family though not in its wealth. The second quotation also comes at a key point, at the end of the first section of the Letter, just before the transition from 'mores' to 'vita': 'Nor when I was involved in ordinary conversation with family or friends was I ever concerned with being eloquent, and I am astonished that Augustus Caesar should have had that concern' (p. 262). This reference is again to Suetonius.[47] Petrarch thus clearly alludes to the beginning and end of Suetonius' life of Augustus at the start and end of the first section of his own autobiographical Letter.

[46] See the index to Francesco Petrarca, *Le familiari*, ed. Vittorio Rossi and Umberto Bosco, 4 vols (Florence, 1933–42), IV, 366. For the *Seniles* see Francis Petrarch, *Letters of Old Age: Rerum Senilium Libri I–XVIII*, tr. Aldo S. Bernardo, Saul Levin, and Reta A. Bernardo, 2 vols (Baltimore and London, 1992), II, 698. See also De Nolhac, *Pétrarque et l'humanisme*, II, 33–4.

[47] Probably *Augustus*, 84, or perhaps *Augustus*, 87: see Marziano Guglielminetti, *Memoria e scrittura: L'autobiografia da Dante a Cellini* (Turin, 1977), pp. 150–51, n. 11.

Other elements of the self-portrait with which the Letter opens also derive from the Suetonian picture of Augustus: the Emperor had an 'excellent physique, [. . .] bright and clear eyes, though in old age he saw less with his left eye [. . .] and his complexion was between dark and pale' (*Aug.* 79). Petrarch of course claims that he 'did not have an excellent physique', but he does say that his 'vivid complexion was somewhere between light and dark', and that he had 'sharp eyes and very keen eyesight, but after surprisingly lasting for so long, it started to fail after [his] sixtieth year so that reluctantly [he] had to resort to glasses' (p. 258). Petrarch's Letter to Posterity, then, like all his other works, links closely with other texts, biographies in this case: Boccaccio's embryonic life of the poet and Suetonius' life of *Augustus*. The presence of Augustus, almost as much as that of Augustine, haunts Petrarch's autobiographical writings.

One passage from Suetonius' life will have a particular resonance in early humanist autobiographical texts. In *Familiares*, 23.2.17, another letter to the Holy Roman Emperor, Petrarch says: 'This concept [of not procrastinating] is useful to everyone, but for you is so essential that without it, however much effort and virtue you employ, you will not be able to give a proper account of your stewardship of the Empire'. Here Petrarch is quoting Suetonius' statement that Augustus, when on one occasion he thought of giving up imperial rule, gave an account of the state of the empire ('rationarium imperii') to both magistrates and the senate (*Aug.* 28); this is a well known passage to Petrarch, not only because it occurs in the chapter that ends with the most quoted phrase in this life (Augustus' boast about finding Rome brick and leaving it marble), but it is cited again in the letter-treatise on the ideal ruler (*Seniles*, 14.1). The very word 'rationiarium' is later used as the title of the substantial autobiographical work written by Petrarch's disciple Giovanni Conversini in the late 1390s, *Rationarium vite* (the Latin title meaning something like an 'account book of my life').[48]

Giovanni's opening words—'Weak little man, what is the point of your daily labour?' ('Quo diuturnus iste labor, homuncio?')—clearly echo the start of Petrarch's autobiographical *Secretum* ('Quid agis, homuncio?'), as does the work's insistence on turning from writing and reading about others towards the self. The word 'rationarium' is immediately used in terms that link it with the biblical notion of 'stewardship': ' "Come, wicked servant, render an account of your stewardship"; [. . .] recount your adversities in a sincere, truthful style. For no one knows anyone better than yourself, no one is a more reliable witness of your life, as long as blind error does not

---

[48] Quotations in what follows are from Giovanni Conversini, *Rationarium vite*, ed. Vittore Nason (Florence, 1986).

deceive your conscience nor constant shame cloud it' (Conversini, ed. Nason, p. 51). Subsequently this biblical image is enriched with a secular mercantile metaphor: 'just as [the good father] writes in his account book the income and outgoings, so I going over in the sighing of my heart the years that are past, will embrace the whole sequence of years that have gone by' (p. 67). One of the last chapters also opens with a reminder of the account-book metaphor: 'As I prepare to write down at the end of this account book the end of this wearying journey' (p. 172). But there are sufficient Suetonian intertexts throughout Conversini's memoir to suggest that he is also aware of the term's use in the life of Augustus: at one of the more dramatic moments, when he is planning to kill his uncle, the Bishop of Grado, Conversini says his anger cooled as quickly as asparagus cooks, one of Augustus' favourite sayings, reported by Suetonius ('Ut Cesarem Augustum de se predicasse legi, durabat vix dum asparagi coquerentur', p. 146; cf. *Aug.* 87). And Giovanni's many family problems cause him to identify with the first Roman emperor: 'this made me almost like Augustus, for whom everything in the world went according to his wishes, but in the members of his family he only found cause for grief' (p. 161; cf. *Aug.*, 65). However, the overall confessional tone to the work derives from Augustine's work: like the saint, Giovanni's losing of the right path was the cause of his conversion (pp. 102–3); he later echoes the prayer of Augustine's mother (p. 156); and many chapters open, like those in the *Confessions*, with a plea to God, or a mention of the subject's sins. Conversini's *Rationarium vite* is an interesting 73-chapter life-story, inspired by biblical /Augustinian ideas of repentance and conversion from several deadly sins (including lust and contemplated murder), and containing comic and erotic overtones from the *novella* tradition (e.g. Chapters 26 and 32) as well as clear echoes of Petrarch's *Secretum* and Suetonius' life of Augustus.

Later Quattrocento humanists such as Leonardo Bruni and Pius II wrote lengthy *Commentarii* which dealt with their own lives and the events they lived through, but this was a mixed genre which veered more towards a history of their own times than to autobiography.[49] Artists too, as well as learned humanists, favoured this term: Ghiberti's *Commentarii* (1447–55) were a mixture of autobiography, the artistic workshop book, and the contemporary merchants' memoirs tradition.[50] After a history of ancient art traced in Book I, largely following the elder Pliny and Vitruvius, Ghiberti charts the development of 'modern' art in Italy down to his own time, at

---

[49] On the fashion for *Commentarii* in the second half of the Quattrocento, see Gary Ianziti, *Humanistic Historiography under the Sforzas: Politics and Propaganda in Fifteenth-Century Milan* (Oxford, 1988), pp. 145, 175–7.
[50] See Lorenzo Ghiberti, *I commentarii* (Biblioteca Nazionale Centrale di Firenze, II.1.333), ed. Lorenzo Bartoli (Florence, 1998).

which point, in the last few pages of Book II he gives an account of his own artistic development, before moving on in the last book to a technical discussion of optics and perspective.

Much more substantial is Alberti's autobiography, his *Vita*, probably written in the 1460s,[51] which in many ways anticipates the 'Renaissance man' autobiography epitomized by Cellini's *Vita* (1558–66). Written in the third person, like Caesar's *Commentarii*, it has only recently been securely attributed to Alberti himself, so this too is a text that hovers between biography and autobiography. It is clearly unfinished, as it begins *in medias res* with no introduction, and stops abruptly in the midst of a second series of the subject's famous sayings. However, the work does have a discernible structure: first a chronological account of the life, then a description of character and 'mores' which is interrupted by a lengthy list of witty sayings, and finally a physical description and another list of sayings.

The very first sentence mentions Alberti's 'pueritia' (Fubini and Menci Gallorini, p. 68) and the first paragraph deals with his wide-ranging education, which embraces arms, horsemanship, and physical exercise, as well as music, literature, painting, and sculpture. The second paragraph immediately moves on to the beginning of his maturity, his university studies (of law), his illness, his first literary work, his turning to physics and mathematics 'because he realized that they required not so much memory as intelligence' (p. 70). There then follows a paragraph about his mature literary works, followed by a long account of his relations with those who criticized them (the views of critics also had a prominent place in the lives of Virgil), and his difficult, even violent relations with his relatives. The emphasis here is on character, on Alberti's Stoic, taciturn endurance of these wrongs, and his reluctance to take revenge by calling on the help of those many rulers who admired him (p. 71). When even his relatives ignore his major dialogue, *Della famiglia*, he is inclined to burn the work; and although that detail may come from the lives of Virgil, one absolutely original element here is the portrait of Alberti's delight in any rare piece of knowledge he can glean from artisans ('fabri'), architects, shipwrights, tailors, and cobblers—this is all the more unusual in that the first group and last two groups were constantly used to epitomize the unlearned audience attacked by Alberti's fellow humanists.[52]

---

[51] For the dating and the edition, see Riccardo Fubini and Anna Menci Gallorini, 'L'autobiografia di Leon Battista Alberti: Studio e edizione', *Rinascimento*, XII (1972), 21–78.

[52] Petrarch defines the unlearned audience as 'dyers, weavers and artisans' (*Familiares*, 24.12.31), or as 'cobblers and bakers' (*Prose*, 60); Bruni singles out 'woolworkers, cobblers and agents, people who have never read literature' (*Opere*, ed. Viti, 126); and Giovanni Brancati mentions 'tailors, cobblers, barbers and all the other lowly and unlearned people' (quoted in Roberto Cardini, *La critica del Landino*, Florence, 1973, p. 181, n. 56).

The second section, on his mores, claims that though he never suffered from avarice, he was prone to anger: the mention of these two deadly sins might suggest that the life has a Christian orientation, as earlier biographies clearly did, but this is not the case: this is a secular text, with no mention anywhere of Christianity or God. A list of artworks (including his camera obscura) and writings on art follows, before we return to his contemplative character and his lack of pride. There then comes the first list of his witty sayings (pp. 73–6), punctuated by another passage about his lack of envy (p. 74).

The final section begins with Alberti's almost miraculous abilities: his capacity to prophesy the future, to tell immediately whether men were his friends or enemies, as well as his modesty in attributing to others his own good deeds. Then comes a physical description: we are told of his ability to withstand bodily pain, his susceptibility to cold, his dislike of garlic and honey, and the last sentence of this section on character and physique claims that he provided an example to other men that they can do anything they like if they have the will power (p. 77). The last paragraphs before the final list of sayings (with which the work concludes) deal with the moral lessons he derived from nature: when he went out and saw artisans about their work he was reminded that he too should be busy; when he saw the countryside coming into bloom in spring or the fields ripe with crops in summer he would chide himself about productivity, and such sights were able to restore his health. A more unusual note is struck when we are informed that he found pleasure in any aesthetic spectacle: old men moving with dignity, or the delights of nature, or elegant animals. It is at this point that he tells us that he wrote a Latin funeral oration for his dog: though Burckhardt listed this as yet another illustration of the virtuosity of 'Renaissance man', the context of this passage and the description of the dog as 'magnificent' ('lepidissimo', p. 77) suggest a different emphasis, the sensitive artist's appreciation of nature and animals. One final individual note is sounded when he tells us that in literature he appreciated good content ('historiam') so much that 'he even declared inelegant writers to be worthy of praise' (p. 77).[53] The work ends abruptly with another two pages of sayings. The Stoic emphasis and the long list of clever *dicta* show this biography's debt to Diogenes Laertius' *Lives of the Philosophers*, but it stands out for its originality rather than anything else: notably Alberti's open celebration of the importance of all kinds of skill (including cobblers and tailors), which is reflected both in his taste for all kinds of writers and in his emphasis on all-round versatility, man's capacity

---

[53] For Alberti's appreciation of writers for their content, see McLaughlin, *Literary Imitation*, pp. 149–50.

to achieve anything. This is completely in harmony with that optimism about the present's capacity to rival the past which was evident in Alberti's dedicatory letter to his own *Della pittura* (1436). And that optimism carries through into the next century, exemplified by Vasari's major biographies and Cellini's autobiography, both of which celebrate a narrative of progress towards a present that is, in artistic terms, perfect.

This survey has highlighted the enormous quantity as well as the particular qualities of biographies and autobiographies written during the Italian Renaissance. It is clear that famous works, such as Vasari's *Vite*, and Cellini's and Cardano's autobiographies do not arise *ex nihilo* but spring from a well-ploughed biographical furrow, which stretches back to Plutarch, Suetonius, and the Late Antique lives of the poets. Suetonius' *Augustus* has emerged as a particularly influential source, partly also, one suspects, because this was the first complete life in the Suetonian corpus (the life of Julius Caesar is incomplete). Diogenes Laertius' *Lives of the Philosophers*, translated into Latin by Ambrogio Traversari around 1432, is also influential, especially in the quotation of letters, or of the will and famous sayings of the subject.

As for Christian influence, there seems to be a gradual emancipation from the Augustinian-religious dimension in writing about the self after Petrarch and Conversini. There is an interest in the secular nature of life, less emphasis on the deadly sins, as Humanism leads to an interest in the 'human' as well as the 'humane' existence, and we see particularly in Petrarch's Posterity Letter and Alberti's *Vita* evidence of the urge towards self-fashioning and the construction of a particular image.

Another 'secular' trend is the emergence of the lives of artists and writers to a position of parity with those of rulers and saints, and the gradual decline of the *De viris illustribus* tradition in favour of the life of the single, contemporary 'individual', not a figure from the remote past, however illustrious. This shift is concomitant with the decline of 'ancient' Latin and the rise of the 'modern' vernacular. The new status enjoyed by artists is particularly evident, and was no doubt aided by the confluence of the humanistic impulse to write the model life and the Italian, particularly Florentine, mercantile and workshop tradition of writing *ricordi*. Cellini's *Vita* would be unthinkable without these traditions behind it.

Nevertheless, autobiography is in a sense a genre whose time had not yet come: it still has very close links with biography, and in any case Cardano's autobiographical work (1575) was not printed until the seventeenth century, and Alberti's and Cellini's lives not until the eighteenth. The tight linkage between writing about others and writing about the self is evident in the close interplay between Boccaccio's life of Petrarch and

Petrarch's own Posterity Letter, and in Alberti's third-person autobiography. Conversely, it is clear from Bruni's biographies that whether writing about Cicero, Dante, or Aristotle, he is in a sense also writing about himself and his own contemporary ideals. Cellini in his *Vita* (1558–66) is also indebted to previous writers of biography, and thanks to them has a clear idea of the difference between writing history proper and writing a life (*Vita*, I, 35, 37, 38, 90; II, 43, etc.)—indeed his autobiography has another close link with biography, since one of the motives for writing the work was the fact that he had not been included in Vasari's *Vite*; but his text is full of heterogeneous matter, such as sonnets (Proem; I, 84; I, 123) and other verse (I, 119, 128; II, 89). Cellini's emphasis on his religious conversion and miraculous escape from prison (carefully placed as the climax to Book I) also reveals a debt to Augustine's autobiography (and perhaps also to Boethius), while the link between artists and the comic tradition is evident in a number of novella-like chapters, notably the Black Mass in the Colosseum (I, 46).[54] Cardano too appeals to previous writers of autobiography such as Marcus Aurelius, Galen, Sulla, Julius Caesar, and Augustus (proem), but he had access only to the first two mentioned; in fact he talks more about biographers than autobiographers, including an attack on Suetonius for organizing his lives by topics ('per species') and not including a brief summary of the life as Cardano does in his fourth chapter.

Finally, the titles used by the authors of the various autobiographical works considered here also show how in the absence of an established genre, writing about the self has to come from adjacent genres before acquiring a more autonomous status: epistles (Petrarch's Letter to Posterity), diaries or account books (Conversini's *Rationarium*), commentaries (Bruni's, Pius II's, and Ghiberti's *Commentarii*), the latter being linked via Caesar's model with Alberti's *Vita*, which initially seems to be a third-person biography. It is only around the middle of the sixteenth century that we find the title *Vita* being used in the vernacular for Cellini's autobiography, while Cardano's Latin title (*De propria vita*) can be seen as the closest forerunner of our own word 'autobiography'.

[54] For the literary nature of Cellini's *Vita*, see Paolo L. Rossi, '*Sprezzatura*, Patronage, and Fate: Benvenuto Cellini and the World of Words', in *Vasari's Florence: Artists and Literati at the Medicean Court*, ed. Philip Jacks (Cambridge, 1998), pp. 55–69.

4

National Biography and the Arts of Memory: From Thomas Fuller to Colin Matthew

IAN DONALDSON

The arts of memory and of biography have always been closely allied, as the language of life-writing often reminds us. A 'memoir' (for example) is an act of remembrance in a curiously double sense, looking as it does to the past and to the future: selecting from the stream of memory to form an enduring record—a 'memorial', as it once was called—by which people and events can be remembered in the years to come. Memoirs and memorials were popular forms in Restoration England, when the word 'biography' makes its first recorded appearance.[1] Charles II's return to England in 1660 initiated a period of intense interest in the chronicling of lives, especially of those who had played a major part in the great political and religious events of the preceding decades, or who now were regarded as significant or aspiring figures within the new society forming under the restored monarchy. After the trauma of Civil War came a strong wish for the commemoration of notable individuals and social groups. Edward Hyde, 1st Earl of Clarendon, presented his *History of the Rebellion* as an

---

[1] The *OED*'s first citation of the word 'biography' is from Dryden's *Life of Plutarch* (1683), but the word was already in common usage twenty years earlier: see, for example, *The Life of the Reverend Divine, and Learned Historian, Dr Thomas Fuller*, attributed to J. Fell (1661), p.105; and Donald Stauffer, *English Biography before 1700* (Cambridge, MA, 1930), pp. 218–19.

act of biographical remembrance: 'that the memory of those few, who, out of duty and conscience have opposed and resisted that torrent which hath overwhelmed them' might not 'lose the recompense due to their virtue'.[2] Along with the need to remember went the need to forget. Charles II's Act of Indemnity and Oblivion prohibited the calling of 'any name or names, or other words of reproach tending to revive the memory of late differences or the occasions thereof'. Hyde himself, commending the Act to fellow members of the Convention Parliament in September 1660, urged them on the king's behalf to teach their neighbours how 'to learn this excellent art of forgetfulness'. Writing in the aftermath of these 'late differences' about an earlier and greater act of rebellion, John Milton (*Paradise Lost*, I. 361–3) imagines the fallen angels as forgotten souls, lacking all forms of commemoration:

> Though of thir Names in heav'nly Records now
> Be no memorial, blotted out and ras'd
> By thir Rebellion, from the Books of Life.[3]

Hell, in this vision, is a place without biographers; heaven is where the records are kept, and memory is eternal.

If the wish to commemorate the lives of famous men and women acquired particular momentum and significance in Restoration England, the origins of this enterprise are of course more ancient. So too is the association of such writings with the concept of memory. Introducing his translation (1579) of Plutarch's *Lives of the Noble Grecians and Romanes, Compared*, Sir Thomas North explained that the purpose of these *Lives* was to 'stay the fleeting of our memorie, which otherwise would be soone lost, and retayne litle', and to preserve 'the notable doings and sayings of men' from 'the death of forgetfulness' and 'horrible darknes'.[4] North's sentiments are not original: he is simply rendering Jacques Amyot's address 'Aux lecteurs' prefixed to the French translation of Plutarch (1559) from which North's translation as a whole is cribbed. Amyot in turn is simply rehearsing the familiar commonplaces of Cicero and others on the function of history, and of Horace on the enduring power of poetry.[5] What is distinctive here, however, is the application of these traditional sentiments to a particular branch of writing for which there is not yet a satisfactory

---

[2] Edward Hyde, Earl of Clarendon, *History of the Rebellion and Civil Wars in England*, 7 vols (Oxford, 1839), I, 1.

[3] Arthur Bryant, *King Charles II* (London, rev. edn 1955), p. 90; *The Poetical Works of John Milton*, ed. Helen Darbishire (Oxford, 1958).

[4] Thomas North, 'Amiot to the Reader', *The Lives of the Noble Grecians and Romanes, Compared* (1579), iii[v].

[5] Jaques Amyot, *Les Vies des hommes illustres, Grecs & Romains* (Paris, 1555), A[IV]; Cicero, *De oratore*, II. ix. 36; Horace, *Odes*, iii. 30.

name: biography. This still vaguely designated art—'une Histoire elo-quente', 'an eloquent history'—provides, it is claimed,

> the surest, safest, and durablest monument that men can leave of their doings in this world, to consecrate their names to immortalitye. For there is neither picture, nor image of marble, nor arch of triumph, nor piller, nor sumptuous sepulchre, that can match the durableness of an eloquent history, furnished with the properties which it ought to have.[6]

This notion of biography as a durable monument was itself to be remembered and repeated by compilers of biographical dictionaries for many years to come.

As the idea of remembrance was of such importance in Renaissance biography, it is not surprising that those endowed with powerful memories were regarded with particular veneration, and played a significant role in its development. John Aubrey sought out informants with long memories, and reported that as a boy he *'did ever love to converse with old men, as Living Histories'*. In 1660 Sir Thomas Browne told Aubrey of his meeting with a 91-year-old 'understanding-singing man' who could describe from memory more than a hundred brass inscriptions that had been stolen from a local church, and seemed himself 'a living memorial of ecclesiastical history'.[7] Such phrases reify these elderly witnesses as enduring objects, like the written records whose creation they assisted. In a similar spirit, Izaak Walton expressed his admiration for Dr Robert Sanderson, whose life he wrote; whose 'memory was so matchless and firm, as 'twas only overcome by his bashfulness'. For Sanderson 'the study of old *Records, Genealogies,* and *Heraldry,* were a recreation, and so pleasing, that he would say they gave rest to his mind'.[8] In the following century Walton would in turn be praised for his industry 'in collecting biographical memoirs and historical facts, and in rescuing from oblivion the memory and writings of so many of his learned friends'.[9] Thus the biographical process and the biographical product, the author and his subject, were curiously related and identified in a single pursuit: the cultivation and preservation of memory.

The most remarkable memorialist of the period, however, widely famed for his scholarship and his astonishing feats of mental recall, was the Reverend Dr Thomas Fuller: a figure who is today, ironically, almost totally forgotten by the general public and even by more specialized readers. Fuller

---

[6] *Les Vies des hommes illustres,* iii^v.
[7] *Aubrey's Brief Lives,* ed. Oliver Lawson Dick (Harmondsworth, 1962), p. 12; Sir Thomas Browne, letter of 24 August 1672, *Letters,* ed. Geoffrey Keynes (Cambridge, 1946), p. 395; Graham Parry, *Trophies of Time* (Oxford, 1996), p. 259.
[8] Izaak Walton, *The Life of Dr Robert Sanderson* (1678), *Lives* (Oxford, 1927), pp. 398–9.
[9] Izaak Walton, *The Complete Angler,* ed. Sir John Hawkins (1791), p. xxi.

was chaplain to Charles II, and author of many historical works including *A History of the Worthies of England*: the most significant dictionary of national biography to be attempted in early modern times. His biographical methods were closely linked to his own habits of remembering. Samuel Pepys records a meeting with him in a London tavern on 22 January 1661, at which Fuller told him about

> his last and great book that is coming out: that is, his history of all the families of England—and could tell me more of my owne then I knew myself. And also to what perfection he hath brought the art of memory; that he did lately to four eminently great Schollars dictate together in Latin upon different Subjects of their proposing, faster than they were able to write, till they were tired.[10]

John Aubrey was similarly impressed by Fuller's powers of recall. 'His naturall memorie was very great', wrote Aubrey of Fuller, 'to which he had added the *art of memorie*: he would repeat to you forwards and backwards all the signes from Ludgate to Charing-crosse'.[11] Pepys and Aubrey both speak of Fuller's skills in 'the art of memory', the system of mnemonic techniques devised in Classical times and still widely known in the Renaissance.[12] Yet Fuller himself was ambivalent about this art, which he regarded as a kind of trickery, speaking disparagingly of the 'Memory-mountebanks' who professed to be its masters. To one who claimed to have taught him the art of memory during his time at Sidney Sussex College, Fuller is said to have replied 'that it was not so, *for I could not remember that I had ever seen his face*—which, I conceive, was a real refutation!'[13]

There were certainly memory-mountebanks abroad. Fuller had good reason to be cautious of the recommendations and suppositions of a writer such as John Willis, a new edition of whose *Mnemonica; or, the Art of Memory, Drained out of the Pure Fountains of Art and Nature*, was published in 1661, the very year of the encounter between Pepys and Fuller at the Dog Tavern. Willis believed that memory was weakened by a variety of factors. Bad air was deleterious to the memory, especially if it was windy, or (alternatively) still, or indeed if it was moist, or smoky. Food was equally harmful—beans, peas, garlic, onions, cheese, milk, pork, young chickens 'before they are feathered', and 'any food that hath a slimie tast'. Sleep

---

[10] *The Diary of Samuel Pepys*, ed. R. C. Latham and W. Matthews, 11 vols (London, 1971), II, 21.

[11] John Aubrey, *Brief Lives*, ed. Andrew Clark, 2 vols (Oxford, 1898), I. 257. The story is confirmed in *The Life of [. . .] Dr Thomas Fuller* (1661), p. 76.

[12] Frances Yates, *The Art of Memory* (London, 1966); Mary Carruthers, *The Book of Memory: A Study of Memory in Medieval Culture* (Cambridge, 1990).

[13] Thomas Fuller, *The Holy State* (1648), p. 163; *The Appeal of Injured Innocence* (1659), p. 447.

likewise: especially if over-indulged or taken in a windy place or 'under *Lunar raies*' or 'in the day, most of all with shoes on, or being miry', or 'upon the back, for it preventeth expulsion of Excrements, at mouth and nostrils'. Other factors were equally injurious to the memory: 'perturbation of mind'; 'Filthy desires'; 'Rash answers'; 'Disorderly reading of books'; 'Night study'; 'Wearing head-hair over long'; 'Dipping or washing the head in cold water'; 'Distraction of mind about several studies at one time'. Willis's tips for those who wished to improve their memory included exposure to wholesome air, sweet scents, and the breath of flowers; consuming the brains of partridges, sparrows, hares, conies, and hens; 'Washing the feet once a moneth in water moderately heated, wherein *Bawm, Cammomill, Bay leaves*, and other oderiferous hearbs have been boyled'; exercise, especially if taken 'In delightfull places, not subject to wind', and the belly, bladder, and nostrils are properly evacuated in advance. Combing the hair backwards assisted the memory (so Willis believed), as did spitting, and eating twelve raisins each morning without drink—a regimen that also miraculously preserved one's youth.[14]

If Fuller was duly sceptical of such prescriptions, he was not entirely innocent of the arts of memory, as Aubrey's mention of his ability to recite the London street signs 'forwards and backwards' suggests. To repeat what one had learnt both forwards and backwards was a standard memorial exercise of the day, derived from the practice of the ancients, and demonstrating total mastery of a subject.[15] William Lily in his *Shorte Introduction of Grammar* (a standard textbook of the time) had insisted that it was profitable for a student 'not onely that he can orderly declyne his Noune and his Verbe, but every way, forwarde, backeward, by cases, by persons: that neither Case of Noune, ne person of Verbe can be requyred, that he can not without stoppe or study tell: and unto thys tyme I counte not the scholler perfect, nor ready to go any further, thene that he hath already learned'.[16]

Even the Bible itself might be conned in this manner, until the devout

---

[14] John Willis, *Mnemonica; or, the Art of Memory, Drained out of the Pure Fountains of Art and Nature. Digested into Three Books* (1661), pp. 136–43.

[15] Cicero, *Rhetorica ad Herennium*, tr. Harry Caplan, Loeb Classical Library (London and Cambridge, MA, 1968). The elder Seneca, famed for his exceptional memory, could listen to two hundred students each reciting a single line of poetry, and repeat the lines in reverse order: Marcus Annaeus Seneca, *Controversiarum Libri*, I. ii. Fuller himself recalls Augustine's story of his friend Simplicius 'who being ask'd, could tell all Virgills verses backward and forward, and yet the same party, vowed to God, that he knew not that he could do it till they did try him': *The Holy State*, p. 164; Augustine, *De anima*, IV. vii. Hugh Platte in his *Jewell House of Art and Nature* (1594), § 98, pp. 81–5, describes the classic 'house of memory' technique by which each subject 'both forwarde and backewarde is easily brought to minde'.

[16] William Lily, *A Shorte Introduction of Grammar*, n.d. [*c.* 1570], A2ᵛ-3.

reader knew the divine texts, quite literally, backwards as well as forwards.[17] Curious, if not blasphemous, though the technique may seem, it
had a sound rational justification, as Lily explained in relation to the
learning of grammar. Students should not be hurried too rapidly to the next
stage of learning until they had thoroughly mastered their current lesson;
if moved too fast, they would be unable either to progress or to retreat.
To retain true mental agility and freedom, it was necessary therefore to
know at all times how any single fact was related to the larger structure
of knowledge that needed to be mastered: and to be able to move at any
time in any direction through that structure, backwards or forwards. In
the hands of a literal-minded teacher, this methodology clearly might be
abused, leading to purely mechanical learning. Fuller's scepticism about the
arts of memory may have developed at an early age while he learnt his
Latin grammar (as his first biographer tells us) 'under the ill menage of a
raw and unskilful schoolmaster' and was 'often beaten for Lily's sake'.[18]
Whatever the case, the basic technique of learning 'forwards and backwards' is one that evidently stayed with Fuller in his later years.

As an undergraduate at Queens' College, Cambridge, Fuller had studied
with the gifted mathematician and divine Edward Davenant, a cousin of
Fuller's who possessed the same exceptional powers of memory. Aubrey,
who knew Davenant well, and derived much of his knowledge of Fuller
from him, describes Davenant's 'excellent way of improving his children's
memories, which was thus: he would make one of them read a chapter
or &c., and then they were (*sur le champ*) to repeat what they remembred,
which did exceedingly profitt them; and so for sermons, he did not let them
write notes (which jaded their memorie) but gave an account *viva voce*'.[19]
Davenant must have imposed the same discipline on Fuller, who in later
life is said never to have used notes for his own prayers and sermons, 'other
than the beginning word of each Head or Division'.[20] Evidently possessed
of what today would be called a photographic memory, Fuller habitually
noted headwords in this way to ensure perfect recall. His first biographer
notes his ability to memorize words 'of different Languages, and of hard
and difficult prolation, to any number whatsoever', and his curious manner
of recalling extended passages in a form of writing

---

[17] Abiezer Coppe, *Some Sweet Sips, of Some Spiritual Wine* (1649), in *A Collection of Ranter
Writings from the Seventeenth Century*, ed. Nigel Smith (Junction, UT 1983), p. 61. Cf.
Augustine searching through his own memory, looking for God: 'Place there is none; we go
backward and forward, but place there is none' (*et nusquam locus, et recedimus et accedimus,
et nusquam locus*): *Confessions*, X. 26, tr. William Watts (1631), Loeb Classical Library, 2
vols (London and Cambridge, MA., 1961).
[18] *The Life of . . . Dr Thomas Fuller*, 1661, p. 2; *History of the Worthies*, II, 461.
[19] *Brief Lives*, ed. Clark, I, 202–3.
[20] *The Life of . . . Dr Thomas Fuller* (1661), p. 56.

which something like the *Chineses*, was from the top of the page to the bottom: the manner thus. He would write near the Margin the first words of every Line down to the Foot of the Paper, then would be beginning at the head againe, fill up every one of these Lines, which without any interlineations or spaces but with the full and equal length, would so adjust the sense and matter, and so aptly Connex and Conjoyn the ends and beginnings of the said Lines, that he could not do it better, as he hath said, if he had writ all out in a Continuation.[21]

In addition to this technique, Fuller had a number of additional simple rules to assist the memory which he sets out briefly in *The Holy State* (1648). The most significant of these in relation to Fuller's own biographical work is his insistence on the need for a methodical distribution of facts into discrete locations, or parcels of knowledge. '*Marshall thy notions into a handsome method*. One will carrie twice more weight trust and pack'd up in bundles, then when it lies untowardly flapping and hanging about his shoulders. Things orderly fardled up under heads are most portable'.[22] The 'handsome method' that Fuller recommended for ease of mental recall served equally as an organizing system for *The History of the Worthies of England*.

Fuller was not the first author to attempt a history of English 'worthies'. In 1619 Ben Jonson told the Scottish poet William Drummond of Hawthornden 'that he had ane intention to perfect ane Epick Poeme intitled Heroologia of the Worthies of his Country, rowsed by fame, and was to dedicate it to his Country, it is all in Couplets, for he detesteth all other Rimes'. The project came to nothing, though there are indications elsewhere in Jonson's work how the subject might have been handled.[23] In the following year, 1620, the London bookseller Henry Holland produced a similarly titled work *Heroologia Anglica*, a series of brief lives of statesmen, scholars, churchmen, navigators, etc., from the time of Henry VIII to the early years of James I. The lives are all in Latin, and accompanied by fine quality engravings. Holland's work, with its loosely chronological structure, formed a simple model that later compilers of biographical dictionaries, such as Thomas Birch in his *Heads of Illustrious Persons of Great Britain*

---

[21] Ibid., p. 77.

[22] Ch. 10, 'Of Memory', *The Holy State* (enlarged 2nd edn 1648), p. 164. 'Method is the mother of memory' was one of Fuller's favourite sayings: see e.g. *Worthies*, p. 161. *Methodus mater memoria* declares the decorative ribbon fluttering above David Loggan's portrait of Fuller, reproduced as frontispiece to the 1662 edition of the *Worthies*. Most of Fuller's advice concerning the use of the memory is taken without acknowledgement from Cicero's *Ad Herennium*.

[23] *Conversations with William Drummond of Hawthornden*, lines 1–5, in *Ben Jonson*, ed. C. H. Herford and P. and E. Simpson, 11 vols (Oxford, 1925–52), I, 132. Jonson celebrates 'worthies' from Britain's past in *Prince Henry's Barriers* (1610), *The Masque of Queens* (1609), and from among his contemporaries in *Epigrams* (1616).

(1743), illustrated by Jacobus Houbraken and George Vertue, were content to follow.[24]

The structure of Fuller's *History of the Worthies of England* is altogether more ambitious than such works as these. Its basis is geographical, or (to invoke a popular term of the day) chorographical: Fuller inspects the whole of England county by county, following the example of such works as William Camden's *Britannia* and John Speed's *History of Great Britain*. Fuller acknowledges his debt to these earlier antiquaries in the opening paragraph of *The History*, while simultaneously hinting at another, much older, mnemonic model that he is also following.

> England may not unfitly be compared to a House not *very great*, but *convenient*, and the several Shires may properly be resembled to the *rooms* thereof. Now as learned Master *Camden* and painful Mr *Speed* with others, have discribed the *rooms* themselves; so it is our intention, God willing to discribe the *Furniture* of those *rooms*; such Eminent Commodities which every County do produce, with the Persons of Quality bred therein, and some other observables coincident with the same subject.[25]

The house with its various rooms to which Fuller here likens England bears a strong resemblance to the many-roomed 'house of memory' described in Classical treatises on the art of memory, still in common use in Renaissance times. Such writings recommended that the items to be remembered should be imaginatively distributed to fixed places within some familiar but reasonably intricate location, such as a house, from which they could later be retrieved through a process of simple association: by mentally revisiting each room in turn, one recalled in precise order, 'backwards or forwards', the items previously deposited there. These memorial locations were selected, as Quintilian explained,

> and characterized with the utmost possible variety, such as a spacious house divided into a number of rooms. Everything of note therein is carefully committed to the memory, in order that the mind can run through all the details without let or hindrance. [. . .] This done, as soon as it is necessary to revive the memory of these things, all of these places are visited in turn, and what has been deposited is summoned in, as the various images remind one of their particular characteristics.[26]

It was important, as Cicero advised, that memory *loci* should be 'of moderate size and medium extent, for when excessively large they render the

---

[24] George Vertue studied Holland's work with close attention, as is revealed in the detailed annotations in his personal copy of *Heroologia Anglica* (now in Cambridge University Library, Keynes D. 5. 19).

[25] Fuller, *A History of the Worthies of England* (1662), p. 1.

[26] Quintilian, *Institutio oratoria*, XI. ii, tr. H. E. Butler, Loeb Classical Library, 4 vols (London and Cambridge, MA, 1968); translation adjusted.

images vague, and when too small the arrangement of images will be overcrowded'.[27] England, being (in Fuller's view) a house 'not very great, but convenient', was a perfect memorial *locus*: sufficiently substantial to be treated in this extended manner, yet sufficiently compact to be retained coherently in the mind.

Fuller in short takes over a well-known model for the exercise and improvement of human memory and re-uses it as the organizing principle of his book. The house of memory becomes his house of fame, in which the English worthies may be fittingly remembered.[28] For a central aim of *The History of the English Worthies* is, as Fuller declares, 'to preserve the memories of the dead'. Physical monuments (he continues, in a passage closely reminiscent of the words of Sir Thomas North) will in time decay, but the written word will endure. Biography is thus the finest vehicle for human remembrance.

> It hath been the lawful desire of men in all ages to perpetuate their Memories, thereby in some sort revenging themselves of Mortality, though few have found effectual means to perform it. For Monuments made of Wood are subject to be burnt; of Glass, to be broken; of soft stone, to moulder; of Marble and Metal (if escaping the teeth of Time) to be demolished by the hand of Covetousness; so that in my apprehension, the safest way to secure a memory from oblivion is (next to his own Vertues) by committing the same to writing to Posterity.[29]

Despite (or perhaps on account of) its elaborate structure, which Fuller takes eighty folio pages to explain, *A History of the Worthies of England* is a curiously wayward and piecemeal work, its biographical intentions constantly overlaid with miscellaneous information of other kinds concerning local wonders, buildings, manufactures, proverbs, and natural commodities. It is intriguing and frustrating by turns, as Pepys discovered when he chanced upon a newly published copy in St Paul's Churchyard in February 1662, a year after his meeting with Fuller, who had not lived to see his great work in print. Pepys and Fuller had much in common: a Cambridge background, an insatiable curiosity about genealogies and current events, and a determination to employ systematic techniques—of memory, and of shorthand—to cope with the large quantities of infor-

[27] Cicero, *Rhetorica ad Herennium*, III. xix. 31; translation adjusted.
[28] For Jonson's *The Masque of Queens* (1609) Inigo Jones had designed a House of Fame based in part on Giulio Parigi's Palazzo della Fama: see John Peacock, *The Stage Designs of Inigo Jones: The European Context* (Cambridge, 1995), pp. 72–3, plates 20 and 21. For the earlier history of the House of Fame, see J. A. W. Bennett, *Chaucer's House of Fame* (Oxford, 1960).
[29] Fuller, *A History of the Worthies*, pp. 1–2.

mation with which they were obliged to deal in their everyday work.[30] Pepys picked up *The History of the Worthies* with high expectations, 'and so I sat down reading in it, till it was 2 a-clock before I thought of the time's going'. He was 'much troubled', however, by what he had found in Fuller's great book, or, more to the point, by what he had failed to find; for '(though he had some discourse with me about my family and armes) he says nothing at all, nor mentions us either in Cambridge or in Norfolke'. Though Fuller had remembered the Pepys family well enough, he had evidently not reckoned them worth memorializing. Not everything that Fuller's voracious memory retained needed, he believed, to be remembered by posterity, and the process of selection was as important as that of retention. For what Pepys had first imagined to be 'a history of all the families of England' had proved to be something rather different: a history of the *worthies* of England: of people whose social or intellectual distinction had in some manner or another earned them a niche in this national house of fame. Turning the matter over, Pepys reluctantly conceded the logic of Fuller's procedure, for 'our family were never considerable'.[31]

Fuller's biographical methods were governed by two principal factors: a sense of pragmatism, and a sense of what might very loosely be described as piety. Pragmatism, in that the number of people to be included in his book, if they were genuinely to be remembered, needed to be kept to a manageable, or 'convenient', size.[32] Piety, as these people must also be, through some distinction of birth or achievement, *worthy* of commemoration, as the very title of his book insisted. The question of who did, and who did not, warrant inclusion in a biographical compendium of this sort was much debated at this time.[33] The criteria by which Fuller judged his

[30] The arts of memory and of shorthand had certain aims and features in common. The memorialist John Willis commended shorthand as 'exceeding profitable for the committing of a long speech quickly to memorie': *The School-Maister to the Art of Stenographie* (1622), A6ᵛ. Cf. Quintilian, *Institutio oratoria*, XI. ii. 25.

[31] Pepys, *Diary*, ed. Latham and Matthews, III, 26–7.

[32] Acutely conscious of what he had not been able to include, Fuller actually entitled one chapter of *The History of the Worthies* 'An Apologie for the unvoluntary Omissions in this Book'. In a similar fashion William Camden, for whom the office of the historian ('to commend to their posteritie such notable and good acts as were worthie to the memorie') closely resembled that of the herald (who 'ought to preserve to perpetual memorie, all facts and notable designments of honour and arms'), felt obliged to explain in the preface to the 1610 edition of *Britannia* that he could not be expected to remember *every* family, 'for their names would fill whole volumes'. See W. H. Herendeen, 'William Camden: Historian, Herald, and Antiquary', *Studies in Philology*, LXXXV (1988), 192–210, and Stuart Piggott, 'William Camden and the *Britannia*', *Proceedings of the British Academy*, XXXVIII (1951), 199–217.

[33] In Ben Jonson's comedy *The Devil is an Ass* (1616) the jeweller Gilthead, who is passionately addicted to Plutarch's *Lives*, christens his own son Plutarchus, 'In hope he should be like him:/ And write the lives of our great men!' (III. ii. 24–5). Jonson plays on current uncertainties about the exact social status of the readers, writers, and subjects of biography.

worthies to be worthies were allowed to remain agreeably vague. After noting the outstanding princes, saints, martyrs, confessors, popes, cardinals, prelates, statesmen, judges, lawyers, soldiers, seamen, sheriffs, writers, and musicians (etc.) for the various counties of England, Fuller arrived at a category of what he simply designated 'memorable persons': persons who have 'an extraordinary (not vicious) remark upon them', and

> are not clearly reducible to any of the former *Titles*. Such therefore, who are *over, under,* or *beside the Standard* of common persons for *strength, stature, fruitfulnesse, Vivacity* or other observeable eminence, are *lodged* here under the NOTION of *Memorable Persons*, presuming the pains will not be to *Me* so much in *marking,* as the pleasure to the *Reader* in *knowing* them.[34]

'*Over, under,* or *beside the Standard* of common persons': the formula was sufficiently flexible to allow Fuller to include practically anyone he chose. Pepys's consciousness that his family might be reckoned insufficiently 'considerable' to be included in the *History* was only partly justified, for Fuller's attitude was remarkably unfettered by considerations of class. He was ready to accept as 'memorable persons' not only those of distinguished birth but people of lower social rank, including 'all such *Mechanicks* who in any *Manual Trade* have reached a *clear Note* above others in their *Vocation*'. It was not just on account of their civic or moral virtues that such folk were to be commemorated. Many of Fuller's memorable persons were included because of some physical achievement or colourful trait, such as might have gained them entry in more recent times to *The Guinness Book of Records* or that section of *The Reader's Digest* devoted to 'The Most Unforgettable Character I've Ever Met'. Among the 'memorable persons' of Cornwall listed in Fuller's *Worthies*, for example, were one John Bray, who in 1608 had carried on his back 'by the space well near of a *Butt length,* six *Bushells* of *Wheaten Meal,* reckoning *fifteen gallons* to the *Bushell,* and upon them all the *Miller,* a *Lubber* of *four and twenty years of age*'; John Roman, 'his *Contemporary,* a short *Clownish Grub*', who, like Milo of Crotona, could carry an ox; a man named Kiltor, who, lying on his back in the castle green at Launceston, could throw 'a stone of *some pounds* weight, over the *Tower's top* (and that I assure you is *no low one*), which leadeth into the *Park*'; and Edward Bone, a deaf and dumb mute who 'yet could learn, and express to his master any news that was stirring in the Country'. Edward Bone, like Fuller himself, was blessed with an unusual memory: 'he would not only know any party, whom he had once seen, for ever after, but also make him known to any other, by special observation and difference.'[35] Fuller's own 'special observation and

---

[34] Fuller, *A History of the Worthies*, p. 40.
[35] Ibid., pp. 205–6.

difference' makes these tiny portraits of memorable persons themselves indeed deliciously memorable; and *The History of the Worthies* itself, for all its unwieldiness, a treasure house of miscellaneous biographical pleasures.

Fuller's biographical work was none the less driven by a clear ideology of remembrance; an ideology succinctly expressed by the biblical text quoted on the title page of his 1651 publication *Abel Redivivus, or the Dead Yet Speaking: The Lives and Deaths of Modern Divines*. The text is from Proverbs 10,7: 'The memory of the just is blessed: but the name of the wicked shall rot'. In determining which names were to be blessedly remembered and which would be left to rot, the biographer here acts like the recording angel in Milton's vision, writing and fiercely amending the great book of life.

    This same ideology of remembrance is clearly evident in the large-scale biographical dictionaries which were undertaken in various parts of Europe during the following century, and which attempted, in the manner of Fuller's *History of the Worthies of England*, to assemble information about their nation's most distinguished citizens. And who would these people be? Who should be gathered into the national pantheon? Whose name deserved to be remembered, and whose should be left to rot? Here is how the editors of the *Biographia Britannica* explained their motivating ambition in 1747:

> [I]t was in order to collect into one Body, without any restriction of time or place, profession or condition, the memoirs of such of our countrymen as have been eminent, and by their performances of any kind deserve to be remembered. We judged that this would be a most useful service to the publick, a kind of general MONUMENT erected to the most deserving of all ages, an expression of gratitude due to their services, and the most probable means of exciting, in succeeding times, a spirit of emulation, which might prompt men to an imitation of their virtues. This was the first and great motive to the attempting such a collection, towards which, indeed, we saw there were considerable materials ready prepared, though no sign of such building's being ever traced, or that there had ever been a thought, either to the expediency or possibility of erecting such a structure; a BRITISH TEMPLE OF HONOUR, sacred to the piety, learning, valour, publick-spirit, loyalty, and every other glorious virtue of our ancestors, and ready also for the reception of the WORTHIES OF OUR OWN TIME, and the HEROES OF POSTERITY.[36]

Piety and pragmatism ('we saw there were considerable materials ready prepared') are once again nicely blended here, along with a stiff dose of civic usefulness. The house of fame has now become a neoclassical edifice

[36] *Biographia Britannica* (1747), I, viii.

like the Temple of Ancient Virtue or the Grenville Monument at Stowe.[37]
Yet the *Britannica* (so it is implied) is superior to these edifices, which,
being simply material in nature, will in time inevitably decay. Recognizably
Augustan though the *Britannica*'s vision may be, it repeats the view of
biography offered by Jacques Amyot and Thomas North almost two centuries earlier: that, of all the various means by which the memory of a
human life may be prolonged, biography, the written word, will prove the
most enduring. Into this British Temple of Honour is gathered a band of
heroes and worthies selected 'without any restriction of time or place,
profession or condition', for the admiration and remembrance of posterity.
The company may seem a little less lively than Fuller's 'memorable
persons'—not much stone-throwing or ox-lifting is in prospect—but the
criteria for admission are still remarkably egalitarian. The main condition
for entry is that the lives of the biographical subjects should be in some
sense suitable for emulation, and 'will prompt men to an imitation of their
virtues'.

   The *Biographia Britannica* was one of the principal models for Leslie
Stephen's *Dictionary of National Biography*, which was indeed originally
known as the new *Biographia Britannica*. It is perhaps unsurprising therefore that Stephen's fellow editor, Sir Sidney Lee, speaking on the subject of
'National Biography' in 1896, should find himself echoing the sentiments
of the *Britannica* (and, more distantly, of Fuller, and North, and Amyot,
and Cicero) in declaring the basic aims and function of the new Dictionary.

> Pyramids and mausoleums, statues and columns, however fitting it may be
> to encourage them in the interests of art, all fail to satisfy one or other of
> the conditions of permanence, publicity, and perspicuity. Monuments in stone
> and brass may preserve a man's name for two or three centuries, but little
> purpose is served by the preservation of a man's bare name. [. . .] It is to the
> prosaic, yet more accessible and more adaptable, machinery of biography
> that a nation must turn if her distinguished sons and daughters are to be
> accorded rational and efficient monuments. Biography is of its essence public
> and perspicuous; it is not less certainly permanent. The marble statuary that
> surmounted the burial places of the heroes of Greece and Rome has for the
> most part crumbled away, but 'Plutarch's Lives' remain.[38]

While Lee's vision of biography responding to 'a whole nation's commemorative aspirations' may seem curiously modern, anticipating in some ways

---

[37] See Philip Ayres, *Classical Culture and the Idea of Rome in Eighteenth-Century England*
(Cambridge, 1997), esp. pp. 75–83.
[38] Sir Sidney Lee, *National Biography: A Lecture Delivered at the Royal Institution*, 31
January 1896, pp. 13, 14–15. Leslie Stephen's somewhat more ambivalent views on the value
of commemoration are expressed in 'National Biography', in *Studies of a Biographer* (1898), I.

Maurice Halbwachs's theories of collective memory,[39] his belief in the
enduring power of biography stretches back to the Renaissance, and ultimately to Classical Antiquity. Lee's 'rational and efficient monuments',
however, speak for a new age, in which biography is seen to possess a
'machinery' that is 'more accessible and more adaptable' than that of the
visual arts. Britain's distinguished daughters were explicitly welcomed to
this new national pantheon along with her distinguished sons, and the
general criteria for admission were widened in other ways.

Yet only a fraction of the 'whole nation' could ever of course be represented in the *Dictionary of National Biography*. In recent years attempts
have been made to recover certain categories of persons who are 'missing'
from the original *DNB*—the successful engineers and businessmen, for
example, who seldom gained entry to the *DNB*'s pages, and, in particular,
its missing women: for despite Lee's gallant flourish, the nation's 'distinguished daughters' amounted to no more than 3 per cent of the total entries
in the original *DNB*. The central question that exercised the compilers
of early biographical dictionaries—who should be remembered in these
collections, and who may safely be forgotten?—has a continuing force.[40]
The New Dictionary of National Biography, scheduled for publication in
2004, strenuously attempts to broaden the boundaries and categories of
biographical remembrance. Yet as the late Colin Matthew, first editor and
chief architect of the *NDNB*, was quick to point out, Leslie Stephen's
biographical coverage was in fact very enterprising and eclectic, judged by
the standards of its day,

> including several categories of subjects which in the 1880s were quite outside
> 'scholarly' interest, particularly sportspeople, murderers, journalists, actors
> and actresses, deviant clergymen, transvestites, fat men, old women and, not
> surprisingly given Stephen's personal history, a close attention to agnostics
> and secularists.[41]

For the compilers of *The New Dictionary of National Biography*, the

---

[39] Lee was concerned that 'the whole nation's commemorative aspirations [. . .] be so contrived, so contracted, that the collected results may not overwhelm us by their bulk': *National
Biography: A Lecture*, p. 15. On Maurice Halbwachs's *Les Cadres sociaux de la mémoire*
(1925), see in particular Peter Burke, 'History as Social Memory', in *Memory: History,
Culture, and the Mind*, ed. Thomas Butler (Oxford, 1989), pp. 97–113.
[40] C. S. Nicholls, ed., *The DNB: Missing Persons* (Oxford, 1993); Gillian Fenwick, *Women
and 'The Dictionary of National Biography'* (Oxford, 1994). The contributors in the collection
National Biographies and National Identity (ed. Iain McCalman with Jodi Parvey and Misty
Cook, Canberra, 1996) address many of the ideological issues involved in the making of
dictionaries of national biography.
[41] Colin Matthew, *Leslie Stephen and 'The New Dictionary of National Biography'*, Leslie
Stephen Lecture, 25 October 1995 (Cambridge, 1995), p. 13.

very word 'memory' is no longer synonymous (as it was in Fuller's day)
with the mental powers of a single remarkable individual, or group of
individuals. What Sidney Lee casually termed 'the machinery of biography'
has become a team of powerful supercomputers, stored in a pleasantly
capacious Victorian North Oxford house, 'not very great but convenient',
that are capable of digesting and processing huge quantities of biographical
data—50,000 entries, running to 45 million words in length—at brain-
dazzling speed, the electronic chip having replaced the human mind as the
ultimate source and repository of biographical memory. With perfectly
calibrated knowledge of the data they command, the laser printers shuttle
at high speed from the left-hand margin of the page to the right-hand
margin, then from the right-hand margin to the left, backwards and forwards, as Fuller once rapidly scribbled his Chinesey notations;
boustrophedon, as the Greeks used to say, as the ox ploughs the field,
backwards and forwards in a continuous motion.

Such memory work might seem largely mechanical were it not tempered
by a humane vision. Colin Matthew's own concept of remembrance was
significantly different from that of biographical editors before him, for it
included what Matthew called 'the more general context of popular
national memory'. This 'general memory of the British past' included the
popular afterlives, as well as the firmly attested lives, of the dictionary's
biographical subjects, embracing, for example, the various legends adhering
to such names as Arthur, Alfred, Robin Hood, Shakespeare, Byron, and Sir
Walter Scott, and the manner in which their lives and creations have been
reinvented and reimagined in novels, plays, films, and television.[42] The truly
influential figures from the nation's past, Matthew realized, live on not as
monuments, fixed and unchanging in stature, but in a more dynamic and
creative way, teasing the imagination, refashioning themselves as the centuries pass, never remaining entirely the same. The duty of the national
biographer, as Matthew perceived it, is to observe and record the transform-
ational power of such figures, as well as the strict historical facts and
circumstances of their actual lives.

Like Thomas Fuller, Colin Matthew has not lived to see his great
dictionary in print. When it is finally published, the *NDNB* will indeed be
(as was observed at his funeral service) 'a monument' to Matthew's own
vision and diligence, 'as large and as enduring as any scholar could ever
hope to have'. But it should also be what George Smith, the enterprising

---

[42] Ibid., p. 28.

publisher of the original *DNB*, had hoped his dictionary would be: 'a living organism'. This was a phrase that Matthew endorsed, and proudly applied to the *NDNB*.[43]

---

[43] Address by Sir Keith Thomas at the funeral of Colin Matthew, 4 November 1999; Matthew, *Leslie Stephen and 'The New Dictionary of National Biography'*, p. 21.

5

From Eulogy to Biography: The French Academic Eloge

PETER FRANCE

> We have had, it is true, a few masterpieces, but we have never had, like the French, a great biographical tradition; we have had no Fontenelles and Condorcets, with their incomparable *éloges*, compressing into a few shining pages the manifold existences of men.

So wrote Lytton Strachey, in the preface to *Eminent Victorians*.[1] It may seem paradoxical that Strachey, the great debunker, should cite French encomiastic writing as a model. No doubt it was less the commitment to praise than the French virtues of brevity and elegance which appealed to the author of *Landmarks in French Literature*. Even so, his strategically placed remarks may encourage us to return to a neglected French genre, which continues to raise important questions about the relation between eulogy and biography.

Life-writing, whether of the famous or the obscure, is no doubt largely born of curiosity. Like Ranke's historian, impelled by the desire to know 'how it really happened', the curious biographer seeks answers to such questions as: 'What was this person's experience of life?' or 'What sort of a person was he/she?'—questions often spontaneously asked by those who have admired the work or achievement of the person in question. The fundamental imperative, then, would seem to be the urge to tell the truth, the unvarnished truth—perhaps even the 'whole truth', in so far as this is compatible with the inevitable selection of data for a well-documented modern life. This truth will be attested by evidence of the type familiar to

---

[1] Lytton Strachey, *Eminent Victorians* (London, 1918), Preface.

historians: archival and printed documents and oral testimony (the truth value of such material rarely being self-evident).

There is, of course, more to truth than facts. The modern biographer usually feels obliged to search also for an inner, often hidden, psychological truth.[2] Given the difficulty of knowing even those closest to us, this is obviously an even harder task than chronicling the events of a life; it is this fatal unknowability that unsettles the biographer hero of Sartre's *La Nausée*—even if Sartre himself was to become one of the great speculative biographers of the twentieth century.[3] But although the biographer will sometimes admit ruefully the applicability to his or her art of Barthes' remark in his 'autobiographical' essay, 'all this must be regarded as being said by a character in a novel',[4] the readers of both biography and autobiography are probably as attached to truth as the readers of history.

But history, as we know only too well, is not only about truth. The same applies to biography, particularly when one looks back to such proto-types of the genre as the academic eulogy. The very title *éloge*, often used synonymously with *vie* in seventeenth- and eighteenth-century France, attests to a different, and vital, component of biography, the urge to *celebrate*. Ancient rhetoric classed speeches in three categories: the deliberative (political debate about what should happen), the judiciary (legal debate about what happened), and the demonstrative or epideictic (praise or blame). Written biography, although aspiring also to a category omitted in this ternary classification—the scientific or informative—can arguably be seen as a close relative of such epideictic genres as the funeral oration or hagiography.

The biographer's task in this perspective is to provide moral lessons through a narrative which offers examples to be followed or avoided. Some twenty-five years after Watteau's death in 1721, the Comte de Caylus declared in a 'life' of the painter read aloud to the Académie Royale de Peinture et de Sculpture: 'I regard the life of artists as a picture sincerely painted for painters present and to come with the aim of constantly offering them praise or blame in a form which has all the liveliness of action'.[5] The reference to blame is meant to justify Caylus' criticisms of Watteau; more

---

[2] Richard Holmes describes biography as an essentially Romantic genre, based on sympathetic identification (*Dr Johnson and Mr Savage*, London, 1993, p. 230). Against this one may set Bernard Crick's scepticism about the typically English 'affable pretence of being able to enter into another person's mind' and his preference for what he sees as the more formal French approach (*George Orwell: A Life*, London, 1980, p. xxiii).

[3] On Sartre as biographer, see Chapter 15 below.

[4] Roland Barthes, *Roland Barthes* (Paris, 1975). The quotation figures in handwritten form, white on black, on the inside front cover. All translations in this chapter are my own.

[5] Comte de Caylus, *La Vie d'Antoine Watteau*, in *Vies anciennes de Watteau*, ed. Pierre Rosenberg (Paris, 1984), p. 54.

normally, however, praise overshadows blame in the writing of lives. Biography here is celebration, and the subject of biography is a Carlylean hero, as in the series of popular books produced in the Soviet Union, 'Lives of Remarkable People'—a modern version of the tradition of exemplary lives which goes back to Plutarch and beyond.

The celebration of a life may be seen then as one of the most potent forms of moral teaching, but eulogy has other functions. One of these is to pay a debt of gratitude, whether on the part of humanity, the nation, or some more limited group. The French Panthéon, a massive stone embodiment of the praise of heroes, bears the inscription: 'Aux grands hommes la Patrie reconnaissante' (To our great men the gratitude of the Fatherland).[6] But to praise the dead is also to empower the living; laudatory biography is, as we shall see, a vital element in the construction, by groups such as writers, artists, and scientists, of an edifice of corporate self-representation. Historians have shown that biography plays an essential part in the emergence of such modern genres as the history of literature or the history of science.[7] In both these cases, the history of the discipline subsequently frees itself from the biographical model to a greater or lesser extent, but certainly the early historiography of science in France is in large measure made up of the lives (*éloges*) of members of the Académie des Sciences. For all these reasons, then, it is worth examining how biography developed in the eulogies of the various French academies.

The *éloge* flourished in France from the seventeenth to the nineteenth century, and it is still not dead today. Its origins go far back through medieval hagiography to ancient biography, and most notably to Plutarch, whose *Lives* were a central point of reference in European culture and education until quite recently.[8] Plutarch was one of the models for the secular biographies, including biographies of artists, writers, and scholars, which flourished in the Renaissance, and most notably in Italy.[9] The title of Cornelius Nepos' *De viris illustribus* ('Of Illustrious Men') is echoed in countless works such as those of Paolo Giovio (*Eulogies of Men Famous for their Martial Virtue, Eulogies of Men Famous for their Writings*, etc.).

Many of these Renaissance lives, like Giovio's, were written in Latin, although Giovio was apparently one of those who encouraged Vasari to

---

[6] On the Panthéon, see Mona Ozouf, 'Le Panthéon', in *Les Lieux de mémoire*, ed. Pierre Nora, Part I, *La République* (Paris, 1984), pp. 139–66.
[7] See, for instance, René Wellek, *The Rise of English Literary History* (Chapel Hill, 1941); Robert Escarpit, 'Histoire de l'histoire de la littérature', in *Histoire des littératures*, ed. Raymond Queneau, 3 vols (Paris, 1958), III, 1735–1812.
[8] See Chapter 2 above.
[9] See Chapter 3 above.

compose his *Lives of the Artists* in Italian. If there were obvious reasons
for making the lives of saints widely available in translation (e.g. the *Golden
Legend* of Jacobus de Voragine), it might seem less important for the lives
of the learned. The fact that in seventeenth-century France such lives began
increasingly to be written in the vernacular says something about the greater
social visibility of writers and scholars. Eulogistic biography moved beyond
the self-glorification of a limited group to satisfy the curiosity of a broader
educated public, who had previously tended to despise men of letters. Thus
Scévole de Sainte-Marthe's Latin *Eulogies of Learned Men* of 1598 were
recycled in French some thirty years later for a more worldly audience by
Guillaume Colletet, an early member of the Académie Française. Claude
Cristin has shown how this movement accelerated at the end of the seventeenth century, when Antoine Tessier extracted his *Eloges des hommes
savants* from the great sixteenth-century Latin history by Jacques-Auguste
de Thou.[10]

By the early eighteenth century, then, there was in France an increasing
quantity of vernacular biographical writing about what Carlyle was to call
'the hero as man of letters'. This ranged from the full-scale life (e.g. Adrien
Baillet's voluminous *Vie de Monsieur Descartes*, 1691), through introductory notices at the head of complete works (this was often the destiny of
Louis Racine's hagiographic life of his more famous father), to brief entries
in compilations such as Moreri's *Grand Dictionnaire historique* (first
edition 1674), a type of publication whose popularity grew by leaps and
bounds. What gave French biography its specificity, however, was the development of the academies and the place occupied in them by eulogies of the
dead.

The academies owed their existence to the nationalistic cultural policy
of Cardinal Richelieu, Louis XIV, and the latter's right-hand man, Jean-
Baptiste Colbert. The first to emerge was the Académie Française, given its
charter by Richelieu in 1634 and charged with establishing and maintaining
linguistic and literary standards. It was joined in Louis XIV's reign by
academies of science, fine art, music, and 'inscriptions and belles-lettres'.
Most of these bodies would listen from time to time to eulogies, but from
our point of view the most important are the Académie Française and in
particular the Académie des Sciences.

A striking feature of these bodies, but one that seemed entirely natural
to most contemporaries, is that academicians were men only. There were
suggestions that women might become members, but in the period that

---

[10] Claude Cristin, 'Aux origines de l'histoire littéraire française: "Les éloges des Hommes
sçavants Tirez de l'histoire de M. de Thou par Antoine Tessier" (1683-1715)', *Revue d'histoire
littéraire de la France*, XXII (1972), 238–46.

concerns us nothing came of them, and the first female member of the Académie Française, Marguerite Yourcenar, was elected as late as 1980. Consequently, the already dominantly masculine nature of the *éloge* was yet further reinforced. These were lives of the 'great men' by other 'great men', contributing to the patriarchal biographical tradition later represented in the *Dictionary of National Biography* and subverted by its editor's daughter, Virginia Woolf.[11]

The first member of the Académie Française to die was the now forgotten moralist Pierre Bardin. On his death in 1637, his surviving colleagues decided that whenever an 'immortal' died there would be 'a succinct eulogy, without excessive praise, which would be a kind of summary of his life', together with two epitaphs, in prose and in verse.[12] This was done for Bardin, but the tradition was not maintained, except for the most illustrious members, and the eulogy of the deceased academician was generally pronounced in a session of the Académie, as it still is today, by his successor and by its current director. Thus it fell to Jean Racine, as director in 1684, to sing the praises of his former rival Corneille.

These speeches, while they may contain biographical information, are more akin in their eloquence and generality to the funeral orations of a Bossuet than to anything we could call biography. In 1653, however, the young Paul Pellisson published an *Histoire de l'Académie Française* which was so favourably received that it earned him the next vacant place in the Académie. The greater part of his slim volume is made up of *éloges* of dead academicians, though there are also tactful notices on the living. Pellisson's work, with its simplicity and good taste, was still being cited as a model of the *éloge historique* 150 years later.[13] His very brief lives (three or four pages on average) are written in an agreeably natural style, free of the excessive eloquence of the oration; they contain a sketch of the person, his origins and career, and a list of his main works together with critical remarks. Anecdotes enliven the account, which also makes room for such matters as sources of wealth or cause of death.

Pellisson's lives cover only the first eighteen years of the Académie's existence; his work was continued, for the period 1652–1700, by the Abbé d'Olivet. His biographies are a little longer than his predecessor's, but less attractive. It sometimes seems as if he is going through the motions without conviction, and this is borne out by the fact that he burned the pages he wrote on the period 1700–1715, explaining that there were too many

---

[11] See Hermione Lee, *Virginia Woolf* (London, 1996), pp. 3–20.
[12] Paul Pellisson and Pierre-Joseph Thoulier d'Olivet, *Histoire de l'Académie Française*, ed. Ch.-L. Livet, 2 vols (Paris, 1858), I, 161.
[13] M. Dussault, 'Sur les éloges historiques', *Le Spectateur français au XIXe siècle*, IV (1806), 321.

uninteresting academicians—it might be appropriate to give them a flattering *éloge* when they died, but not years later.[14]

The creation of a biographical record of the Académie had thus run into the shallows, and it was not until Jean le Rond d'Alembert became Secrétaire Perpétuel of the institution in 1754 that things took a turn for the better. D'Alembert, who was trying to make the Académie a stronghold of the new philosophy, felt the need to improve its image by writing its history, which consisted largely of the lives of the academicians. He set to and wrote over sixty *éloges historiques* of members who had died since 1700. In 1779 he published a selection devoted to the most illustrious figures (Bossuet, Fénelon, etc.), all of which he had previously read aloud in the Académie. This was a trial run for his six-volume *Histoire des membres de l'Académie Française morts depuis 1700 jusqu'en 1771* (1785–7).

D'Alembert's *éloges* are considerably longer than Pellisson's or d'Olivet's, between twenty-five and sixty pages. They are based, he says, on each academician's works, on written records, and on conversation with the subject and those who knew him. He is aware of the perils of monotony in such a genre, and declares that he has attempted to vary his style: 'the essential thing would have been to give to each of the pieces the character of those whom we had to depict'.[15] So while his eulogy of the Oratorian Jean-Baptiste Massillon is serious, but rather short on biographical detail, the piece on Boileau is immediately more joky, making room for stories and witticisms, and that on the scandalous Abbé de Choisy, while passing quickly over his cross-dressing as unworthy of the attention of this 'grave assembly', paints a sharp picture of the world of knaves and fools he lived in.

Some readers or listeners found d'Alembert's *éloges* too frivolous and too satirical, 'a collection of caustic and frigid epigrams' in the words of M. Dussault, who preferred the good taste of Pellisson.[16] In particular, critics deplored the use of the genre, by d'Alembert and others, to score points off their adversaries: 'the eulogy of the dead consists above all in the satire of the living,' wrote an anonymous correspondent to the *Spectateur français* in 1808.[17] And it is certainly the case that d'Alembert sometimes used his *éloges* to political ends, enlisting his heroes in the continuing

---

[14] Pellisson and d'Olivet, *Histoire de l'Académie*, II, 385–93 (letter from d'Olivet to President Bouhier, 27 August 1733).

[15] Jean le Rond d'Alembert, *Eloges lus dans les séances publiques de l'Académie Française (Paris, 1779)*, 'Avertissement sur les éloges qui suivent', p. iv.

[16] Dussault, 'Sur les éloges historiques', p. 322.

[17] Anon., 'But philosophique des éloges académiques', *Le Spectateur français au XIXe siècle*, (1808), 55.

struggle of light against darkness. This is particularly true of a text which was not at first meant for the Académie, the *Eloge de Montesquieu*.

Montesquieu died in 1755, and his *éloge* was published that year, at the head of Volume V of the great *Encyclopédie*, of which d'Alembert was co-editor. It is a substantial text, meant to be read silently rather than heard—as is obvious from the presence of a 'footnote' which is as long as the main text and offers an analysis of Montesquieu's masterpiece, *L'Esprit des lois*. As d'Alembert explained, this is particularly appropriate in the context of an instructive work such as the *Encyclopédie*, but in any case, 'the history of famous writers is simply that of their ideas and their writings'.[18] The writings do indeed dominate in this as in most *éloges*, but they are set here in the story of a life, the life of a hero of the mind, not only a great scholar, but a good citizen of whom the nation can be proud.

Such exemplary lives, like the lives of saints, tend to follow a similar pattern. D'Alembert is conforming to this when he apologizes for beginning with details of his hero's birth and family; properly speaking, a philosopher needs no ancestors. The *éloge* goes on to recount such standard elements as youthful promise (working on his masterpiece at the age of twenty), early recognition (elected to the Academy of Bordeaux at twenty-six), and dedication to his task (excessive reading cost him his sight). In particular, the intellectual hero, like the saint, should face persecution, and it is here that the eulogy of the dead is made to serve the struggles of the present. At the time of writing, the *Encyclopédie* was under persistent attack from its enemies, the same kind of enemies who had tried to keep Montesquieu out of the Académie. So the eulogist, as so often happens with biographers, identifies with the person he is celebrating, seeing in his heroic life an episode in an on-going campaign. The exemplary life serves to boost the corporate self-image of a group or party.

Elsewhere in the *Encyclopédie*, in his entry 'Eloges académiques', d'Alembert offers some theoretical remarks on the genre. In particular, he distinguishes between two types of eulogy practised in the academies. One of these is the *éloge historique* given by the Secrétaire Perpétuel of the institution; in such texts the speaker or writer 'gives a detailed account of the whole life of an academician', but omitting 'low, puerile details which are unworthy of the majesty of a philosophical eulogy'. The stress will be on the works rather than the man; truth is the aim, but facts are mingled with general reflections ('the soul of this type of composition'). Such are the classic *éloges* of Fontenelle, to which I shall turn in a moment.

D'Alembert distinguishes this historical sub-genre from the *éloge ora-*

---

[18] D'Alembert, 'Eloge de M. le Président Montesquieu', in *L'Encyclopédie, ou Dictionnaire raisonné des sciences, des arts et des métiers*, V (Paris, 1755), p. viii, note a.

toire, generally given at sessions of the Académie to honour the newly deceased—a kind of lay funeral oration. This, he says, tends to be general in character, neither too factual nor too critical. The same description fits another type of *éloge oratoire* instituted shortly after the writing of this article, the prize eulogy. In 1758, the Académie Française, which had since its founding given a prize for eloquence, set up an annual competition for the best eulogy of a famous figure from the past. Jean-Claude Bonnet has written very interestingly of the implications of this new prize. Whereas the funeral oration had praised royalty, aristocracy, politicians, and generals ('les grands') while insisting on the Christian lesson of *memento mori*, the Académie was setting out, as if in anticipation of the establishment of the Panthéon, to celebrate the great creative figures ('les grands hommes') of the nation or of humanity. As Bonnet puts it, 'through ever more biographical and individualized accounts of exemplary destinies, the great romance of the nation is written'.[19]

This innovation was disliked by some critics, who mocked the idea of academicians assuming the role of arbiters of value, particularly when, after the Revolution, they sought to distribute patriotic honours. One anonymous writer of 1808 mocked the 'religious adoration of *great men*'. It is certain, however, that for several decades after 1758, *éloges* were extremely popular and the public flocked to the academy sessions at which they were declaimed. The same writer, referring to the 'thousands of panegyrics' produced towards the end of the eighteenth century, remarked that 'it seemed that the whole of France was occupied in erecting statues'. The press of the period, including the influential manuscript *Correspondance littéraire* distributed to the élite of Europe, is full of discussions of these eulogies. Some competitions at the Académie Française developed into *causes célèbres*, notably the debate in 1775 about the rival eulogies by Guibert and La Harpe on the seventeenth-century Marshal Catinat, who is painted as an ideal Enlightenment figure, not just a warrior, but a citizen, a philosopher, a friend of humanity.[20] And when Voltaire died three years later, the flurry of eulogies provoked a short published essay, described as 'impartial reflections on the eulogies of Voltaire which competed for the prize of the Académic Française in 1779'.[21]

The champion of this genre was Antoine-Léonard Thomas (1732–85). Contemporaries were far from unanimous in their admiration of him but

---

[19] Jean-Claude Bonnet, 'Les Morts illustres: oraison funèbre, éloge académique, nécrologie', in *Les Lieux de mémoire*, Part II, *La Nation*, 3 vols (Paris, 1986), III, 217–41.

[20] On this episode, see Bonnet, 'Les Morts illustres', pp. 223–4.

[21] Louis Laus de Boissy, *Réflexions impartiales sur les éloges de Voltaire qui ont concouru pour le prix de l'Académie française, en l'année 1779* (Paris, 1780), reprinted in *Les Voltairiens*, ed. J. Vercruysse, III (Nendela, Liechtenstein, 1978).

he won the Académie's prize on five different occasions, and wrote a lengthy historical and theoretical essay on the *éloge*. His idea of the genre is essentially moralizing and celebratory; the *éloge* is the equivalent of a monument erected to the great dead so as to inspire emulation in the living. Thomas therefore disagreed with those who claim that a eulogy should be a plain account interspersed with philosophical reflections, eschewing eloquence in favour of a 'historical style'. On the contrary, he wrote, the point is to 'awaken great ideas or great sentiments', and this calls for eloquence: 'Everything that you want to inspire in me must be painted forcefully. Do you want to exalt me? Be grand in your writing. Do you want to make me admire virtues, labours, great sacrifices? Display that same admiration in such a way as to strike me and astonish me'.[22]

Lest this eloquence should seem hollow, the eulogist must show a solid knowledge of his subject. Above all, he should ideally be able to unify his account round what Sartre might have called an original 'project': 'discover [...] what is the single, underlying idea which gave rise to all his ideas' (p. 281). The account of a life is less a chronicle than a demonstration.

One can see what this means in practice by looking at Thomas' *Eloge de Descartes*, which won the prize in 1765 and was much praised by such members of the 'philosophical' party as Voltaire and Diderot.[23] This offers an exalted narrative of Descartes' intellectual career, presenting him as a single-minded hero of liberation, whose ideas have triumphed over the hostility and neglect he suffered in his life. The eulogy, devoted 'to philosophy and to truth', is a belated homage to a man who could not be praised in his own day. It finishes with an apostrophe to the 'men of genius' who endured persecution, but now form 'a single people, a single family, with all the great men of the past and the future'.[24]

The text is clearly constructed to serve its ideological objective. The opening section, roughly chronological, deals with Descartes' formative experiences (education, war, travel, etc.) and his character, showing how Nature prepared him for his mission, the pursuit of truth. A central section, much the longest, is devoted to an exposition of his ideas, ending with a summary of his achievement. And the final part, before the peroration, is devoted to the ingratitude he met with.

Can this be seen as in any sense a biography? The narrative element, though present in the first section and to a certain extent in the last, is

---

[22] A. L. Thomas, *Essai sur les éloges*, in *Oeuvres*, 4 vols (2nd edn Amsterdam and Paris, 1773), II, 271–3.
[23] Voltaire, in an open letter to Thomas, wrote: 'People no longer read Descartes, but they will read his eulogy, which is at the same time your own eulogy' (Thomas, *Oeuvres*, IV, 183). More privately, however, he mocked Thomas for his inflated style.
[24] Thomas, *Oeuvres*, IV, 110.

virtually absent from the exposition of his thought, which is thematic rather than chronological. Clearly Thomas is less interested in telling the story of a life than in depicting an exemplary mind and its products. And in so far as he does follow Descartes' career, it is in highly general and allusive terms. As he put it in his *Essai sur les éloges*: 'if the reader is at all well informed, he will already know the facts about great men' (II, 271); the eulogist need not bother with detail: 'I shall not dwell on his education' (IV, 16). The contrast with Adrien Baillet's minutely documented *Vie de Monsieur Descartes* (1691) is striking, even if Baillet's book too was described by a subsequent biographical dictionary as an *éloge*.[25]

Nevertheless, if we compare it with the very unfactual eulogies of Descartes by Gabriel-Henri Gaillard and Louis-Sebastien Mercier which competed for the same prize,[26] Thomas' text does at least gesture towards biography. In particular, like d'Alembert, he provides a lot of information in footnotes.[27] These are as long as the text itself, and are clearly intended for publication rather than for oral performance at the Académie, since their relative factuality would lower the tone of the eloquence. Thomas does not quote his sources, but although his text shows no sign of original research, he clearly used the existing authorities—his phrasing and choice of anecdote occasionally echo those of Baillet. Even these notes, however, are fairly perfunctory about biographical detail, and several of them simply extend the philosophical discussions which are such an important part of the main text.

The prize eulogy, then, although a very significant cultural phenomenon, should not really figure prominently in a history of biography in France. If we are to understand why Lytton Strachey saw the French *éloge* as a possible model, we must return to the historical eulogies written by the Secrétaires Perpétuels of the academies. Apart from the work of d'Alembert, the Académie Française is fairly barren territory. More interesting are the Académie des Inscriptions et Belles-Lettres, for which Claude Gros de Boze composed three volumes of *éloges*, and above all the Académie des Sciences, the setting for the eulogies written by Fontenelle, Condorcet, Cuvier, Arago, and other eminent scientists.

---

[25] See the bibliography to the entry on Descartes in *Nouvelle Biographie générale*, ed. M. le Dr Hoefer, 46 vols (Paris, 1855–66), XIII, 758, note 3.

[26] Gabriel-Henri Gaillard, *Eloge de René Descartes* (Paris, 1765); Louis-Sebastien Mercier, *Eloge de René Descartes* (Paris and Geneva, 1765). To the disgust of contemporaries, Gaillard shared the prize with Thomas.

[27] These notes were described rather backhandedly by Guibert, himself an exponent of the genre, as 'a supplement which is perhaps superior to the work itself', less eloquent, but simple, clear, and scientific (*Eloges*, Paris, 1806, p. 260).

Bernard Le Bovier de Fontenelle was the person who did most to make the *éloge* an important and popular genre. In 1699, at the age of forty-two, he was appointed Secrétaire Perpétuel of the newly reorganized Académie des Sciences, a position he was to keep for nearly half a century. He had displayed his talent for popularizing science in the *Entretiens sur la pluralité des mondes* (1686), an attractive presentation of the new astronomy in dialogues between a philosopher and a society lady. Now he devoted himself wholeheartedly to the task of spreading the good word among educated audiences. To this end he wrote not only a retrospective history of the Académie up to 1699 (partly a rewriting of a text by his predecessor Duhamel), but above all an on-going history consisting essentially of annual reports on new scientific work and of some sixty *éloges* of recently deceased academicians.[28]

Whereas Duhamel had written his history in Latin, it was essential to Fontenelle's enterprise that he write in French, and this had to be the clear, natural French of contemporary literature. His success in this was beyond doubt, even if subsequent generations came to see his language as too flowery. More than a century later his distant successor as secretary, Pierre Flourens, still described his work as a standard of perfection, citing 'this precise, clear turn of phrase, this elegant way of writing, this simple, concise style whose only fault is a certain affectation'—an affectation more obvious to later generations than to contemporaries.[29] In a different register, Garat, whose own *éloge* of Fontenelle won the Académie Française prize in 1784, had declared that his picture of the heroic progress of modern science was perhaps the only modern text to match the glory of ancient history.[30] The *Eloges* enhanced the prestige of science and the Académie, and created a positive corporate image of the scientists, both French and foreign, whose exploits were celebrated. At the same time, Fontenelle provided, as a modern critic has written, 'a sheaf of scrupulously historical, precise, lively, and edifying biographies'.[31]

These brief lives—usually no more than thirty or forty pages—were written quickly. The regulation specified that they were to be read out at the first meeting of the Académie after the subject's death. On one occasion, indeed, when an academician (Dodart) died only seven days before a meeting, Fontenelle could not produce his text in time and a colleague

[28] References to Fontenelle's *Eloges* are to the text in his *Oeuvres complètes*, ed. A. Niderst, 7 vols (Paris, 1990–96).

[29] See Pierre Flourens, *Recueil des éloges historiques lus dans les séances publiques de l'Académie des Sciences*, 3 vols (Paris, 1846–52), I, 7–8.

[30] Dominique-Joseph Garat, *Eloge de Bernard de Fontenelle: Discours qui a remporté le prix de l'Académie Française en 1784* (Paris, 1784), p. 56.

[31] Alain Niderst, in Fontenelle, *Oeuvres*, VI, prefatory note.

improvised a funeral oration, leaving him to produce a written text at leisure. This was instant biography, its necessary brevity (since it had to be read aloud) placing it somewhere between the obituary and the full-scale life.

Unlike the later authors of prize eulogies, moreover, Fontenelle generally had no existing biography to draw on and had to do his own research, relying on published works, papers, his own memories, and conversations with colleagues. The seriousness with which he approached the task is evident from his correspondence with John Conduitt, Isaac Newton's nephew by marriage. Newton, who was a corresponding member of the Académie, died in 1727, and Conduitt offered to provide information for his *éloge*. Fontenelle accepted eagerly and wrote stating his requirements: 'I need everything you can find about M. Newton without exception.' He then gave a long list, including date and place of birth, parents' names, early signs of genius, anecdotes of youth or childhood, formative influences, reading, reasons for becoming a mathematician, composition of works, experiments, opposition encountered, praise received from scholars and princes, career and fortune, behaviour in public offices, private life, friendships, contacts, character, opinions on life, government, and literature, occupations in old age, death (VI, 32–3).

This clearly implies a standard pattern for the heroic biography of a scientist, with its obligatory mention of early signs of genius and the encounter with opposition. The rubrics go well beyond the purely scientific, however, and an examination of the Newton *éloge* shows that Fontenelle made use of information belonging to most of the categories listed above. Even so, the bulk of this short biography (some twenty-five pages) is concerned with Newton's scientific work rather than other aspects of his life. After a brief account of his family background and education, Fontenelle deals in chronological order with Newton's early mathematical work, the *Principia*, and the *Optics*, explaining them as simply as possible for a lay audience. Only then does he revert to the career, integrating the work on chronology and on currency into the narrative. After a description of Newton's admirable death and the post-mortem honours he received, the *éloge* concludes with a physical and psychological portrait, remarks on his religion and some details on his fortune and the charitable way he spent it.

An important feature of the genre, often highlighted by later commentators, is the way in which biography is interspersed with reflections from the author, whose personal presence is strongly felt. In particular, comparing Newton's prosperous career and many honours with the persecution undergone by Descartes, Fontenelle loses no opportunity of grinding his own axe, presenting England as a model in the way it encourages and rewards its scientists. At the same time, since he was notoriously attached to Descartes' cosmology, he presents the notion of attraction with some scepticism; Voltaire, who wrote his own comparison of the two great men a few years later, mentioned that at a reading of a translation of Fontenelle's text 'the whole Royal Society rose up in arms' because he had failed to give the supremacy to Newton.[32]

As we see, this eulogy, perhaps more than most, had an impact on the public. In France it was admired as one of Fontenelle's best. Certainly we can see in it the features that made his writing so effective. Without shirking his difficult scientific task, Fontenelle writes an easy, elegant prose, citing literary texts such as Lucan or mythological figures such as Prometheus, but also allowing a gentle smile to play around his exposition, as when he notes ironically that the 'marvellous phenomenon' of the tides seems to be 'degraded' by the apparent obviousness of Newton's explanation (VI, 120). He includes the occasional anecdote (but not the story of the apple, which seems to have been launched by Voltaire) and notes little humanizing facts such as Newton's thick white hair when he removed his wig, and the fact that he never wore spectacles and only ever lost one tooth. As he puts it, 'his name must serve as justification for these little details' (VI, 133).

Above all, as later commentators noted, his simple account presents an inspiring picture of human achievement. Newton is an outstanding figure, one of the three or four transcendent geniuses produced by each century (VI, 114), but he shares the qualities of the ideal man of science who is figured forth by the whole body of the *Eloges*. He does not, like some other heroes, have to endure persecution and poverty, but like them he displays a strong sense of vocation, astonishing precociousness, an attachment to truth, patriotic loyalty, willingness to work for the public good, quiet modesty, and the qualities that go to make a good colleague. In the case of Newton, we see less perhaps of the individuality and the attractive unworldly eccentricity which, according to Garat, Fontenelle was adept at displaying in his scientists, but we certainly see a sublimity calculated to provoke the reader to emulation: 'What a magnificent spectacle the imagination discovers on gathering together these facts recounted with so much modesty!'[33]

Fontenelle's followers did not radically change the pattern he had established. His immediate successor, Dortous de Mairan, failed to live up to the standard Fontenelle had set; his text is described by the *Correspondance littéraire* as dry: 'where Fontenelle had gathered flowers, he found only

[32] Voltaire, *Letters Concerning the English Nation*, ed. N. Cronk (Oxford and New York, 1994), p. 62.
[33] Garat, *Eloge de Fontenelle*, pp. 50–51.

thorns'.[34] More successful was Jean-Antoine-Nicolas Condorcet, Secrétaire Perpétuel of the Académie from 1776 until its closure under the Revolution. Condorcet was in his own right a philosopher-scientist with greater authority than Fontenelle. Before becoming secretary he had filled a gap left by Fontenelle with a book of *éloges* of academicians who had died between 1666 and 1699. After 1776, he composed a total of some fifty further *éloges* of the recently dead.[35]

It is striking how the distance in time allows for a much less respectful treatment of the seventeenth-century figures. The so-called eulogy of Marin Cureau de la Chambre, for instance, notes that his scientific works are totally forgotten and ridicules his metaphysical theories, according to which 'the soul of a man is larger than that of an elephant, a whale, or the largest trees' (II, 2–3). More clearly than Fontenelle's work, Condorcet's *éloges* have a philosophical agenda; they are full of 'enlightened' reflections on philosophy, religion, education, and politics. Speaking of Etienne Mignot de Montigny, Trésorier de France, he stresses the importance of science for the efficient government of the country:

> Whenever the government concerns itself with agriculture, industry, manufacturing, trade, public works, communications, or the effects of taxation . . . it can only find a solid foundation for these operations in the physical sciences. (II, 585)

As with Fontenelle, the scientific work takes the lion's share of the eulogies, but Condorcet also paints an individualized image of the dead man, usually an edifying one in spite of the blemishes. Sometimes, where the actual scientific work is unremarkable, Condorcet compensates for this by describing the life. This is most evident in the fascinating *Eloge de M. de la Condamine*, written before Condorcet became secretary, and read out to the Académie in 1774 by d'Alembert. As the *Correspondance littéraire* notes, this is not so much a eulogy as 'a short history of his life', done with simplicity and wit rather than eloquence.[36] La Condamine had not been in the front rank of scientists, but he had made a ten-year-long scientific voyage to South America, and this gave Condorcet the opportunity to tell a gripping tale of adventure (based on La Condamine's own account) in which we see the hero in the Andes 'climbing up crevices in the rock, and crossing torrents on immense mats of lianas which act as bridges and which, attached to two rocks, bend beneath the traveller's weight and allow him

---

[34] *Correspondance littéraire*, ed. Maurice Tourneux, 16 vols (Paris, 1877–82), I, 140.
[35] Condorcet's *éloges* are cited from his *Oeuvres*, ed. A. Condorcet O'Connor and François Arago, 12 vols (Paris, 1847).
[36] *Correspondance littéraire*, ed. Tourneux, X, 422.

to sway in the wind' (II, 170). Here again is a hero who has dedicated himself to the cause.

If celebration is the main motive behind the *éloge*, it does not rule out criticism. One orator after another repeats that his function is to tell the truth about a person without flattery or concealment. More than this, the life may be exemplary almost as much by its deplorable features as by its positive qualities. An interesting example of this is the eulogy of Joseph Priestley read out to the Académie (then called the Institut) in 1805 by the great zoologist Georges Cuvier.[37] (The date is perhaps important; after the short-lived Peace of Amiens, France was again at war with Britain, but this did not prevent French men of science from honouring their English corresponding member. Although Académie Française eulogies often obeyed a patriotic impulse, those of the Académie des Sciences were often devoted to non-French nationals, the implication no doubt being that this internationalism redounded to the glory of France.)

As Cuvier puts it, Priestley's life shows two quite different men, the scientist and the theologian. His task, as he sees it, is to depict the whole man; even if Priestley's science is what will most interest his hearers, he feels bound to discuss the theology and related political questions—and indeed this takes up half the text. The first half, beginning with a rapid sketch of Priestley's early years, offers a clear and enthusiastic account of Priestley's pioneering work as a chemist (noting nevertheless that he was a prisoner of the chemistry of his time and so failed to make the conceptual breakthrough of a Lavoisier). So far, so good, and the modest, dedicated, inventive Priestley seems to fit the traditional mould of the scientist perfectly. But at this point, Cuvier announces: 'I have arrived, gentlemen, at the painful part of my task'. However, even though Priestley's ill-fated ventures into theological controversy may seem inappropriate to a scientific academy, he feels that 'this terrible example deserves to heard with some interest' (p. 115).

What follows is a fairly careful, if sceptical, account of Priestley's religious progress, his strange Christian materialism, and what could only strike Cuvier and his audience as the mad conclusions he reached, including his prophecies. Here the orator remarks: 'I would have concealed from you, gentlemen, such extraordinary details, if our eulogies were not historical, with the obligation to give the pros and the cons, as the first and most famous of our predecessors [Fontenelle] expressly stipulated'. What is more, 'the errors of so great a genius offer a clearer warning than the actual evils that beset him' (p. 121). These evils—the Birmingham riots

[37] Georges Cuvier, *Eloges historiques* (Paris, 1867), pp. 99–130.

and Priestley's enforced exile—are nevertheless depicted in dramatic terms, so that what had begun as an inspiring eulogy finishes as a cautionary tale.

One of the features of the academic eulogy tradition is that those who composed them were in their turn eulogized by their successors. There is an *éloge* of Fontenelle by d'Alembert, one of d'Alembert by Condorcet, and, as we shall shortly see, one of Condorcet by Arago. As they honoured their predecessors, the orator-biographers enacted the handing on of the torch of learning. What is more, the dead academician often helped his future eulogist by leaving memoirs. In his *éloge* of Cuvier, first read to the Académie des Sciences and later reissued with additional biographical details, Pierre Flourens, the current secretary, quotes Cuvier: 'knowing from experience how difficult it is for the authors of this kind of work to obtain detailed information about the life of their subjects, I intend to save my eulogist this labour'.[38] Academicians could thus determine their biography in advance, not out of vanity, says Flourens, but as a service to the history of science.

One notices here a strong biographical concern: 'Everything is of interest in the life of a great man' (p. liii). Elsewhere Flourens had written that the term *éloge* was really a misnomer, quoting to this effect Fontenelle's preface to the second volume of his *Eloges*: 'The title of *Eloges* is not really accurate; that of *Vies [Lives]* would have been better, since these are really nothing but Lives, as they might have been written from the simple desire to do justice. I can guarantee their truth to the public'. This could of course be seen as a rhetorical move, since to be effective the eulogy must be believable, but it does point to some discomfort with a word which seems to undermine the activity of life-writing in an age which is no longer quite at home with the old rhetorical categories. Flourens comments: 'The word *Vie* is the correct, natural and simple term; *éloge* is merely the accepted term belonging to a particular moment in literary history'.[39]

What is missing here is the word 'biography', still a new word in the eighteenth century, when the large-scale biographies of a Descartes or a Voltaire were described as 'Vie' or 'Histoire'. It seems appropriate, therefore, to conclude this investigation with a nineteenth-century text which seems to belong to the category of the *éloge*, but to which its author gives the title 'biographie', the life of Condorcet by François Arago, one of the Secrétaires Perpétuels of the Académie des Sciences. The full title of this work is revealing: *Biographie de Jean-Antoine-Nicolas Caritat de Condorcet, Secrétaire Perpétuel de l'ancienne Académie des Sciences, par M. Arago, lue à la séance publique de l'Académie des Sciences le 28 décembre*

---

[38] Flourens, 'Eloge de George Cuvier', in Cuvier, *Eloges*, p. li.
[39] Flourens, *Recueil des éloges historiques*, I, 58.

1841. We see here the desire to establish a continuity between the old pre-Revolutionary Académie and its modern reincarnation. Like the old *éloges*, this one was read aloud to the Académie, but clearly not in its entirety, since it is 171 pages long; the full text was published at the head of an edition of Condorcet's works.[40] And Arago insists that this is not a eulogy, but a 'biographie'.

The difference, as he explains in the opening pages, lies partly in the length. This is a 'meticulous, detailed biography' (p. ii). Arago hints, without pursuing the question, that the needs of science may require this of future secretaries of the Académie, but concentrates on explaining why an *éloge* would not have been sufficient for Condorcet. His distant predecessor, he claims, as an active participant in the Revolution (which claimed his life), has been the subject of much slanderous gossip, and has to be defended in the eyes of posterity. And this calls for detailed evidence:

> I could not expect to be simply taken at my word. If for every characteristic trait I had been content to gather together and keep to myself all that established the truth of my impression, I should not have done enough: I was obliged to put the public in a position to judge equitably between me and most of my predecessors. (p. iii)

What one immediately notices here is that the move to biography is motivated not by some disinterested search for the whole truth, but by the rhetorical aim of justification. In that praise and blame are the essential categories, the text is still an *éloge*. Indeed, Arago says as much at the outset, noting that because of the time and circumstances of his death nearly fifty years before, Condorcet has still not received the eulogy to which he was entitled. His text, with all its detail, is a work of rehabilitation and celebration. This is achieved partly by the use of quotations, accompanied by comments such as 'This loyal, noble language will serve to rectify many false ideas [about Condorcet]' (p. xli). The biographer is a defence advocate. More than simply doing posthumous justice to Condorcet, Arago is using this life to keep the republican flame alive and to perpetuate the ideal image of the philosopher-scientist as responsible citizen. Arago praises Condorcet's *Eloges* in terms that could be applied to his own work: 'The history of the human mind is seen from an elevated perspective. In the choice of details, the author is constantly concerned to instruct and to be useful even more than to give pleasure' (p. liii).

By the time Arago came to write about Condorcet, biography had developed strongly in France in a variety of forms. There were plenty of full-length *vies*; Sainte-Beuve was beginning his new-style *portraits littér-*

---

[40] Condorcet, *Oeuvres*, ed. Condorcet O'Connor and Arago, I, i–clxxi.

aires and his group biographies; and the obituary had found its place, sometimes in specialized publications (an early example being the eighteenth-century *Nécrologe des hommes célèbres*).[41] In the nineteenth century there was a new flourishing of biographical dictionaries with two large-scale publications, the fifty-five-volume *Biographie universelle* (1811–33; 2nd edn 1843–61) of Louis-Gabriel Michaud, and the fuller, less personal forty-six-volume *Nouvelle Biographie générale* (1855–66) directed by Dr Hoefer. Like the *éloges* of the Académie des Sciences, these were cosmopolitan in scope, though they served at the same time as dictionaries of national biography.

The introduction to the *Nouvelle Biographie générale*, discussing the sources used, gives a special place to the 'mass of *éloges*', noting that the records of provincial academies are full of these 'biographies'.[42] The *éloge* is thus a tributary stream (and, as already noted, an entirely male one) to the greater undertaking of general biography. The word *éloge* was something of an embarrassment to some authors, who were anxious to distinguish their work from the deceits and flattery of the funeral oration ('to lie like a funeral oration' is a phrase noted by the seventeenth-century lexicographer Furetière). And certainly Fontenelle, Condorcet, and their fellow eulogists did provide broadly reliable information, though not in great detail. Yet a eulogy remains a eulogy; the aspiration to truth does not seriously interfere with the aim of offering an exemplary life-story.

Can a life-story be other than exemplary, one wonders. Obviously the characteristic modern biography, with its wealth of details, does not present itself as an exercise in praise or blame, but as an attempt to find and tell the historical and psychological truth. In some cases the revelations of the misery and weakness of a great creative figure could be held to undermine the value of his or her achievement, which an earlier tradition would have celebrated more wholeheartedly. Nor can a life-story addressed to a broad reading public be expected to model itself on a genre designed for oral performance in an all-male academy. Even so, and whatever the intention of the biographers, readers of modern biographies are surely not wrong if they continue to find in them a stimulus to personal reflection or emulation, an example or a lesson such as was offered by the *éloges* of a Fontenelle

---

[41] *Le Nécrologe des hommes célèbres de France par une société de gens de lettres*, 17 vols (Paris, 1767–82). The leading spirit in this periodical publication was the anti-*philosophe* Charles Palissot de Montenoy. The obituaries, entitled *éloges*, vary between three and thirty pages; like the academic eulogies, they concentrate on the work rather than the life, preferring critical discussion to anecdote.
   On Sainte-Beuve, see Chapter 8 below.
[42] *Nouvelle Biographie générale*, ed. Hoefer, I, iii.

or a d'Alembert. And in a time of exhaustingly voluminous biographies, one may still share Lytton Strachey's admiration for the concision and elegance of these 'brief lives'.

6

Adding Stones to the Edifice: Patterns of German Biography

ROGER PAULIN

Despite disavowals in its country of origin, there *is* such a thing as a great German biographical tradition. Why, then, do we not hear more of it, and what has happened meanwhile to the art of biography in the German-speaking lands? Inevitably, comparisons are made with the Anglo-Saxon tradition of biographical writing and scholarship. These are of only limited help. For German comment on Anglo-Saxon literary or scholarly traditions tends to notice only two things. One is the sense of continuity, the unbroken succession of literary modes, the straightforward acceptance of institutions that are deemed satisfactory and that 'work'. The other is a certain lack of depth or bottom, a tendency to dwell on the surface, even to pursue readability and general accessibility at the expense of high seriousness and reflection. Thus in the art of biography, the Anglo-Saxons, it is said, get on with the business of writing, insouciant of charges of reductionism or positivism, and even deserve a measure of grudging admiration for such moving and doing.

The Germans, it is maintained, do not have such an uninhibited relationship to past traditions in any field of intellectual endeavour. Political considerations are made partly responsible for this. While one should not lightly underestimate their effects, they are not the only factors for discontinuity. In purely formal terms, biography has never been fully accepted into the scheme of German poetics. To some extent, the answer lies in the nature of the German biographical tradition itself. It has always been seen as part of historiography, so that its development belongs rather to *Wissenschaftsgeschichte* than to *belles-lettres*. Thus Carlyle belongs fairly and

squarely to English literature as well as to historical writing, whereas
Ranke, the most readable of the German historian-biographers, does
not.

Then there is the function of this biographical tradition. It is not just
the record of great names, but a hierarchy of cultural role models, canonical
literary figures, and representative individuals. As a determiner of national
moral values—spiritual and political—it does more than merely mem-
orialize. It is one of the many intellectual institutions before 1871 that
speak for a German nation not yet politically in being but which coalesces
in cultural terms around a shared linguistic and historical heritage. 'Representatives of the nation' can thus become focal points for all kinds of
aspirations not yet underwritten by actual political institutions. Gustav
Schwab's much-read biography of Schiller, for example, aligns itself with a
visible sign of national greatness, the first statue erected to the poet's
memory, in 1840.[1] And it is not by chance that so many German liberal
aspirations before 1871 centred on public celebrations of Schiller's life and
works, of which biographies are one important manifestation.[2]

It is also not fortuitous that the great age of the German biography is
roughly 1830–90, spanning the period that gave us works as disparate
as Droysen's life of Alexander the Great (1833),[3] Hermann Grimm's of
Michelangelo (1860–63),[4] Ranke's of Wallenstein (1869),[5] and Erich
Schmidt's of Lessing (1884–92),[6] the years leading through reaction and
revolution up to the *Gründerzeit* ('founding period') of the Second Empire
and its apogee. All relate in their several ways to these processes and refer
to them. Droysen reflects on the nature of the 'monarchic organism',[7]
Grimm on the role of great men in the events of history, Ranke similarly
on the relationship of the individual to the general development of an
epoch, Schmidt on the emergence of German literary culture. Each one is
a kind of monumental 'representative man' for which Carlyle's *Life of
Friedrich Schiller* (1825) provided an early model. This would link the
German biography to the high seriousness of the Victorians. But the German
biographies also reflect the nineteenth century's awareness that the Life

---

[1] Gustav Schwab, *Schiller's Leben in drei Büchern* (Stuttgart, 1841) (1st edn 1840).

[2] Thomas Nipperdey, *Deutsche Geschichte 1800–1866: Bürgerwelt und starker Staat* (Munich, 1984), p. 722.

[3] Johann Gustav Droysen, *Geschichte Alexander des Grossen* (Berlin, 1833).

[4] Hermann Grimm, *Leben Michelangelo's* (Hanover, 1860–63).

[5] Leopold von Ranke, *Geschichte Wallenstein's* (Leipzig, 1869).

[6] Erich Schmidt, *Lessing: Geschichte seines Lebens und seiner Schriften*, 2 vols (Berlin, 1884–92).

[7] Droysen, op. cit., p. 538.

forms an entity in itself around an 'organizing centre'[8] that aggregates and co-ordinates the individual events that befall it. In that sense, nineteenth-century biographers are heirs to the insight, enshrined in German idealist and Romantic thought, that the individual is the visible and tangible representative of the total forces—intellectual, moral, historical—of an age or culture. Thus the Life and the Works reflect one another, support each other, and in the final analysis bear the same relation to the *Ganzes*, the totality.

Seen in these terms, the German biographical tradition might appear to be the product of national liberalism, its function to annex the lives of the great for the sake of overarching cultural and political ends. Erich Schmidt's monumental life of Lessing could serve as a prime example. It is not for the faint-hearted: it is huge, 'philological', painstaking, supremely *wissenschaftlich*, and it sets the capstone (if that is the right image for so weighty a work) on nearly a century's proclamation of Lessing as the founder of modern German literature and thought.

But had the biography, the heir to both positivism and historicism, become crushed under the weight of its erudition? Nietzsche, speaking of a 'biographical epidemic',[9] seemed to think so. And others, who shared Nietzsche's disdain for diligent philology as an end in itself and applauded his remarks on mere progress or utilitarianism—the harnessing of art or scholarship to an 'official' culture—would have concurred. Instead, if there were to be 'Lives', they must be of the aristocrats of the mind, representing timeless poetic genius; they should be sufficient in themselves, adequate in their powers of utterance, beholden to no tradition; they should transcend mere influence and be explicable only in terms of the epoch on which they stamped their individuality—figures such as Goethe, Beethoven, or Wagner. The German biographical tradition comes to an end as it bifurcates into accounts of unapproachable genius (e.g. Friedrich Gundolf's studies of Caesar, Shakespeare, Goethe, or Stefan George) or popular (and immensely readable) accounts by the likes of Emil Ludwig or Stefan Zweig.

All along, however, the biography had had a competitor in the form of the scholarly apparatus to those historical-critical editions, or the volumes of edited correspondence, that are in many ways the greatest German contribution to scholarship. There is an unwillingness to make this corpus of material readily available to the non-specialist reader, an unease at the

---

[8] Wilhelm Dilthey's phrase: 'die organisierende Mitte', quoted in Ulfert Ricklefs, 'Leben und Schrift: Autobiographische und biographische Diskurse. Ihre Intertextualität in Literatur und Literaturwissenschaft', *Editio: Internationales Jahrbuch für Editionswissenschaft*, IX (1995), 37–62, ref. 47.

[9] Friedrich Nietzsche, *Werke*, ed. Karl Schlechta, 3 vols (Munich, 1969), III, 366.

potential loss of scholarly standards. There are inhibitions at material being allowed to float freely in the narrative mode. A good example would be August Wilhelm Schlegel, of whom there has never been a biography: Schlegel, *cicisbeo* to Madame de Staël, following her from Coppet to Moscow and back, whose *Lectures on Dramatic Art and Literature* had proclaimed Romantic doctrine 'from Cadiz to Edinburgh, Stockholm and St Petersburg'.[10] Comtesse Jean de Pange, coming from another biographical tradition (and perhaps a little too close to its André Maurois wing) documented Staël and Schlegel.[11] But Germany has produced volume after volume of edited correspondence, its apparatus fairly bristling with biographical facts. Schlegel was captious, vain (Byron disliked him, a sure sign), generally unattractive as a person (so was Staël), but his Life has never been structured or documented except through the letters. This is not an isolated example.

After 1945, commentators were in fairly broad agreement that there was no going back to what many now claimed was a nineteenth-century discipline. Friedrich Sengle's *Wieland* (1949) remains the only large-scale literary biography combining readability, empiricism, and scholarly reassessment.[12] It has not found many successors, if any. German biographies often are anti-biographies, breaking with older, discredited conventions, amalgams of fiction and autobiography. The conventional form requires some sense of conviction. Thus, in the eyes of one critic (and historian of biography), Golo Mann's splendid *Wallenstein* (1971) takes us little further than the nineteenth century![13] This remark was not intended to be a compliment: it was not the same as a modern Anglo-Saxon biographer hearing a flattering comparison with Mrs Gaskell or Hallam Tennyson. It illustrates the discontinuous and problematic tradition of historical or literary biography in Germany. Indeed, the potential German biographer might instead be told that he or she is breaking taboos, is entering a terrain not accessible to theory or scholarly criticism, is challenging modern anti-narrative positions, is positing an 'individual' where Freud or Foucault have told us that there is, properly speaking, no such thing. Above all, he or she may learn that this kind of thing is best left to the Anglo-Saxons and their tradition

---

[10] Georg Hirzel, 'Ungedruckte Briefe an Georg Andreas Reimer', *Deutsche Revue*, XVIII, (Oct.–Dec. 1893), 98–114, 238–53, ref. 249.

[11] Comtesse Jean de Pange, ed., *Auguste-Guillaume Schlegel et Madame de Staël; d'après des documents inédits* (Paris, 1938).

[12] Friedrich Sengle, *Wieland* (Stuttgart, 1949).

[13] Helmut Scheuer, 'Biographie: Überlegungen zu einer Gattungsbeschreibung', in *Vom Anderen und vom Selbst: Beiträge zu Fragen der Biographie und Autobiographie*, ed. Reinhold Grimm and Jost Hermand (Königstein im Taunus, 1982), pp. 9–29, ref. 10.

of the Lives of the Poets.[14] I do not rate highly the chances of a revival of German biographical writing, but I am encouraged by an increasing willingness to explore what there once was. The rest of this chapter therefore focuses on one aspect of that 'German biographical tradition', one that involves the relationship between hagiography and national literary canon.

The emergence of German literary biography—Lives of the Poets—in the late eighteenth century has to be seen in the context of a national identity that was not fully realized until three or four generations later. Its background is a tentatively emerging national canon, centred on but a few commanding figures. There was, of course, agreement on a supranational canon—Homer, Dante, Tasso, Ariosto, Shakespeare, Cervantes, Ossian— but Germany had produced nothing commensurate. The different critical schools in the German-speaking lands could not agree on indigenous models. Outstanding figures were few. The many lives of Luther[15] reflected the concentration of German spiritual and intellectual culture in the Protestant heartlands; and Sandrart's memorialization of Dürer accorded a German painter a pre-eminent status, akin to Raphael or Michelangelo.[16] Much of the biographical activity of the period was, in any case, conducted in the spirit of learned compendia or necrologies. One might have to search diligently among the dross to find nuggets of excellence.

Where individual names did provide the focus for an emergent literary canon, other traditions of biography had to be invoked. The first German poet to become part of this new canon was Friedrich Gottlieb Klopstock, the author of *Der Messias* (1749–73) and as such the most translated German author of the eighteenth and nineteenth centuries.[17] In Klopstock converge the Homeric, the Miltonic, the Youngian, all strands of 'original composition'. But this achievement can only be fused with the Life through another strain of biography: hagiography. It is, of course, no longer vener-

---

[14] See esp. Gerhart von Graevenitz, 'Geschichte aus dem Geist des Nekrologs: Zur Begründung der Biographie im 19. Jahrhundert', *Deutsche Vierteljahrsschrift für Literaturwissenschaft und Geistesgeschichte*, LIV, 2 (1980), 105–70, ref. 105–10; Ernst Ribbat, 'Der Dichter und sein Monograph: Zu den Aussichten einer fragwürdigen Gattung', in *Germanistik: Forschungsstand und Perspektiven* (Vorträge des Deutschen Germanistentages 1984), 2. Teil. Ältere Deutsche Literatur. Neuere Deutsche Literatur, ed. Georg Stotzel (Berlin and New York, 1985), pp. 589–99.

[15] Between 1546 and the end of the eighteenth century some fifty biographies of Luther had appeared.

[16] Joachim von Sandrart, 'Albrecht Dürer Mahler/Bildhauer/Kupferstecher und Baumeister von Nürnberg', in *L'Academia Todesca delle Architectura, Scultura & Pittura: Oder Deutsche Academie der Edlen Bau- Bild- und Mahlerey-Künste*, 2 vols (Nuremberg, 1675–9), I., II. Theils III. Buch, III. Capitel, pp. 222–9.

[17] He would be in competition with the even more translated Johann Arndt, *Vier Bücher vom wahren Christentum* (1605).

ation *per se*, but the structuring and schematizing of a life around considerations of edification, amplification, and transfiguration. The rich seam of pietism can be tapped and merged with the inspirational theory of poetry and the aspirations of national cultural renewal. Thus Klopstock is also the first major modern German poet to be the subject of a biography during his own lifetime.[18] And it is Klopstock more than any other canonical figure who receives the accolade of 'divine',[19] analogous to the Renaissance 'alter deus' or 'divino artista' but now harnessed to the religious connotations of genius. Like the prophetic patriarch Edward Young, to whom Klopstock had once addressed an early ode, age and venerability (Klopstock lived to be seventy-nine) go hand in hand with the biblical virtues which his Life illustrates.

The 'minor canonizations'—in the form of biographical prefaces—of poets from the Klopstock circle who died young and without the fulfilment of age show a similar insistence on the association of life and works.[20] It informs much of the discussion of individual poets or artists as suitable models for a literature that is not merely national in name but which illustrates the national virtues (also sung by Klopstock) of honesty, loyalty, or forthrightness of mind. Schiller's stringent review of the works of the *Sturm und Drang* poet Gottfried August Bürger (1791) also makes this link, placing severe obligations on the poet's individuality if he is to rise to the supreme challenge of reflecting humanity as a whole. And the Romantic imitation of Vasari, Wackenroder and Tieck's *Herzensergiessungen eines kunstliebenden Klosterbruders* (1796) ('Heart's Outpourings of a Lay Brother Devoted to Art') regarded all personal aberrations or freakishness as a barrier to ultimate artistic greatness.

Klopstock's life centred on the fulfilment of *Der Messias*. After his death, the religious poet and his epic poem could merge in symbiotic form under the heading 'representative of the German nation'.[21] The same could not, however, be said for Lessing. Lessing had died in 1781, not much over fifty. In contrast to Klopstock, he had led a shifting and unstable existence, subject to exigencies and deprivations, some of his own making, often due to his generosity. Yet his life, too, could be made to suit the record of his works, an achievement which an early biographer saw fit to compare with

---

[18] Carl Friedrich Cramer, *Klopstock: Er, und über ihn*, 5 vols (Hamburg, Dessau, Leipzig and Altona, 1780–92).

[19] 'Von diesem Göttlichen'; see Klamer Schmidt, ed., *Klopstock und seine Freunde* (Halberstadt, 1810), p. iv.

[20] As in the biographical prefaces to the works of Nikolas Dietrich Giseke (1767) and Ludwig Heinrich Christoph Hölty (1783).

[21] As the preface to his works states: Friedrich Gottlieb Klopstock, *Sämmtliche Werke*, 10 vols (Leipzig, 1854–5, 1st edn 1844–5), I, xxx.

Columbus's or Cook's.[22] Still, the individual uniqueness of Lessing's life could be subsumed under the commonplaces of hagiography and the cult of genius. While Klopstock's works would, in the eyes of his contemporaries, be dominated by the supreme *Messias*, much of Lessing's oeuvre remained to be revealed. Thus the first Lessing biography is a two-volume introduction to works not published during his lifetime.[23] The works thus suspend the arbitrariness and relative brevity of the life. In the extraordinary letter from Moses Mendelssohn to Lessing's brother, with which the first volume of the life ends, his achievement is likened to Copernicus, who 'discovered a new system, and died'.[24] He had achieved everything in the realm of the senses, and had passed into the supersensory realm: 'Like the sons of the prophets, they looked in wonderment at the place from which he went up and was seen no more'.[25] The Jewish hagiography (II Kings 2, 11)—easily merged with its Christian counterpart—equates acceptance into the canon with Elijah's translation in the whirlwind. It is too good a quotation for Schink, Lessing's next biographer, to miss and he duly repeats it.[26] But Schink's concern as a biographer is couched in terms of a different, if ultimately also religious, image, that of the monument. Indeed his biography forms part of a three-volume *Pantheon der Deutschen*, and his stated task is to add 'a few stones to the edifice begun by German patriotism, leaving the columns themselves to posterity'.[27] Schink's biography stands free of the works themselves (it is he who is prepared to press the analogies with Columbus and Cook). But to fulfil the patterns of edification, to make the life appear more exemplary and yet more humanly accessible, he adds two plates: one shows the young Lessing's obedience to his parents, the other his integrity as a pursuer of truth, and both are as such obliquely hagiographic.

Both Klopstock and Lessing enter the canon foremost as German writers in an established German line of achievement. 'He stands as the first column of German originality',[28] states an early nineteenth-century Klopstock biography, also finding the monumental image congenial. They illustrate how language and culture establish national bonds, not the scattered multiplicity of political institutions that called themselves the 'German lands'. Part of

[22] Johann Friedrich Schink, 'Charakteristik Gotthold Ephraim Lessings', in Karl Gottlieb Hofmann, *Pantheon der Deutschen*, 3 vols (Chemnitz and Leipzig, 1794–5), II, 1–192, ref. 5f.
[23] *Gotthelf Ephraim Lessings Leben, nebst seinem noch übrigen litterarischen Nachlasse*, ed. K. G. Lessing, 3 vols (Berlin, 1793–5).
[24] Ibid., I, 451.
[25] Ibid., I, 452.
[26] Schink, 'Characteristik Gotthold Ephraim Lessings', p. 192.
[27] Ibid., p. 7.
[28] [K. Nicolai], *Klopstock: Ein Denkmahl zur Säcularfeier seines Geburtstages am zweiten Julius 1824* (Quedlinburg, 1824), p. 6.

the anecdotal—and incidental—material on Klopstock's and Lessing's lives recounts how they moved as equals among kings and princes, yet spurned preferments that might inhibit their genius. (This would overlook the negative role of Frederick the Great in the establishment of German literature, or the hopes both placed in the young reforming emperor Joseph II.) It is a variation on Renaissance commonplaces, relevant to readers aware that it was culture, and not so much rulers, that held the nation together. Christoph Martin Wieland, a contemporary of Lessing and Klopstock, found less automatic entry into the German literary pantheon. For some, he might appear too cosmopolitan to deserve the accolade of 'deutscher Dichter'. But the nearly thousand-page biography which his editor, Gruber, appended to his edition of the works, removes such doubts by recounting Wieland's meeting with Napoleon in 1806.[29] They converse on the basis of equality, not deference; worldly authority (it is just after the battles of Jena and Auerstädt) acknowledges the power of the intellect—across national borders. Again, this somewhat implausible point is too good for others to miss. Schiller's sister-in-law Caroline von Wolzogen, in her biography of 1830, embellishes his life-story with the fantasy that Schiller, had he lived, would have encountered the 'world conqueror' with equal dignity and composure,[30] as the representative of 'Humanität'. (It is also a tactical ploy to get round Schiller's marked progression from rebellious and anti-authoritarian youth to respect for crowned heads in maturity.)

The biographical commonplaces—of hagiography, of traditional pan-egyric, of the 'divino artista'—that accompany this early stage of German Lives of the Classical Poets, can be concentrated so as to make life and works one 'single entity', one 'symbolic form', one 'individuality'. These are phrases taken from Friedrich Schlegel's *Ueber Lessing* of 1801,[31] not a biography as such, but a 'Charakteristik', the attempt to reduce to their essentials the adventitious and cluttered details of personality and writings. This symbolic unity is the ideal, not the norm or the reality: 'the golden age of literature will be when prefaces are no longer needed' (one might say, biographical introductions).[32] As yet, however, the Life was deemed necessary as an accompaniment or corroboration of the Works.

---

[29] J. G. Gruber, *C. M. Wielands Leben*, 4 vols (Leipzig, 1827–8), IV, pp. 420–28. This forms vols L–LIII of *Sämmtliche Werke*, 53 vols (Leipzig, 1824–8).

[30] [Caroline von Wolzogen], *Schillers Leben, verfaßt aus Erinnerungen der Familie, seinen eigenen Briefen und den Nachrichten seines Freundes Körner*, 2 vols (Stuttgart and Tübingen, 1830), II, 297. Cf. Lesley Sharpe, ' "Wahrheit allein sollte mich leiten": Caroline von Wolzogen's Schiller Biography', *Publications of the English Goethe Society*, LXVIII (1999), 70–81.

[31] Friedrich Schlegel, 'Ueber Lessing', August Wilhelm Schlegel and Friedrich Schlegel, *Charakteristiken und Kritiken*, 2 vols (Königsberg, 1801), I, 170–270: 'Beziehungen aufs Ganze', p. 266; 'symbolische Form', p. 263; 'Individualität', p. 193.

[32] Ibid., p. 241.

Shortly after Schlegel's essay on Lessing, Goethe attempted something similar to this 'Charakteristik'. He, too, was concerned to elevate his subject, the art historian Johann Joachim Winckelmann, to canonical status. He had no less serious a purpose than had Lessing's or Klopstock's sponsors. As an account of the father of modern European neoclassicism, it is not free of an ideological or even polemical—anti-Romantic—intention. But it records that Germany's greatest living poet saw the function of biography as a means of making a public statement. His *Skizze zu einer Schilderung Winckelmanns* (1805) is not free-standing, but forms the introduction to a collection of Winckelmann's letters. Goethe's approach is different from Schlegel's, in that it refers less to 'das Ganze', the whole,[33] than to a series of abstract categories, superimposed on the mass of biographical detail ('ancient art', 'friendship', 'beauty', 'Rome', 'passing'). They structure a life that already conforms in some respects to hagiographic patterns (humble origins overcome through higher intervention, leading to career and ultimate apotheosis). We do not read the essay to be informed of the mere facts of Winckelmann's life: there is not a single date in the text. Such account of the life as there is, and of its various stages, is determined completely by the work, and not vice versa: 'everything that he produces is extraordinary and estimable because his character was revealed in it'.[34] Goethe embellishes and harmonizes. Like Raphael, Winckelmann dies at the apogee of his career: the squalid circumstances of his life in Rome and especially of his death (he was robbed and murdered in Trieste) are passed over. Instead, we have this extraordinary final section:

> Thus, at the summit of the good fortune he could only have wished for himself, he was removed from this world. His native country was expecting him, his friends awaited him with outstretched arms, all the expressions of affection, so essential to him, all the terms of public recognition, so important for him, waited for his advent, to overwhelm him. And in this sense we may call him fortunate, that he has gone up from the summit of human existence to join the immortals, that a brief moment of terror, a quick second of pain snatched him away from the living. He did not experience the infirmities of age, the diminution of his intellectual powers; the dispersal of art treasures, that he said would happen, if perhaps in another sense, did not happen before his eyes. He lived as a man, and as a man at the height of his powers he has departed this life. Now in the memory of those he has left behind he enjoys the good fortune of appearing always forceful and worthy through and through: for in the shape that a man leaves the world, so he walks among

---

[33] Cf. Hans-Martin Kruckis, '*Ein potenziertes Abbild der Menschheit': Biographischer Diskurs und Etablierung der Neugermanistik in der Goethe-Biographik bis Gundolf*, Probleme der Dichtung, Bd 24 (Heidelberg, 1995), p. 47.

[34] Johann Wolfgang Goethe, 'Winckelmann und sein Jahrhundert', *Sämtliche Werke*, 18 vols (Zurich, 1977), XIII, 407–50, ref. 443.

the shades, and thus Achilles remains ever present for us as a young man, ever striving.[35]

That remarkable image of Achilles, like its biblical equivalent in the lives of Lessing, was not to be restricted to Winckelmann alone. Goethe is clearly making a legend of Winckelmann, laying down the essentials of artistic existence and their application. Winckelmann becomes a symbol, in that Goethe fuses the particular, the Life, with the ancient world and its afterlife, the general. It comes therefore as no surprise to find the Achilles passage invoked as part of much more potent cultural myth-making: Gustav Schwab's life of Schiller (1840). It belongs to the retouching of detail which is so necessary for the construction of literary monuments. The quotation is (correctly) attributed to Goethe and dated 1805, the year of its appearance and of Schiller's death.[36] The biographer must somehow reconcile Goethe's attested close friendship with Schiller with his failure to attend Schiller's funeral. Goethe, as is well known, hated the panoply associated with death and could not bring himself to join the sparse number of mourners at Schiller's hurried burial. The resourceful Schwab makes a virtue out of necessity by stating that 'Goethe stepped forward and spoke to the nation'.[37] But Schwab is merely continuing a hagiography that had even extended to Schiller when living. He recounts the false report of Schiller's death in 1791, which had caused his Danish friends to create a secular memorial around 'Freude, schöner Götterfunken',[38] and later to rejoice at the 'resurrection of our immortal and deathless Schiller'.[39] Such veneration and legend-making moves effortlessly among the mythologies and cults and plucks at will the images needed for its purposes.

While Lessing and Klopstock found general acceptance in terms of the symbolic unity of life and works, other figures had a less easy passage into canonicity. The Romantics remembered Schiller as their most implacable opponent and found little pleasure in his sanctification by biographers and editors (especially when these included Goethe and Wilhelm von Humboldt). Hearing the threnodic note of a Schiller dying 'at the height of his powers', they could reflect that their own movement also had its necrology and cult of remembrance, not merely those figures now being enthroned by Goethe and his Weimar acolytes. Ludwig Tieck, as the senior surviving poet of German Romanticism, wished to set the record straight —through the life and works approach. The opportunity was afforded by

---

[35] Ibid., p. 450.
[36] Schwab, *Schiller's Leben*, pp. 633f.
[37] Ibid., p. 633.
[38] Ibid., pp. 366f.
[39] Ibid., p. 368.

the reissue in 1815 of the works of his close friend Friedrich von Hardenberg, known as Novalis. Part of the last section of the short biography reads:

> Before he reached his twenty-ninth year, our friend thus died, whose extensive knowledge, philosophical genius and poetic talent one can only love and admire. He hastened ahead of his time, so that his native country ought to have expected extraordinary things from him, had this early death not overtaken him. The unfinished writings he left have been widely received and many of his great thoughts will in future still inspire, and noble minds and profound thinkers will be illumined and fired by the sparks of his intellect. [. . .] For the more experienced eye his aspect was one of beauty. The outline and expression of his face approached that of John the Evangelist as we see him in the wonderful great picture by A. Dürer, once to be seen in Nuremberg, now in Munich.[40]

Here artistic integrity, religious piety, national pride, and genius are conflated. The reminiscence of the Dürer portrait not only invokes a Christian iconography opposed to Goethe's pagan reference to Achilles; it is a reminder of the religion of art which Tieck himself and his dead friend Wackenroder had propounded as young men, centred on Raphael and Dürer. In the same way as Goethe's vision of Winckelmann makes its subject into the exemplar of the Classicism that Goethe affirms, so Tieck fashions Novalis according to an image that stresses the Romantic poet, seer and visionary.

This pattern of commemoration was especially suited to writers whose brief lives denied them the canonical status of those who had had full use of their powers. Gustav Schwab's accounts of Wilhelm Müller and Wilhelm Hauff,[41] both writers who died in their twenties, conform to its general conventions. It could be turned on its head, as Tieck himself did with his biographical introduction to the works of Heinrich von Kleist.[42] Despite his admiration for Kleist's poetic talent, and his tolerant words for a writer who had taken his own life, Tieck cannot find the unity, the symbolic wholeness that Friedrich Schlegel's account of Lessing had posited. The works and the life diverge and follow patterns of their own, the one leading to the hope of future recognition, the other registering the failure of the

---

[40] Ludwig Tieck, 'Preface to the Third Edition of Novalis' Schriften (1815)', Novalis, *Schriften: Historisch-kritische Ausgabe*, ed. Paul Kluckhohn and Richard Samuel et al., 6 vols (Stuttgart, 1960–88), IV, 551–60, ref. 558.
[41] Gustav Schwab, 'Wilhelm Hauff's Leben' (1827) in Wilhelm Hauff, *Sämmtliche Werke*, ed. Gustav Schwab, 5 vols (Stuttgart, 5th edn 1853), I, 5–20; Gustav Schwab, 'Wilhelm Müller's Leben', in Wilhelm Müller, *Vermischte Schriften*, ed. Gustav Schwab, 5 vols (Leipzig, 1830), I, XVII–LXII.
[42] Heinrich von Kleist, *Hinterlassene Schriften* (Berlin, 1821) and *Gesammelte Schriften* (Berlin, 1826).

person to fulfil the talent with which he undeniably was blessed by nature. This highly influential biographical essay is a factor in the withholding of recognition from Kleist during the nineteenth century and the denial of a place in the canon. His life and works are pulled apart; his qualities of poetic genius are countered by symbolic patterns of light and darkness. Here, Tieck is unable to employ the hagiographic patterns of explication and selective embellishment that hitherto had done service and continued to be potent forces in the establishment of a German national literary canon for the rest of the century. It is not his last word on these matters. Later in the same decade, he was wrapping these biographical devices in a fictional guise, to produce the ultimate ideal 'Life': William Shakespeare's.[43] It was intended to suit all the needs of nineteenth-century cultural ideology. Thus not only Lessing, Klopstock or Schiller, but also the greatest English 'Representative Man' may be annexed for the purposes of national role models.

---

[43] Ludwig Tieck, *Dichterleben* (1826, 1831), most accessible in Ludwig Tieck, *Schriften*, 20 vols (Berlin, 1828–46), XVIII.

7

Shaping Victorian Biography: From Anecdote to Bildungsroman

ELINOR S. SHAFFER

Burckhardt in his comments on biography in *The Civilization of the Renaissance in Italy* (1860) famously said that 'the dominating tendency that distinguishes Italians from other Westerners' is 'the search for the characteristic traits of significant persons'. By the end of the eighteenth century other European countries seemed to have joined the search. In England few doubted that biography in this sense had begun with Dr Johnson's *Lives of the Poets*, and was best exemplified in the *Life of Dr Johnson* himself by the grand individualizer James Boswell. Yet the debate between individualization and edification as goals of biography was not so easily put aside. As the appetite and scope for more facts, of whatever kind, increased, and the need for reshaping them into a matter for national pride became equally imperative, the form of the brief 'Life' was sprung and new models had to be sought.

A Scottish writer early in the nineteenth century, James Field Stanfield, wrote the first full-scale book on biography, *An Essay on the Study and Composition of Biography* (1813). This was at almost the same time as the word *Bildungsroman* was coined in Germany by Karl von Morgenstern. In neither case was the author well-known. But they formulated the terms in which biography and the novel were to be in close proximity, both in likeness and in difference, throughout the century. Stanfield tells us that biography should assist us in understanding human character 'from a patient and extensive survey of living character, in various countries and stages of civilization; and from an early and constant exercise of considering self-movements, in all their springs, courses and apparent destinations'. The aim is to apply the results to 'the improvable points of education and conduct'.[1]

Biography is thus to serve the elucidation of the range of human possibility, in the Enlightenment manner of Herder or Lessing; it will speak to the Education of the Human Race. It is anything but local, provincial, or merely anecdotal. Moreover, and we hear the Victorian age in the offing, it is to be 'improving'. Stanfield goes on to pinpoint the dilemma which will haunt nineteenth-century biography. On the one hand, biography is serious history. He points to the historian's obligation to tell the truth, quoting Robertson's words to Gibbon: the historian 'should feel himself a witness giving evidence upon oath'. But on the other hand, there is a need for censorship (he uses this word), in order to protect certain parts of the audience, especially the young, who should be edified by their reading. The more the aim is 'improvement', of the individual and of the human race, the more care must be taken. A certain latitude is allowed through the discussion of negative examples; biography may lend itself to moral judgement, even condemnation, sparingly applied, and employ a gamut of examples for moral illustration. The potential collision between serious truth-telling and moral edification is perceived by Stanfield, who admits rather wistfully that the novelist has 'greatly the advantage' over the biographer. The novelist is 'the judicious narrator of feigned events', and can 'create and control the characters', and 'fit them to situations calculated to discover the effects of circumstances on disposition' and thus aid the reader's 'development'.[2] The novel as fictitious history was to prove the more successful genre, as Stanfield foresaw, even while recommending the practice of biography. There are many examples of nineteenth-century biography that foundered, either in the making or in the reception, on the clash between its two incompatible aims.

Yet this elevation of its purpose posed a challenge to the novel, a still suspect form, and one deluged at that time in both England and Germany by the sensational and 'Gothick' vogue. As Steinecke has pointed out, so low had the novel sunk that in England the Gothick mode was branded as 'German', and in Germany, with equal disapproval, as 'English'.[3] To call

---

[1] James Field Stanfield, *An Essay on the Study and Composition of Biography* (1813), quoted in J. L. Clifford, *Biography as an Art* (London, 1962), p. 60.

[2] Ibid., p. 71.

[3] Hartmut Steinecke, 'Britisch-deutsche Romanlektüren im frühen neunzehnten Jahrhundert—Hoffmann und Scott zum Beispiel', in *The Novel in Anglo-German Context: Cultural Cross-Currents and Affinities*, ed. Susanne Stark (Amsterdam and Atlanta, GA, 2000), p. 109.

upon the novel to act as the vehicle of this serious historical and moral inquiry might have seemed a futile or quixotic gesture in 1813.

But there were signs of help at hand. Walter Scott published his novel *Waverley* in 1814, which together with Lockhart's biography of Scott was to affect the writing, and the close relationship of the novel and biography, in both Britain and Germany. At nearly the same time the *Bildungsroman* was defined, on the basis of the already existing examples of that genre: drawing on some earlier reflections on *Bildung* by Friedrich von Blancken-burg in his 'Essay on the Novel' (1774), where the main example was Wieland's *Agathon*, Karl von Morgenstern coined the term in two lectures on the 'Essence' and 'History' of this contemporary form, published as 'Ueber das Wesen des Bildungsromans' (1819).[4]

More important than the coining of a term was the example of Goethe's novel *Wilhelm Meister* (1795). In Germany, the term was taken up only later by Wilhelm Dilthey, who wrote a major biography of Friedrich Schlei-ermacher (1868); this was in effect the biography not simply of the man, the Romantic theologian, but of the founding of the modern, secular disci-pline of hermeneutics out of biblical hermeneutics. This major work of 'shaping' was followed by his development of the term *Bildungsroman*, which was developed in German critical practice in the early twentieth century. The term was not in general use in criticism in English until at least the 1930s, when Susanne Howe published *Wilhelm Meister and his English Kinsmen: Apprentices to Life* (1930), and its acceptance might be dated as late as William Buckley's *Season of Youth: The Bildungsroman from Dickens to Golding* (1974). Moreover, Buckley was at pains to point out differences between the paradigmatic examples in English and German (and, indeed, between English and other European literatures). But if the explication of the critical term waited until well after the fact, there was a substantial, long-term and controversial reception of Goethe's novel. Schiller had been enthusiastic; Friedrich Schlegel had immediately greeted it in his prescient essay 'Ueber Goethes Meister' as the model of the future, even if in terms that did not altogether please Goethe. The new form of the novel would become the dominant genre of the future, and incorporate all others within its capacious embrace.

Wilhelm Meister itself had already perceived and made emblematic the close link between biography and the *Bildungsroman*. Late in the novel, as it moves towards a complex resolution, the *Turmgesellschaft*, the secret Society of the Tower that has taken Wilhelm's guidance and destiny on itself, meets in a chapel. The chapel is lined not with religious symbols of

---

[4] The lectures are reprinted in E. Lämmert and Hartmut Eggert et al., ed., *Romantheorie: Dokumentation ihrer Geschichte in Deutschland 1620–1880* (Cologne and Berlin, 1971).

any kind, but with the biographies and accumulated experiences of its members.[5] Here the shaping of the biographies of individuals into a cumulative shared experience for their guidance presents itself as a secular replacement for religion. Ironic though Goethe may be about the Society of the Tower, the *Bildungsroman* probes the nature of moral guidance of the individual in a secular world.

In a late essay, 'Ein Wort für junge Dichter' ('A Word for Young Writers'), Goethe discussed the meaning of the term 'Meister', as one who leads the young through every stage of their craft, imparting the principles by which they can achieve their aim. 'A "Meister" in this sense I have never been', he tells them. Instead, he has been a 'Befreier', a liberator; 'for you have become aware through me that just as the human being must live from within outwards, so the artist must exercise his effects from within outwards, in that he, however he tries, will always bring only his own individuality to light'. Finally, the work springs from the inner life, and in it 'the worth of the life' ('der Werth seines Lebens') is displayed. The full development and expression of the individual's inner life is the consummation of the novel as of the biography.[6]

In Britain *Wilhelm Meister* had a rocky road. Carlyle translated the first part, *Wilhelm Meisters Lehrjahre*, as *William Meister's Years of Apprenticeship*, in 1823; he included the second part, the *Wanderjahre*, in his collection *German Romance* of 1825. Not only was the title of the collection misleading and the other selections unfortunate, but this was a translation of the first version of the *Wanderjahre*, not Goethe's final version; the Goethe–Carlyle correspondence refers to Eckermann politely suggesting that Carlyle translate the later and final version.[7] Carlyle never did so. The correspondence shows Goethe setting out his theory of *Weltliteratur*, as a way of extending the hand of fellowship to writers and translators in other countries; Carlyle responded in kind, drawing Goethe's attention to Burns as deserving of attention outside his native land.

Francis Jeffrey, however, wrote a negative criticism in the *Edinburgh Review* which echoed all the earlier strictures against German literature made by that influential journal since its founding in 1802. He condemned *Wilhelm Meister* as 'almost from beginning to end, one flagrant offence against every principle of taste, and every just rule of composition'. It was

---

[5] Nicholas Boyle, *Goethe: The Poet and the Age*, II: *Revolution and Renunciation (1790–1803)* (Oxford, 2000), p. 377.
[6] Andrew Fineron, ' "Man halte sich an's fortschreitende Leben": Goethe's Late Essays "Wohlgemeinte Erwiderung" and "Ein Wort für junge Dichter" ', *Publications of the English Goethe Society*, n.s., LIX (2000), 44–5.
[7] *Correspondence between Goethe and Carlyle*, ed. Charles Eliot Norton (London and New York, 1887). This edition includes the German originals and translations.

'absurd, puerile, incongruous, vulgar, and affected'.[8] Jeffrey was well known to be a leader of the opposition to German literature; but even De Quincey, a sensitive critic, reasonably well versed in German works, denounced *Wilhelm Meister*: 'No other of Goethe's works is likely to be more revolting to English good sense'.[9] The charges against Goethe, including immorality and vulgarity, were to continue in various forms despite Carlyle's intervention in his favour.

Carlyle himself was in two minds about the work: 'In Goethe's writings [. . .] we all know, the moral lesson is seldom so easily educed as one would wish'.[10] Moreover, many of these early readers found it difficult to grasp the relationship of the various highly differentiated and extended episodes to one another. In the ample but not necessarily representative quotation supplied in Victorian reviews the most popular part of the novel was the Mignon story, the affecting tale of the mysterious waif adopted by Wilhelm.[11]

There was one immediate response to Carlyle's translation of *Wilhelm Meisters Lehrjahre* that was worthy of Goethe, and it came from Coleridge. Surprisingly, this is hardly known, despite Coleridge's prominence as the earliest and most sympathetic of the readers of new German philosophy and literature. Carlyle is often given credit for replying to Jeffrey, and in the pages of Jeffrey's own journal, in his article 'The State of German Literature' (1827), which ranged beyond Goethe's novel to defend German literature against the charge of 'mysticism' and began to turn the tide in favour of at least some German writing. But it was Coleridge who, as he had done time and again during his whole career, grasped the essential nature and possibilities of a German form and turned it to his own creative and intellectual purposes.

Coleridge began by questioning, rightly, Carlyle's translation of the title, 'Bekenntnisse einer schönen Seele', as 'Confessions of a Fair Saint', which ought to read 'Confessions of a Beautiful Soul'. Under cover of criticism of Carlyle's mistranslation, he appropriated Goethe's title and set out in a white heat of composition on his own confessions. He had found a way—in the fictional form of the confessional letters—to present his own inward experience, and his own long nurtured thoughts, and to give an accounting

---

[8] Francis Jeffrey, '*Wilhelm Meister's Apprenticeship*, a Novel', *Edinburgh Review*, XLII (August 1825), 414.

[9] Thomas De Quincey, '*Wilhelm Meister's Apprenticeship*', *London Magazine*, X (August 1824), 190.

[10] Thomas Carlyle, 'Goethe's Works', *Foreign Quarterly Review* (August 1832), *Works*, 30 vols (London, 1902–9), XXVII, 422.

[11] For a sampling of periodical reviews see John Boening, *The Reception of Classical German Literature in England 1760–1860* (New York and London, 1977).

of 'the state of my faith'.[12] More importantly, he had grasped the embedded-
ness of the *Confessions* in a larger enterprise of quest and self-development.
The *Confessions*, which a recent historian of the *Bildungsroman* calls 'the
most sophisticated introjection of otherness in the novel',[13] exemplified
the possibility that Schlegel, in his review of *Wilhelm Meister,* had perceived
and celebrated: the capacity of the new novel form to accommodate a
variety of genres and modes of experience and to orchestrate their d0sson-
ances into a larger whole. For Coleridge, his exploration of his state of
belief revealed that he could no longer hold that the Bible was literally the
Word dictated by the Holy Ghost, for the higher criticism had revealed it
as a human document, a work embedded in a particular history and social
context. But this candid account opened the way to an aesthetic reinterpre-
tation of the sacred text in which the literary merit of the Bible was
comparable with Shakespeare (then a risky and innovative procedure). He
intended to publish this confession as integral to his major work *Aids to
Reflection.*

From the time of Coleridge's receipt, reading, and re-creation of Carlyle's translation in 1824, then, Goethe's *Bildungsroman* was absorbed into
the stream of major Victorian reconstructive thinking about the relations
of personal, intellectual, and spiritual experience. For Coleridge the culmination of his aesthetic philosophy lay in the embodiment of new thinking
in an imaginative form. Schelling had called for this in theory but had not
the creative resources to exemplify it. That Coleridge's absorption of Goethe
took place in so veiled and oblique a way reminds us of the dangers of
invoking the name and example of Goethe in nineteenth-century England
and the pitfalls for biographers and autobiographers who believed in confronting the truths not only of fact but of experience. Nevertheless,
Coleridge's brilliant dealings with the *Bildungsroman* bear out in an unexpected way Stanfield's more pedestrian grasp of the advantages of the novel
form over the biographical.[14]

Goethe continues to play a seminal if often unacknowledged role in the
development of biography and of the relation of the novel to biography in
the nineteenth century. The biography of Goethe himself was an important
milestone in both England and Germany. G. H. Lewes, together with Mary
Ann Evans (not yet George Eliot), set out in 1854, with the support of
Carlyle's contacts in Germany, to gather information about his life and

---

[12] Coleridge, *Shorter Works and Fragments*, ed. H. J. Jackson and J. R. de J. Jackson, 2 vols
(London, 1995), II, 1118.
[13] Michael Minden, *The German Bildungsroman* (Cambridge, 1997), p. 40.
[14] For a fuller account, see E. S. Shaffer, 'The Confessions of Goethe and Coleridge: the
Bekenntnisse einer schönen Seele and the *Confessions of an Inquiring Spirit*', in *Goethe and
the English-Speaking World*, ed. Nicholas Boyle and John Guthrie (London, 2001).

works.[15] Their most important informant was Karl August Varnhagen von Ense. Varnhagen had extensive British contacts and correspondents, including Carlyle (who had provided Lewes's introduction to him, when he had gone to Berlin for the first time in 1838, revisiting in 1843) and Richard Monckton Milnes, Keats's friend and first biographer. Moreover, he was a writer of substance himself, who reviewed and championed German literature over a long period, and is one of the originators of modern biographical techniques. His *Rahel: Ein Buch des Andenkens für ihre Freunde* (1834), a biographical commemoration of his wife, Rahel, through her letters, was a best-seller, and offers the combination of the extensive quotation from the writer's own words with the placement of the writer in his or her milieu that became characteristic of the Victorian 'Life and Letters'.

Rahel had shaped her own environment, the literary salon in early nineteenth-century Berlin, to a remarkable degree. Moreover, Varnhagen's own practice as a biographer was modelled on Goethe's autobiographical *Dichtung und Wahrheit* ('Poetry and Truth') and especially on Goethe's biographical essay *Winckelmann und sein Jahrhundert* (1798; 'Winckelmann and his Century'). Varnhagen himself pointed also to Goethe's *Beylagen zu Cellinis Lebensbeschreibung* ('Notes on the Life of Cellini') as containing the main motif of the *Wanderjahre*, the second part of *Wilhelm Meister*.[16] Again Goethe's biographical work and his novels are seen to come from the same impulse. In 1965 an English critic pointed out that Monckton Milnes in turn used Varnhagen as his model when 'introducing the modern biography to English literature', in his *Life, Letters and Literary Remains of John Keats* (1848).[17] Varnhagen placed his extensive library at Lewes's disposal, and he was able to consult and borrow books from it over the four months they were there. Marian Evans and George Lewes were therefore not merely conversing with a well-informed personal friend of Goethe, they were drawing on the experience of a major biographer, whose practice was shaped by Goethe's. The *Life of Goethe*, then, was instrumental in planting Goethe's own biographical practice in Victorian Britain.

Lewes's correspondence with Varnhagen, which stretches over the whole

[15] For an account of the collaboration of Lewes and Eliot on the biography of Goethe and its influence on her later practice as a novelist, see E. S. Shaffer, 'George Eliot and Goethe: "Hearing the Grass Grow"', *Publications of the English Goethe Society*, n.s, LXVII (1997), 3–22.

[16] Karl August Varnhagen von Ense, 'Im Sinne der Wanderer' [*Wilhelm Meisters Wanderjahre oder Die Entsagenden*], 2te Fassung, 1829, *Literaturkritiken*, ed. Klaus F. Gille (Tübingen, 1977), p. 65.

[17] Philip Glander, 'The Letters of Varnhagen von Ense to Richard Monckton Milnes', *Anglistische Forschungen*, XCII (1965), 6.

period since their first meeting, shows that Varnhagen's advice, his recommendations of books by and about Goethe, and not least his example
played a considerable role in Lewes's wish to write a biography of Goethe.
Writing to Varnhagen about the latter's *Life of Zinzendorf*, Lewes remarks,
'As a bit of biography it is quite a model; but in that department you are
passé maître'.[18]

If Varnhagen's own reviews of Goethe's work may at times be thought
overly deferential, this seems to be due to his very just appreciation of
Goethe's importance in creating and establishing a German literature. As
he wrote in 1855, in a review of a commentary on the 'classic' pastoral
Hermann und Dorothea (which remained the favourite among Goethe's
Victorian readers), 'Our German literature, of whose very existence August
Wilhelm Schlegel spoke only doubtingly in his Berlin Lectures of fifty years
ago, has since then, as no one will deny, gradually grown into a substantial
possession'.[19] Goethe is 'at once the core [. . .], the richest cornucopia
and the highest adornment of this literature'.[20] Varnhagen's judgements,
although tending to the affirmative mode, were weighty and searching.

The *Life of Goethe*, the first biography of Goethe in English or German,
was a great success, and went into a number of editions. The experience
of immersing herself in Goethe's life and writings was formative for George
Eliot's own career as a novelist. The German translation followed the first
publication immediately; the German version was into its sixteenth edition
by 1892.[21] It was undoubtedly a sympathetic treatment of Goethe, but
Lewes did not mince words and showed himself not too far ahead of the
English reading public in his dismissal of some aspects of *Wilhelm Meister*.
The *Confessions* he dismisses as having nothing to do with the rest of the
work and finds that it simply interrupts the story in 'a most inartistic
manner'.

On the crucial point of Goethe's morality, he found a defence in a subtle
distinction:

> But while asserting *Wilhelm Meister* to be in no respect a Moral Tale, I am
> bound to declare that deep and healthy moral meaning lies in it, pulses
> through it, speaking in many tones to him who hath ears to hear it. As

---

[18] T. H. Pickett, 'G. H. Lewes's Letters to Varnhagen von Ense', *Modern Language Review*,
LXXX (1985), 525.
[19] Karl August Varnhagen von Ense, 'Erläuterungen zu den deutschen Klassikern' (Jena, 1855),
in *Literaturkritiken*, ed. Klaus F. Gille (Tübingen, 1977), p. 106.
[20] Ibid., p. 107.
[21] The first German edition, entitled *Goethes Leben und Werke*, appeared in 1856 (ed. Julius
Frese); the 16th edition, *Goethes Leben und Schriften*, in 1892, edited and with a Preface by
Ludwig Geiger.

Wordsworth says of *Tam O'Shanter*, 'I pity him who cannot perceive that in all this, though there was no moral purpose, there is a moral effect'.[22]

This was a cunning piece of special pleading on Lewes's part, invoking Wordsworth, the highly respectable poet laureate, whose death in 1850 had recently been mourned by the nation, in defence of Burns and by extension of Goethe.

In his Preface to the revised edition of 1863, in which he reports having sold 13,000 copies in the two countries, Lewes takes up the contrast between Goethe's own autobiographical account in *Dichtung und Wahrheit* and the facts as they had gradually been emerging in the ensuing years. Lewes is firm that he is giving the facts; but the facts are not the most important matter. It is 'the abiding inaccuracy of *tone*, which, far more misleading than the many inaccuracies of fact, gives to the whole youthful period [. . .] an aspect so directly contrary to what is given by contemporary evidence, especially his own letters'. He concludes with an ironic sally that nevertheless disarms criticism: 'Jupiter serenely throned upon Olympus forgets that he was once a rebel with the Titans'.[23] It may be argued that Goethe in *Dichtung und Wahrheit* had written another *Bildungsroman*, namely, one in which he as protagonist finds his mission in creating the literature of his country, and in which his personal development is at one with that of his society and culture. Poor Wilhelm Meister (and his heirs) had no such glorious mission. In any case, the question of 'tone' and its role in lulling, misleading, and smoothing over uncomfortable matters in biography as in autobiography became a major one in Victorian life-writing. If, as we might now hold, a 'fact' may be only a shared or consensual fiction, the tone in which it is rendered may significantly alter it, as well as the judgement that might follow on it.

Thus Goethe's own biographical and autobiographical writings, and the biographical activity around Goethe of those who had known him, whether Eckermann, or more importantly Varnhagen von Ense, fed into the biographical and novelistic work of Lewes and Eliot, and also found its way through other channels such as Monckton Milnes into English life-writing.

Goethe had died in 1832, and by the time of his first biography was gaining his permanent place in the canon. But the biographies of living authors, or those newly dead, posed greater problems. The case of J. A. Froude's much-disputed biography of Carlyle is a peculiarly interesting example. It shows that the criticism of Goethe's morality, in life and in his

---

[22] George Henry Lewes, *The Life of Goethe* [1855](London 1908), with an introduction by Havelock Ellis, pp. 414–15. This Everyman edition uses the text of the revised version of 1863, which included new material, including Goethe's letters.
[23] Lewes, *Goethe* (rev. edn 1863), p. xvi.

novels, continued in a surprisingly tenacious way to affect the judgements
made on those who supported or emulated him. Even more, it shows that
'German thought' continued to be found dangerous, in particular with
reference to religion (as the reception of Coleridge's *Confessions* shows).
These dangers also touched the more secular branches of biography and
history. In Froude's case German thought, biography, and novelistic practice
led him to a sophisticated view of historical fact that did not wash well
with his historian colleagues. The virulence of the pursuit of Froude by his
enemies is quite astonishing. Yet much was at stake.

John Anthony Froude (1818–94) was the younger brother of Hurrell
Froude, who threw in his lot with the Tractarians, though he remained a
High Anglican, never following Newman to Rome. As a young man at
Oxford J. A. Froude published a novel, *The Nemesis of Faith* (1849), and
some short fiction, indebted to Goethe's *Die Wahlverwandtschaften*. Froude
himself was the first to translate Goethe's novel into English, as *Elective
Affinities* (1854). Goethe's novel was the occasion of some of the strongest
moral criticism directed against him, more than *Wilhelm Meister*, and it
carried over into criticism of any fiction writer suspected of borrowing
his themes or sharing his concerns.[24] Even modern readers will probably
remember that *Elective Affinities* treats two potentially adulterous married
couples, and features an adulterous act which is imagined by the partners.
Froude's novel, however, is an example of the novel of spiritual crisis, the
'loss of faith', which was to be a flourishing sub-genre of Victorian fiction.
It contains the protagonist's 'Confessions of a Sceptic', in the manner of
Wilhelm Meister's 'beautiful soul' and Coleridge's 'inquiring spirit'. The
novel is, as one of George Eliot's biographers puts it, a 'tale of a young
man who, having been persuaded against his true feelings to take orders,
admits his disbelief in Revelation, and falls into an adulterous love with
the wife of a friend'.[25] It was, moreover, autobiographical. His loss of faith
made it impossible for him to sign the Thirty-Nine Articles of the Church
of England, which he would have had to do to take orders. Froude's novel
was publicly burnt in his college at Oxford, and he was forced to resign
his Fellowship. More than this, however, his loss of faith was attributed in
the novel to his reading of George Eliot's translation of D. F. Strauss's *Das
Leben Jesu* (1835). *The Life of Jesus* was itself perhaps the major biography
of the nineteenth century, raising questions of fact and value, and history
and mythology, in the context of a once sacred text.[26] Eliot wrote a friendly

---

[24] Shaffer, 'George Eliot and Goethe', pp. 11–15, outlines this continued criticism of *Die
Wahlverwandtschaften*, in particular as it bore on George Eliot's *The Mill on the Floss*.
[25] Gordon S. Haight, *George Eliot: A Biography* (Oxford, 1968), p. 68.
[26] E. S. Shaffer, 'The Hermeneutic Community: Coleridge and Schleiermacher', in *The Coleridge Connection*, ed. Richard Gravil and Molly Lefebure (London, 1990), pp 200–29.

criticism of Froude's novel; he sought her out at the *Westminster Review*, of which she was an assistant editor, and began to contribute to the journal. He naturally was interested in Carlyle's affirmative treatment of German literature and thought, and in 1849 approached him. Carlyle knew Froude's story, and wrote of the novel at first in the most negative terms: 'a wretched mortal's vomiting up all his interior crudities, dubitations, and spiritual, agonizing bellyaches into the view of the public, and howling tragically, "See!" '[27]

Froude seems to have been a rather likeable young man, who suffered honest doubts and was open about them. Despite his initial reservations Carlyle became friendly with Froude, and gradually over thirty years entrusted him with editorial power over his papers, and empowered him in his will to act according to his own best judgement. Froude agreed too to write a biography of his friend and mentor, for though Carlyle would have preferred to have none, he knew it would be better to choose his own biographer. After leaving Oxford Froude had set about making a career as an historian, notably as author of the twelve-volume *History of England* (1858–70). Despite competition from Macaulay's *History of England* the books were successful. He extended one of the earliest national histories, Fuller's *Worthies*, to some naval exploits of the sixteenth century, which also gained popular favour. His books were criticized for embracing Carlyle's own notions of 'hero-worship', which naturally won Carlyle's approbation. Carlyle could hardly have found, or hoped for, a more suitable biographer.

Froude, following his *History of the First Forty Years of Carlyle's Life* (1882), opened his biography *Thomas Carlyle: A History of his Life in London 1834–1881* (1884) with a chapter entitled 'Duty of his Biographer'. Here he stated: 'I, for myself, concluded, though not till after long hesitation, that there should be no reserve, and therefore I have practised none'.[28] His justification is that Carlyle had been a truth-teller, and that only the truth would do him justice. Nevertheless, he spends seven pages discussing whether or not to be candid.

The biography reads extremely well. It shows a respect and admiration for the man, often lets him speak through his own splendid letters (though he was criticized for not attempting to render Carlyle's pithy conversation in the manner of Boswell's *Johnson*), and despite considerable detail moves ahead at a firm, lively pace. Any reader coming fresh to it would come to

[27] *New Letters of Thomas Carlyle*, ed. Alexander Carlyle, 2 vols (London, 1904), II. 59; letter to John Forster, 1848.
[28] J. A. Froude, *Thomas Carlyle: A History of his Life in London 1834–1881*, 2 vols (London, 1884), I, 7. See also his comments in II, 408–12. Later he felt obliged by continuing controversy to return to the subject in *My Relations with Carlyle* (1895).

feel affection for the man despite his humours, quirks, and peccadilloes. Towards the end of the first volume he reaches the point at which he had made Carlyle's acquaintance. The account he gives is carefully edited. He and Clough had left Oxford because 'we were out of place in an Article-signing University'. He doesn't mention the *Nemesis of Faith* except obliquely: 'I had written something, not wisely, in which heterodoxy was flavoured with the sentimentalism which he so intensely detested'. He does not give Carlyle's sharpest indictment of it, but simply reports him as saying a 'man should eat his own smoke, not exhale it on the public'.[29]

Froude gives a detailed account of Carlyle's writing of his *Life of Frederick the Great* (1858), of his two trips to Germany (1851 and 1858) to find materials and visit the sites, and of its eventual success. This leads into an account of Carlyle's historical method. Among his works to have paved the way for the biography of a controversial national figure were his brief accounts of German literary figures, in particular the *Life of Schiller*; his stimulating history of the French Revolution; and the *Life and Letters of Oliver Cromwell*, as well as a lecture on Cromwell in *Heroes and Hero-Worship*. But in the *Life of Frederick* he attempted biography on a large scale.

History, Froude wrote, is about the 'actions of men'. But 'the actions without the motives are nothing'. He immediately goes on to speak of Shakespeare, not of the history plays, but of Hamlet and Lear. History too requires 'dramatic portraiture' of the 'inner nature' of the characters. Yet it must be true to 'ascertained fact'. The potential conflict between the literary portrayal and the ascertained fact is resolved, it is implied, if the power of the character-drawing is adequate. The invocation of Shakespeare is significant; as Coleridge's *Confessions* invoke Shakespeare as the secular literature worthy of comparison with the literature of the Bible, for Froude, Shakespeare has come to stand for 'creative power'. Moreover, Froude takes up the moral question. 'Nature is not a partisan', but produces infinite variety; 'and when, as in Shakespeare, nature is represented truly, the impressions left upon the mind do not adjust themselves to any philosophical system'. History, like *Hamlet*, is 'undoctrinal and dramatic'.

Finally, as the culmination of his argument, Froude compares Carlyle with a novelist: his Frederick the Great was 'as peculiar and original as Sterne's Walter Shandy'.[30] *Tristram Shandy* was a favourite in Germany as in England; Carlyle's art has in the same way as the novelist's captured an individual. Even the large-scale historical biography, setting a national leader in his context, is measured by the attainment of the aim of the novel form, the permanent aesthetic value Carlyle had located in Shakespeare and Dante in his lecture on the 'Poet as Hero'.

An extraordinary imbroglio arose from Froude's undertaking these tasks on Carlyle's behalf. Nothing could better illustrate the dilemmas and dangers that beset the Victorian biographer. The first set of objections came from a member by marriage of the Carlyle family, who challenged his right to the papers. The second set of objections came from those who felt he had not used his stewardship wisely in following Carlyle's instructions to publish his *Reminiscences* immediately after his death. The *Reminiscences*, especially the chapter on Carlyle's wife Jane, are a striking case in themselves of the whole range of the biographical form from 'anecdote' to *Bildungsroman*. The anecdotes came first from the novelist Geraldine Jewsbury, a close friend of Carlyle and his wife, and an early practitioner, in *Zoe* (1845) and *The Half Sisters* (1848), of the *Bildungsroman* form which she learned from *Wilhelm Meister*. The anecdotes dramatically revealed Jane's unhappy situation, in particular one in which Jane is shown carrying the whole burden of the house and farm, while Carlyle sits impassively by. Carlyle, while castigating Jewsbury's as 'mythical stories', felt impelled to weave his own face-saving anecdotes, stressing Jane's talent for domesticity and her unfailing good humour in the face of crises, yet here and there revealing his sense of having treated his wife badly: 'her grief [at her mother's death] was still poignant, constant:—and oh how inferior my sympathy with her, to what hers would have been with me; woe on my dull hard ways in comparison!'[31] A number of reviewers felt that Froude as a responsible editor and executor should have kept these admissions back. The *Reminiscences* as a whole, each chapter on a different figure, show Carlyle at his best when talking of those—for example Leigh Hunt and J. S. Mill—whose intellectual influence had helped him in the life-long self-education that required all his thought and attention. Jane's indispensable role in keeping his poor house for him while he fulfilled his private and public mission takes on an increasing irony. When *Letters and Memorials of Jane Welsh Carlyle*—her 'terrible letters', as Froude called them—were published in 1883, as Carlyle had wished, Froude came in for criticism from those who felt he had merely hinted in his biography at sexual matters he must have known about, Jane's affair, Carlyle's impotence. Others denied their truth. He should have said less; or he should have said more. Carlyle had complained of English biography, 'how delicate, decent it is, bless its mealy mouth'. His biographer was made to pay the price for Carlyle's 'posthumous penance'.

Froude defended himself publicly by invoking Carlyle's own ringing

---

[31] Carlyle, *Reminiscences*, ed. K. J. Fielding and Ian Campbell (Oxford, 1997), p. 101.

defence of Lockhart's forthright treatment of Scott in his biography. In a private letter, he referred to Goethe, whose autobiography was 'a shock to foolish idolaters; yet who would part with it? In wise men's eyes it detracts nothing from Goethe. Yet Goethe tells things of himself a thousand times worse than the worst that can be known of Carlyle'.[32]

A third set of objections came from some members of the historical profession, who had already made their opposition to several of his works plainly known. Froude's twelve-volume *History of England from the Fall of Cardinal Wolsey to the Defeat of the Spanish Armada* (1856–70) was attacked for its Carlylean approach to history through 'great men'. In some influential quarters there was a strong move to separate biography from history. The most important of his opponents was W. E. H. Lecky, best known for *The Rise and Influence of the Spirit of Rationalism in Europe* (1865), who had written a cutting review of Froude's *The English in Ireland in the Eighteenth Century* (1872–4), and followed it up in his own *The History of England in the Eighteenth Century*. His opponents banded together to make the name of Froude a synonym for historical inaccuracy, for failure to get any fact right. This failure was dubbed 'froudacity' or 'froudulency' and was able to rouse certain gentlemen to great hilarity.[33] His various opponents made common cause; Lecky supported Mary Carlyle, an in-law, who laid claim to the papers; the American art-historical scholar Charles Eliot Norton joined the historians' 'froudacity' campaign, criticizing the slight revisions Froude had made in Carlyle's letters and papers for the sake of clarity and readability, declaring that in comparing the published texts with the manuscripts he found 'an error a page', or even 'an error a sentence' in Froude's biography. In 1903 a book entitled *The Nemesis of Froude* was published. As late as 1911 Froude was again castigated, as the historian James Bryce put it, as 'a brilliant stylist, who had begun his career as a writer of stories, and chose thereafter to display in the field of history his gift for picturesque narration'.[34] His Goethean fiction of more than half a century previous was neither forgiven nor forgotten. More seriously still, his absorption of the higher criticism through George Eliot's translation of Strauss had made him wary of claims to historical 'fact'. As he wrote as early as 1844, and restated in 'The Science of History', in his provocative *Short Studies on Great Subjects*: 'Even ordinary history, except mere annals, is all more or less fictitious; that is, the facts are related, not as they really happened, but as they

[32] Froude, Letter to Olga Norikoff, II, 328.
[33] Waldo Hilary Dunn, *Froude and Carlyle: A Study of the Froude-Carlyle Controversy* (London, 1930), pp. 137–8.
[34] Quoted in Dunn, *Froude and Carlyle*, p. 110.

appeared to the writer; as they happen to illustrate his views or support his principles'.[35]

Perhaps Froude's most interesting treatment of the status of historical fact occurs in his 'Essay on the Lives of the Saints'. At Oxford he had been asked to help with the 'Lives' by Newman, and had withdrawn on discovering the dubious status of these 'histories'. Once again the relations of sacred history, fact, fiction, and biography are closely interwoven. He adopts the view that the 'Lives' are nonsense; yet they are imaginative nonsense that should not be simply dismissed. 'Miracles' and mythic materials are instructive of the modes of the imagination and the lives of nations. Froude's self-defence voices the argument familiar to him as a reader of Coleridge and of Eliot's translation of Strauss:

> There are two kinds of truth, the literal and external truths corresponding to the eternal and as yet undiscovered laws of fact; the other, the truth of feeling and of thought, which embody themselves either in distorted pictures of the external, or in some entirely new creation; sometimes moulding and shaping real history, sometimes taking the form of heroic biography, of tradition, or popular legend, sometimes appearing as recognized fiction in the epic, the drama or the novel.

Ultimately, he says, this rests on human biological and psychological fact: 'It is useless to tell us that this is to confuse truth and falsehood. We are stating a fact, not a theory, and if it makes truth and falsehood difficult to distinguish, that is nature's fault, not ours'.[36]

Froude's refusal, like Coleridge's, of the plenary inspiration of the biblical text, his awareness of Strauss's view that tradition and expectation in a society moulded what it held to be the case, his support for Carlyle's attempts to dramatize inward history, all these condemned him to suffer a campaign against his veracity, his very competence. In the *DNB* entry for Froude the negative judgements were given a status approaching the permanent. The author, identified as A. F. Pollard, summarized views on his Carlyle biography: while his literary merit was as always great, 'its ruthless exposure of his master's weaknesses caused widespread dismay'; 'the historical accuracy of the portraits he drew of Carlyle and his wife was denied by the majority of those who were in a position to know the facts'. The judgement on his historical writings is still more negative, again excepting his literary merits: 'his faculty for dramatic presentation, and command of the art of picturesque description have secured for his

---

[35] Quoted by William C. Hutchison, Introduction to J. A. Froude, *The Nemesis of Faith* (London, 1904), p. xvii.

[36] Froude, *Essays in Literature and History*, Introduction by Hilaire Belloc, 2 vols (London, 1905), I, 131–2.

"History" a permanent place in English prose literature'. Yet he has failed
to convince of 'the fidelity of his pictures or the truth of his conclusions'.
Indeed, he 'hardly seems to have regarded truth as attainable in history',
and 'derided its claims to be a science'. While his Oxford reading of Lessing,
Neander, Spinoza, and Schleiermacher is cited earlier as rousing the fears
of his clerical masters, his views on historical truth are attributed to no such
commanding intellects but dismissed as the motto of the wily Talleyrand, 'Il
n'y a rien qui s'arrange aussi facilement que les faits'. [37]

In the new generation of twentieth-century biographers, Lytton Strachey,
often seen as representing the decisive turning-away from Victorian biography, depicts Froude (together with the poet Arthur Hugh Clough, who
also left Oxford on the grounds of his unwillingness to sign the Thirty-
Nine Articles) as rather a hero. From his witty and devastating portrayal
in the opening chapter on 'Cardinal Manning' in *Eminent Victorians* (1918)
of the whole group of dim, self-deluding, place-seeking Tractarians,
including Froude's brother Hurrell, only Froude and Clough emerge with
honour, both intellectual and moral. Strachey offers a vignette of the young
Froude at Oxford, doing research for Newman on the Lives of the Saints
and finding it impossible to swallow the claims for the miraculous resusci-
tation of St Neot—'historical humbug', as Strachey put it. Clough figures
again in Strachey's 'Florence Nightingale' as the honest man wracked by
doubts. Together they represented for Strachey the sacrifice of genuine
inquiry to the labyrinthine hypocrisies of the Victorian establishment. His
championship of Froude and Clough marked the beginning of a new kind
of biography.

It is a strange turn of events that the most recent edition of Carlyle's
Reminiscences still preserves a hostile attitude towards Froude, without
exhibiting any awareness of the sources of the opposition to him in his
controversial religious and historical stance, much less his Goethean
fictions. The editors conclude their Introduction: 'What all this confirms is
not only the fact that Froude's editing is untrustworthy, but the widely
prevailing sense of his much more general unreliability'. In a further twist
of historical irony, the change in biographical standards is confirmed, even
while the hostility to Froude is maintained, as they claim that Carlyle's
Reminiscences 'broke through much more forcibly into authenticity in
experience and style' [than mid-Victorian autobiography].[38]

Finally, however, the best biographers were not the group of conscious
followers of Goethe—Carlyle, Froude, Jewsbury, Lewes, nor the practitioners of the 'Life and Letters' form—but the biographers who as

---

[37] [A. F. Pollard], 'Froude, James Anthony', *DNB*, Supplement, II (London, 1901), pp. 254–62.
[38] Introduction to Carlyle, *Reminiscences*, pp. xxv, xiii.

novelists had absorbed the new form of the novel of self-education. Elizabeth Gaskell's *Life of Charlotte Brontë* (1855), a biography by a novelist about another novelist, is undoubtedly a masterwork. It has all the qualities of a novel, the sustained building of suspense, the powerful empathy with the central character, the creation of a milieu in intimate detail; and it commands the complete absorption of the narrator, the character and the reader. The strenuous effort of the protagonist to create a life as a writer, to climb from provincial obscurity to recognition in the capital, resembles an epic novel on the scale of Balzac; the brevity of the life, on the Romantic model of Keats, is all the more shocking. The powerful combination of epic magnitude and tragic untimely end joins two of the major biographical modes of the nineteenth century. It is also specifically a *Bildungsroman*, in which self-creation has never seemed more difficult, the distance travelled from the obscure hinterlands to social and literary success never so far, and the precise niche in society open to the protagonist never so ambiguous. The vivid sense of the difficulty and the distance is partly derived from the difference between a male career and a female, and the sufferings undergone by a woman attempting to combine them. This biography is a female *Bildungsroman*; and part of its intensity comes from the author's passionate advocacy, which nevertheless is carefully controlled through the narrative voice of one for whom the difficulty and the distance were not so overwhelming.

Not surprisingly, perhaps, Lewes was one of the enthusiastic commentators on it, as he had been one of the first to praise 'Currer Bell's' *Jane Eyre*, and then to perceive the still greater merit of Brontë's *Villette*. He now perceived Mrs Gaskell's *Life* as having the permanence of fiction: 'The book will, I think, create a deep and permanent impression [. . .] [T]hanks to its artistic power, [it]makes us familar inmates of an interior so strange, so original [. . .] so picturesque [. . .] that fiction has nothing more wild, touching and heart-strengthening to place above it'.[39]

Another admirer from within the Goethean camp was none other than Varnhagen von Ense. He noted down his reading of the biography in his diary on 13 August 1857: 'So much power of feeling and spirit, so much lovely talent, which wear themselves down in striving and struggle, gaining nothing through endurance and victory but renewed striving and struggle!' Deeply moved, he spoke of it as belonging to *Weltliteratur*, that Goethean conception of the literature that would speak to all the world: 'The book

[39] Lewes, Letter to Elizabeth Gaskell, 15 April 1857, in *The George Eliot Letters*, ed. Gordon S. Haight, 7 vols (London, 1954), II, 315–16; quoted in Winifred Gérin, *Elizabeth Gaskell* (Oxford, 1976, reprinted 1990), p. 257.

belongs in the rank of those which, like Stilling's history of his early years, like Rousseau's *Confessions*, open up and illuminate unnoticed regions of human nature'.[40]

The book was widely hailed; but it did not escape criticism. The immediate 'hornet's nest', as Mrs Gaskell termed it, was stirred up by the protests of living persons who threatened legal action, in particular, the woman represented as having brought about the moral downfall of the young Branwell Brontë, his employer's wife, then Mrs Robinson, now Lady Scott. The Gaskells' lawyers counselled a public apology; others then came forward to protest at the depiction of the Clergy Daughters' School, presented as the model for Lowood in *Jane Eyre*, while Patrick Brontë (who had commissioned the book and continued to champion it) asked for some alterations in the depiction of his behaviour towards his daughters. Whatever the rights and wrongs of the claims, Mrs Gaskell quickly revised her book and it was republished within months. Some modern critics have taken the tack that Mrs Gaskell had been overzealous on behalf of her subject: she had not sufficiently stressed the negative responses to Brontë's work, the attacks for vulgarity and sensationalism, nor had she told the full facts about Charlotte Brontë's passionate attachment to her employer and tutor, Monsieur Héger, during her stay in Brussels (the material on which Brontë had drawn in her novel *Villette*). Moreover, and this is the most weighty charge, Gaskell had juggled with the dates in order to make Branwell's downfall (rather than Charlotte's own affair of the heart) appear the source of her unhappiness in Brussels.[41]

It is plain enough that Victorian contemporaries were more concerned about the representation of living persons in a negative light, while modern critics wish the biographer to be even more daring in her revelations. In this case, however, the biography partakes so powerfully of fictional truth that both sets of complaints seem to pale in significance. In this sense the *Bildungsroman* stands as an 'ideal' form which could resolve the clash between unvarnished fact and edification. The power to shape and transform the facts through an imaginative portrayal, which Coleridge and Froude reserved for religious literature and Shakespeare, was in the course

---

[40] K. A. Varnhagen von Ense, *Tagebücher*, XIV (Hamburg, 1870), p. 46. Quoted in Norbert Bachleitner, 'Die deutsche Reception englischer Romanautorinnen des 19. Jahrhunderts', in *The Novel in Anglo-German Context*, p. 184. The reference is to J. H. Jung-Stilling, *Heinrich Stilling's Jugendgeschichte*, the first part of which was published at Goethe's instigation in 1777, the last in 1817.

[41] Gérin, *Elizabeth Gaskell*, p. 171. Gérin presents charges against the biography in two chapters, 15 (pp. 159–78), and 17 (pp. 189–201). Similar views have been expressed by Lyndall Gordon, Jenny Uglow, and others.

of the nineteenth century accorded, not without struggle, to the new dominant form, the novel, in particular the *Bildungsroman*, and its near relation, the biography.

8

Sainte-Beuve: Biography, Criticism, and the Literary

ANN JEFFERSON

The work of modern criticism is to put Art back on its pedestal.

Flaubert[1]

It is not commonly supposed that biography has much to say about literature, and still less about its literariness. Biographers may tell us about the
authors of literary works; and in some instances, biography may be read
as literature; but for anyone confronting the question 'What is literature?',
biography would seem to have little to offer in comparison to the kind of
writing we call 'theory', or even to literature itself. From this perspective,
biography is perceived as being at best marginal to literature, and at worst
as positively antithetical to the literary. This negative relation is particularly
marked in the French tradition where writers themselves have repeatedly—
and often very vociferously—protested against what they present as an
extraneous imposition of the 'life' on to the literary 'work'. One thinks
here of Flaubert, Mallarmé, or Proust; and indeed Flaubert was one of the
first and most vehement in arguing for the need to separate biographical
concerns from the literary.

Much of Flaubert's correspondence with Louise Colet, his mistress and
a writer herself, is concerned with this issue, and it is expressed in words
of advice such as, 'do not believe that the pen has the same instincts as the
heart'.[2] Flaubert clearly thought that Louise Colet's own work was marred
by her inability to keep these two instincts apart, and this is one of the

---

[1] Gustave Flaubert, letter dated 17 May 1853, *Correspondance*, ed. Jean Bruneau, Bibliothèque de la Pléiade (Paris, 1980), p. 328.
[2] Ibid., p. 139 (letter dated 27 July 1852).

reasons why he keeps returning to the subject. He concludes this particular
letter with the rather stern assertion that 'Art has no truck with the artist!'
If this statement was intended chiefly as an admonition to a fellow writer
who supposedly allowed her heart to override her pen, its minatory force
applied as much to the readers of literature as to its practitioners. When
Mallarmé, thinking broadly on the same lines as Flaubert, writes to his
friend Cazalis: 'I am now impersonal and no longer the Stéphane you once
knew',[3] his comment is not advice on how to write, and still less a report
on his current state of mind. Rather, it is an indication of how his new
poetic practice may be best read and understood by the few friends he
thought capable of doing so. Specifically, his instruction is that they are
not to read his poetry as having its origin in the life of the Stéphane they
once knew. It was with this readerly and critical perspective in mind that
Proust in his essay 'La Méthode de Sainte-Beuve' insisted that 'the social
self' with its 'habits, society and vices' is not to be confused with 'the
writer's self' who, he says, exists only in his books. He makes it clear that
he is as much concerned with how critics should proceed as with what art
should be: 'perhaps I shall manage to say a few things to which I have
often given thought, about what criticism should be and what art is'.[4] The
result is his famously ferocious attack on Sainte-Beuve, which is above all
an attack on a critical method supposedly based on the false premise of
biographical anecdote. 'In what way does the fact of having been Stendhal's
friend allow one to be a better judge of him?' asks Proust (p. 158). In
the particular case of Stendhal, he goes on to suggest that Sainte-Beuve's
acquaintance with the man, and the second-hand information that he had
sought out from some of the novelist's other friends and contemporaries,
actually contributed to a gross misjudgement on Sainte-Beuve's part when
he (Sainte-Beuve) concluded that 'Stendhal's novels [. . .] are frankly
detestable'.

The issue I want to address here is not that of the status to be accorded
to the author in the literary text,[5] but more precisely whether biography
has any critical validity in the study of literary texts when the prime concern
of those texts is considered—either by their authors, or by a critical *parti
pris*—to be aesthetic. For it is not just the writers I have cited who seem
to be saying that the answer to this question is 'No'. The thrust of a good
deal of twentieth-century critical writing seems to be just as adamantly
negative. The French critic Gérard Genette characterizes the tradition of

[3] Stéphane Mallarmé, *Correspondance 1862–1871*, ed. Henri Mondor (Paris, 1959), p. 242.
[4] Marcel Proust, 'La Méthode de Sainte-Beuve', in *Contre Sainte-Beuve*, ed. Bernard de Fallois
(Paris, 1954), pp. 150–80 (p. 151).
[5] For an excellent discussion of this issue, see Seán Burke, *The Death and Return of the
Author* (Edinburgh, 2nd edn 1998).

what the French call 'the man and the work' (and the English, with a slight difference of emphasis, the 'life and works') as 'the two caryatids of traditional literary studies',[6] as if to suggest that this critical model has now been superseded. In arguing for what he calls 'pure criticism', Genette states that criticism's interest in literature needs to be an interest in essences rather than persons. Or, in the words of Philippe Sollers, whom he quotes in support of his claim, 'the essential question nowadays is no longer that of the *writer* and the *work*, but of *writing* and *reading*'.[7] The focus of critical attention has been diverted from an outmoded concern with individual writers to writing as such, in a manner which would appear to make biography entirely extraneous to the central concerns of modern literary study—concerns which have to do, precisely, with the literary.

However, the sheer polemic contained in the notion of purity as well as in the oppositions that both these critics adduce (persons vs. essences, writers vs. writing, then vs. now) might prompt us to pause and ask whether these terms are as mutually exclusive as the critics maintain, and whether the concerns of so-called 'traditional' criticism—and in particular of biographically based criticism—were in fact as antithetical to those of modernity as they (and many other contemporary critics and theorists) assert. In what follows, I want to go back to Sainte-Beuve, the acknowledged founder and exemplar of the biographical approach to literary criticism, in order to examine whether and how his method acquired general critical validity, what its critical presuppositions were, and in particular, how it conceived of literature and the literary.

Charles-Augustin Sainte-Beuve (1804–69) is widely regarded as the inventor of modern literary criticism (modern in the commonly accepted sense, rather than in the polemical sense I have just been quoting). He was also considered by many of his contemporaries to be one of its finest practitioners. This view was not confined to France. Matthew Arnold called him 'the most notable critic of our time'; for Henry James (no mean critic himself) he was 'the acutest critic the world has ever seen', and 'a man of extraordinary genius'; and according to Lytton Strachey, it was with Sainte-Beuve that 'criticism, as we know it, came into existence for the first time'.[8] In a somewhat fuller appraisal delivered as a lecture in 1904, Gustave

---

[6] Gérard Genette, *Figures II* (Paris, 1969), p. 156. Translated by Alan Sheridan in *Figures of Literary Discourse* (Oxford, 1982), p. 148.

[7] Genette, 'Raisons de la critique pure', *Figures II*, pp. 7–22 (pp. 17–18).

[8] Matthew Arnold, 'Sainte-Beuve', *Five Uncollected Essays*, ed. Kenneth Allott (Liverpool, 1953), p. 66; Henry James, 'Sainte-Beuve's First Articles', *Literary Reviews and Essays*, ed. Albert Mordell (New York, 1957), pp. 79, 83; Lytton Strachey, *Landmarks in French Literature* (London, 1912, reprinted 1949), p. 143.

Lanson, whose own work dominated critical practice in France for many decades, described Sainte-Beuve as 'the patron of critics and literary historians'.[9] And despite his strictures about the need to keep biographical preoccupations out of art, Flaubert too admired Sainte-Beuve, and keenly regretted that his death in October 1869, just a month before the publication of *L'Education sentimentale*, deprived him of one of the readers he had most desired for his strange novel.

For all these people it would seem that, despite the fact that the critical genre he developed was what he called the 'portrait', Sainte-Beuve was first and foremost a critic rather than a biographer. Most of these 'portraits' originally appeared as articles in literary journals—*La Revue de Paris, Le Globe, La Revue des deux mondes, Le National, Le Constitutionnel, Le Moniteur*, and *Le Temps*—and were subsequently published in book form in *Critiques et portraits littéraires* (1836–46), *Portraits de femmes* (1844), and *Portraits contemporains* (1846).[10] They tended to deal with individual authors rather than individual works, and to discuss them in a broadly biographical frame. The *Causeries du lundi*, which he began in 1851 and continued until his death, were less biographically orientated, but were nevertheless grounded in the same general principles as the earlier portraits. Like the portraits, they were subsequently published in book form, and the first volume appeared in 1851. Sainte-Beuve claimed that his particular brand of criticism and its format in the portrait were directly attributable to the nature of the literary journals for which he wrote. But the portrait also formed the basis of the university lecture courses that he gave during his tenure of a series of university teaching posts,[11] and almost all of which led to the publication of a major book: *Port-Royal* (1840–59), *Chateaubriand et son groupe littéraire* (1860), and *Virgile* (1857). In

---

[9] Gustave Lanson, 'Sainte-Beuve', *Essais de méthode, de critique et d'histoire littéraires*, ed. Henri Peyre (Paris, 1965), p. 427. It should, perhaps, be said that Lanson, who had his own critical and methodological battles to fight, was not always so generous towards his patron. For a fuller account of 'lansonisme', see Antoine Compagnon, *La Troisième République des lettres* (Paris, 1983).

[10] Sainte-Beuve's work was re-edited and republished several times both during and after his lifetime. I shall be referring to a number of recently edited editions of his work, in particular the *Portraits littéraires*, ed. Gérald Antoine (Paris, 1993), a selection of his critical writings published under the title *Pour la critique*, ed. Annie Prassoloff and José-Luis Diaz (Paris, 1992), and *Portraits de femmes*, ed. Gérald Antoine (Paris, 1998), as well as to the two-volume *Oeuvres*, ed. Maxime Leroy, Bibliothèque de la Pléiade (Paris, 1949–51). Despite his popularity with English writers, very little of Sainte-Beuve's work exists in English translation. All translations here are my own and the references are to the published French editions.

[11] Sainte-Beuve held teaching posts at the Académie de Lausanne (1837–8), the Université de Liège (1848–9), the Collège de France (where as Professor of Latin Poetry he actually lectured only between 1854–5), and the École Normale Supérieure (1857–61).

addition to his critical work, Sainte-Beuve published four collections of poetry—*Vie, poésies et pensées de Joseph Delorme* (1829), *Les Consolations* (1830), *Pensées d'août* (1837), and *Livre d'amour* (1843)—and a single novel, *Volupté* (1834). I shall be returning to his creative writings below.

What emerges from this brief survey of Sainte-Beuve's critical output is first, that, institutionally speaking, he practised forms of writing that are still recognized and have currency today: journalistic articles and essays, university lecture courses, books. But in seeking to understand what has given Sainte-Beuve's criticism its status as origin and—to some extent—as the model for subsequent critical practice, we need to look beyond the familiarity of its institutional forms. One might, as a first gesture, consider Sainte-Beuve's own individual critical virtues: his huge appetite for reading, his prodigious capacity for hard work (the *Causeries du lundi* were produced week in week out for almost thirty years), and his own experience as a writer, which according to him had given him '[a] keener sense of beauty'.[12] But this would require us to overlook what were also evident shortcomings as a critic. Proust alone provides a pretty damning catalogue: not only his misjudgement of Stendhal, but also his preference for Feydeau and Béranger over Flaubert and Baudelaire, his inability to recognize—or at least to publicly acknowledge—the great figures of his day (e.g. Balzac), his destructive jealousy of Hugo (whose wife Adèle was for a while Sainte-Beuve's mistress), and so on. And while he wrote perfectly decent prose, he is not normally praised as a stylist.

Yet, just as his individual merits do not necessarily explain the importance of his criticism, his demerits may not disqualify it either. The issue, in other words, is not whether he succeeded in backing the winners in the stakes of literary posterity, or even whether he worked hard enough to earn serious professional status for a new breed of literary critics. Rather, it is this: Sainte-Beuve's critical enterprise owes both its strength and its importance to the fact that it is, in all its complexity, a response to the radical transformation in the conception of literature and of the literary that took place at the turn of the nineteenth century. This change may be summarized by the words of the poet André Chénier, quoted by Sainte-Beuve on a number of occasions: 'art only makes verses, the heart alone is the poet'.[13] Chénier's formula is a rallying cry for the renewal of literature known as Romanticism. But what is distinctive about Sainte-Beuve's response to it is that, instead of confining his critical enterprise to a defence

---

[12] Quoted in Antoine, Introduction to *Portraits littéraires*, p. xli.
[13] E.g. 'Mathurin Régnier et André Chénier', *Portraits littéraires*, pp. 110–22 (p. 118).

of the literature which emerged from this view,[14] he recast the basic procedures and presuppositions of criticism itself so as to take account of the
new conception of literature that it articulated. In the process he radically
redefined the scope and function of literary criticism, and created a legacy
which is still operative today—and, arguably, in even the 'purest' forms of
criticism.

For as long as literature was viewed as the expression of an eternal
beauty inseparable from truth and reason (the classical view), and as long
as literary expression was evaluated primarily in terms of rhetorical precept,
there was little for criticism to do except to measure individual works
against the aesthetic blueprint of a universally accepted and pre-established
ars poetica. One of the last and most powerful proponents of this kind of
criticism in France, Jean-François de La Harpe (author of a nineteen-volume
Cours de littérature ancienne et moderne known as *Le Lycée*, 1799–1805),
asserts quite simply that 'the beautiful is the same at all times, because
nature and reason do not change'.[15] The chilling consequence of this view
(at least chilling to the modern mind, and that is the point here) is that
Quintilian, Cicero, Horace, and Boileau between them provide the student
of literature with 'a perfect legislation which may be justly applied in all
cases, an imprescriptible code whose verdicts will serve forever to tell
us what should be condemned and what applauded'.[16] In contrast, the
implications of Chénier's claim meant that for Sainte-Beuve, art was
the product neither of the rhetorical rules of verse nor of some abstract
and universal beauty, but of *genius*. What made a literary work literary was
not its conformity to aesthetic or rhetorical precept, but the fact that it
was the work of a genius whose influence might be felt in every aspect of its
construction, right down to particular images and linguistic formulations.

The notion of genius was not itself new: Diderot's entry on that topic
(1757) in the *Encyclopédie* had already made a powerful case for its
imaginative and mimetic powers.[17] Moreover, Diderot had also grounded
genius in feeling and presented it as inherently disruptive of the laws of
taste which La Harpe was still defending nearly fifty years later. But what
Sainte-Beuve brings to the concept of genius is a sense of the uniqueness
of each of its manifestations. For him, unlike Diderot, there is no language

---

[14] Though for a while he also did exactly that through his association with *Le Globe*, which
began in 1827 with his article on Hugo's *Odes et Ballades*.

[15] Quoted in Roger Fayolle, *La Critique littéraire* (Paris, 1964), p. 247.

[16] Jean-François de La Harpe, 'Éloge de Boileau, ou éloge de la critique dogmatique', from
Le Lycée, reproduced in Raphael Molho, *La Critique littéraire en France au XIXe siècle*
(Paris, 1963), p. 43.

[17] Denis Diderot, 'Article Génie', *Oeuvres esthétiques*, ed. Paul Vernière (Paris, 1959), pp.
9–17.

that could describe genius outside the particular forms that it takes, and these forms are always associated with a particular individual: 'I call genius what comes from the person: the rest is talent'.[18] Because it always has its source in the individual, its characteristics are not immediately given, and it therefore becomes the function of criticism to identify what Sainte-Beuve calls the 'dominant quality' or the 'general formula [of the] mind' of a writer.[19] In contrast to La Harpe's 'imprescriptible code', which equipped the student of literature with an unvarying and pre-existing notion of the aesthetic, Sainte-Beuvean criticism has always to discover from scratch what the defining characteristic of a given literary genius is: 'Let us try to find [the] characteristic name of each individual which he bears engraved partly on his brow and partly in his heart.'[20] Literarity becomes something to be defined afresh with each new critical engagement.

Moreover, it would seem that it is easier for the critic than for the writer to identify this particular form of the literary, and that it comes most clearly into focus when it is the object of critical discourse. Criticism becomes the guardian of the distinctiveness of literature (the literarity of each genius) by separating itself off from it and constituting literature as its 'other'. This is in significant contrast to the rhetorically based approach to literature which, alongside the legislative function promulgated by La Harpe, had made the *study* of literary rhetoric an extension of its *practice* (and vice versa). When the heart—or the individual genius—came to be seen as the source of literary art, the notion that literary texts could be studied as examples of rhetorical skill which the student might emulate began to disappear, and with it any sense of the continuity between the study of literature and its practice.[21] As commentary replaced emulation, the relation between a newly constituted critical discourse and its object made literature simultaneously more elusive (its defining quality always has to be discovered anew) and more elevated (literature and criticism are different orders of discourse). Criticism becomes a kind of necessary sup-

---

[18] Quoted in Antoine, Introduction to *Portraits littéraires*, p. lix.

[19] See 'M. Ampère', *Portraits littéraires*, pp. 223–50 (p. 223) and Gérald Antoine, Introduction to his edition of *Vie, poésies et pensées de Joseph Delorme* (Paris, 1956), p. lx. Although Sainte-Beuve devoted a number of portraits to women writers (see his *Portraits de femmes*), he was not particularly concerned with issues of gender, and his paradigm for the emergence of genius in a writer is generally a male one. I shall therefore refer to writers and critics as 'he'.

[20] Sainte-Beuve, 'Chateaubriand jugé par un ami intime en 1803', *Nouveaux lundis*, 13 vols (Paris, 1863–70), III, 31.

[21] This shift was not applied across the board, and rhetoric remained the basis of the teaching of literature in schools and universities for the rest of the nineteenth century. On this, see Genette, 'Rhétorique et enseignement', *Figures II*, pp. 23–42. For a fuller discussion of the role of rhetoric in nineteenth-century French education, see Françoise Douay-Soublin, 'La Rhétorique en France au XIXe siècle: Restauration, renaissance, remise en cause', in *Histoire de la rhétorique dans l'Europe moderne*, ed. Marc Fumaroli (Paris, 1999), pp. 1071–1214.

plement of literature, with all the ambiguity that supplementarity entails: it is both surplus to and constitutive of the literary.[22]

None of this is presented in systematically theoretical terms by Sainte-Beuve, but I shall be trying to put together various elements of Sainte-Beuve's thinking about criticism and literature (scattered in the form of passing comments in his critical accounts of individual writers) in order to support the suggestion that the strength of Sainte-Beuve's criticism lies not in its readings of individual writers so much as in the fact that it was a very fully elaborated response to the shift in the conception of the literary from rhetoric and poetics to genius and the heart. In seeking to establish the elements of Sainte-Beuve's critical principles I shall concentrate chiefly on the *Portraits littéraires* and his first collection of poetry, the *Vie, poésies et pensées de Joseph Delorme*, since I want to suggest that between them they constitute the framework of Sainte-Beuve's literary aesthetic. For one of the consequences of Sainte-Beuve's critical position and of its construction of the literary is that the creative and the critical prove to be so mutually—if paradoxically—implicated that it becomes impossible to maintain a clear distinction between the two. When one looks at the beginnings of Sainte-Beuve's career as a writer, the critical project and the creative project appear to have been developed alongside each other—or even as versions of each other. His earliest critical work, the articles that appeared in book form under the rather long-winded title *Tableau historique et critique de la poésie française et du théâtre français au XVIe siècle* in 1828, was written at the same time as the first poems of the *Joseph Delorme* collection. And *Joseph Delorme* itself was finally published just one day before the first of Sainte-Beuve's literary portraits (on Boileau), which appeared in the newly founded *Revue de Paris* on 5 April 1829. But aside from this chronological overlap, the most striking feature that Sainte-Beuve's critical portraits and *Joseph Delorme* share is the biographical format that they both adopt.

The Boileau portrait represents a very bold if somewhat understated move on Sainte-Beuve's part, precisely through its use of biography. For more than any other, Boileau's name had been associated with the rhetorical precepts which had dominated literary thinking and practice since the

---

[22] This ambiguity of the supplement is the one exemplarily described by Derrida in *Of Grammatology*, tr. Gayatri Chakravorty Spivak (Baltimore, 1976). For an illuminating discussion of the role of criticism and literary self-consiousness, see Philippe Lacoue-Labarthe and Jean-Luc Nancy, *L'Absolu littéraire* (Paris, 1978). They specifically exclude the French tradition from their discussion, but while there are many differences between the theoretical concerns of German Romanticism and the biographically based criticism of Sainte-Beuve, the function of criticism in relation to literature seems to be broadly, and significantly, similar in each.

publication of his *Art poétique* in 1674. To treat Boileau as the object of a biographically conceived critical study is to set the precepts of Boileau's own poetics on one side, and to evaluate his work in quite other terms than those which he himself had promoted. In his introduction to the portrait Sainte-Beuve promises to 'study [Boileau] in his private life, [...] examining him in detail from our perspective and the ideas of our time, moving in turn from the man to the author, from the *bourgeois* of Auteuil to the poet of Louis le Grand, not evading the serious questions of art and style when we encounter them, and perhaps occasionally shedding some light on them without ever claiming to settle them' (*Portraits littéraires*, pp. 6–7). Sainte-Beuve makes no bones either about his historically relativist *parti pris* or about the biographical basis of his discussion. It is this perspective which makes his move just as radical as—and perhaps ultimately more effective than—the full-scale attack on the rules of classical dramaturgy which had been mounted by Hugo just over a year previously in his provocative *Préface de Cromwell*.

On its publication, the *Vie, poésies et pensées de Joseph Delorme* were presented as precisely that—the life, poems and thoughts of one Joseph Delorme, whose fictional status is nowhere made clear. Sainte-Beuve's name did not appear as that of the author, and an anonymous *éditeur* introduces the collection ascribed to Joseph Delorme with a brief biographical sketch of the poet in which the reader is invited to see the poems as based on episodes in the hitherto unknown life of Delorme. The *pensées* which conclude the volume are also ascribed to Delorme and have the appearance of a kind of personal aesthetic, recorded by him in a series of private notes and musings. Although lives of poets were by no means an unknown phenomenon at the time, no others had quite the same role as that of the fictional Joseph Delorme.

Alfred de Vigny's *Stello* (1832) recounts the lives of three (real) poets, Nicolas-Joseph-Laurent Gilbert, Thomas Chatterton, and Marie-Joseph Chénier (brother of the more famous André). Gilbert and Chatterton had both died young and the effect of their biographies is to create an aura of pathos around a vanished or unrealized body of poetic writing, as well as to plead for the protection of poetry from the destructive effects of political power. Sainte-Beuve knew Robert Southey's account of the life of the English poet Henry Kirke White, the macabrely titled *Remains of Henry Kirke White* (1807); and he was also clearly familiar with Samuel Johnson's *Lives of the Poets*, which he admired for the quality of the critical comments in them. This critical element of biography was for Sainte-Beuve its most vital component, and in his view, lives of writers had to be much more than stories in which their literary creations appear simply as biographical events like any other. Because of the need to take account of the special features of genius as Sainte-Beuve understood it, biographies of poets could not simply replicate the biographies of the heroes and the great men whose social role the poets were usurping.[23] According to him, if biographer-critics omit to grasp the unique character of a poet's genius, they will end up merely 'keeping the registers of the temple, and will not be priests of the god'. In short, their books will be 'useful, accurate, undoubtedly worthy, but not works of high criticism and art' (*Portraits littéraires*, p. 25). Evidently Sainte-Beuve had something much more ambitious in mind than either pathos or mere historical accuracy when it came to the issue of literary biography.

These comments, which appear in Sainte-Beuve's essay on Corneille, were written in the same year that he conceived of the tripartite arrangement of his *Vie, poésies et pensées de Joseph Delorme* and wrote the introductory life for it. Admittedly this life has its share of Romantic pathos: Delorme dies young of a characteristically Romantic combination of tuberculosis and 'an affection of the heart' (p. 21), and is revealed to have lived out his poverty-stricken existence in an equally Romantic state of melancholy and suffering. However, there is much more to this biography than the construction of a conventionally wretched Romantic poet. What is striking is the fact that the life is treated as essential for a proper understanding of the poems: 'the poems on their own, without the history of the feelings to which they relate, would have been no more than a half-understood enigma' (p. 2). Equally, though, the poetry is presented as a record of the (inner) life which would otherwise have remained unknown: 'his poems suffice to enable us to understand the active feelings which were sapping him at that time' (pp. 18–19). The life explains the poetry, but at the same time the poetry provides the only complete history of the life, creating a circularity in which each is necessarily presupposed by the other. The implicitly critical dimension of the biographical introduction is further emphasized by its concluding remarks, where the anonymous editor places Delorme's work in the poetic tradition founded by André Chénier, and also tries to identify the distinctive qualities of Delorme's poetry: its subject matter, its lexis and the 'individuality [. . .] of its conceptions' (p. 26). The occasional footnote in the poems serves as a continuing reminder of an editorial presence and the critico-biographical context. Sainte-Beuve is not alone in using the fiction of an editorial frame: Chateaubriand and Constant use versions of it in *René* and *Adolphe*. But where they do so in order to try and negotiate the question of autobiographical readings of their texts

---

[23] On this change in status and role of the writer, see Paul Bénichou, *Le Sacre de l'écrivain 1750–1830* (Paris, 2nd edn 1996).

and to encourage readers to focus on the moral problems raised in each of them, Sainte-Beuve's biographizing strategies seem designed above all to create a (literary-)critical perspective on his work. In the process he takes this editorial topos far further than other writers of the time; indeed, in subsequent editions he actually duplicates the critical frame that the editor creates by including samples of the book's real critical reception after its publication in 1829.[24]

The centrality of this critical perspective is made very evident in the first of the 'Pensées', which directs the reader firmly towards a critical and biographical approach to the text. It does this by addressing the problem of the limitations of language and its implications for all literary expression:

> Truth in all things, if it is taken in its purest and most absolute sense, is ineffable and ungraspable; in other words, a truth is always less true when expressed than when conceived. In order to get it to the state of clarity and precision which language requires, one has more or less, but necessarily and invariably, to add to it and to subtract from it, to heighten the colours, remove the shadows, sharpen up the outlines; it is for this reason that there are so many *expressed* truths which resemble *conceived* truths no more than clouds made of marble resemble real clouds. (p. 130)

However, instead of developing this thought into a Romantic scenario that would highlight the poet's suffering at his inability to express his ineffable experience, Sainte-Beuve sees the issue as one which concerns the reader even more than the writer, and which makes critical response an essential component both of reading and of writing:

> whatever the idea is that one is expressing, one cannot be too mindful of what one is leaving out and what one is including, and one must add, mentally at least, all the qualifications which the trenchant speed of language removes, and have constantly in one's mind's eye the vast and amorphous model out of which it was carved. If the writer-philosopher and -critic has to proceed in this way to gain a proper understanding of himself, and avoid becoming the dupe of his own formulae, *how much more must the well-intentioned reader acquire the habit of seeing the things that lie beneath the words, of taking into account as he reads a thousand unspoken circumstances, of following the broad middle way with his author, rather than clinging like a rebellious child to the brambles in the ditch.* (pp. 130–31, my emphasis)

The limitations and crudeness of language impose on the poet the need for a *critical* vigilance, requiring him in the very moment of composition to act as his own critic. But they also require the reader to supplement the

---

[24] The 1840 edition of Sainte-Beuve's *Poésies complètes* contains a bibliographical note with references to the critical reception of *Joseph Delorme*; the 1861 edition of *Joseph Delorme* itself includes a selection of critical articles on it. Sainte-Beuve did the same thing with subsequent editions of his novel *Volupté*. Sainte-Beuve himself reviewed the second edition of *Joseph Delorme* in *Le Globe*, November 1830.

inevitably partial forms of literary expression with the 'thousand unspoken circumstances' in which they took shape, and to keep in mind a sense of the larger authorial project. This is the underlying principle of Sainte-Beuve's own critical portraits which seek, precisely, to articulate what the finished text could at best only imply.

If the poet is isolated, misunderstood, and mocked by his public, this does not make him a victim of political philistinism, as Chatterton is for Vigny or of straightforward poetic philistinism, as with Baudelaire's 'L'Albatros'. Rather, it is a sign that his readers have failed to supply the critical context which will make sense of the poet's work. So, for instance, in the poem 'L'enfant rêveur', the poet addresses the dreaming child and future poet with these words of warning:

> Personne sous tes chants ne suivra ta pensée,
> Et de loin on rira de ta plainte insensée. (p. 99)

> ('No-one will follow your thoughts beneath your songs,/ And from afar people will laugh at your absurd lament'.)

The word 'follow' (*suivre*), used here to describe the ideal relation of the public to the poet's thought, also occurs as a key element in Sainte-Beuve's notion of critical response, as we saw in Joseph Delorme's comments about the well-intentioned reader, who is to '*follow* the broad middle way with his author'. It is also used in the portraits to describe how Sainte-Beuve himself sees the role of the critic, which is 'to try to *follow* [the writer] in his origins, in his active development, his range, digressions, diversions, the way he mixes things together, unfolding his various phases, his intellectual vicissitudes, and the riches of his soul' (*Portraits littéraires*, p. 225; my emphasis). In any case, the poem certainly suggests that the poet remains highly vulnerable if he does not have a critical counterpart.

Such is the importance of this critical or quasi-biographical dimension that its absence is often presented in the poetry as potentially disastrous, even where it is not deliberately withheld by the outside world. So, when the poet turns in on himself in a movement of introspection which excludes the outer world, this merely reveals chaos and confusion. As the child in 'L'enfant rêveur' plunges into his own inner world, what he sees are:

> [. . .] précipices sans fond,
> Arêtes de rocher, sable mouvant qui fond,
> Monstres de toute forme entrelacés en groupe,
> Serpents des mers, dragons à tortueuse croupe,
> Crocodiles vomis du rivage africain,
> Et, plus affreux que tous, le vorace requin. (p. 99)

> '([. . .] bottomless chasms,/ Rocky mountain ridges, moving sands

which dissolve,/ Monsters of every shape entwined in groups,/ Sea serpents, dragons with twisted rumps,/ Crocodiles vomited up from the shores of Africa,/ And, most horrible of them all, the voracious shark'.)

Delorme's inner world is described in very similar terms (p. 17), and these images of internal chaos suggest that without a critical dimension of context or response, the inner self is bound to lack coherence and to collapse into frightening turmoil.

Equally, however, a simple, straightforward ardour that rushes headlong towards the world is almost always presented as no less disastrous for the writer. The poet who is too *avid* will inevitably destroy the object that he reaches out for, as in 'Rêverie', where he shatters the image of the stars reflected in the lake's surface by rushing to seize hold of it. And if poetic inspiration is evoked as the upward thrust of a creative *essor* in the poem 'À mon ami V[ictor] H[ugo]', the speaker is nevertheless troubled by the thought that the thrusting, soaring poet might be deaf to the very crowd who grant him critical recognition as a poet:

> Entends-tu ce long bruit doux comme une harmonie,
> Ce cri qu'à l'univers arrache le génie
>   Trop longtemps combattu,
> Cri tout d'un coup sorti de la foule muette,
> Et qui porte à la gloire un nom de grand poète,
>   Noble ami, l'entends-tu?[. . .]
>
> Poussant ton vol sublime et planant, solitaire,
> Entre les voix d'en haut et l'écho de la terre,
>   Dis-moi, jeune vainqueur,
> Dis-moi, nous entends-tu? la clameur solennelle
> Va-t-elle dans la nue enfler d'orgueil ton aile
>   Et remuer ton cœur? (p. 49)

('Do you hear the long sound, sweet as harmony,/ The shout wrung from the universe by genius/ Too long opposed,/ A shout suddenly erupting from the silent crowd,/ And which sings in praise of the name of a great poet,/ Noble friend, do you hear it? [. . .] //Pursuing your sublime, soaring, solitary flight,/ Between the voices from on high and the earth's echo,/ Tell me, young victor,/ Do you hear us? Will the solemn clamour/ Make your wing swell with pride among the clouds/ And move your heart?')

The anxiety here is that the crowd's recognition will go unacknowledged by the poet, and his heart remain unmoved (the heart, of course, having now become the source of poetic creativity). In a later (unpublished) essay on Hugo, this anxiety becomes outright denunciation, as the poet's *essor* has evolved into the blind self-assertion of a 'cyclops'. Rather than listening and responding to the world around him, Hugo merely projects himself into it, 'making and seeing the world in his own image';[25] and he is now also incapable of reading any poet other than himself: 'He no longer hears Virgil any more than Petrarch; he sees all things and all people in himself' (p. 233). In *Mes Poisons* this crude creative assertiveness is described quite simply as 'the *priapism* of amour-propre' and is the mark of 'our poets [who] are in a perpetual state of useless personal exaltation, and an infatuation which they cannot conceal'.[26] In these images of an over-assertive creativity, the poet is castigated for his blindness to his own (critical) context: the world in which he lives, the literary tradition in which he writes, and the reader-critics who receive him. In short, it would seem that without a critical component, poetry will find itself on a suicide course and cease to be poetry at all.

A second, contrastingly positive image of poetic creativity in *Joseph Delorme* presents it as not only more reflective (like the poet contemplating the lake at the end of 'Rêverie'), but as actively calling for an interpretative response. 'Retour à la poésie' sums up this second version of creativity in its last stanza:

> Tel est le destin du poète;
> Errer ici-bas égaré;
> Invoquer le grand interprète;
> Écouter la harpe secrète,
> Et se mirer au lac sacré! (p. 55)

> ('This is the destiny of the poet;/ To lose his way and wander here below;/ To invoke the great interpreter;/ To listen to the secret harp,/ And see his reflection in the sacred lake!')

The poet is always lost because even if he resists the blind thrust of Hugolian inspiration, his picture of himself in his own context can never be complete; his poetry is based on listening (to the secret harp) and reflection (in the sacred lake), and is dependent on the completing response of a third-party 'interpreter'. In other words, the poet relies on the critical attitude not only for a proper reception of his work, but for its very construction.

It seems axiomatic in Sainte-Beuve that the subject can never fully grasp itself, and that every speaker needs a listener or interpreter to make sense of what he himself cannot. Thus the address to Victor Hugo in 'A mon ami V. H.' ends with the fantasy that the thrusting poet might eventually prove capable of giving ear to the lesser mortal that the speaker figures himself as being ('I, poor fallen being'):

> [. . .] mais si, comme un bon frère,
> Du sein de ta splendeur à mon destin contraire

---

[25] Des gladiateurs en littérature', *Pour la critique*, p. 234.
[26] Sainte-Beuve, *Mes Poisons* (Paris, 1926), pp. 130–31; emphasis in original.

Tu veux bien compatir;
Si tu lis en mon cœur ce que je n'y puis lire,
Et si ton amitié devine sur ma lyre
Ce qui n'en peut sortir;

C'est assez, c'est assez: jusqu'à l'heure où mon ame,
Secouant son limon et rallumant sa flamme
A la nuit des tombeaux,
Je viendrai, le dernier et l'un des plus indignes,
Te rejoindre, au milieu des aigles et des cygnes,
O toi l'un des plus beaux! (pp. 50–51)

('[. . .] but if, like a good brother,/ From the heart of your splendour
so different from my own destiny/ You are willing to sympathize;/ If
you read in my heart what I cannot read in it,/ And if your friendship
divines on my lyre/ What cannot emerge from it; // It is enough,
enough; until the hour when my soul,/ Shaking off its yoke and
rekindling its flame/ At the darkening of the tomb,/ I shall come,
the last and one of the most unworthy,/ To join you, amidst the eagles
and the swans,/ Oh thou, one of the finest!')

In order to become a poet in his turn, the speaker needs the established
artist to become a critic-interpreter as well, and to lend an ear to the secrets
of the heart that the speaker himself cannot fully decipher or articulate.

The critical perspective associated with *Joseph Delorme* is also powerfully evoked within the poems themselves as a repeatedly fantasized
biography scenario (or to be more accurate, obituary scenario). It would
seem that the poet can only imagine the self within the frame of a biography
narrated by a third party. In a number of poems he anticipates his own
death and imagines himself as the object of another's biographizing speculation. Or rather, he repeatedly figures himself as a corpse, only to discover
as a painful absence that there is no other there to write his obituary. In
'Adieux à la poésie' he recognizes that when he dies there will be no
'distraught lover' to weep over his dead body and lay his head in his coffin.
And in 'Les rayons jaunes', a poem inspired by the death of the aunt who
had helped to bring him up, he constructs a similar non-scene, acknowledging the impossibility of there ever being a 'young fiancée' to mourn
him after his own death. More elaborately in 'Le creux de la vallée', the
poet narrates his own suicide and the subsequent discovery, months later,
of his unrecognizable body by strangers. These figures—as unknown to
him as he is to them—speculate fleetingly and vainly about the poet's life
as they trundle his remains to an unmarked grave in the local cemetery
and abandon him to anonymity. These poems all suggest that Sainte-
Beuve conceives of identity not as based in self-presence, but as an object
precariously dependent on an external biographical gaze. In any case, such
obituarizing fantasies are in sharp contrast to the priapic self-assertion of

the cyclops-poet who constructs the world and his others simply as projections of himself.

This brief glance at *Joseph Delorme* would seem to confirm the idea that the critical stance and the biographical perspective are integral both to its construction and to its outlook. One could, of course, attribute this to Sainte-Beuve's own particular mind-set and emotional proclivities, and see it simply as heralding his ultimate choice of an exclusively critical career (in other words, to interpret the phenomenon purely biographically). But there does seem to be something more at stake here. For it returns us to the idea that at this juncture in the history of literature and the idea of the literary (for that too has its history), the critical perspective becomes inseparable from the construction and conception of literature itself. I shall now move on to explore this claim from the angle of the more overtly critical 'portraits'.

The genre of the 'portrait' which Sainte-Beuve adopted for his own purposes did not originally have a literary-critical function. Widely practised in the seventeenth century, it was primarily a social pastime, rather than a critical or a literary form. (Some of the most striking instances of the portrait have survived as 'literature' in La Bruyère's *Caractères*, Saint-Simon's *Mémoires*, and in the comical 'scène des portraits' in Molière's *Misanthrope*.) In Sainte-Beuve's hands, the portrait was recast and adapted to the new critical task of defining the genius of the writer. The reason he chose the term 'portrait' in preference to 'biography' or 'life' may in part be because he saw the biographies of poets and artists as different in essence from the records of the lives of other great men. And it may be for this reason, too, that he also says that his portraits are a 'transformation of the academic *éloge*' practised in the eighteenth century, since they too were dedicated to 'great men' and not specifically to writers.[27] For in the realm of literature the individual genius of the writer is as much determining as it is determined, and this makes the great writer fundamentally different from 'statesmen, conquerors, theologians, and philosophers'. Indeed, it is the unpredictable nature of individual genius that makes any conventionally causative account of it problematic. As Sainte-Beuve says in his review of Hippolyte Taine's *Histoire de la littérature anglaise*: 'there is nothing [. . .] more unpredictable than talent, and it would not be talent if it were not unpredictable' (*Pour la critique*, p. 180). And he goes on to criticize Taine's 'method' precisely for its inability to capture the unique qualities which constitute genius:

---

[27] Preface to *Critiques et portraits littéraires*, II, *Oeuvres*, I, 651–2. Sainte-Beuve's portraits are more insistently realistic than the avowedly celebratory *éloge*. On the *éloge* see Chapter 5 above.

'there is only one soul, one particular cast of mind capable of creating this
or that masterpiece. [. . .] There is only one version of each poet'.

Moreover, the particular cast of mind identified by the literary portrait
is something which the poet-genius is incapable of identifying himself, so
that it becomes the critic's task to reveal it to the poet. Sainte-Beuve states
this quite categorically in another essay on Taine, in which he describes
criticism as a kind of dialogue or 'causerie' where the critic mentally
addresses his comments directly to their subject, as if he were actually
present: persuading the writer of the validity of the critic's insight, catching
him by surprise, and ultimately leading him to a greater understanding of
himself and his talent. In this imaginary dialogue, the critic becomes

> invigorated by a flattering notion and a powerful motive, the thought that
> one is teaching him [the writer] as well, that one is taking him a step further
> in his knowledge of himself and of the place he occupies in literary renown;
> one would delight in thinking that one is developing an aspect of his repu-
> tation and that one is lifting a veil which had hidden a part of it from him.[28]

He makes a similar point in a letter to George Sand when he praises her
for qualities which he assumes that she is no better able to explain than he
is: 'There is a side of you [. . .] that I do not properly know or understand
[. . .], an area which remains mysterious; it is related to your genius, to
your secret, to something that you would undoubtedly not be able
to explain yourself'.[29] If he is modest about his own capacities to define
the author's genius here, the presupposition of the portraits is precisely that
this *is* what the critic can do. The critical portrait provides knowledge
that neither the political historian (who writes biographies of statesmen
and conquerors), nor the literary historian (who, like Taine, describes the
characteristics of a period rather those of an individual), nor even the writer
himself could possess. In the case of the living poet, the insights provided
by the critic may be absorbed by the writer as a form of self-knowledge,
and potentially feed back into his literary practice, thus suggesting yet
another way in which critical activity becomes integral to the literary.

The critical portrait is, however, inherently biographical, since for
Sainte-Beuve, the genius which constitutes literature can only ever be
grasped as a temporal phenomenon, and the biographical overview becomes
the critic's unique prerogative and the basis for his exclusive purchase on the
literary. That is to say that despite its occasional appearance as Hugolian
essor, genius can never be purely spontaneous self-affirmation: it is the
effect of a conjunction of circumstances with which it interacts, and it also

---

[28] 'Divers écrits de M. H. Taine', *Causeries du lundi*, 15 vols (Paris, 1851–62), XIII, 211.
[29] Letter dated 21 July 1839, *Correspondance générale*, ed. Jean Bonnerot, 19 vols (Paris, 1935), I, 374.

has its own evolving dynamic. Amaury, the hero of Sainte-Beuve's *Volupté*, speaks of the 'individual *connection* with the things surrounding it' that even the humblest existence reveals.[30] For Sainte-Beuve, the most important component of this connection of the poet's existence to the things surrounding it are his *origins*: 'In order to know an eminent character, the study of his origins and education is essential (*Portraits littéraires*, p. 923).' First, there are the poet's ancestors and his geographical roots; then his parents (and in particular his mother); then his siblings and even his children.[31] Sainte-Beuve's portraits always begin with the writer's family background, and then go on, as he recommends here, to consider the writer's education and to examine his circle of friends at the moment when his talent first appears in adult form (his 'generation'). The critic's goal in this exploration of the writer's emergence is, however, not some explanatory model that would reveal the determining causes of his genius; for if Sainte-Beuve's understanding of genius is temporal, it is not in any real sense of the word determinist.[32] The primary aim of what he calls 'the biographical critic' is to identify the particular moment when the poet's genius comes into its own, since this moment relates to all that precedes it and to all that comes after it and is the key to the wider biographical picture which it is the critic's business to reveal:

> If you understand the poet at this critical moment, if you unravel the node to which everything will be connected from that moment on, if you find what you might call the key to this mysterious link made half of iron and half of diamonds joining his second, radiant, dazzling and solemn existence to his first, obscure, repressed and solitary one (the memory of which he would more than once like to swallow up), then one could say of you that you thoroughly possess and know your poet. ('Pierre Corneille', *Portraits littéraires*, p. 24)

In a letter of 9 June 1861, Sainte-Beuve writes of the poet's distinguishing feature as an 'integral molecule',[33] a metaphor which nicely combines a notion of uniqueness and configuration, individual feature and broader relation. For him, as he says in his review of Hugo's *Feuilles d'automne*, the single work or the singular feature have always to be placed in a wider context, which is pre-eminently a chronological or temporal one, and it is the particular role of criticism to do this:

> after the uncontested and universal triumph of the genius to which it devoted

---

[30] Sainte-Beuve, *Volupté*, ed. André Guyaux (Paris, 1986), p. 290; my emphasis.
[31] Sainte-Beuve, 'Chateaubriand jugé par un ami intime en 1803', *passim*.
[32] As Jean-Pierre Richard puts it in his remarkable essay on Sainte-Beuve, the life is as much an expression of the writer's genius as is his work. See 'Sainte-Beuve et l'objet littéraire' in his *Études sur le romantisme* (Paris, 1970), pp. 227–83.
[33] Quoted by Antoine in his Introduction to *Joseph Delorme*, p. lx.

itself from the outset, and whose glorious monopoly it sees slipping from its grasp, criticism still retains an honourable task, an attentive and religious concern: to embrace all the different parts of the development of the poetry, to point out the connections with the earlier phases, to place the evolving work as a whole back in its true light, where its more recent admirers see the latest manifestations too prominently. (*Pour la critique*, p. 126)

It is because the poet's work always emerges in a given temporal context and has its own temporal vicissitudes that biography is the most suitable format for critical commentary. Sainte-Beuve's poet acquires his identity as what one might call a 'subject in process' (to borrow Julia Kristeva's term); but it is the critic's larger view and his biographical frame which enable him to capture that sense of process, and to see beyond the poet's own limited view of the immediate circumstances in which he makes his personal choices and develops his characteristic forms. Time and again Sainte-Beuve reminds his readers that the biographer-critic has a longer perspective than the poet, since the poet is caught up in the immediate, liable inevitably to lose sight of his past self, to be necessarily ignorant of his own future, and to have at best only a partial view of the tradition within which his work is created. The biographical overview allows the critic to identify the vital moment when literary genius comes into being, and to hold on to its full significance by maintaining a sense of its context and its evolution. In other words, the priest knows more of the divinity that he guards than the gods themselves who embody it.

But if the view that the critic has of his subject embraces a temporal dimension which the subject himself can never fully grasp, and if the critic ends up with insights into the poet-subject's work that the poet cannot match, criticism itself turns out also to have its own temporality. In an extended metaphor for the role of the critic, Sainte-Beuve describes litera-ture as a kind of landscape whose separate and mutually isolated features can nevertheless be linked by a critical trajectory which is figured as a journey down a river:

> Art which meditates and edifies, art which lives in itself and in its work may be visualized as some venerable and ancient castle washed by a river, as a monastery on a river bank, as a motionless and majestic rock; but from each of these rocks or castles the view—though immense—does not reach the other points, and many of these monuments and marvellous landscapes are not, as it were, aware of each other; so *criticism, whose principle is mobility and sequence, moves from place to place* like the river below, surrounding them, washing them, reflecting them in its waters, and effortlessly transporting the traveller who wishes to get to know them, from one to the other. ('Adam Mickiewicz', *Oeuvres*, I, 537; my emphasis)

Although criticism is credited here with the ability to relate the individual literary monuments to each other, it is nevertheless represented as a river that meanders (through space, through time), and not as a single vantage point that takes in the whole landscape. The diversity of literature is such that no one perspective can encompass it in a single gesture. For this reason, criticism is condemned to perpetual mobility and transformation as it responds to its often very disparate objects:

> And let no-one say that if criticism had a central viewpoint, if it judged according to an absolute principle or truth, it would spare itself a large part of the tiring effort of this movement and these forced shifts, and that, from the top of the hill where it might sit like a king in an epic poem or like the judge Minos, it would enumerate with ease and pronounce its oracles with true unity. To my knowledge there is, at present, no viewpoint that, if adopted, would be sufficiently central to allow one to embrace the infinite variety unfolding in the plain below. (Ibid., pp. 536–7)

The critic is in a paradoxical position whereby on the one hand the validity of his enterprise requires him to have a greater knowledge of the literary than literature itself, and on the other hand, that validity would be lost if criticism sought to turn its greater insight into universal principle and theoretical precept. For to do so would be to revert to the position exemplified by La Harpe, in which the critic judged all works by external rather than intrinsic criteria. Indeed, this was the nub of the objections that Sainte-Beuve made to Taine, for whom criticism was also no more than 'different applications and different aspects of the same thought, [. . .] the fragments of the same whole which he keeps redistributing' (*Pour la critique*, p. 171). On this score, Taine's literary history turns out to have all the drawbacks of La Harpe's poetics.

The paradox is that if criticism were to formulate its knowledge of literature as system or as theory, it would lose all connection with the object it claims to illuminate, and its knowledge would become void. By putting Sainte-Beuve's ideas about criticism and literature together, and by suggesting that they constitute a coherent project, one runs the risk of removing Sainte-Beuve from the meandering river and transporting him to the mountain top—in short, of turning him from traveller to judge. It is one of the chief merits of biography and the portrait that each one deals successively with the singularity of a given genius whose own evolutionary temporality works against the tendency of critical knowledge to become theoretical system. Moreover, each portrait is itself composed over a period of time, however brief, in a process which Sainte-Beuve evokes very vividly in the account of his working method that introduces his portrait of Diderot. The biographical portrait is presented here as something to be painstakingly composed and constructed, rather than as a pre-formed repository for facts and information about its subject's life:

> You shut yourself away for two weeks with the writings of a famous dead philosopher or poet; you study him, you turn him round and round, you question him at leisure; you get him to pose for you; it is almost as if you were spending a fortnight in the country creating the bust of Byron, Schiller, or Goethe. [. . .] Each feature is added in its turn and finds its place in the physiognomy which you are trying to reproduce; it is like each star appearing in succession before one's eyes and beginning to shine at its allotted point in the texture of a beautiful night sky. (*Portraits littéraires*, p. 166)

Gradually abstraction and generality (the currency of theory and system) are replaced by 'an individual, precise reality, with its own increasing accentuation and sparkle; you sense a likeness emerging and developing'. By submitting to this compositional process, the critic will eventually capture 'the familiar tic, the revealing smile, the indefinable crack in the skin, the intimate and painful wrinkle concealed in vain beneath the already thinning hair' which sum up and reveal the writer. In the same instant, criticism and creation merge: 'analysis disappears in creation, the portrait speaks and lives, and one has found the man' (ibid.). The moment when the biographer-critic reaches his goal and identifies the characteristic that constitutes literary genius is also the moment when criticism itself could be said to become a form of literature.

Just as poetry seemed repeatedly to presuppose criticism in Sainte-Beuve's conception, so the critical portrait finds itself unavoidably embroiled in a variety of encounters with literature. Biography as practised in these portraits constantly negotiates the line where criticism constitutes literature as its object by revealing what literature and the poets who create it do not know and could not themselves articulate. And at the same time, it steers a delicate path between the theoretical abstractions towards which its own knowledge tempts it on one side, and, on the other, the literary creativity which brings that knowledge to life but within which the distinctiveness of critical insight would eventually be lost. In brief, there is something uncannily modern (in the sense that Genette or Philippe Sollers might understand the word) in a critical practice which is not only devoted to identifying the literary, but which is also so actively and ambiguously involved in creating it.

9

Yury Tynyanov and the 'Literary Fact'

AVRIL PYMAN

Russian Formalist *theory* was opposed not so much to biography as to the biographical approach to the history of literature, which, the Formalists considered, should be studied 'scientifically' as the history of form rather than of personalities, ideas, or content. The study of literature, in other words, is not philosophy, psychology, sociology, theology, or mythology, but an exact science dealing with the primary matter of text: the word as such, language, speech, the stylistic device. Later some concessions were made to the 'function' of the text, and terms such as 'system', 'evolution', and 'structure' were added to the Formalists' vocabulary and promptly appropriated by their Structuralist followers. Biographies of authors were thought of as belonging to a separate 'series' parallel to, but by no means of the essence of, the evolution of literature—any more than biographies of composers or artists are essential to the study of music or art.

In *practice*, however, the lives and times of writers were often found not so much to run parallel to as to be contingent upon the texts they produced, in a way that made it increasingly difficult to preserve the clinical purity of the 'science' of literature. To deal with this, the Formalists introduced, sought to define, and argued about new terms such as 'literary fact' and 'literary milieu'. Increasingly, the more imaginative and intuitive of them succumbed to the seductive charm of biography. Yury Tynyanov, the central figure of this chapter, sought to distinguish his books about writers' lives from his 'scientific' works of theory and research by writing them in the form of novels, closely associated with the historical fiction and film scenarios on which he was also engaged. It is, however, a fact of Tynyanov's own biography that, in his culminating achievement, the unfinished

Pushkin, the genres of literary-historical research, biography and fiction begin to merge. The following account of how this came about does not seek to argue for or against the original Formalists' position on the biographical approach, which had great value as a corrective and still serves to remind us that the primary object of literary study must always be the text, but rather to celebrate the way in which their achievements surpassed their theorizing and the irresistible vitality of literature.

Theory

Opoyaz, the Society of Poetic Language, was founded, according to Roman Jakobson, in February 1917 over pancakes at Lili Brik's.[1] *De facto*, the society had been active since 1914[2] as an informal grouping of friends devoted to the study of literature as pure form. Among the best-known names were Osip Brik (1880–1945), Boris Eikhenbaum (1886–1959), Boris Tomashevsky (1890–1957), Viktor Shklovsky (1893–1984), Yury Tynyanov (1894–1943), and Roman Jakobson (1896–1982), whose primary affiliation was with the allied Moscow Linguistics Circle. Tynyanov joined Opoyaz in 1918. His nursery was Professor S. A. Vengerov's seminar at St Petersburg University, more like a literary debating society than an academic seminar. Although truly attached to Vengerov, an inspirational teacher who had known Turgenev, Tynyanov identified with the school of Russian Formalism, elaborated by Opoyaz and the Moscow Linguistics Circle in direct opposition to his teacher's empirical methods. Formalist insistence that the study of literature should be conducted as a science, not 'a conglomeration of cottage industries',[3] was influential far beyond the bounds of Russia. It led directly to the discrediting of the biographical approach to individual authors and what they called the 'Abraham begat Jacob' approach to the history of literature. Vengerov's compilative multi-volume *Critico-Biographical Dictionary of Contemporary Writers*[4] seemed to them a model of how not to study literature, for they differentiated, where Vengerov and his colleagues did not, between different disciplines or 'series'—in Russian, *ryady*: the evolution of poetic language was one series, whereas biography, history, sociology, psychology, and economics belonged

[1] *Iakobson—Budetlianin, Sbornik materialov*, ed. Bengt Jangfeldt, Acta Universitatis Stockholmiensis, Stockholm Studies in Russian Literature, XXVI (1992), p. 32.
[2] See Michael O'Toole, 'Russian Literary Theory: From the Formalists to Lotman', *Reference Guide to Russian Literature*, ed. Neil Cornwell (London and Chicago, 1998), p. 40.
[3] Roman Jakobson, quoted in O'Toole, 'Russian Literary Theory'.
[4] S. A. Vengerov, *Kritiko-biograficheskii slovar' sovremennykh pistalelei i uchenykh (ot nachala russkoi obrazovannosti do nashikh dnei)*, 6 vols (St Petersburg, 1889–1904).

to different series which, though each might contribute in an auxiliary fashion to cultural history, were, they thought, essentially extraneous to the study of the 'literary process'.

Between 1918 and 1922 Formalist insistence on the importance of the 'matter' of language, coming as it did as a reaction against Symbolist emphasis on metaphysical superstructure and hidden *realiora* ('the more real', i.e. 'noumena', 'forms'), was welcomed in revolutionary circles as 'materialist' and anti-mystical. Formalists debated hotly with advocates of the classical Marxist approach and usually won the argument. Scholarly, innovative, persuasive, and iconoclastic, they seemed more revolutionary by far than opponents who clung to the nineteenth-century Marxist conviction that literature, like everything else, is firmly rooted in economics and reflects the class struggle. Tynyanov, in his autobiography, states expressly that 'had there been no Revolution I could not have understood literature'.[5] It was not until manipulative political ideologues who shared Lenin's view that literature should not only mirror reality but also serve the interests of the Bolshevik party, for the most part men and women who had no professional training in the arts, gained a controlling influence in publishing and editing that Opoyaz found itself with no regular journal. Formalist works, however, continued to come out in book form and in periodicals and literary newspapers. Tynyanov's last collection of articles, *Arkhaisty i novatory* ('Archaists and Innovators'), was published in Leningrad in 1929.

Nevertheless, the purity of Formalist doctrine had by then been considerably eroded and not only by outward circumstance. In 1923 Tomashevsky published an article on literature and biography in which he categorically restates the Formalist tenet that the biography of a writer should be seen as 'external' (even though necessary) material of an auxiliary nature to the study of literature and literary history. Yet from the eighteenth century onwards, he conceded, there had been strong demand from readers for lives of writers, heroes to admire, places to visit: a Ferney, a Yasnaya Polyana. Fiction, too, had created its own places of pilgrimage: the pond where Karamzin's 'poor Lisa' was said to have drowned herself, for instance. Such contamination of one 'series' by another is, therefore, an undeniable fact. The business of the literary historian who is concerned also with writers' lives is to delineate which are and which are not 'literary facts'. Tomashevsky suggested that what the literary historian really needs is the biographical legend created by the author himself. Only such a legend is a literary fact.

The inadequacy of such a definition of literary fact was clear from the

---

[5] Iurii Tynianov, 'Avtobiografiia', in *Iurii Tynianov, pisatel' i uchenyi: Vospominaniia, razmyshleniia, vstrechi*, ed. G. Pomerantsev (Moscow, 1966), p. 19.

critic's acknowledgement in the same article that various approaches are required to various types of 'biographical legend'. For the Romantics, he goes on, the life, its real setting and the created legend are all, equally, 'literary fact'. An intimate confessional writer such as Vasily Rozanov invites the scholar to examine how much the minutiae of everyday life described in the work of literature amount to true autobiography, how much is literary construct. 'Blok's legend is an inescapable concomitant to his poetry'. As to Mayakovsky and the Futurists, the Formalists' closest associates in contemporary creative literature, they had made their own personalities so central to their poetry that the literary construct 'intersects the path of the future biographer, who will have to try to construct a different, extra-literary biography'. The Pushkin era, on the other hand, the era to which Tynyanov was to devote his seminal academic studies and his best fiction, produced a 'group-created biography'. 'Now Pushkin writes to Baratynsky from Bessarabia, now Yazykov writes to Pushkin. And then all three of them become the themes of lyric poems.'[6]

Tynyanov, at much the same time (*c.* 1923–5), produced his own article on the literary fact (later reprinted in his *Archaists and Innovators*)[7]. In his academic work, he arrived at a new and seminal understanding of Pushkin's contribution to the formation of poetic language. He did this not so much by analysing the poet's texts, for perfection defies analysis, as by examining their interaction with lesser texts by more one-sided writers and, inevitably, Pushkin's interaction with the writers of these texts in the context of their lives. This context is made up of what Tynyanov calls 'literary facts', facts of everyday life and behaviour which are 'literary' in one epoch, but not necessarily so in another. His pivotal example, like Tomashevsky's, is the letter, but he is more explicit. Eighteenth-century private letters, he maintains, are of interest to the cultural historian but have no bearing on the literary system, whereas the architecture of the ornate and lofty state apartments where poets declaimed their resounding odes could well be designated 'literary fact'. In Pushkin's time, when a new, less solemn and resonant literary language was in the process of evolving, the friendly epistle becomes a 'literary fact', as do games of charades, *bouts rimés*, acrostics, epigrams, occasional verse in albums, polite conversation, the etiquette of the duel, and the ballroom. 'At a time when any kind of genre

---

[6] Boris Tomashevskij, 'Literature and Biography', tr. Herbert Eagel, in *Readings in Russian Poetics: Formalist and Structuralist Views*, ed. Ladislav Matejka and Krystyna Pomorska (Cambridge, MA and London, 1971), pp. 47–55, first published as 'Literatura i Biografia', *Kniga i revoliutsiia*, IV (1923), 6–9.

[7] Iu. N. Tynianov, 'Literaturnyi fakt', *Arkhaisty i novatory*, Nachdruck der Leningrader Ausgabe von 1929, mit einer Vorbemerkung von Dmitrii Tschizewskii, Slavische Propyläen, XXXI (Munich, 1967), pp. 6–9. All translations from this article are mine.

is disintegrating it moves from the centre to the periphery, and in its place a new phenomenon swims up into the centre out of the depths, the back-yards and the trivia of literature'. Yet even as elegant frivolity bubbled up into the centre once occupied by stately grandiloquence, even as the Baroque allusions of the eighteenth century are replaced by the impassioned republican Roman virtue which provides 'the key semantic coloration of the political and artistic speech of the period', Pushkin is seen to be eliminating periphrastic conceits, French phrases and gallicisms in search of a new simplicity, even a certain coarseness, and rejoicing, in his letters and epi-grams, in a deliberate sprinkling of the Russian equivalent of Anglo-Saxon words. 'The literary fact, now swimming up out of everyday life, now diving back into the depths', is, like any other constructive principle, subject to 'automization'.

The term 'automization' probably originates with Shklovsky, though the terminology of Formalism was worked out in discussion and regarded as common property. Tynyanov, applying it to the literary fact, sees that once the fact has passed into common literary usage it begins to lose vitality and gradually ceases to contribute to literary evolution. This occurs slowly and can take many years to affect the literary process as a whole. In the mind of the genius, however, evolution can be 'catastrophic', as it was with Pushkin. Scourge of stiff eighteenth-century grandeur, exquisite retailer of social trivia, poet of friendship and romantic love, he not only proceeded to reinvent a poetic language capable of embracing the epic and the sublime, but then moved on into journalism and had no hesitation in dredging up the prosaic literary fact of the poet's pay packet. 'I write for myself and publish for money and not in the least for a smile from the fair sex'. This was a whole new vocabulary and originated not from books, but from life.

In the article 'On Literary Evolution', published in 1927, Tynyanov still insists 'that a literary work is a system, as is literature itself'. He perceives the history of literary evolution not as 'a history of generals' but as the study of 'the mutations of systems'.[8] Such mutations, however, as is clear from the earlier article, are brought about in conjunction with constantly evolving literary facts. Tynyanov's concept is more elastic than Tomashev-sky's. The domestic, cultural, religious, or historical 'fact' becomes 'literary' not only when and if it becomes the subject of a work of literature or a part of a writer's 'legend' but when and as it enters into a closely contingent relationship with 'dynamic speech structure'.

[8] I. Tynianov, 'On Literary Evolution', tr. C. A. Luplow, in *Readings in Russian Poetics*, pp. 61–2, first published as 'O literaturnoi evoliutsii' in 1927 and reprinted in *Arkhaisty i novatory*, pp. 30–47.

Tynyanov's analytic grasp of the interplay between life and literature so scrupulously anatomized in his theoretical articles was, in fact, also highly imaginative. He was an inspired talker and brought the characters of Pushkin's time so vividly to life in conversation that a friend, Korney Chukovsky, asked him in 1924 why he could not project this empathy for his authors into lectures and critical articles. The very idea was contrary to the Formalist ethos, but from it sprang Tynyanov's historical novels. Chukovsky obtained a commission for a fictionalized life of Wilhelm Küchelbecker for a children's series and, by the end of the following year, Tynyanov had completed his first *biographie romancée* or, as his colleague Eikhenbaum preferred to call it, historical novel. *Kyukhlya* is the story of an almost forgotten poet and literary critic, an 'archaist' whose attempts to write antique tragedies and heroic poems against the spirit of the time and to reimbue the poetic language with weight and dignity Tynyanov considered seminal (together with those of his allies Griboedov and Katenin) for Pushkin's incomparably more successful revival of epic form. Not only did Küchelbecker's life make a rattling good story, but it positively sparkles with the vitality of the literary fact. Tynyanov, surprised by success, insisted that the work, as fiction, in no way contaminated his Formalist approach to the study of the literary process.

Some of his colleagues, notably Eikhenbaum, found it more difficult to separate the study of text from the study of environment and individuals. Pressures from non-literary 'series' were, as early as 1925, felt to be brutally deforming the literary process; it was as if Tynyanov's 'dynamic speech structure' were no longer evolving according to purely literary laws. The question of 'how to write' was replaced or complicated by another question: 'how to be a writer'.[9] On 25 July 1925 Eikhenbaum was confessing his longing for biography in a letter to Shklovsky. Personality, it seemed to him, had become of cardinal importance, if only as the repository of creative resistance to pressures exercised by the literary and non-literary environment. The interplay between personality and environment, he had begun to feel, was perhaps, after all, a part of the literary process and a legitimate object of study. For himself, he had no wish to forsake scholarship for fiction 'like Tynyanov' though he thought his friend's new departure 'a splendid way out of our professorial dryness'.

---

[9] O. M. Chudakova, 'Sotsial'naia praktika: Filologicheskaia refleksiia i literatura v nauchnoi biografii Eikenbauma i Tynianova', *Tynianovskii sbornik*, Akademiia Nauk Latviiskoi SSR, Institut Filosofii i Prava (Riga, 1986), pp. 103–31. All translations from this article, including Eikhenbaum's diary and his fellow Formalists' letters, are mine. An excellent account of the crisis of Formalism, not only from the point of view of the Formalist attitude to biography, is given by Victor Erlich in his classic *Russian Formalism: History—Doctrine* (The Hague, 1965) in the chapter 'Crisis and Rout (1926–1930)', pp. 118–39.

'And somehow I keep returning to the thought of biographies', wrote Eikhenbaum,

> only not about one (writer) but about many—not on the plane of psychology and natural history (like Ostwald) but on the plane of historical environment. To interweave the way a person constructs his or her own life (creative work seen as action) with the period, with history. [. . .] I feel that a book of this sort, orientated towards the human being, is historically needed and is essential to me personally. It will be literature and action both.[10]

Eikhenbaum's diary leaves no doubt that his urge to explore the biographies of writers in conjunction with 'literary environment' (*byt*) as distinct from 'literary fact' was, like Tynyanov's initiative in film scenarios and fiction, a response to the time. This does not mean to say that it was a surrender to outward pressure, as is perhaps too often supposed when Russian Formalism is under discussion. It was rather what Tynyanov, in the context of the development of poetic language, called 'dynamic interaction',[11] a reaction comparable to Shklovsky's famous 'knight's move',[12] against the immediate predecessor (in this case their own strict Formalism) and a harking back to one more distant, less directly related: a purified, more stringently selective version of the empirical approach.

Nevertheless, Eikhenbaum's new theoretical formulations were resisted by his friends. They struck Tynyanov as 'Germanic' and Shklovsky as a heresy against Opoyaz. Eikhenbaum's next book on *The Literary Career of Lev Tolstoy*[13] disturbed them further. Tynyanov, now himself deeply concerned with the relationship of biography to the literary process, considered Eikhenbaum's seamless combination of the two to be merely 'flirting' with the problem. Shklovsky complained you could not see 'the instrument' in the work or feel 'the resistance of the material'. Eikhenbaum would have done better, he felt, to write a novel about Tolstoy, following Tynyanov. To the author himself he was more encouraging: 'the book is good, the most interesting part is not about Tolstoy, but about everything round about him. The achievement lies in the fact that this "round about" passes into Tolstoy without a jolt, that he is correctly shown as the point

---

[10] This extract from Eikhenbaum's diary for 15 December 1925 is translated from Chudakova's quotation from archival sources; see Chudakova, 'Sotsial'naia praktika', p. 111.

[11] Iu. Tynianov, *Problemy stikhotvornogo iazyka*, *Voprosy poetiki*, Vypusk V, Academia (Leningrad, 1924), p. 10. The Russian word is *vzaimodeistvie*.

[12] Viktor Shklovskii, *Khod konia* (Berlin and Moscow, 1923). The knight in chess is free to move backwards or forwards across the board, one square straight, the second diagonally; at a tangent, that is, from the original direction. Shklovsky compares this pattern to the development of author-figures across the board of the 'literary process'.

[13] B. Eikhenbaum, *Literaturnaia kari'era L'va Tolstogo*, published as *Lev Tol'stoi*, 2 vols (Leningrad, 1928–31).

of intersection of lines of force.'[14] He added, however, that the biographical element as such should have been approached with more rigour and suggested that Eikhenbaum should have explained precisely why he had excluded some aspects of Tolstoy's life instead of simply passing over them in silence.

What the friends really objected to was the ease with which Eikhenbaum recombined the 'series' so recently and so painstakingly separated. It was in large part on this disagreement that their grand project to produce a collective study of the history of Russian literature from the Formalist point of view eventually foundered. The principal contributors to such a study were to have been Eikhenbaum, Jakobson, Tynyanov, and Shklovsky. As we have seen, Eikhenbaum was already impatient of the constraints of pure Formalism. Tynyanov visited Jakobson in Czechoslovakia in 1928–9 and, encouraged by Shklovsky, they produced the *Prague Theses*, intended as a manifesto to resurrect Opoyaz with all the original membership but also as a defence of Formalist doctrine against erosion from within. Viktor Zhirmunsky, the chairman of the Series of History of Verbal Arts who had published *Voprosy poetiki*, was inclining to Eikhenbaum, whose 'literary environment' amounted to 'the most vulgar Marxism', as Shklovsky put it in a letter to Jakobson on 16 February 1929.

The *Prague Theses* of 1928 stated that the present crisis could only be resolved 'by way of analysis of the relationship between the literary series and other historical series' and denounced any such analysis undertaken 'without taking into account the immanent laws of each system' as 'methodologically pernicious'. In other words, the purists required that the literary fact be admitted as a proper subject for study only when its precise contribution to the literary process could be clearly delineated, whereas Eikhenbaum's literary environment created atmosphere and stimulated the literary process in a way which could be intuited and left vague. On 5 March 1929 Tynyanov wrote to Shklovsky: 'It is essential to be aware of biography in a way that sees it harnessed to the history of literature and not running alongside like a foal'.[15]

This was all very well for Tynyanov, whose biographical novels in the free fictional genre behave precisely like loose foals running gloriously free of the 'history of literature', kicking up their heels for sheer joy. 'Where

---

[14] These and other fragments from the correspondence are quoted in Chudakova, 'Sotsial'naia praktika', while partially published earlier as a supplement to Shklovsky's memoirs and in *Voprosy literatury*, XII (1984), 185–218. Shklovsky (*Khod konia*, p. 22) had already made the point that the creator of a work of art is 'simply the geometrical point of intersection of forces operative outside him'.

[15] See n. 14.

the document runs out is where I take over', he said.[16] But he was steeped in the documents[17] and too much in love with his heroes to abuse his freedom:

> The urge to get to know them better and to understand them more deeply— that was what my fiction was to me. And I think still that artistic literature is distinguished from history not by 'making things up' but by a greater, closer, and more involved understanding of people and events, by greater concern for them.[18]

Essentially, the *Prague Theses* insisted on the difference between the live foal and the anatomical drawing, not between the foal and its decorously harnessed dam who must surely, after all, belong to the same 'series'.

The task of writing a collective *History of Russian Literature* would thus have proved beyond them, even had exterior pressures not intervened in the form of opposition to Formalism on the part of the authorities. By 1930 Opoyaz was no longer a geographically or ideologically cohesive group. Jakobson remained abroad, concentrated increasingly on linguistics, and eventually emigrated to the United States. Brik, always a bureaucrat at heart, steered a dodgy course between the life of a literary functionary and the Cheka (secret police), though, to his credit, he defended his friends and the posthumous reputation of Lili's lover Mayakovsky as best he could. Shklovsky, who said of himself that, had he been stranded on a desert island, he would have become not Robinson Crusoe but a monkey, adapted. Zhirmunsky, Tomashevsky, and Eikhenbaum pursued distinguished academic careers and evolved towards a methodology that preserved standards and considerable integrity, yet did not openly challenge the Marxist approach. Tynyanov, who early fell victim to multiple sclerosis and found it difficult to visit libraries as his physical condition deteriorated, dedicated himself increasingly to film and fiction. The failure to revive Opoyaz, if failure it was, exceeded such details of biography and group biography. It was indeed a part of the 'literary process'. The fact that Mikhail Bakhtin, a friend and colleague who developed separately from the Formalists but in full awareness of their contribution to the theory of literary criticism, came to stress the 'dialogical relationship' between life and literature, and that Yury Lotman, founder of the Tartu school of semiotics, extended the study of text to the study of 'semiosphere', suggests that the problem of isolating the 'literary series' has proved persistently

[16] Tynianov, *Kak my pishem* (Leningrad, 1930), p. 160.
[17] This point is made with great expertise by A. Belinkov, *Iurii Tynianov* (Moscow, 2nd edn, 1965), pp. 501–2 and *passim*.
[18] Tynianov, *Sochineniia v trekh tomakh*, ed. B. O. Kosteliants (Moscow and Leningrad, 1959), I, 9. All quotations from Tynyanov's novels in the second part of this essay refer to this three-volume edition (hereafter *Soch.*). Translations are my own.

intractable. So also does Tynyanov's practice as a writer of historical novels about writers which, with *Pushkin*, comes close to literary biography.

Practice

Tynyanov's three historical novels, *Kyukhlya*, *The Death of Vazir-Mukhtar* (about Aleksandr Griboedov), and the unfinished *Pushkin*, were intended as a trilogy.[19] They are all firmly rooted in Tynyanov's specialism, although the interaction between specialism and fiction differs, as we shall see, from book to book. In early papers for Vengerov's seminar and in a series of articles published between 1920 and 1929, Tynyanov examined in minute detail Pushkin's literary relationship with Küchelbecker and Griboedov and clearly felt a compulsion to cover the same period and *dramatis personae* in a series of interconnected novels. However, whereas he discovered Küchelbecker's lost archive and edited and published his *Lyrics and Poems*, *Dramatic Works* and *Verses* after writing *Kyukhlya*, Tynyanov had done substantial work on Pushkin before embarking on the poet's life. Academic research continued in tandem with his work on the first two parts: 'Childhood' and 'The Lycée'. Not surprisingly, further discoveries about Küchelbecker tend to invade *Pushkin* and it is possible that, had he lived, Tynyanov would have revised not only *Pushkin* Part 3 but all his previous work. But then we should have had different books.

What we do have must suffice: a masterly evocation of an epoch in which few facts were not 'literary'. Even those that appear at first reading unwieldy, dreary, and dull (Kyukhlya's life in exile; Pushkin's boring and unnerving day withstanding police attempts to enlist him as an informer; Griboedov's tortuous politicking and preoccupation with his mother's debts) are shown as anti-literary rather than a-literary. The novels contain only glancing references to written works, with which it is assumed the reader is familiar, albeit that some works are little known, even to the Russian reader. Yet the interplay between action and poetry is constant, not only because the protagonists live to write and everything is grist to their mill (or, in the case of Griboedov, food for apathy and spleen), but also thanks to Tynyanov's mastery of device and the nervous rhythms of

---

[19] *Kyukhlya* was first published in Leningrad in 1925; *The Death of Vazir-Mukhtar* first appeared in serialized form in the Leningrad journal *Zvezda* in 1927–8 and as a book in 1929; *Pushkin* was partially serialized in journals during the author's lifetime, and then published with the unrevised third part 'Youth' as vol. III of Tynianov's *Selected Works* (*Izbrannye proizvedeniia*) in Moscow in 1956. Belinkov considers that 'Youth' should have been published under some such title as 'Extracts and Sketches' or 'Rough Drafts' (see his *Iurii Tynianov*, Moscow, 1965, p. 512).

his prose. Immediacy is achieved by the cinematic cross-cutting of scenes from close-up to crowd and often startlingly angled 'shots' (as in Rodchenko's photographs or Eisenstein's films). Expectation is aroused by the use of poetic and mythic signs, rhythmically repeated. Suspense is exacerbated by digression and 'retardation'; tension is relieved by humour. In the cases of Küchelbecker and Griboedov, the quixotic heroes are supported and offset by archetypal Sancho-Panza-like body servants, who provide a commonsensical double-take on their impractical aristocratic masters. Direct speech is freely imagined, effortlessly and unobtrusively stylized so that we are neither jolted by anachronism nor slowed down by clumsy archaisms.

Anecdotal incidents familiar to the Russian reader are 'made strange'. For instance, when the schoolboy Pushkin recites the famous stanzas for which he was 'blessed on his way' by Derzhavin, we do not hear the expected words. The incident, described in both *Kyukhlya* and *Pushkin*, is brought to life in the first by Küchelbecker's jealous rivalry and, in the second, by the suddenly aroused attention of a senile, weak-bladdered Derzhavin who is having difficulty sitting through a wearisome ceremony in his uncomfortable court clothes. Similarly, Pushkin's encounter with the ox-cart bearing Griboedov's mutilated remains from Tehran to Tiflis, the subject of a famous picture by Martiros Sarian, is given weight by its positioning at the end of *The Death of Vazir-Mukhtar*. But the scene is presented kinetically (Pushkin is past the cart by the time realization dawns and he turns his head to look after the plodding oxen) and interwoven with the fabric of the trilogy by the conceit that the playwright is truly present not in the vegetable-box-like coffin containing the composite body of 'Griboed' (of which only one arm and beringed hand in fact belong to the tsar's ambassador), but in the thoughts and dreams of those who valued him: of Küchelbecker in his prison cell; of the young Georgian wife pregnant with his stillborn child; of his Petersburg lover; and of Pushkin himself. Interrelated as they are, each book is complete in itself (*Pushkin* remained unfinished at 554 pages owing to Tynyanov's illness and early death, but that is a different kind of incompleteness). Each book has not only a different integral narrative structure and plot but deals with a different subject, not in the Formalist sense of 'siuzhet' as 'plot', but in the sense of underlying theme. *Pushkin* is perhaps a different genre.

The subject of *Kyukhlya* is the essential importance of the disinterested, creative human being—whether or not he appears a failure to his contemporaries. It comes across all the more strongly because presented in the form of a string of vivid, exotic, exciting, and richly comic incidents, related at breathtaking pace. The narrative, the misadventures of Wilhelm Küchelbecker, begins with a failed elopement at the age of fourteen interwoven with a family conference at which the fateful decision is taken to send 'dear Vilya' to the new Lycée in Tsarskoe Selo. The Lycée, dreamt up by Alexander I's liberal minister Speransky to educate citizens worthy of a country on the brink of introducing democratic representative government and abolishing serfdom, is the key formative environment for both Küchel-becker and Pushkin. In the first novel, it is presented from a point of view very close to that of the youthful Kyukhlya, enlarged by aperçus into other minds: for example, the speech made by the radical teacher Kunitsin at the opening ceremony is followed by the reactions to it of the royal family and ministers unfriendly to Speransky. The schoolboy journal, *The Lycée Sage*, permitted as a controllable outlet for the abundant creativity of the pupils, provides material from which Tynyanov takes off merrily into direct speech and vivid description to establish Kyukhlya's position as a likeable butt, quick-tempered, vulnerable, at times suicidal, but never one to bear a grudge. The stammering, gangling lad first finds refuge in poetry but gradu-ally forms friendships with other poets among the boys: notably Anton Delvig and Pushkin. The narrative tempo, sped on by staccato simple sentences, is suddenly slowed to stopping-point by a rare quotation. 'I wrote it for you to remember us by, Wilhelm', Pushkin says, and recites his mellifluous 'Separation' in a 'different', hesitant voice:

> He finished; Kyukhlya shut his eyes. He burst into tears, then impetuously jumped up and hugged Pushkin, who was shorter than he by two heads, to his chest,—and so they stood for a moment, saying nothing, lost.
> That was the end of the lycée. (*Soch.*, I, 53)

Uncertain what he wants to do, but consumed by ambition to serve some great civic cause (whether in Italy, Greece, or Russia) and to write great poetry in the archaic style, 'Khlebopekar' (as General Yermolov translates the German surname in affectionate acknowledgement of the young poet's slavophile enthusiasms) travels abroad and in the Caucasus, falls foul of the tsar's secret service, the Third Department, survives several cloak-and-dagger attempts on his life inspired by their agents, and tries his own hand at political assassination during the Decembrist uprising, only to discover, at the critical moment, that he has failed to keep his powder dry. Police at first arrest the wrong man, washing the indignant suspect's hair repeatedly because the colour is the only feature that does not correspond to their official description, penned by Kyukhlya's colleague, the pusillaminous journalist Bulgarin. Aided and abetted by peasants on the family estate, his sister, and his innocent Dulcinea-like lady love, Kyukhlya embarks with his man-servant on a tragi-comic dash to the border, where he is taken and returned to years of solitary confinement in the Peter-Paul fortress. His Dulcinea, a faithful intercessor and correspondent throughout this period, cannot face the humdrum life of exile in the Siberian village to which the poet is finally consigned. Her image, as she came to speed him on his escape in the wintry woods, is with him always, 'bright-cheeked from the frost with cold lips, laughing and crying' (*Soch.*, I, 271), but Kyukhlya weds an unprepossessing Aldonsa and engenders a family who, after his death, succeed in losing the manuscripts on which, throughout all his vicissitudes, he had never ceased to work.

Küchelbecker's obscurity allowed Tynyanov's imagination free play, yet knowledge of the period infuses every sentence: 'Complete certainty that that is precisely how it was and not otherwise is necessary for the work' he once wrote, adding: 'for the novelist the most important thing is to have a sufficiently clear attitude to what is already known and in the public domain, to be able to make *in*tensive use of what, in reading, is normally used *ex*tensively'.[20] Neither pastiche nor parody, *Kyukhlya* is a tragic *bouffonnerie* which builds up to a bold, strategically envisaged crisis, 'the war of the squares' where the Decembrist rising foregathers, disintegrates, and crumbles. The hero's subsequent fate is recounted with tact, affection, and restraint.

The Death of Vazir-Mukhtar corresponds more closely to Eikhenbaum's definition of the trilogy genre as 'historical novels' rather than 'literary biography', and it is not hard to understand why the English translator, A. Brown, called his abridged version *Death and Diplomacy in Persia* (1938). Griboedov, the Vazir-Mukhtar of the title, writes nothing but letters and reports in the period covered by the book, neither is the story a biography in the true sense of the word. The action begins in December 1825. Griboedov, the author of the sparkling comedy in verse *Woe from Wit* and several failed tragedies, is already a spent force, although he does not fully realize this. In *Kyukhlya* he figures briefly in the Caucasian chapters as a friend of Küchelbecker and the maverick General Yermolov. Disgusted by the sight of his own heavy Moscow furs, already touched by some inward lethargy, Griboedov refuses at the last moment to accompany his friend back to the capital and so misses the Decembrist rising. An advocate of the 'biographical approach' might have played on the notion that Griboedov's Chatsky, the hero of *Woe from Wit*, is in part modelled on Küchelbecker, but this is emphatically not Tynyanov's way. An intimacy is established— no more.

As the second novel opens, Griboedov, having completed a peace mission to Persia, is introduced to the reader as a successful diplomat about to set out from Georgia, where he enjoys the protection of a powerful relative, to harvest the fruits of his labours in St Petersburg and to propose

---

[20] Tynianov, *Literaturnyi Leningrad*, LVIII (21 November 1934), here quoted from B. Kostelants's notes to Tynianov's *Pushkin*, *Soch.*, III, 559.

an eminently sensible project for the extension of trade between Persia, Russia, and the Caucasus. Medals and money come his way, but the 'project' is stillborn and he himself, a friend to many Decembrists and author of a subversive play, is regarded with suspicion. The upshot of his attempts to serve his country is to be sent back to Persia on a mission impossible. Here, with the connivance if not at the instigation of the British mission, he is murdered and dismembered by a fanatical mob.

Such is the narrative. The subject is death, a lingering poetic death of the spirit flowing towards sensational political assassination as towards an end long foreseen which there is no point in trying to evade. 'He was embittered and good-natured', is how Tynyanov describes the man as he goes through the motions of visiting his mother and his old patron Yermolov, of taking new lovers and meeting old friends. Griboedov allows himself to be cut out by his own half-brother and servant with a village wench, absentmindedly espouses an exquisite Georgian princess, plays the part of ambassador to the shah with dignity and dash—but without enthusiasm. A dead soul, with doom and poetry all about him. Through the account of the long journey from north to south, ill omens which accompany the setting out of the Russian host in the Igor lay ring like a refrain and the reader is painfully conscious also of the Gogol-like subtext. Even Griboedov's chosen form of transport, the *brichka*, is the same as that of Gogol's hero, Chichikov, the pedlar of 'dead souls'. As in Gogol's epic *poema*, the long narrative tapestry of the journey is embroidered with Homeric incident:

> An old soldier was sitting in a sentry box by the wayside, asleep.
> 'Grandad, what are you doing here?'
> 'On guard.'
> 'What are you guarding?'
> 'The road.'
> 'Who set you to guard the road here?'
> 'On the orders of Emperor Paul.'
> 'Paul?'
> 'Thirty years now I have been on guard. I went to the town to enquire, they say there's a paper about rations, but the order's lost. So I stay on guard.'
> 'So they left you at your post?'
> 'What else? I told you, the order was lost. I sent in a petition five years ago—no answer. They issue the rations.' (*Soch.*, II, 158)

A longer set-piece within the main story is the 'soldier's tale' about the legendary Russian deserter Samson, the extradition of whose person and retinue Griboedov is under orders to negotiate with the shah. The harem and the eunuch's story provide colourful oriental digressions.

Griboedov's entry into Tehran, without his pince-nez, astride a borrowed black stallion, is superbly told from the point of view of a shortsighted man conscious of the imperative to present a dignified figure even when confronted with a kneeling elephant, massed bands and dancers, and a crowd which wails unaccountably: 'Ya Hussein! Va Hussein!' and melts before him. Griboedov did not know that the slayer of the holy Imam Hussein, the accursed Ibn-Saad, had entered the city on a black stallion.

As in *Kyukhlya*, the climax is a brilliant, cinematic, multiple-viewpoint crowd scene. Only the end, the brief encounter with Pushkin already described, restores the almost puppet-like Griboedov in his stiff diplomatic garments and steel pince-nez to his true setting: the hearts and minds of his scattered friends and the freedom of literature.

In these two complete novels, Tynyanov achieves his aim of keeping separate the artistic and imaginative *in*tensive use of documentary material from the *ex*tensive study of the literary process. With Pushkin, this task was to prove more difficult. There was a wealth of new material exhumed by Tynyanov and others in connection with the centenary of the poet's death in 1937. While working on his 'fictional' *Pushkin*, he wrote his articles 'Pushkin and Küchelbecker' (1934) and 'Pushkin's Prose' (1937), as well as 'Nameless Love' (1939), which treats academically the essentially biographical problem of the identity of the addressee of one of the poet's most beautiful elegies, a problem which, in the heyday of Formalism, Tomashevsky had been content to regard as a literary construct, a poetic mystification. Tynyanov envisaged *Pushkin* as a work of more than one volume which would explore the poet's ancestry, then follow him from the cradle to the grave and beyond: 'For you see, Pushkin himself as the greatest literary phenomenon of the last century does not end with his physical death', Tynyanov told a correspondent of *Literaturny Leningrad* in November 1934. If the book as it was planned can be said to have a narrative structure or plot, it is the life and times of Aleksandr Pushkin. If the book as it stands can be said to have a subject or theme it is the interaction, albeit the tangential interaction, of life and literature. Tynyanov does not quote from well-known works nor show us Pushkin writing specific masterpieces, but he re-creates the life through the poetry as well as through the documents so that every incident is vibrant and alive, a part of the creative process. The book differs from Elaine Feinstein's *Pushkin* (1998) not only in that it is much fuller but because it is written with empathy rather than detachment. The life is allowed to tell itself, free of comment or interjection from the biographer.

Yet, in spite of the inevitable contamination between the study of literature and the historical novel, Tynyanov's *Pushkin* is different, and not only because it is free of academic apparatus. Less episodic than *Kyukhlya*, less selective than *The Death of Vazir-Mukhtar*, more conventionally biographical, the book is also more 'literary'; for Pushkin, consumed by

literature, changed everything he touched and all that touched on him to
'literary fact'. Yet Pushkin the human being is more compellingly present
in Tynyanov's 'novel' than in any conventional literary biography. This is
achieved, I think, by showing, in a very physical and intimate way, the
gradual build-up of conflicting pressure between the poet and his epoch,
the interaction of the individual with great historical events such as the
burning of Moscow, the defeat of Napoleon, the sickeningly gradual erosion
of the high hopes for liberalization in Russia fostered by the whole ambience of the Lycée.

'War! War!' Pushkin mutters to himself, determined to combat this
erosion of Lycée principles, if only on the field of literature. A less *engagé*
biographer might have given us something in the nature of 'Pushkin from
then on engaged in constant literary polemics'. Constantly the poet's genius
breaks the frame of the merely literary, reflecting, albeit obliquely, the
travail of his time and country. Tynyanov, also reflecting the 'literary facts'
of his own time and place, sick to death and hungry in the evacuation
during World War II as he completed the third part of his *Pushkin*, was no
longer in total control of the genre he had invented for the minor characters
of his trilogy. Indeed, it must be remembered that Tynyanov died before
he could see the third part into print and while still making alterations to
the published 'Childhood' and 'Lycée' sections. Nevertheless, whether or
not the result was one of which the authors of the *Prague Theses* would
have wholeheartedly approved, it does offer a remarkable synthesis of life
and literature, not coldly juxtaposed, but smelted in the emotional furnace
of the biographer's commitment to his subject.

Pushkin the child is ill with poetry. He chews his pencils. When a stupid
tutor reads out his verses at the family table, the boy attacks him physically.
His illiterate nanny slips Voltaire into his satchel as though his father's little
book were a favourite teddy bear. The satanic verses he writes at the Lycée
end in high fever, resolved only by a visit from his mother. The creative
process is felt as delirium:

> [I]t was like an illness; he was in a state of torment, chasing words, beset by
> rhymes. Then he would read through and be astonished: the words were not
> what he wanted. He would cross out word after word. The rhymes remained.
> He began to grow used to the words being not what he wanted, to there
> being too many of them. He could not stop writing, but then in deep despair
> he would tear it up. [. . .] He read nothing to anyone. It seemed as hard for
> him to admit to poetry as to a crime. (*Soch.*, III, 294)

The school nickname of 'Monkey with Tiger' is amply justified by the sheer
physicality of the swarthy, passionate youth. As his fencing master says,
Pushkin fights in earnest, as though practice with foils were a real duel.

With a rapier, as in poetry, he is 'aggressive, evasive, sudden and swift'. (*Soch.*, III, 392)

Great historical events are not allowed to overwhelm the personal. For the students at the Lycée, the young men mustering to fight Napoleon are personified by Kaverin, a friend of the liberal teacher Kunitsyn, whom they experience as an older brother going off to war:

> [A] young volunteer-officer galloped by flat out along the verge, almost running them down; he was chopping at the wet branches with his sabre, the branches sprang back in his face, his eye closed, he was laughing. [...] a green branch was caught up in his cross, water and tears flowed down his cheeks. He was chewing a green leaf with his white teeth and was, it appeared, drunk. His face was utterly childish. He smiled. (*Soch.*, III, 341-2)

Later that night, after Kaverin has returned to his unit, 'Pushkin suddenly wanted to go and catch him up—looking out on the road, he began to think where he might get hold of a horse. Then, reluctantly, went back to sleep' (ibid.).

Pushkin's frivolous parents and the butterfly uncle Vasiliy Lvovich, who escorted him to the Lycée and wrote light verse, flee the fire of Moscow, abandoning their homes, clothes, and possessions. The director of the Lycée explains this is nothing to worry about:

> 'It will soon be over now', he said calmly. 'Everyone thinks it was the French burnt Moscow. They're wrong. The French aren't mad. Moscow is being burnt by the Russian. They hurt him to the quick, maddened, wounded, goaded him, and he'll burn everything, die in the flames himself, but the guests won't come out of it alive either.'
> Aleksander, mouth open, stared at him. That was something quite new, and he didn't yet understand. (*Soch.*, III, 366)

Everyone thinks that the Lycée is to be evacuated on its first anniversary, but instead the pupils are assembled to hear the good news: 'On the anniversary of this Lycée, the nineteenth day of October, Napoleon Bonaparte quit Moscow' (*Soch.*, III, 383). Before the spring thaw, Russian troops are in Paris and the first director of the Lycée dies in harness, happy that under him the school has been 'free of the spirit of sycophancy' (*Soch.*, III, 392). Kunitsyn and his pupils expect from day to day the emancipation of the serfs and sweeping reforms, but already Arakcheev is in the ascendant and the tsar, when he can spare a moment from Foreign Affairs, is anxious only to maintain the status quo.

When Pushkin eventually leaves the Lycée, he is already a fully fledged member of Arzamas, a protégé of Karamzin's, and, according to Tynyanov's unproven theory, hopelessly in love with the old historian's thirty-six-year-old wife. Unlike Tynyanov, the young Pushkin identifies conservatism in literature (as advocated by the journal *Beseda*) with creeping conservatism

in politics and listens spellbound to the witty and sceptical Westernizer
Chaadaev. Some of his friends are already preparing themselves for resistance, but Pushkin, absorbed by the poetic battle, is not of their councils.
A visit to Mikhailovskoe, the scene of a later exile, allows him to complete
his first great success, the poem *Ruslan and Lyudmila* but, before he can
see it published, the newly emancipated schoolboy has become involved
with courtesans and theatrical intrigue and has fallen foul of a minister
thanks to a bawdy epigram. The Establishment decides the reprobate poet
should be sent for a soldier or exiled to Spain, perhaps, or to Siberia.
Thanks to Karamzin, he is merely packed off to the Crimea to serve in a
government department under the care of a family friend. Tynyanov makes
of the journey into exile a hymn to the promise of Russia, not the
country of dead souls traversed by Griboedov *after* 1825, but a vast land
of infinite variety, with great rivers, healing waters, the exotic beauty of
the Crimean coast. Sailing the Black Sea, Pushkin writes the elegy for his
impossible love with the freedom of one who may be putting pen to paper
for the last time: 'As one accursed, not daring to mention her name, he
sailed on, full of power, drunk with the recollection of everything that had
been forbidden, that would remain for ever unfulfilled.' (*Soch.*, III, 554).

The symbol of this pre-1825 Russia is not an old soldier left on guard
by a forgetful government, but the escape attempted by two convicts the
poet witnesses on the way south:

> And now he, Pushkin, had been exiled here, so that here and nowhere else
> he might witness the thirst for freedom that could make two men shackled
> together swim forward at furious speed.
> Long live the Lycée! (*Soch.*, III, 554)

Having brilliantly debunked 'the biographical approach', the Formalists
themselves and Tynyanov among them proved unable to resist the attrac-
tions of biography *per se*, or to separate the life of a man who lived to
write from his work. In practice, this was neither failure nor compromise.
The liberation of the imagination in Tynyanov's 'historical novels', coupled
with his own insistence on the significance of the 'literary fact', imbued his
last unfinished biography of Russia's greatest writer and his evocation of
one of the most hopeful periods of her history with unrivalled poetic
intensity and artistic control. There is no obligatory optimism here, no
astute premonition of, and compliance with, Zhdanov's 'no-conflict' theories, as has been implied by some critics. The third part of *Pushkin* is a
product not of extra-literary political pressure but of a combination of
'literary facts' contingent on the life of the biographer: World War II, when,
for a short period, as Pasternak tells us, the weather cleared and writers

wrote what they felt. Like his Pushkin in the Crimea, but with more reason, Tynyanov was writing 'as though it were the last thing he was destined to write' (*Soch.*, III, 553).

10

Freud and the Art of Biography

MALCOLM BOWIE

'When psycho-analysis puts itself at the service of biography, it naturally has the right to be treated no more harshly than the latter itself' (XXI, 212), Freud announced in his speech of acceptance on being awarded the Goethe prize in 1930.[1] The defensive note that is to be heard in this remark had often sounded in his earlier accounts of artistic creativity: if psychoanalysis fails to throw any light on the riddle of the artist's 'miraculous gift' (XXI, 211), then it is no more culpable than biography, which is routinely defeated by the same riddle. The artist's gift makes his works worth studying, and his life-story worth narrating, but it is precisely this element in his character that is most resistant to being understood. Writing in this mood, Freud has no words of encouragement for biographers as a professional community. They are bound by the bleak imperative that he had issued to his fellow analysts at the start of his essay on 'Dostoevsky and Parricide' (1928): 'Before the problem of the creative artist analysis must, alas, lay down its arms' (XXI, 177). If creativity is inscrutable, and the artist's gift a mere given, then there is little hope that the appreciation of art-works themselves could be enhanced by either group of practitioners. Biographers and analysts are alike not only in the curiosity they direct at Goethe, Dostoevsky, or Shakespeare but in the feelings of hostile rebellion that often accompany their empathizing enthusiasm for such figures. If the

---

[1] With two exceptions (see n. 4), my quotations from Freud's writings are taken from *The Standard Edition of the Complete Psychological Works*, translated from the German under the general editorship of James Strachey, 24 vols (The Hogarth Press and the Institute of Psycho-Analysis, 1953–74). Volume and page references to the Standard Edition are given in my main text.

two groups are equals in ambivalence, and in the certainty of defeat, in a sense their story ends there, and there is little point in adding plaintive postscripts to it.

What is surprising about Freud in this mood is that he seems to want to disconnect himself from the life-historical components of his own doctrine, and to understate the role that the writing of lives has had in clinical psychoanalysis from the beginning. But if we re-establish this larger perspective within Freud's career, and pay attention first of all to the ordinary rather than to the illustrious lives against which he tested his theory, psychoanalysis may be seen to offer the biographer a series of new insights and incitements—and a call to arms rather than to surrender.

The whole of clinical psychoanalysis belongs, in one notable sense, to the biographical arts, for the encounter between 'analysand' and analyst involves the writing and rewriting of a life history on the empty air of the consulting-room. The two parties are uneasy collaborators. Where the one offers a report on experience and on the associations to which key images and episodes give rise, the other is required by the conventions of his professional association to comply imperfectly with the analysand's wishes, and sometimes to be plain awkward.

The analyst's aim is to allow his conversational partner to recollect material that had previously been repressed, and in so doing reconstruct a lost epoch of his childhood history. Yet, precisely because the material involved is painful, the patient may be expected to resist the onset of full recollection and new knowledge of his own past; as the analyst gets close to the traumatic core of the patient's early experiences, the patient may react 'with an unmistakable aggravation of his symptoms and his general condition' ('Constructions in Analysis', 1937, XXIII, 265).

The spoken contributions of the practitioner, to say nothing of his silences, are therefore likely to be double-edged instruments for anyone who enters analytic therapy in search of a smooth, through-composed autobiographical narrative. On the one hand those contributions may seem to offer useful connective tissue and an overall sense that the patient's narrative is on the move towards a satisfactory dénouement, but on the other they may block, divert, or disfigure the emerging pattern and induce panic in the patient. The words of the analyst, even when they place benign constructions or interpretations upon the patient's self-descriptive speech, may strike their recipient as misguided or inept. Suddenly, the analyst is a rival storyteller rather than a co-worker. He is telling the wrong tale.

The consulting-room is a tension-filled biographical workshop, therefore, and the lessons it contains for the writer of biographies do not at first seem in themselves particularly rewarding. The psychoanalytic dialogue as announced, practised, and codified by Freud in the early years of the twentieth century suggests that the raw materials of an individual's life always occupy disputed territory and that a plurality of interpretations could play upon them indefinitely. The clearest practical guideline to be derived by the biographer from Freud's own accounts of the therapeutic method he pioneered is that a certain elasticity of personal response to one's protagonist is always likely to be beneficial. Do not impose a premature scheme upon him or her, avoid simplistic plot-structures, and give your own hard work of construal a role in the story you are setting out to tell. Unexceptionable imperatives such as these do not, however, take us very far in understanding either the air of impending scandal that surrounds the teachings of psychoanalysis or the proliferation of biographical works claiming some sort of Freudian allegiance or pedigree. To begin to grasp the reasons why Freud's 'talking cure' should have come to seem both disreputable and alluring to the writer of lives, both a cautionary tale and an inspiration, we need to look beyond the clinical consultation itself and the benign-seeming conversational contract that governs it.

Freud as the deviser of a distinctive clinical technique speaks of its two golden rules, and of the symmetry that exists between them: the patient says 'whatever he likes' (*Five Lectures on Psycho-Analysis*, 1910, XI, 32), and the analyst listens with 'evenly-suspended attention' ('Recommendations to Physicians Practising Psycho-Analysis', 1912, XII, 111). No coercion, no officious striving towards a preordained goal, is to cast its shadow over this sunlit scene of interlocution. The dangerous excitement offered by psychoanalysis to participants and outside observers alike comes, however, from a different source and concerns the intellectual rather than the social and interpersonal manners that it enjoins upon its adherents. Throughout his long career, Freud insisted upon the principles of simplicity and parsimony both in scientific explanation and in the therapeutic process. Nature, for Freud as for Newton, did not luxuriate in superfluous causes, and when it came to that corner of the natural order in which human minds and their characteristic sufferings were to be found, one causal fountainhead took priority over all others: the early life of the child within the family group. It was in the force-field of the family as experienced by the young child that the explanation for neurotic misery was to be discovered, and it was by way of an experimental re-creation of that field that psychoanalytic therapy was able to alleviate or in some cases eliminate the patient's ills.

Without becoming excessively parsimonious in the attempt to explain Freud's appeal to certain biographers, one could say that this recourse to early childhood as the seat of psychological causes has obvious practical advantages for them as they organize their narratives. An adult life is such a tangled affair, with so many disparate strands running through it, that almost any simplifying mechanism will be welcome. Particularly welcome will be a mechanism that is not imposed from without, or borrowed from some imaginary pattern-book of typical life-shapes, but derived directly from the inner fabric of the biographical subject's experience. Through the thicket of the adult subject's professional and personal lives, through the jungle of affective, economic, and socio-political forces in which his individuality is forged and modified, the Freud-inspired biographer can travel with a reliable navigational aid. The early configurations of the individual's libido as contained or discharged within the family group hold the key to his later erotic career. The domestic politics of child and parents confined within a household are to be rediscovered in later life projected on to the wider screen of the individual's public life. If we add to these intellectual benefits the spectacle of the young child as the hero of the Oedipal drama and therefore as a creature of intense and conflicting passions, the charm of psychoanalysis as a biographical aid will begin to seem irresistible. It will be both a scientific procedure and a dramaturgical device. It will allow us to construct hypotheses and theorems that are intellectually convincing but at the same time dark, fateful, and incest-fringed.

Looked at from the viewpoint of life-writing practice, Freud's own case-histories are still remarkable for their exploitation of this double advantage. On the one hand, the merits of Freud's new approach to neurosis were epistemological, and could be laid out before his patients in those terms as their treatment proceeded. Freud was often dealing with educated and sharp-witted patients in the early years, and it made practical sense for him to explain to them his own principles of explanation. 'I took the opportunity of giving him a first glance at the underlying principles of psychoanalytic therapy', Freud announces in the opening chapter of his 'Notes upon a Case of Obsessional Neurosis' (1909), and much of the later reported discussion between clinician and patient has the tone of a leisurely tutorial or seminar:

> I then made some short observations upon *the psychological differences between the conscious and the unconscious*, and upon the fact that everything conscious was subject to a process of wearing-away, while what was unconscious was relatively unchangeable; and I illustrated my remarks by pointing to the antiques standing about in my room. They were, in fact, I said, only objects found in a tomb, and their burial had been their preservation: the destruction of Pompeii was only beginning now that it had been dug up. (X, 176; emphasis in original)

In the ensuing exchanges between Freud and the patient now celebrated as the 'Rat Man', two cool-headed, inquisitive partners in dialogue contemplate together an archaic order of things, and weigh up its possible implications for the present and future. For a moment the tone and indeed the subject matter of their discussion begin to resemble those of the transcendentalized tutorial that is Plato's *Meno*. How much of the individual's present knowledge of the world can be held to derive from an anterior state of his mind or soul? Where Socrates appeals to an antenatal preexistence in which the soul already had full knowledge of the world, Freud appeals to a lost postnatal period of the individual's personal history, but in both cases new knowledge is acquired by a disciplined return to the past. The acts of remembrance triggered by the analytic dialogue, like the slower and more laborious steps by which Socratic recollection is achieved, involve not simply the recovery of lost part-meanings but the restoration of meaning itself in a form that is stable, complete, and immune to doubt. The essential difference between the two modes of retrospection is that where the one plays upon past success, the other plays upon early scenes of inner conflict. Much of Freud's reported conversation with the Rat Man is taken up with the attempt to persuade him that the remembering of terrifying early events can indeed bring a fortunate epistemic outcome rather than a simple rekindling and prolongation of his pain.

On the other hand, however, Freud's narrative draws upon a whole gamut of Jacobean intensities and transgressions in its portrayal of his patient's troubled family history, bringing the quest for scientific knowledge bizarrely close at times to melodrama and *grand guignol*:

> Once when the patient was visiting his father's grave he had seen a big beast, which he had taken to be a rat, gliding along over the grave. He assumed that it had actually come out of his father's grave, and had just been having a meal off his corpse. The notion of a rat is inseparably bound up with the fact that it has sharp teeth with which it gnaws and bites. But rats cannot be sharp-toothed, greedy and dirty with impunity: they are cruelly persecuted and mercilessly put to death by man, as the patient had often observed with horror. He had often pitied the poor creatures. (X, 215–16)

Reportage slips seamlessly into interpretation in writing of this kind. However faithfully the patient had adhered to the rule of free association during his sessions, Freud's report is the product of an elaborate selection procedure and firmly applied criteria of relevance. The mundane concerns of the patient and the ambient life of the imperial capital are winnowed away in favour of 'key' incidents, fantasies, and dream-images. And the enigma that these selected biographemes are expected to unlock has as much to do with the central theoretical claims of psychoanalysis itself as with the tenor, by turns frightened and defiant, of the subject's behaviour. Even as rats scurry across a father's grave, a new science is being asserted. Its principles are interleaved as maxims into Freud's empirical account, and its humanistic purport is highlighted by references to literature. Real dramas come to the aid of an already dramatized psychological theory: Ibsen's

Little Eyolf has been mentioned earlier in the paragraph quoted, and the third scene of Goethe's *Faust*, Part I is attached in a footnote to the sentence describing the penetrative power of rat's teeth. Even as the Rat Man is being depicted as a main actor in his own nightmares, and anchored to a precise local scene, he is being transferred into the company of Mephistopheles and Ibsen's Rat-Wife, and becoming a lesser character in an altogether different play. This play has the emergence of a new mental science as its theme, and a combined researcher and clinician as its hero.

It would be unwise to make too much of the foreshortening to which Freud subjects his biographical material here and in the equally famous case-histories of 'Dora' and 'Little Hans'. All three works belong to the first, highly inventive phase of the psychoanalytic project, during which a new kind of theory required a new and still uncertain kind of corroborative support. Abstract claims about the causes of neurosis needed to be tested in the crucible of individual lives, and it is hardly surprising that those claims should be present as a series of eager iterations inside Freud's biographical reports proper. The commentator who looks back with a century of hindsight to the characteristic style of argument to be found in these documents will of course find that they have elements of violence, hyperbole, and self-fulfilling prophecy. Such a style is perhaps to be expected from any author having startling new propositions to announce and many detractors standing vigilantly by.

Yet even when allowances have been made for the assertiveness of a young science, to say nothing of the distinctive 'branding' that a new therapy may require, there is still something strange about the speed with which Freud withdraws, in these narratives, from the troublesome textures of ordinary experience. The psychoanalytic view of things calls for an elaborate two-way mapping between reconstructed childhood scenes and the emotional contours of later life, and this process involves sifting through large quantities of potentially instructive material. But the selectivity of this approach is uncompromising: material that proves upon examination to have no value of this retrospective-prospective kind is simply discarded. Biographical data deemed irrelevant to the patient's obsessional idea is not kept in a separate archive pending its inspection through a different lens, but removed once and for all from the scene of enquiry. This does not mean that the case-history overall is undernourished by empirical data. On the contrary, it is alive with literary, linguistic, and geographical lore. Weasels rather than rats plague the principal Viennese cemetery, Freud notes; the association between rats and erotism is to be found in the engravings by Alfred Le Poittevin known as *Diableries érotiques*; and verbal bridges connect *Ratten* ('rats') with *Raten* ('instalments'), *Spielratte* ('gambler'), and *heiraten* ('to marry'). But information of this kind, while giving the patient's main symptoms an extraordinary cultural depth and density, blots out the rest of him. The symptom is an ingeniously coded message, and glory belongs to whoever has the ingenuity—and the cultural knowledge—to decipher it.

During the period of the classic case-histories (1901–9), in which the lives of ordinary people presenting themselves as patients were being reduced and schematized in this way, Freud was already beginning to sketch out the seemingly quite different set of biographical opportunities with which the present essay began. Perhaps the new science indeed had some-thing of importance to say about celebrated lives too. At the scientific meeting of the Vienna Psychoanalytic Society held on 11 December 1907, for example, Freud was in no doubt that psychoanalysis offered major new insights into the process of artistic creation. The minutes of the meeting record the following as Freud's first response to a paper that had just been read by Max Graf on the psychology of poets: 'Every poet who shows abnormal tendencies can be the object of a pathography. But the pathog-raphy cannot show anything new. Psychoanalysis, on the other hand, provides information about the creative process. Psychoanalysis deserves to rank above pathography'.[2] It is already clear from these reported remarks, and from Freud's contemporaneous published writings on the theme, not only that the great creative artist is the very type of the hero, but that a potent second-order heroism may be claimed by anyone who succeeds in fathoming his creativity. Psychoanalysis studies ambition, and exemplifies it too.

Freud is already, in these early years of the twentieth century, deeply immersed in a pattern of self-flattering identifications that was to remain with him for the rest of his career. It was at this time that he commissioned *The Myth of the Birth of the Hero* (1909) from his follower Otto Rank, and offered his own short paper on 'Family Romances' (IX, 237–41) for inclusion in the volume. The studies of Leonardo and Michelangelo were to follow in 1910 and 1913. The figure of Moses was to become a lifelong personal obsession and emblem. The Moses story, whether narrated in the book of Exodus, renarrated by Rank as the cornerstone of his study, or compressed by Michelangelo into his eloquent statue, was the archetypal tale of heroic action overcoming the inertia of stone, stupidity, or com-placent collective opinion. And it was a tale of family conflict long before it moved on to the public stage. In *Moses and Monotheism* (1939), his last completed book, Freud was still looking back to Rank's tribute and giving prominence to the 'average legend' which connected his own life-story, as

---

[2] Minutes of the Vienna Psychoanalytic Society, vol. I: *1906–1908*, ed. Herman Nunberg and Ernst Federn (New York, 1962), p. 265.

recounted in *The Interpretation of Dreams* (1900) and elsewhere, to the heroic careers of antiquity: 'A hero is someone who has had the courage to rebel against his father and has in the end victoriously overcome him' (XXIII, 12). This 'myth' or 'legend' had the peculiarity of always emerging unscathed from any attempt to discredit it. It was the indestructible and ever-tensile mainspring of creative endeavour. Long before questions of knowledge, skill, technique, or training arose to challenge and delay an emerging singular talent, an attitude, a slant of personality, had to be in place. Before apprenticeship, defiance.

The case-histories and the often fragmentary accounts of great artists show Freud's campaign on behalf of his scandalous new doctrine in two complementary registers. While in the former he descends with relish into the underworld of individual desire, basing his claims for psychoanalysis on its ability to extract meaning from the common stink of humanity, in the latter he propels himself towards the salubrious summits of human achievement. Freud was not at all squeamish in discussions with his patients about the 'low' bodily functions that permeated their dreams and fantasies, and not at all impatient or contemptuous when they seemed to want to preserve rather than demolish their obsessional ideas, but 'grubbing about in human dirt' (*The Interpretation of Dreams*, 1900, V, 470), as he himself called it in a moment of professional soul-searching, could nevertheless be a dispiriting business, especially when its yield of new knowledge or therapeutic benefit was slow to emerge. The psychoanalytic study of high culture and its heroes brought welcome respite from clinical toil. And it conferred intellectual dignity on the entire enterprise. What had begun as a new approach to the neuroses and to no other class of mental affliction was gradually acquiring such breadth of vision that it could look beyond affliction altogether and contemplate the triumphs of the human mind. 'Information about the creative process', as the minutes of the Viennese meeting modestly call it, was the loftiest reward to which Freud aspired and second only to the understanding of dreams among the foundations of his science.[3]

Freud's *Leonardo da Vinci and a Memory of his Childhood* (1910) is extraordinary in many ways, and not least because it contains a lucid lesson on the art of biography, from which all modern practitioners could still benefit. Looking back on his own biographical performance, Freud begins his concluding chapter with a series of general reflections on the biographer's choice of subject. Where other writers could accuse the psychoanalyst of being a simple pathographer and of wishing to reduce a great man to a mere 'nerve case', a far commoner failing among biographers, for Freud,

---

[3] Minutes, p. 265.

is that of removing not just nervous symptoms but all other signs of character and idiosyncrasy from their subjects:

> Biographers are fixated on their heroes in a quite special way. In many cases they have chosen their hero as the subject of their studies because—for reasons of their personal emotional life—they have felt a special affection for him from the very first. They then devote their energies to a task of idealization, aimed at enrolling the great man among the class of their infantile models—at reviving in him, perhaps, the child's idea of his father. To gratify this wish they obliterate the individual features of their subject's physiognomy; they smooth over the traces of his life's struggles with internal and external resistances, and they tolerate in him no vestige of human weakness or imperfection. They thus present us with what is in fact a cold, strange, ideal figure, instead of a human being to whom we might feel ourselves distantly related. That they should do this is regrettable, for they thereby sacrifice truth to an illusion, and for the sake of their infantile phantasies abandon the opportunity of penetrating the most fascinating secrets of human nature. (XI, 130)

These remarks are all the more telling for containing Freud's own *mea culpa*, caught up in his attack on the idealizations and wishful misperceptions in which others indulge. He too has a tendency to idealize his great men, to strip them of their local characteristics, and to offer them up as bland exemplars either of a disembodied creative power or, tautologically, of greatness itself. The challenge that faces any biographer, whether or not he attempts to use a psychoanalytic method in arranging his material, is that of preserving the individuality of his subject while also offering a convincing general vision of the human mind in action.

Freud's study of Leonardo does both things. It examines the minute and contemplates the vast. It clings to the oddities of the Leonardo case and looks beyond them to the fortunes of the *Wisstrieb*, or the 'drive to know', playing itself out in world-historical time. It pursues a great man, corners him, and lets him go. The rhythmic alteration between viewpoints, and the sudden expansions and contractions of Freud's analytic language, make the Leonardo essay into a special sort of fable. Freud himself was prepared to think of the work as a 'psychoanalytic novel' (XI, 134), but it makes more sense in the context of the present volume to think of it as a case-history of the biographical impulse.

For Freud, as he sets to work upon the documentary and pictorial data that Leonardo bequeathed us, eccentricity exists at three levels, each of which harbours an intellectually stimulating puzzle. The first is that of Leonardo's personality: he finds it difficult to finish his projects, spawns an ungovernable wealth of potentialities in his sketches and studies, and vacillates between the artistic and scientific vocations. He looks upon the plenitude of natural forms that the Creator has set before him, now celebrating their variety, now brooding upon his own limited ability to call them to order. The second level is that of his works: he returns often to images of an ambiguously smiling woman, and on occasion—in the *Madonna and Child with St Anne*, for example—to compositions in which this motif is strangely reduplicated and reinforced. Third, there is the singular childhood memory, recorded by Leonardo in one of his scientific notebooks, around which Freud constructs his main tissue of speculation. 'While I was in my cradle', Leonardo had written, 'a vulture came down to me, and opened my mouth with its tail, and struck me many times with its tail inside my lips' (XI, 82). If there are three puzzles in the material, Freud's hope is that there will be one solution, and that a single bold inferential pathway will allow him to connect the personality, the work and the self-contained fragment of reminiscence. Yet far from rushing to the point at which a close interlock between the levels can be achieved, he lingers over philological, textual, and historical details, just as he had in the 'Rat Man' case-history, accumulating corroborative evidence and improvising on a variety of side-issues. Each *explicandum* is alive with curiosities, and these are allowed to scatter before a complete explanatory hypothesis magnetizes them into their final shape. Freud speaks about an insatiable *Wisstrieb*, and enacts it in the erudite excursions of his text. With the flair of a great detective he gathers Leonardo's vulture, the insistent ambiguity with which he depicts the feminine, and the litter of his incomplete projects into a single hypothesis that is the summation of all the learning previously amassed. Freud's *Eureka!* is uttered from inside the tangible detail of his account: the vulture is an overwhelming phallic breast, the instrument of a maternal tenderness that had veered in Leonardo's infancy towards excess and menace (XI, 87, 115, 135); and the consequences of that original tender intimidation are everywhere to be observed in the Leonardo oeuvre.

In the alternative dimension of Freud's study, however, Leonardo has the role not so much of a singularity—a genius, a great man, a sublime oddity towering above ordinary mortals—as of an entry-point to the world of shared experience. Leonardo's epistemological and artistic quest has a perfectly familiar point of origin—in the infantile sexual researches by which the young of the species seek to understand the difference between the sexes, the behaviour of their parents, and the sexual topography of their own bodies. The genius begins where everyone else does, and is different from the multitude of human beings only in so far as his quest takes him further than his fellows along the road of sublimation: he begins as an infant voyeur and ends as a visionary. Freud brings tireless rhetorical exuberance to this theme:

In reality Leonardo was not devoid of passion; he did not lack the divine

spark which is directly or indirectly the driving force—*il primo motore*—
behind all human activity. He had merely converted his passion into a thirst
for knowledge; he then applied himself to investigation with the persistence,
constancy and penetration which is derived from passion, and at the climax
of intellectual labour, when knowledge had been won, he allowed the long
restrained affect to break loose and to flow away freely, as a stream of water
drawn from a river is allowed to flow away when its work is done. When,
at the climax of a discovery, he could survey a large portion of the whole
nexus, he was overcome by emotion, and in ecstatic language praised the
splendour of the part of creation that he had studied, or—in religious phraseology—the greatness of his Creator [. . .]. Because of his insatiable and
indefatigable thirst for knowledge Leonardo has been called the Italian Faust.
But quite apart from doubts about a possible transformation of the instinct
to investigate back into an enjoyment of life—a transformation which we
must take as fundamental in the tragedy of Faust—the view may be hazarded
that Leonardo's development approaches Spinoza's mode of thinking. (XI,
74–5)

In passages of this kind, Freud is fusing a number of separate narratives
into a single elevated trajectory: the passage from infancy to adulthood is
echoed in the transformation of sexual bafflement into religious awe, of
hard work into ecstasy, and of the mere academic journeyman into a
supreme intellectual adventurer or sage. By way of this composite story of
human growth and maturation, Freud's reader is invited to move in imagination from the first stirrings of infant sexual feeling through doubt and
self-division to the pantheistic serenity of Spinoza's *Ethics*. Moreover Freud
himself has a part to play in his *Bildungsroman* of the human species.
Freud's 'drive to know' was not a matter of common knowledge, but his
personal discovery; explanations of the kind offered by psychoanalysis
derived not from a lightly adjusted common sense, but from an insight
that he alone had reached and an investigative method that he alone had
pioneered. Who else but Freud had found himself suddenly able to 'survey
a large portion of the whole nexus' of childhood experience? Revealing
the secret of Leonardo's creativity is much more than a vindication of the
psychoanalytic method: as narrated here, Leonardo's career is the self-
realization of the entire intellectual project of psychoanalysis given clinching
allegorical form. Besides, Freud not only identifies with the 'Italian Faust'
but fills a major gap left in his scientific investigations. Leonardo had been
a relentless explorer of external nature and an eager student of human
anatomy, but his research curriculum had little room in it for the inwardness
of human thought and desire (XI, 76–7). The psychologist that Leonardo
was not, Freud himself had already become. In psychoanalysis, Leonardo's
science finds its completion.

What makes Freud's essay still so fascinating to students of biography
is that a tension between empirical observation and grand theory is plainly

visible within it at every turn, and that this classic conflict sometimes achieves a dangerously hyperbolic form. The work contains both a fantasy of intellectual omnipotence and a series of all too falsifiable conjectures. Freud makes blunders, and the most celebrated of these—involving a mis-translation of the Italian *nibio* as 'vulture' rather than 'kite'—is aggravated by the long, gratuitous excursus on Egyptology to which it gives rise. But a more correct and less fantastical book would have been much less instruc-tive than the text we in fact possess. This is in one sense a perfectly disreputable biography of a great man, in that the biographer's own career not only appears as an occasional descant against that of his subject but sometimes drowns it out. In the closing paragraphs of the work, Freud bemoans the lack of first-hand observational material under which Leonardo's biographers labour, and suggests that if he had had more data at his disposal he would have written a more convincing book. The evidence provided by Freud's other extended exercises in biography does not, however, support this view. Certainly if the biographer's priority is to preserve the singularity of his subject against the insipid idealizing portraiture that Freud himself castigated, then a dearth of data can offer a real advantage. He can become a novelist, an inventor of characters rather than a simple reporter of those that already exist.

Two other works should be mentioned at this point. The first is Freud's account of the judge Daniel Paul Schreber (1842–1911), first published in 1911 ('Psycho-Analytic Notes on an Autobiographical Account of a Case of Paranoia', XII, 1–82). This work is not a case-history in that Freud was never to meet, and hear spoken testimony from, the paranoid sufferer on whom he wrote so eloquently. It is a discussion of Schreber's own autobiographical writings, which had been published eight years earlier, and contains a detailed sketch of a psychoanalytic theory of the psychoses. Strictly speaking, Freud reminds his reader, the primary materials offered by the Schreber case are doubly unsatisfactory: they are too few on the one hand, and of the wrong kind on the other. Yet Freud is undeterred by this, and produces a dramatic portrait of his subject's strangeness, and by literary means that could scarcely be more strange. Identifying powerfully with certain elements of Schreber's delusional system, he finds himself replicating them in a transposed form. Schreber's fantasies of omnipotence, and his sense of universal connectedness within the cosmos, are reported with such intelligence and nuance in the sufferer's own memoirs that the ambitions of psychoanalysis are confronted with an unexpected mirror. Uncanny echoes begin to pass between text and commentary; each is a gloss on the other: 'Schreber's "rays of God", which are made up of a condensation of the sun's rays, of nerve-fibres, and of spermatozoa, are in reality nothing else than a concrete representation and projection outwards of libidinal cathexes; and they thus lend his delusions a striking conformity with our theory' (XII, 78). Limited information about the biographical subject has again given free rein to the biographer's self-absorbed reverie. Schreber's delusions not only 'confirm' psychoanalysis but cause Freud to wonder, in the closing sentences of his essay, whether his own vision of universal connectedness might not prove, in some respects, delusional.

The second work I have in mind has an anomalous place in the Freud canon, and is included neither in the German nor in the English editions of his complete psychological writings. Freud's *Woodrow Wilson: A Psychological Study* was written in collaboration with William C. Bullitt in the 1930s and remained unpublished until 1966.[4] At first glance, the complementarity between the two authors is remarkable: Bullitt had been a member of the United States delegation at the Paris peace conference at the end of World War I, had known Wilson personally, and had access not only to all the main documents but to a wide circle of the late president's intimates and acquaintances; Freud was the instigator of a now celebrated theory of human personality. Bullitt was able to supply Freud with the treasure-house of information that he had so conspicuously lacked in writing about Leonardo, and Freud brought to the enterprise the very powers of psychological understanding that his co-author lacked. Wilson's story, like so many recounted by Freud, including Schreber's and his own, has the father-son relationship as its principal axis, and tracing the destinies of that relationship from the small world of Wilson's childhood home to the large geopolitical arena in which his presidency was eventually to be conducted gave Freud an extremely promising plot. The fact that this promise went, for the most part, unrealized may be attributed to the working method that the collaborating authors chose. Bullitt began by providing a lengthy 'digest of data on the childhood and youth of Thomas Woodrow Wilson', and Freud by providing one of the brief, semi-popular outlines of psychoanalysis at which he had become adept in his later years. The two kinds of material, having been inertly counterposed at the start of the book, were never to achieve full combustion.

Freud's contributions to this Woodrow Wilson project are written with great vigour, and with many flashes of wit, but their distribution is reiterative rather than developmental. A pattern of admiration, self-abasement, and repressed hostility is to be discerned early in the history of the son's reactions to his father, and this pattern simply migrates intact from one

---

[4] On the circumstances surrounding the production of this work, see Ernest Jones's *Sigmund Freud: Life and Work* (London, new edn, 1957–8), II, 214, 225; III, 117, 160, 173. The Wilson biography was first published by Houghton Mifflin (Boston, 1966) and has been reprinted by Transaction Publishers (New Brunswick and London, 1999). My quotations are from the later edition and page numbers are given in the text.

phase to the next of Wilson's public life. Describing Wilson's imperious behaviour during his Presidency of Princeton in the early years of the new century, Freud writes:

> The original source of all these character traits was, of course, little Tommy Wilson's passivity to his 'incomparable father'. The Reverend Joseph Ruggles Wilson, who incidentally is not to be recommended as a model for fathers, had made his son love him so deeply and submissively that the flood of passivity he had aroused could be satisfied by no other man or activity. To find outlet for it was not easy for a man whose Super-Ego demanded that he should be all masculinity: God Himself. The Professor Extraordinary of Rhetoric, dead, continued to overwhelm his son. (113)

And the consequences of Wilson's attachment to this overwhelming and unrecommendable parent are continuing to play themselves out during the peace talks fifteen years later. Wilson had denied having prior knowledge of the secret treaties into which the allies had entered before the talks began, and Freud comments: 'But one recalls that the terms of the secret treaties were the terms of the Treaty of Versailles and that he was striving to repress his knowledge of the terms of the Treaty of Versailles in order to preserve his identification with Christ and to escape the scourgings of his Super-Ego' (283). Again two separate orders of fact or apparent fact are being set against each other without producing an interference zone. There is no active interface between politics and the mental life of individuals. In writing of this kind, which is plentiful in the volume as a whole, the separation is still as plain as it had been in the co-authors' independent introductory essays. Political deeds, in this account, are determined both by externally visible power relations and by the psychological constitution of the politicians concerned, but not intricately so. There is no play between causal systems, and there are very few moments of difficulty or interpretative conflict in the smoothly self-confirming Freud-Bullitt narrative.

What is to be seen in the Wilson biography, and in many of Freud's public writings, is a sustained flight from uncertainty and ambiguity. If psychoanalysis was to become a significant conceptual instrument in social and political debate, its explanations needed to be clear and decisive, just as its therapeutic procedures needed to be demonstrably efficacious in the alleviation of mental suffering. Deep-seated ambiguity would have been a weak rallying cry in either campaign. Yet a cult of ambiguity had been present in the founding documents of the psychoanalytic movement. Dreams, jokes, and 'Freudian' slips all occupied an uncertain border territory between incompatible systems, and the complex polyphony of meanings that could be found in dreams in particular was the very source of their troubling beauty. Intricate over-determination of the kind that the Wilson biography so firmly excludes is a main characteristic of the dreamwork, and available on terms of strict equality to presidents and paupers:

> Not only are the elements of a dream determined by the dream-thoughts many times over, but the individual dream-thoughts are represented in the dream by several elements. Associative paths lead from one element of the dream to several dream-thoughts, and from one dream-thought to several elements of the dream. [. . .] In the case of every dream which I have submitted to an analysis of this kind I have invariably found these same fundamental principles confirmed: the elements of the dream are constructed out of the whole mass of dream-thoughts and each one of those elements is shown to have been determined many times over in relation to the dream-thoughts. (*The Interpretation of Dreams,* 1900, IV, 284)

The cat's cradle of associations between Freud's 'dream-thoughts' and 'dream-elements' offers a powerful model of mind as a perpetual play between interfering systems, by virtue of which all manner of reinforcements, lateral connections, short-circuits, oscillations, and feedback loops are made possible from moment to moment in the history of an individual human subject. The transferential encounter between analysand and analyst, and especially the mobile meshing that can take place between the free associations of the one and the suspended attention of the other, produces in the interpersonal field a similar image of causal complexity. It is disappointing that Freud as a biographer so often turns his back on opportunities such as these, and prefers to narrate the lives of his subjects as the linear passage of a childhood paradigm through an indefinite series of adult scenes. One early cause produces an unceasing procession of later effects.

Freud became a biographer of note only in his study of Leonardo, but the lessons of psychoanalysis in general for the modern practice of life-writing are none the less profound. In the case of Leonardo, an archetypal 'great man' whose creative gift began to be intelligible only when brought into alignment with a disturbing childhood memory, Freud produced a masterpiece of ambiguity: his identification with an indomitable predecessor advances and recoils as the narrative proceeds; his subject is now the supreme hero of the Italian Renaissance, now a rather derisory modern nerve-case; and the plot of the work, being concerned at one moment with the knowledge-seeking drive of humankind at large, seems at the next to dwindle into a promotional exercise on behalf of a still unaccredited psychological theory. Starved of information about Leonardo, Freud gave his own hesitation between rebellion and admiring acquiescence a central organizing role in the novelized case-study he assembled.

Overall, psychoanalysis redramatizes one of the paradoxes that the modern biographer confronts from day to day: you need a simplifying model, a schematic life-pattern, in order to give your work an arresting plot and prevent it from becoming a mere chronicle of particulars; but if your model insists too much and alters too little you may lose all sense of a human life being lived, of a motivated individual moving forward in time and occupying, as he travels, a border-zone between inner and outer circumstances. Such is the knife-edge that biographers and analysts alike occupy. Psychoanalysis contains a further cautionary tale on the relationship between the biographer and his chosen subject, for Freud is at once a powerful critic of identification and a helpless victim of its seductions. The writing of a successful biography emerges in the Freudian workshop as an exalted ambition but an almost impossible artistic goal.

11

The Newness of the 'New Biography': Biographical Theory and Practice in the Early Twentieth Century

LAURA MARCUS

The dominance of modernist and avant-garde literature in the first decades of the twentieth century has directed attention away from certain texts and genres. Biography is a prime example of this process. While numerous histories of the biographical genre do exist, few critics have attempted to situate early twentieth-century biography in the broader literary and cultural arena.[1] Those who focus on modernist experimentation rarely consider the ways in which biographers approached the new aesthetics, or address the extraordinary popularity and perceived significance of the genre in the period of 'high modernism'. Yet the marked increase in the popularity of biography during this period—the 1920s and 1930s particularly—was closely connected to the new forms of, and experiments with, the genre. 'It is the day of the biographer', Hesketh Pearson wrote in 1930.[2] The rise in

---

[1] The fullest recent account of early twentieth-century biography is Ruth Hoberman's *Modernizing Lives: Experiments in English Biography, 1918–1939* (Carbondale, IL, 1987). See also Richard D. Altick, *Lives and Letters: A History of Literary Biography in England and America* (New York, 1979); Ira Bruce Nadel, *Biography: Fiction, Fact and Form* (London, 1984); Perry Meisel, *The Myth of the Modern* (New Haven, 1987); William H. Epstein, *Recognizing Biography* (Philadelphia, 1987; Leon Edel, *Writing Lives* (New York, 1984); John Garraty, *The Nature of Biography* (New York, 1957).
[2] Hesketh Pearson, *Ventilations: Being Biographical Asides*, quoted in Altick, *Lives and Letters*, p. 289.

popularity of biographies was linked to the perception that biography had been reinvented for the twentieth century, requiring a new level of critical self-awareness.

David Cecil, for example, writing in 1936, called biography 'the only new form' of modern literature.[3] Its newness and its success were due, he suggested, to the fact that it was the genre most congenial to the 'scientific' modern age, and the one most allied to modern psychology and the study of 'human character'. Biography is, he argued, on the one hand on the side of science, while, on the other, biographers approach their subjects with newly aesthetic aims, taking advantage of a 'literary' space made available by the mutual lack of sympathy between literature (particularly poetry) and scientific modernity. Cecil's argument is clearly flawed (there is no evidence that poets and novelists in the 1920s and 1930s felt peculiarly threatened by science, and many indeed embraced its terms) but it is echoed in numerous discussions of the 'new biography', in which, as we shall see, the relationship between the literary and the scientific, and the importance of the study of 'character', are two of the dominant themes.

Cecil's claims also find a curious echo in an essay by the critical theorist Siegfried Kracauer, an important critique of biography as 'an art form of the new bourgeoisie' (1930). The dissolution of character in the modern novel, Kracauer argues, has led to the elevation and increased popularity of biography: 'The moral of the biography is that, in the chaos of current artistic practices, it is the only seemingly necessary prose form'.[4] Yet, as I go on to explore, it would seem that critics and commentators in the early twentieth century were exploring fictional and biographical 'characters' in tandem, rather than perceiving biographical lives as offering a unity and plenitude no longer made available by the novelists.

A further dimension of early twentieth-century biography, which struck a number of commentators at the time, was the emergence of a new biographical theory and practice which crossed national boundaries and in which common biographical tenets were developed at the same historical moment in the work of writers between whom there was little, if any, actual contact. The central figures were Lytton Strachey, André Maurois, Emil Ludwig, and the more marginal North American biographer or, in his preferred term, 'psychographer', Gamaliel Bradford; later in this essay I also discuss A. J. A. Symons and his 1934 'experiment in biography', *The Quest for Corvo*.

---

[3] David Cecil, Introduction to *An Anthology of Modern Biography* (London, 1936), p. ix.
[4] Siegfried Kracauer, 'The Biography as an Art Form of the New Bourgeoisie' (1930), in *The Mass Ornament: Weimar Essays*, ed. and tr. Thomas Y. Levin (Cambridge, MA, 1995), p. 103.

In an article on 'The New Biography: Ludwig, Maurois and Strachey', published in *The Atlantic Monthly* of March 1929, George Alexander Johnston wrote:

> No feature of the literary history of Europe in the last few years is more remarkable than the simultaneous appearance in Germany, France, and England of a new conception of biography. [. . .] The amazing similarity both in philosophical conception and in literary style and structure of the work of these writers constitutes a problem of the highest interest.[5]

While Johnston was overstating the likenesses—as Mark Longaker wrote in his 1934 study of biography, 'There are marked similarities in the works of Strachey, Bradford, Maurois and Ludwig, but they obviously do not form a congenial group'[6]—we can work fruitfully with Johnston's perception of biographical 'newness' as a widespread cultural and literary phenomenon.

Commentators and critics both offered descriptions and definitions of the 'new biography' and attempted to account for the new or renewed popularity of the biographical genre. In addition to the numerous biographies published in the 1920s and 1930s, during this period there was a spate of critical and theoretical works on biography, many of them written by biographers themselves, including William Thayer's *The Art of Biography* (1920), James Johnston's *Biography: The Literature of Personality* (1927), Harold Nicolson's *The Development of English Biography* (1927), André Maurois's *Aspects of Biography* (1929), Mark Longaker's *Contemporary Biography* (1934), and Emil Ludwig's *Die Kunst der Biographie* (1936), as well as a very substantial body of essays. Biographical works, in particular the collections of 'brief lives' that appeared, were frequently prefaced by more theoretical reflections on the biographer's art, signalling a marked self-consciousness about the biographical form. Emil Ludwig, whose numerous biographies include full-length studies of Goethe and Wilhelm II, André Maurois, whose first biographies were highly romanticized studies of Shelley and Disraeli, Gamaliel Bradford, author of such texts as *Bare Souls* and *A Naturalist of Souls*, and Lytton Strachey, whose *Eminent Victorians* was the defining text of the 'new biography', produced not only biographies but commentaries on the genre. It is true, of course, that such commentaries tended to justify rather than to critique the 'new biographical' methods, and thus it could be argued that a strong and non-partisan biographical criticism did not emerge at this time; a fact which may have contributed to the delayed development of biographical theory, by contrast with, for example, theories of autobiography.

[5] George Alexander Johnston, 'The New Biography: Ludwig, Maurois and Strachey', *The Atlantic Monthly*, CXLIII (March 1929), 133.
[6] Mark Longaker, *Contemporary Biography* (Philadelphia, 1934), p. 20.

What were the tenets and characteristics of the 'new biographers' and the 'new biography'? They included, or were held to include: a new equality between biographer and subject, by contrast with the hero-worship and hagiography of Victorian eulogistic biography; brevity, selection, and an attention to form and unity traditionally associated with fiction rather than history; the discovery of central motifs in a life and of a 'key' to personality, so that single aspects of the self or details of the life and person came to stand for or to explain the whole; and a focus on character rather than events. While Maurois was committed to representations of a personality unfolding through time, Ludwig and Bradford shared an anti-chronological aesthetic. This reaction against chronology may seem paradoxical in the quintessentially narrative genre of biography, but it is made explicable by the focus on an essential self, transcending time, and, most markedly in Ludwig's work, on the equivalences between biography and portraiture. The biographer is, Ludwig asserts, a 'portraitist', whose problem is 'the discovery of a human soul'. His portraitist is properly inductive and intuitive: he 'begins with the concept of a character and searches the archives for what is at bottom the corroboration of an intuition'.

The tenets of modern biography are often defined in contrast to 'Victorian biography', although they were in part shared by a number of later nineteenth-century critics and writers, including the editors of that monumental enterprise the *Dictionary of National Biography*, Leslie Stephen and Sidney Lee. The *DNB*'s instruction to its contributors was said to be 'No flowers by request', and good biographical practice was held to include concision, candour, and analysis and synthesis rather than the accumulation of facts. The representation of a total break between Victorian and modern biography may thus say as much, or more, about the moderns' need to demarcate themselves sharply from their immediate predecessors as about the differences themselves. As Richard Altick has argued, biography was seen as 'the literary emblem par excellence of Victorianism, a product faithful to the old era's habit of misapplied and exaggerated hero worship, with all its attendant hypocrisy and evasiveness'.[7] The 'new biography' comes to represent the radical ideological and cultural rupture between Victorians and moderns.

The break, in English literary contexts, is seen to start with the late nineteenth- and early twentieth-century auto/biographical texts of Samuel Butler and Edmund Gosse, who put paid, metaphorically and textually, to their Victorian fathers. Gosse, in *Father and Son* (1907), wields the Darwinian rhetoric that so agonized his father, the naturalist Philip Gosse, and represents his childhood self as engaged in a struggle for survival against

---

[7] Altick, *Lives and Letters*, p. 289.

his father's fundamentalism, while he depicts Gosse *père* as one of a dying species. For Desmond MacCarthy, Harold Nicolson, and André Maurois, Edmund Gosse was Lytton Strachey's immediate precursor, enacting, as MacCarthy puts it, 'a tragic-comic clash between an age of belief and one of scepticism'.[8] The extraordinary impact of Strachey's *Eminent Victorians*, which was seen on its publication not only to have revolutionized biography but also to represent an absolute division between old and new, derived in the greatest part from its destruction through satire of Victorian heroes or 'fathers'. Furthermore, its critique of 'Victorian values' is so closely linked with its radical rewriting of biographical discourse that it came to mark the end not only of a way of writing lives but of an age. Published in May 1918, five months before the Armistice, *Eminent Victorians* was perceived as the first text of postwar England, opening up to ridicule the workings of power and the blind submission to God and Country which had led to the mass slaughter of World War I.

The rhetoric of warfare emerges, in ironic form, in Strachey's Preface to *Eminent Victorians*, a piece of writing so influential and so often echoed by subsequent biographers that it is worth quoting at some length. Arguing that the very weight of material emanating from the Victorians about their Age had destroyed the possibility of its clear delineation, Strachey writes:

> It is not by the direct method of a scrupulous narration that the explorer of the past can hope to depict that singular epoch. If he is wise, he will adopt a subtler strategy. He will attack his subject in unexpected places; he will fall upon the flank, or the rear; he will shoot a sudden, revealing searchlight into obscure recesses, hitherto undivined. He will row out over that great ocean of material, and lower down into it, here and there, a little bucket, which will bring up to the light of day some characteristic specimen, from those far depths, to be examined with a careful curiosity. Guided by these considerations, I have written the ensuing studies. I have attempted, through the medium of biography, to present some Victorian visions to the modern eye.[9]

Selection, impartiality, and brevity are upheld as the guiding biographical principles. Eschewing any pretence of, or aspiration to, completeness, Strachey insists on the fragmentary quality of 'the truth which took my fancy and lay to my hand', although he somewhat blurs the distinction between the random or 'haphazard' and the particular in his choice of biographical subjects. Cardinal Manning, Thomas Arnold, Florence Nightingale, and General Gordon may serve as representatives of Church, Army, the Public Schools—'the lives of an ecclesiastic, an educational authority, a woman of action, and a man of adventure'—but Strachey's focus, in the body of

---

[8] Desmond MacCarthy, 'Lytton Strachey and the Art of Biography', in *Memories* (London, 1953), p. 37.
[9] Lytton Strachey, *Eminent Victorians* (London, 1918, reprinted Harmondsworth, 1981), p. 9.

the text, on his chosen subjects' egotisms and idiosyncrasies puts the very notion of the representative into crisis.

The import of *Eminent Victorians*, Strachey suggests, is not only historical but biographical: 'Human beings are too important to be treated as mere symptoms of the past. [. . .] The art of biography seems to have fallen on evil times in England. [. . .] With us, the most delicate and humane of all the branches of the art of writing has been relegated to the journeymen of letters; we do not reflect that it is perhaps as difficult to write a good life as to live one'.[10] While biography is firmly claimed as an 'art', Strachey also plays with the concept of the biographer as a biologist examining his specimens with a curious but dispassionate eye.

This aspect of Strachey's Preface is echoed in Emil Ludwig's account of the 'new biography' in his study *Genius and Character*:

> After a period which attempted to define man in terms of descent and breeding, we enter upon an era totally alien to the Darwinian mentality; once again we turn our attention to the personality *per se*, the personality almost devoid of temporal co-ordinates, considering the volume, intensity, and resistance of its vital forces, the restless fluid of its emotional configurations, and the balance between its impulse towards action and its repression through precept. Whereas our fathers asked, 'How did the individual harmonize with his world?' our first question is, 'Does he harmonize with himself?' Questions of success and responsibility have been shifted from the environment back to the individual, so that the analysis which was formerly expended upon the milieu now seeks to penetrate within. Further, the renewed interest in memoirs is biological: and perhaps the portraitist of to-day, who is first of all a psychologist, is much nearer to the biologist than to the historian.[11]

The broader context here is that of the disciplinary and interdisciplinary configurations and disputes of the early twentieth century, to which biography is central. Positioned, like autobiography, on the fault-lines between literature, history, and science, biography came to be perceived as a crucial tool for the scientific and ethnographic data-gatherers of the turn of the century. In 'An Open Letter to Biographers', the psychologist Havelock Ellis urged biographers to fulfil their proper role: 'In every man of genius a new strange force is brought into the world. The biographer is the biologist of this new life. I come to you to learn the origins of this tremendous energy'.[12] The obsession with 'genius'—also pursued in Ludwig's biographical projects—was in one sense continuous with the nineteenth-century preoccupation with 'Great Men', satirized so fully and frequently

---

[10] Ibid., p. 10.
[11] Emil Ludwig, *Genius and Character*, tr. Kenneth Burke (London, 1927, reprinted 1930), p. 14.
[12] Havelock Ellis, 'An Open Letter to Biographers', *Selected Essays* (London, 1936), p. 111.

by Virginia Woolf, but had also undergone a radical change with the development of interest in the psychology and even pathology of genius.

In 1928, Leonard and Virginia Woolf's Hogarth Press published Harold Nicolson's *The Development of English Biography*. In the final chapter of his study, 'The Present Age', Nicolson argues that biography's lack of a distinct generic identity of its own and its consequent entanglement 'with other interests—with that, for instance, of history, fiction, and science', have made it uniquely sensitive to 'the spirit of the age': 'over no form of literary composition have the requirements of the reading public exercised so marked and immediate an influence. The development of biography is primarily the development of the taste for biography'.[13] When an age demands heroes, biography will supply them; when it asks for funeral monuments, this is the shape into which biography will transmute. In an age of scepticism, such as the one Nicolson inhabits, 'the reading public become dominantly interested in human behaviour, and biography, in order to meet this interest, becomes inductive, critical, detached and realistic. [. . .] The less people believe in theology the more do they believe in human experience. And it is to biography that they go for this experience'. While the 'scientific' interest in biography demands an immensity of detail about the biographical subject, the desire for 'literary' biography requires that this material be organized with 'the perfection of literary form'.[14] The two approaches are, Nicolson argues, incompatible:

> I would suggest, in the first place, that the scientific interest in biography is hostile to, and will in the end prove destructive of, the literary interest. The former will insist not only on the facts, but on all the facts; the latter demands a partial or artificial representation of facts. The scientific interest, as it develops, will become insatiable; no synthetic power, no genius for representation, will be able to keep the pace. I foresee, therefore, a divergence between the two interests. Scientific biography will become specialised and technical. There will be biographies in which psychological development will be traced in all its intricacy and in a manner comprehensible only to the experts; there will be biographies examining the influence of heredity—biographies founded on Galton, on Lombroso, on Havelock Ellis, on Freud; there will be medical biographies—studies of the influence on character of the endocrine glands, studies of internal secretions; there will be sociological biographies, economic biographies, aesthetic biographies, philosophical biographies. These will doubtless be interesting and instructive, but the emphasis which will be thrown on the analytical or scientific aspect will inevitably lessen the literary effort applied to their composition. The more that biography becomes a branch of science the less will it become a branch of literature. [. . .] [I]n general literary biography will, I suppose, wander off into the imaginative, leaving the strident streets of science for the open fields of fiction. The

[13] Harold Nicolson, *The Development of English Biography* (London, 1928), p. 135.
[14] Ibid., pp. 142–3.

> biographical form will be given to fiction, the fictional form will be given to
> biography. When this happens 'pure' biography, as a branch of literature,
> will have ceased to exist.[15]

Nicolson's account of the increasingly novelistic dimensions of biography
in one of its aspects—opposed here to an equivalent growth in highly
specialized 'scientific' biographies—is an aspect of, or anticipates, a range
of twentieth-century intellectual and disciplinary debates, in which language
is divided into its 'referential' and 'emotive' dimensions and functions,
and in which 'science' and 'art'—'the two cultures'—become increasingly
polarised.

In 1928 André Maurois delivered the Clark Lectures at Cambridge
University, published in English as *Aspects of Biography* in 1929, and
named Nicolson's *Development of English Biography* as one of his central
sources. He takes issue, however, with Nicolson's equation of the exact
and the historical sciences, arguing that the writing of history and of
biography should be brought into the literary domains of creativity and
imagination:

> I hope to be able to show you that art and science can be reconciled. A
> scientific book, perfectly constructed, is a work of art. A beautiful portrait is
> at once a portrait resembling its subject and an artistic transference of reality.
> It is perfectly accurate to say that truth has the solidity of stone and that
> personality has the lightness of a rainbow; but Rodin and the Greek sculptors
> before him have at times been able to infuse into marble the elusive curves
> and the changing lights of human flesh.[16]

In the chapter 'Biography Considered as a Work of Art', Maurois defends
the biographical methods he adopted in his biographies of Shelley, *Ariel:
The Life of Shelley* (1924), and of Disraeli, arguing that 'poetry' and
'rhythm' are as central to biography as to other forms of art, and are to
be located in 'the recurrence, at more or less distant intervals, of the
essential motifs of the work':

> A human life is always made up of a number of such motifs: when you study
> one of them, it will soon begin to impress itself upon you with a remarkable
> force. In Shelley's life the water motif dominates the whole symphony. [. . .]
> In Disraeli's life there is a flower motif [. . .] there is an Eastern motif
> [. . .] and there is the antagonistic rain motif, that terrible English rain which
> sets out to extinguish the over-brilliant Eastern flame and succeeds.[17]

In 'Biography Considered as a Science', Maurois argues against Nicolson's
postulated future for biography and for 'that profounder truth which is

---

[15] Ibid., pp. 154–5.
[16] André Maurois, *Aspects of Biography*, tr. S. C. Roberts (London, 1929), p. 38.
[17] Ibid., pp. 71–2.

poetic truth'. Maurois' belief, at least in the early stages of his long literary career, in the 'key to character', the attention paid to the details of a life, his representations of inner thoughts and feelings, and his focus on the biographer's strong affective and empathetic identification with his subject, were, as I have noted, some of the central tenets of the 'new biography'.

Maurois had entered the Bloomsbury orbit when he came to London in the early 1920s to renew wartime acquaintances and to research his Shelley biography; he met the writer Maurice Baring, who introduced him to Harold Nicolson and Desmond MacCarthy. The centrality of biography to Bloomsbury culture and to its cult of the civilized individual is an important, and clearly highly class-inflected, dimension of the 'new biography' that I cannot explore fully here. *Aspects of Biography* is in many ways a 'Bloomsbury' text: the lectures were delivered a year after E. M. Forster's Clark Lectures, which subsequently became *Aspects of the Novel*, and which made the question of 'character' and 'personality' central to the analysis of fiction. *Aspects of Biography* also contains numerous laudatory references to Lytton Strachey, and closely debates with Harold Nicolson, as we have seen, and, less overtly, with Virginia Woolf. When Maurois refers, in the passage quoted above, to the claim 'that truth has the solidity of stone and that personality has the lightness of a rainbow', he is alluding to Woolf's essay of 1927, 'The New Biography', one of the earliest namings of the genre. Woolf describes the divorce between Victorians (represented by Sir Sidney Lee) and moderns:

> 'The aim of biography', said Sir Sidney Lee, who had perhaps read and written more lives than any man of his time, 'is the truthful transmission of personality', and no single sentence could more neatly split up into two parts the whole problem of biography as it presents itself to us today. On the one hand there is truth; on the other there is personality. And if we think of truth as something of granite-like solidity and of personality as something of rainbow-like tangibility and reflect that the aim of biography is to weld these two into one seamless whole, we shall admit that the problem is a stiff one and that we need not wonder if biographers have for the most part failed to solve it.[18]

'The New Biography' was in part a review-essay of Harold Nicolson's *Some People*. Like Woolf's *Orlando* (1928), *Some People* is a hybrid work, a combination of autobiography, biography, and fiction, whose guiding idea, as Nicolson explained, 'was to put real people in imaginary situations, and imaginary people in real situations'.[19] Such an admixture of fact and fiction was, for Woolf, the most striking feature of modern biography, as

---

[18] Virginia Woolf, 'The New Biography' (1927), in *The Essays of Virginia Woolf*, vol. IV, ed. Andrew McNeillie (London, 1994), p. 473.
[19] Nigel Nicolson, Introduction to Harold Nicolson, *Some People* (Oxford, 1983), p. vii.

well as the most troubling, for although she applauded the creativity it afforded, she also expressed doubts about the combining of historical fact and artistic invention: 'Let it be fact, one feels, or let it be fiction; the imagination will not serve under two masters simultaneously'.[20] The balance between fact and fiction, she nonetheless suggests, has shifted in the modern age: 'it would seem that the life which is increasingly real to us is the fictitious life; it dwells in the personality rather than the act'.[21] Thus, by implication, biography is at one and the same time the modern genre *par excellence* and deeply in thrall to fiction and fiction-making.

The paradox that we 'know' characters in fiction far more fully than we do 'real life' figures, that they are imbued with far richer personalities and interiorities than we have access to in other contexts, increasingly became a rationale for the appropriation of novelistic strategies in biographical writing. Fictional characters, E. M. Forster wrote in *Aspects of the Novel*, 'are people whose secret lives are visible or might be visible: we are people whose secret lives are invisible'.[22] The 'perfect knowledge' we acquire of people in novels is 'a compensation for their dimness in life'.[23] While Forster sought to differentiate between fiction and history, novel and memoir, biographers were seeking, unsurprisingly, to represent that visibility of the secret life of the biographical subject that Forster reserved for fictional characters alone. Lytton Strachey's technique, for example, was to take phrases from letters and reported conversations and to turn them into representations of his subjects' thoughts and feelings; Maurois, in *Ariel* and *The Life of Disraeli*, simply laid claim, often without the felt necessity of written evidence, to knowledge of his subjects' inner lives. Calling upon E. M. Forster's distinction in *Aspects of the Novel* between the real man (*homo sapiens*) and the character in a novel (*homo fictus*), the critic George Johnston claimed that the new biographer's empathy with his subject amounted to a form of creation allied to that of the author of a novel:

> The new biography has so completely understood the principal actors in the history of the periods portrayed that it describes them as if it had created them. Thus we reach the paradox that the new biography produces the impression of reality because the principal actors create the illusion that they are the characters in a novel. If the reader of the new biography sometimes feels a sudden doubt whether these people ever lived at all, it is not because they seem improbable, but because they seem too probable to be real.

[20] Woolf, 'The New Biography', p. 478.
[21] Ibid., p. 478.
[22] E. M. Forster, *Aspects of the Novel* (London, 1927, reprinted Harmondsworth, 1962 and 1990), p. 70.
[23] Ibid., p. 69.

> Fiction does not seek to create mere illusion; it seeks to create the illusion of reality. And it is because the writer of fiction has been so successful in producing the sense of reality, and the traditional biographer, with his appeal to veracity, has been so unsuccessful, that the new biography has adopted the methods of fiction and has, by means of them, brilliantly succeeded in re-creating reality.[24]

The new biography, Johnston insists, employs the methods of fiction, but does not produce works of fiction. This nice distinction is treated with more caution by Woolf in 'The New Biography', in which she argues that the biographer treads the finest of lines when 'he carries the use of fiction too far', risking the loss of both 'the freedom of fiction' and 'the substance of fact'. Nonetheless, she recognizes that the focus on 'personality' and the created life has brought with it a desire for, in her words, 'the novelist's art of arrangement, suggestion, dramatic effect to expound the private life'.[25]

The importance of 'personality' and 'character' in literature and criticism of the early twentieth century may indeed be the central route to an understanding of the centrality and popularity of biography in the period. As Gamaliel Bradford wrote, in the introduction to his study *Wives*: 'The real object of the biographer, all that deeply and permanently interests him, is the analysis and synthesis of his subject's character'.[26] Bradford continues by pointing up the complexity of notions of 'character' and 'quality', and hence the difficulty or even impossibility of the biographer's task, that of giving some form of permanence and interpretative stability to 'this perpetual shift and change in the complexion of men's souls'. James C. Johnston, in *Biography: The Literature of Personality*, a study whose stated aim is to elucidate the purpose and methods of biography, and thus to differentiate 'genuine biography' from the spate of meretricious journalistic biographical productions, writes:

> Herein lies the true province of biography in all its varied forms: indeed, centered upon temperament, individuality, character, personality—the frequently recurring terms in any discussion of genuine biography, particularly that which we are sometimes inclined to term 'the new biography'—the real objective of the biographer becomes that of writing not merely the story of a life, but rather of *life-writing*.[27]

Woolf's much-quoted assertion, in her essay 'Mr Bennett and Mrs Brown', that 'in or about December 1910 human character changed'[28] has

---

[24] Johnston, 'The New Biography', pp. 333–4.
[25] Woolf, 'The New Biography', p. 478.
[26] Gamaliel Bradford, *Wives* (New York, 1925), p. 12.
[27] James C. Johnston, *Biography: The Literature of Personality* (New York, 1927), pp. 18–19.
[28] Virginia Woolf, 'Mr Bennett and Mrs Brown' (1924), reprinted in *A Woman's Essays*, ed. Rachel Bowlby (Harmondsworth, 1992), p. 70.

been understood as her way of marking the birth of the modern, using the date of the first Post-Impressionist exhibition in London, which could be said to have changed modes of perception. Less attention, perhaps, has been paid to the fact that Woolf marks historical change in and through an alteration in 'character'. Modernism (though the term had not fully entered the critical and cultural lexicon) for Woolf, as for so many of her contemporaries, thus becomes strongly identified with questions of subjectivity, and with the problematic of representing 'character' or 'personality'. Her essay is a rejoinder to Arnold Bennett's claims that the moderns, or, in Woolf's appellation, 'the Georgians', are incapable of representing 'character': Woolf plays with the complexities and multiple definitions of 'character', linking the term at one point to 'the character of one's cook', so that 'character' shades off into 'character-reference', the implication being that the Edwardians—Wells, Bennett, Galsworthy—depict their fictional characters in ways that look more like references or testimonials than they do depictions of complex modern subjectivities.

'Mr Bennett and Mrs Brown' is also a commentary on the 'new biography' in that it includes Lytton Strachey as one of the Georgians, alongside Forster, Eliot, Joyce, and Lawrence, finding in his work a radicalism and an aesthetic of rupture that, by contrast with that of the poets and novelists, it has not, perhaps, fully retained. Woolf is by no means uncritical of the moderns (Strachey included), finding their destruction of tradition and convention a necessary way of breaking with outworn conventions and yet damaging to the relationship and dialogue between writer and reader that is for her the point and purpose of the literary text:

> Again, in Mr Strachey's books, *Eminent Victorians* and *Queen Victoria*, the effort and strain of writing against the grain and current of the times is visible too. It is much less visible, of course, for not only is he dealing with facts, which are stubborn things, but he has fabricated, chiefly from eighteenth-century material, a very discreet code of manner of his own, which allows him to sit at table with the highest in the land and to say a great many things under cover of that exquisite apparel which, had they gone naked, would have been chased by the men-servants from the room. Still, if you compare *Eminent Victorians* with some of Lord Macaulay's essays, though you will feel that Lord Macaulay is always wrong, and Mr Strachey is always right, you will also feel a body, a sweep, a richness in Lord Macaulay's essays which show that his age was behind him; all his strength went straight into his work; none was used for purposes of concealment or of conversion. But Mr Strachey has had to open our eyes before he made us see; he has had to search out and sew together a very artful manner of speech; and the effort, beautifully though it is concealed, has robbed his work of some of the force that should have gone into it, and limited his scope.[29]

29 Ibid., pp. 85–6.

For Woolf, the Georgians are transitional writers, and their production of 'the spasmodic, the obscure, the fragmentary, the failure', is to be tolerated because it heralds a new age—'we are trembling on the verge of one of the great ages of English literature. But it can only be reached if we are determined never, never to desert Mrs Brown'.[30] 'Mrs Brown' becomes the figure of 'character' itself: female (as, Woolf hints, the future of fiction may well be) and at once elusive and deeply grounded in experience. For the failure of writers adequately to represent 'character' resides, Woolf suggests, in a failure to measure up to the complex subjectivity to which we all have access. Thus, Woolf reminds her 'common reader':

> You have gone to bed at night bewildered by the complexities of your feelings. In one day thousands of ideas have coursed through your brains; thousands of emotions have met, collided, and disappeared in astonishing disorder. Nevertheless, you allow the writers to palm off on you a version of all this, an image of Mrs Brown, which has no likeness to that surprising apparition whatsoever.[31]

Whereas Forster was to claim that we know fictional characters more fully than we do individuals in the world, Woolf represents the self as the source of, and resource for, our knowledge of the inner life.

The growing impact of psychological and psychoanalytic theories on literary creation and criticism clearly played a central role in shaping the 'new biography', and its emphases on identity rather than event or action. The self-consciousness about form exhibited by biographers is accompanied by the perception, as in 'Mr Bennett and Mrs Brown', that the appropriate measure of psychological complexity in depicting the life of another is the psychological and experiential complexity of the biographer's own existence. 'Consider one's own life', 'Think of your own life', Virginia Woolf and André Maurois respectively enjoin, the one depicting the failure of Victorian biography to grasp and represent lived experience, the other arguing against the view that the self is reducible to a 'scientific' knowledge of its parts. Gamaliel Bradford refers to 'the immediate personal concern that accounts for our passionate interest in formal biography', while Emil Ludwig argues, in a slightly different vein, that the biographer 'must always perceive the rhapsody of his own life as though it were foreign to him. [. . .] If he is to make copies of men, he must see himself mirrored in mankind. It is not until his own life appears to him as symbolic that he is prepared to discern the symbolism behind the lives of others'[32]. Biography, it could be said, begins with self-analysis.

---

[30] Ibid., p. 87.
[31] Ibid., p. 86.
[32] Ludwig, *Genius and Character*, pp. 18–19.

The distinction between biography and autobiography, which had become more marked in the course of the nineteenth century, thus becomes in some ways less absolute. A hundred years previously biography had been the parent genre, with 'self-biography' as a sub-genre in which biographical representation was turned, unusually, upon the self.[33] In the early twentieth century, either autobiographical consciousness, with its difficult self-exploration, has become a first reference point, or the two forms—biography and autobiography—are seen as equiprimordial.

The intense focus on 'character' in biography and in fiction also has an etymological dimension. The term 'character' stems from the Greek *kharratein*, to engrave. In Woolf's writing there is a recurrent play on 'character' as a printing term, and on the relationship between 'character' and 'type', deployed in one of her own 'biographical' experiments, *Jacob's Room*, to subvert received definitions of 'character' as psychological 'type', and to explore the concept of reading character as one would read a map or navigate a city. The novel also explores, as do *Mrs Dalloway*, *To the Lighthouse*, and *The Years*, the question of what survives us, of how and on what we make our mark, inscribe our 'character'. In a different way, an implicit understanding of 'character' as mark or sign emerges in that aspect of the 'new biography', most prominent in North American contexts, in which an idealized model of essential selfhood replaces Stracheyan scepticism. 'Character' becomes inseparable from a concept of the permanency of 'impression' that was central to the psychical researchers of the late nineteenth and early twentieth centuries, whose claims for the afterlife were strongly predicated on the notion of 'a transcendental energy in living men' and 'an influence emanating from personalities which have overpassed the tomb'.[34] The widespread turn to psychical research and spiritualism more generally during and after the mass-slaughter of World War I made its own mark on biography, although it could be said that biography has always been a 'haunted' form of writing, imparting a (textual) afterlife to the dead. Thus James C. Johnston asserts: 'There can be only one legitimate purpose for biography of any kind: to keep alive the man's individuality', and refers approvingly to Laura Spencer Portor's *Haunted Lives*:

> The key to a life, insists Laura Spencer Portor [. . .] lies in the fact that all lives are 'haunted' by certain recurrent thoughts, influences, impressions, or realization, which, if the biographer will but seize and present to his readers, will leave a picture that no number of dates, or even events, can succeed in

[33] See my discussion of the history of the autobiographical genre, and of autobiographical criticism, in Laura Marcus, *Auto/biographical Discourses: Theory, Criticism, Practice* (Manchester, 1994), esp. Ch. 1.
[34] F. W. H. Myers, *Human Personality and its Survival of Bodily Death* (1903; reprinted Norwich, 1992), p. 173.

bringing to our minds. [. . .] The extent to which character is capable of crystallizing would obligate the biographer in any sort of method he might choose to see to it that his story possesses as much unity at least as the life itself holds.[35]

Bradford's 'psychography' (also the term applied by George Saintsbury to Sainte-Beuve's biographical writings) is equally predicated on the concept of a 'crystallizing' of character born out of 'recurrence':

> Out of the perpetual flux of actions and circumstances that constitutes a man's whole life, it seeks to extract what is essential, what is permanent and so vitally characteristic. [. . .] As we observe the actions of different men, we find that they follow certain comparatively definite lines, which we call habits. [. . .] The generalization of these habits of action, sometimes expressing itself very obscurely and imperfectly for the acute observer in features and manifestations of the body, constitutes what we call qualities. And the complex of qualities in turn forms the fleeting and uncertain total which we sum up in the word 'character'. [. . .] Character, then, is the sum of qualities or generalized habits of action. Psychography is the condensed, essential, artistic presentation of character.[36]

Underlying Bradford's aesthetics of biography—caught somewhat uneasily between concepts of the self as fixed or as fluid—we can glimpse the psychology of William James, with its double focus on the fixities of habitual action, in which semi-permanent traces are laid down in the mental mechanism through repetition and we become almost immutably what we are, and on the flux and flow of consciousness, in which there is no repetition: *'no state once gone can recur and be identical with what it was before. [. . .] What is got twice is the* same OBJECT. *[. . .]* our state of mind is never precisely the same'.[37] 'Habit has a physical basis', James insists, and the turning of biographers such as Bradford to habitual action as a key to character is frequently accompanied by an emphasis on habitual gesture, the authenticity of which is grounded in its non-volitional, automatic character. For Emil Ludwig, 'a man's daily habits [. . .] were formerly inserted like curiosities, little bonbons for the reader's palate. [. . .] For us, today, the most trivial habit will often suggest the interpretation for some major trait of character'.[38] 'I long since learned', Bradford writes, 'that such material as the fifteen volumes of Sumner's collected works was of little or no value for my purposes. Again, a careless word, spoken with no intention whatever, a mere gesture, the lifting of the hand or the turning

---

[35] Johnston, *Biography: The Literature of Personality*, p. 242.
[36] Gamaliel Bradford, *A Naturalist of Souls* (Boston, 1926), pp. 5–8.
[37] William James, *Text Book of Psychology* (London, 1904), pp. 154–6; emphasis in original.
[38] Ludwig, *Genius and Character*, p. 16.

of the head, may fling open a wide window into a man's inmost heart'.[39]
The perception of gesture as the mark of the uniqueness of the individual
finds its more radical echo in the Freudian concept of the symptomatic
gesture, and of bodies that speak the truths that minds disallow or disa-
vow.

The intense focus on the gesture and the detail in the 'new biography'
can work to 'crystallize' or essentialize 'character', as in the work of Ludwig
(for whom, famously, the motive and meaning of Wilhelm II's life are
concentrated in his withered arm and in the 'inferiority complex' to which
it led[40]) or, as in the far more radical and subversive writings of Strachey,
to unravel identities. At the close of his *Queen Victoria* Strachey undoes
'the life' by having the dying queen remember her experiences in reverse
chronology, turning back:

> To the Spring woods at Osborne, so full of primroses for Lord Beaconsfield—
> to Lord Palmerston's queer clothes and high demeanour, and Albert's face
> under the green lamp, and Albert's first stag at Balmoral, and Albert in his
> blue and silver uniform, and the Baron coming in through a doorway, and
> Lord M. dreaming at Windsor with the rooks cawing in the elm-trees, and the
> Archbishop of Canterbury on his knees in the dawn, and the old King's
> turkey-cock ejaculations, and Uncle Leopold's soft voice at Claremont, and
> Lehzen with the globes, and her mother's feathers sweeping down towards
> her, and a great old repeater-watch of her father's in its tortoise-shell case,

---

[39] Bradford, *A Naturalist of Souls*, p. 13.
[40] Emil Ludwig, *Kaiser Wilhelm II*, tr. Ethel Colburn Mayne (London, 1926). Freud used
Ludwig's biography of Wilhelm II to point up the inadequacy of the term 'inferiority complex',
which 'haunts the pages of what are known as *belles lettres*. An author who uses the term
"inferiority complex" thinks that by so doing he has fulfilled all the demands of psychoanalysis and has raised his composition to a higher psychological plane. In fact, "inferiority
complex" is a technical term that is scarcely used in psycho-analysis. [. . .] A historical
personage of our own days, who is still alive though at the moment he has retired into the
background, suffers from a defect in one of his limbs owing to an injury at the time of his
birth. A very well-known contemporary writer who is particularly fond of compiling the
biographies of celebrities has dealt, among others, with the life of the man I am speaking of.
Now in writing a biography it may well be difficult to suppress a need to plumb the
psychological depths. For this reason our author has ventured on an attempt to erect the whole
of the development of his hero's character on the sense of inferiority which must have been
called up by his physical defect. In doing so, he has overlooked one small but not insignificant
fact. It is usual for mothers whom Fate has presented with a child who is sickly or otherwise
at a disadvantage to try to compensate him for his unfair handicap by a superabundance of
love. In the instance before us, the proud mother behaved otherwise; she withdrew her love
from the child on account of his infirmity. When he had grown up into a man of great power,
he proved unambiguously by his actions that he had never forgiven his mother. When you
consider the importance of a mother's love for the mental life of a child, you will no doubt
make a tacit correction of the biographer's inferiority theory' (Freud, *New Introductory
Lectures*, Standard Edition, XXII, London, 1960, pp. 65–6). Freud thus uses psychoanalytic
theory to 'correct' Ludwig's inadequately psychoanalytic biography.

and a yellow rug, and some friendly flounces of sprigged muslin, and the trees and the grass at Kensington.[41]

The passage is cinematic in its use of visual images and close-up techniques, and in its replaying in reverse time and motion of all that lived and biographical time have constructed. The images of childhood are at one and the same time enlarged and miniaturized, in accord with Susan Stewart's claim that 'we imagine childhood as if it were at the other end of a tunnel—distanced, diminutive, and clearly framed'.[42] Strachey also opens up an interior world conventionally reserved for the novelist, in which the subject is returned to her beginning, restoring, as Freud described the processes of the 'death drive', 'an earlier state of things'.

Strachey's use of detail also serves to make strange the familiar, and his biographical representations often take on a grotesque and even surreal aspect. The sketch of Lady Hester Stanhope, published in *Books and Characters* (1922), for example, opens thus:

> The Pitt nose has a curious history. One can watch its transmigrations through three lives. The tremendous hook of old Lord Chatham, under whose curve Empires came to birth, was succeeded by the bleak upward-pointing nose of William Pitt the younger—the rigid symbol of an indomitable *hauteur*. With Lady Hester Stanhope came the final stage. The nose, still with an upward tilt in it, had lost its masculinity; the hard bones of the uncle and the grandfather had disappeared. Lady Hester's was a nose of wild ambitions, of pride grown fantastical, a nose that scorned the earth, shooting off, one fancies, towards some eternally eccentric heaven. It was a nose, in fact, altogether in the air.[43]

As Ruth Hoberman argues, Lady Hester's 'nose', although theoretically a synecdoche (the figure of speech in which part stands for whole) in fact operates metonymically, in 'a part-part, not part-whole relation to her self, suggesting her own alienated relationship to her society and her self'.[44] The biographical portrait closes with Lady Hester 'lying back in her bed— inexplicable, grand, preposterous, with her nose in the air'.[45] The part or detail—which, in the writings of Ludwig or Bradford, would ideally serve to represent the whole self—is here rendered 'inexplicable', excessive and absurd. In a related way, Strachey uses synecdoche in *Eminent Victorians* to undermine monumental ambition; the parts bring down (rather than represent or stand for) the whole. Hence Lytton Strachey's description of Cardinal Manning's 'remains':

---

[41] Lytton Strachey, *Queen Victoria* (London, 1921, reprinted Harmondsworth, 1971), p. 246.
[42] Susan Stewart, *On Longing* (Baltimore, 1984), p. 44.
[43] Strachey, 'Lady Hester Stanhope', in *Books and Characters* (London, 1922), p. 241.
[44] Hoberman, *Modernizing Lives*, p. 45.
[45] Strachey, *Books and Characters*, p. 249.

The Cardinal's memory is a dim thing today. And he who descends into the crypt of that Cathedral which Manning never lived to see, will observe, in the quiet niche with the sepulchral monument, that the dust lies thick on the strange, the incongruous, the almost impossible object which, with its elaborations of dependent tassels, hangs down from the dim vault like some forlorn and forgotten trophy—the Hat.[46]

Synecdoche, the central device of Stracheyan biography, is also, in Domna Stanton's phrase, 'the idiolect of dandyism'.[47] 'Camp', Susan Sontag wrote, 'is the modern dandyism. Camp is the answer to the problem: how to be a dandy in an age of mass culture'.[48] Numerous biographies of the 1920s and 1930s, including those of Lytton Strachey and André Maurois, adopt the dandiacal or the 'camp' style, or take as their subjects figures, such as Disraeli and Byron, whose 'dandyism' was combined with a fierce commitment to poetry and to politics. The status of the biographical subject—his factuality as well as his genius—secures the biography for literature and for history, while the style of many 'new biographies' allows them a share in the popularity of historical romances. One answer to the problem of 'how to be a dandy in an age of mass culture' was to become a 'new biographer'.

Against the high seriousness of Victorian biography, the 'new biography', of which Strachey's texts are the chief exemplars, is most typically defined by its uses of satire and irony. In this essay I have discussed some of the characteristic devices of early twentieth-century biography: shifts in size and scale, pointing up the relativity of the subject's status and value; a focus on the detail and the gesture. These related devices indicated, I have argued elsewhere, an uneasy relationship to the 'Great Man', his alternate elevation and diminution signalling an oscillation between hero-worship and debunking.[49] To this I would add that the eccentricities of focus and of the imputation of value, and the homing in on the detail, are also defining details of camp style. As Andrew Ross writes, in his essay 'Uses of Camp': 'Camp [. . .] involves a celebration, on the part of cognoscenti, of the alienation, distance and incongruity reflected in the very process by which hitherto unexpected value can be located in some obscure or exorbitant object'.[50] The Nose and the Hat, we could say, function as just such objects in Strachey's writings.

For a fuller exploration of the biographer as dandy we can now turn

---

[46] Strachey, *Eminent Victorians*, p. 108.
[47] Domna Stanton, *The Aristocrat as Art* (New York, 1980), p. 160.
[48] Susan Sontag, *Against Interpretation* (New York, 1966), p. 288.
[49] See my essay ' "Looking Glasses at Odd Corners": Biography and Psychoanalysis in the Early Twentieth Century', *New Comparison*, XXV (1998), 52–70.
[50] Andrew Ross, *No Respect: Intellectuals and Popular Culture* (New York and London, 1989), p. 146.

to the work of A. J. A. Symons. In his essay 'Tradition in Biography' (1929), Symons argues against 'the timeworn chronological formula'[51] of traditional biography in favour of a more 'telling order':

> The easiest, and one of many sound ways, is to lift the curtains on a hero fully developed and manifesting the idiosyncrasies which make him worth writing about, to follow his career until its end, illustrating meanwhile the changing of his character with the years; and then, at the finishing, to retrace the steps by which he had become what, in the first chapter, he was shown as being.[52]

The book for which Symons—dandy, bibliophile, and self-styled 'speculator'—is best known is his biography of Frederick Rolfe (1932), the turn-of-the-century writer and 'spoiled priest' who took as his alias 'Baron Corvo'. Symons called his text *The Quest for Corvo: An Experiment in Biography*: in the use of the term 'experiment' he was drawing attention, he wrote in a prefatory note, to his attempt 'to fulfil those standards which I endeavoured to set up in an essay on biographical tradition published by the Oxford University Press in 1929'. The nature of the 'experiment' lay to an extent in its ostensible indifference to chronology: Symons wrote that his interest 'in the early years of the eminent is far less than that which the tradition of biographical writing painfully imposes on its devotees' and that 'it is possible to reason backwards as well as forwards, to infer the child from the man; and I proposed to do so'.[53] The experimentation is more substantially based, however, in the foregrounding of the biographer's quest for his subject. This method (which, according to Symons's own biographer, his brother Julian Symons, writing in 1950, was 'emulated very little by later biographers') was in fact adopted by a number of late twentieth-century biographers, including Richard Holmes and Peter Ackroyd. The trope of detection enters in the image of one man tracking another across the territory, following (in) his footsteps. The elements which become more or less explicit are, first, the biographer's identification with or desire for the subject whom he pursues and, second, the nature of the 'evidence' and the means of its gathering.

For Symons, biographical desire is textually mediated through the friend (Christopher Millard, former secretary to Oscar Wilde's friend Robert Ross) by whom he is introduced to Rolfe's work. He opens his biography in this way:

---

[51] A. J. A. Symons, 'Tradition in Biography', in *Tradition and Experiment in Present-Day Literature* (Oxford, 1929), p. 155.

[52] Ibid., p. 156.

[53] A. J. A. Symons, *The Quest for Corvo: An Experiment in Biography* (1934) (London, 1993), p. 51.

> My quest for Corvo was started by accident one summer afternoon in 1925,
> in the company of Christopher Millard. We were sitting lazily in his little
> garden, talking of books that miss their just reward of praise and influence.
> I mentioned *Wylder's Hand*, by Le Fanu, a masterpiece of plot, and the
> *Fantastic Fables* of Ambrose Bierce. After a pause, without commenting on
> my examples, Millard asked: 'Have you read *Hadrian the Seventh*?' I con-
> fessed that I never had; and to my surprise he offered to lend me his copy—
> to my surprise, for my companion lent his books seldom and reluctantly. But,
> knowing the range of his knowledge of out-of-the-way literature, I accepted
> without hesitating; and by doing so took the first step on a trail that led into
> very strange places.[54]

The biography draws to a close with Symons's account of his meetings
with one Maundy Gregory, a man fabulously but mysteriously wealthy,
possessed, for a time at least, by a fascination with Rolfe's writings. Symons
recounts his amazement when Gregory hands him one of Rolfe's missing
novels: 'It had been found, I gathered, by one of his many "agents" who,
at considerable cost, had traced the original printer, and from the depths
of a rat-haunted cellar salved five copies, the only survivors of the whole
edition'. The biographical 'quest' Symons describes is a search for both
'the life' of Frederick Rolfe and for his lost manuscripts; in the end Symons
discovers the final missing novel 'in the depths of a literary agent's
cupboard':

> It was a deep satisfaction still to know that every one of the works which
> had been left and lost in obscurity when Frederick William Serafino Austin
> Lewis Mary Rolfe died suddenly and alone at Venice had been collected
> together by sympathetic hands, and that, alone, of living men, I had read
> every one. Nothing was left to be discovered; the Quest was ended. Hail,
> strange tormented spirit, in whatever hell or heaven has been allotted for
> your everlasting rest![55]

The biographical 'quest' is thus displaced on to the bibliographical search
and, with the discovery of the final missing manuscript, Rolfe can be laid
to rest.

Symons's own history in part explains the shift to bibliographical concerns. He was the largely self-taught son of a 'speculator' father and, as a
young man, 'spent hours in practising calligraphy, copying page after page
from the *Dictionary of National Biography* until he had achieved a tiny,
crabbed but beautiful Gothic script'.[56] (It is a nice irony that this 'new
biographer' invents his personal, decadent style by means of the *DNB*.)
His first entrepreneurial ventures included the creation of the First Edition

[54] Ibid., p. 1.
[55] Ibid., p. 283.
[56] Julian Symons, *A. J. A. Symons: His Life and Speculations* (1950, new edn Oxford, 1986),
p. 27.

Club in the early 1920s, during which time he worked on a 'Nineties Bibliography' and befriended the booksellers William and Gilbert Foyle, who had opened a Rare Book Department in their bookshop and, in 1923, became partners in the Club. Symons's first work on Rolfe appeared in a paper delivered at a meeting of Ye Sette of Odd Volumes, 'a select and distinguished dining Club' according to Julian Symons, and subsequently published in Desmond MacCarthy's magazine *Life and Letters*.

Symons died in 1941 at the age of forty-one, before completing a biography of Oscar Wilde by which, Julian Symons writes, 'he planned to show the distant world of the nineties in which Wilde achieved his successes of conversation, drama and self-advertisement, and which he shocked by his homosexuality'.[57] A. J. A. Symons was motivated to write a definitive life of Wilde, his brother asserts, when he 'began to consider seriously the art of biography and decided that English biography "has failed in beauty as in truth" '. Although he gathered a vast amount of material, including the 'Wildeana' entering the collector's market, the writing of the life did not come easily, and only five chapters had been written by the time of his death. Wilde, or what he represented, was none the less central to Symons. Wilde's son, Vyvyan Holland, remained a close friend after his encounter with Symons at the First Edition Club in 1922, the meeting with which Julian Symons opens the story of his brother's life. The reader's first image of A. J. A. Symons—'a very tall, thin young man, wearing a lavender-coloured suit of an advanced cut', framed in the doorway—thus comes as if through the eyes of Oscar Wilde's son.[58]

Rolfe and his biographer walk one of the more 'out-of-the-way' paths of literary history, and their *sui generis* status as writers might seem to preclude them from functioning as representative texts. But the nexus of Rolfe and Symons, as well as Julian Symons's biography, opens up important aspects of early twentieth-century biography and its reception. First, it emerged along with the new book clubs and literary venues of the 1920s, which were in many cases touched with the aesthetic and aristocratic hedonisms of the late nineteenth century, but were also part of a new commercial and literary culture. Second, for the collectors Symons mentions the 1890s and its literary objects are the primary foci of bibliophilia, and the figure and image of Wilde are central. While Symons represents Rolfe's homosexuality as a fatal flaw and as his ruination, the milieu for and in which Symons writes is markedly homosocial. Books are the traffic between men, and biography in this period—which, despite the presence of women biographers, is almost always represented in the terms of one

---

[57] Ibid., p. 246.
[58] Ibid., p. 1.

man writing the life of another—becomes a particularly charged genre. The belief, imputed to Symons by his brother, that the problems of achieving beauty and truth in biography might be tested, if not resolved, through a biography of Wilde, is a telling one, suggesting a continuity between the *fin de siècle* and the 'new biography' of the 1920s and 1930s in ways which also bear on the periodizing of modernism more broadly.

This moment in literary and cultural history also relates to the ways in which norms of 'proper' masculinity (and femininity) and the moral imperatives of the established 'life course', central to Victorian biography, are radically disrupted in certain texts of the new biography. Symons's eschewal of chronology is not just a formal question; the more 'telling order' which he holds that the biographer should pursue disturbs conventional notions of formation and achievement. As William Epstein notes, Lytton Strachey showed, in his *Eminent Victorians*, how ' "obscure recesses, hitherto undivined" divert the course of the miraculously lamplit pathway of the professional career'.[59]

Deviations from the conventional life-course are explored by Woolf, in 'The New Biography' and in a later essay, 'The Art of Biography', in which she focuses on Lytton Strachey's writings. She argues that the biographer should not flout the law of factuality but exploit the 'proper creativeness' of 'fact', for facts, like fictions, are open to multiple interpretations. They are also subject to historical contingency and change and, as she writes in 'The Art of Biography', to 'changes of opinion: opinions change as the times change':

> What was thought a sin is now known, by the light of facts won for us by the psychologists, to be perhaps a misfortune; perhaps a curiosity, perhaps neither one nor the other, but a trifling foible of no great importance one way or the other. The accent on sex has changed within living memory. This leads to the destruction of a great deal of dead matter still obscuring the true features of the human face. Many of the old chapter headings—life at college, marriage, career—are shown to be very arbitrary and artificial distinctions. The real current of the hero's existence took, very likely, a different course.
>
> Thus the biographer must go ahead of the rest of us, like the miner's canary, testing the atmosphere, detecting falsity, unreality, and the presence of obsolete conventions. His sense of truth must be alive and on tiptoe. Then again, since we live in an age when a thousand cameras are pointed, by newspapers, letters, and diaries, at every character from every angle, he must be prepared to admit contradictory versions of the same face. Biography will enlarge its scope by hanging up looking glasses at odd corners. And yet from all this diversity it will bring out, not a riot of confusion, but a richer unity.[60]

---

[59] Epstein, *Recognizing Biography*, p. 148.
[60] Woolf, 'The Art of Biography', (1939), reprinted in *The Crowded Dance of Modern Life: Selected Essays*, ed. Rachel Bowlby (London, 1993), pp. 149–50.

The passage, and the essay from which it was drawn, raises a number of crucial points, which I will use to address some final remaining questions and issues.

Woolf's allusion to the pointing cameras is a reminder that the 'new biography' developed alongside the new media of the early twentieth century. There are important connections to be made, though I cannot pursue them here, between biography and the new arts of publicity and journalism that were also devoted to the representations of lives, though in ways that often appeared to threaten biography as a high art form. The emergent art of film is a further crucial context.[61] George Johnston's article notes that in its focus on vivid details and 'brightly colored tableaux', 'the new biography is undoubtedly akin to the best traditions of the cinemato-graph. The aim of cinematographic art is to concentrate on brilliant images, on significant incidents, on episodes important for the comprehension of the character portrayed. This is precisely what the new biography does'.[62] It may be that the new biography is inflected by the cinematic devices of detail, gesture and close-up and by cinematic subversions of linear time and chronology (in, for example, parallel editing or flashback), but we might also note the ways in which film borrowed from biography the trajectory of a life as an appropriate cinematic theme and structuring principle. Mark Longaker's book *Contemporary Biography* (1934) notes:

> In the past decade, the drama and the motion pictures have shown an unprecedented interest in the lives and personalities of historical figures. [. . .] George Arliss's characterizations of Alexander Hamilton, Disraeli, and Voltaire; and Hartau's admirable interpretation of character in the French film *Napoleon* indicated that the motion pictures may in time afford an excellent medium not only for popularising biography, but also for creating a vivid kind of portraiture.[63]

The second issue that concerns us here is Woolf's allusion to the changed 'accent on sex'. The example she gives of the changing nature of 'fact' is, we can assume, the 'fact' of (homo)sexuality, while the passage serves to erode the absolute nature of sexual difference: 'neither one nor another [. . .] of no great importance one way or the other'. Woolf's own mock-biography *Orlando* (1928), which is, in Leon Edel's words, 'a fable for biographers'[64], stretches the boundaries of the individual beyond breaking-point: Orlando is alive during the three centuries of text-time, first as a man and then as a woman. Lytton Strachey's *Elizabeth and Essex*, published in the same year, suggests that the sexual identity of the queen is ambiguous

[61] See Chapter 16 below.
[62] George Johnston, 'The New Biography', p. 340.
[63] Longaker, *Contemporary Biography*, p. 5.
[64] Edel, *Writing Lives*, p. 192.

—'was she a man?'—and turns to a Freudianism that tells a story in which the (male) child, when confronted with a naked queen or a naked mother, will rapidly endow her with the 'manhood' she is observed to lack, made out of the materials of appearance: 'the huge hoop, the stiff ruff, the swollen sleeves, the powdered pearls, the spreading, gilded gauzes'.[65] Both *Orlando* and *Elizabeth and Essex* were strongly influenced by and contributed to contemporary debates about androgyny and sexual identity.

Woolf was nevertheless critical of *Elizabeth and Essex*, deeming it a failure. She does not refer to Strachey's use of psychoanalysis in the text, though his 'psychobiographical' portrait of Elizabeth met with Freud's full approval. As Freud wrote to Strachey:

> You are aware of what other historians so easily overlook—that it is imposs-ible to understand the past with certainty, because we cannot divine men's motives and the essence of their minds and so cannot interpret their actions. With regard to the people of past times we are in the same position as with dreams to which we have been given no associations—and only a lay man could expect us to interpret such dreams as these. As a historian, then, you show that you are steeped in the spirit of psychoanalysis. And with reser-vations such as these, you have approached one of the most remarkable figures in your country's history, you have known how to trace back her character to the impressions of her childhood, you have touched upon her most hidden motives with equal boldness and discretion, and it is very possible that you have succeeded in making a correct reconstruction of what actually occurred.[66]

Freudian sexual theories provided Strachey with one answer to the question posed in *Elizabeth and Essex*: 'By what art are we to worm our way into those strange spirits, those even stranger projects?'[67] The 'correct reconstruction' of Elizabeth's motives and inner life is made through the 'universal story', the Oedipus legend. Yet Strachey also pursues a deviation from the life-course inscribed by the Oedipus narrative itself, a deviation generated by his explorations of women with power. As Perry Meisel notes, 'the book's psychoanalytic project is its beginning, not its end'.[68]

Strachey and Freud were, it could be argued, the two primary influences on biography in the 1920s, and their interrelation has a central bearing on the history of the British reception of psychoanalysis and of English-lan-guage Freud, with James Strachey, Lytton's brother, largely responsible for the work of translation. Biography was one of the major conduits by means

[65] Strachey, *Elizabeth and Essex* (London, 1928, reprinted Harmondsworth, 1971), p. 13.
[66] Freud, letter to Lytton Strachey, 25 December 1928, in *Bloomsbury/Freud: The Letters of James and Alix Strachey 1924–25*, ed. Perry Meisel and Walter Kendrick (New York, 1985), pp. 332–3.
[67] Strachey, *Elizabeth and Essex*, p. 12.
[68] Meisel, *The Myth of the Modern*, p. 216.

of which psychoanalytic theory reached a general readership, and responses to Freud, positive and negative, emerged to a very large extent as responses to the new ways in which 'lives' were represented and interpreted. Freud was in fact notoriously ambivalent towards biography, warning his would-be biographer Arnold Zweig that 'biographical truth does not exist and if it did we could not use it',[69] but writing to Jung in 1909 that 'We [the psychoanalytic movement] must take hold of biography'.[70] Freud also produced the first 'psychobiography' in his 'Leonardo da Vinci and a Memory of his Childhood' (1910), the text in which he gives his most sustained account of biography as a genre, including the distortions caused by the biographer's identifications with and idealizations of his subject, and uses biographical speculation in, paradoxically, the service of 'correct reconstruction'. Freud, the founder of psychoanalysis, is also the founder of psychoanalytic biography as a genre.[71]

The development of 'psychobiography', strongest in the United States, is a crucial aspect of the history of the 'new biography'. While a number of biographers in the 1920s retained a critical distance from Freudian theory, others, in John Garraty's words, 'began to see the possibilities—the insights into hidden motives, the escape from the limits of 'factual' biography, the sensationalism inherent in an approach that emphasized sex, with its healthy effects on sales'.[72] Garraty, like many biographical critics, is clearly cynical about the development of psychobiography. The sustained attacks on Freudian biography in the 1930s might well have contributed to its decline (though it re-emerged in the United States under the influence of ego-psychology): Bernard DeVoto's influential and highly positivist critique, for example, described psychobiography as an approximation to 'the art of the detective story, whose clues are also invented and whose deductions are also made to fit'.[73] The Freudian biography of the 1920s and 1930s may now seem both quaint and absurd, but there are surely interesting dimensions to the desire for and fascination with the new method by means of which lives could be told differently, and the texts of

---

[69] Freud wrote to Arnold Zweig, 'Anyone who writes a biography is committed to lies, concealment, hypocrisy, flattery and even to hiding his own lack of understanding, for biographical truth does not exist, and if it did we could not use it'. Letter from Freud to Zweig, 31 May 1936, in *The Letters of Sigmund Freud and Arnold Zweig*, ed. Ernst L. Freud (New York, 1970), p. 127.

[70] Letter from Freud to Jung, 17 October 1909, in *The Freud/Jung Letters* (abridged), ed. William McGuire (Harmondsworth, 1991), p. 161.

[71] See Chapter 10 above.

[72] Garraty, *The Nature of Biography*, p. 116.

[73] Bernard DeVoto, 'The Sceptical Biographer', in *Biography as an Art: Selected Criticism 1560–1960* (Oxford, 1962), p. 149.

this period also made their contribution to the deeply imbricated histories of biography and of psychoanalysis.

I would suggest, in conclusion, that the phenomenon of the 'new biography' and the significance of biography in the first decades of the century are not exhausted topics. There has been an extraordinary recent growth of interest in modernism and modernity, and in the literature and culture of the early twentieth century more generally. Any attempt to reconstruct the priorities of this period would need to give biography a much more central place than it has yet received in literary and cultural histories. I have examined some of the preoccupations of biographers and their readers, including the focus on 'character' and 'personality' as a way of inscribing a 'modern' subjectivity. I have also suggested that the category of the 'new biography' often serves to hold together writers and texts with attitudes towards this subjectivity that are widely opposed. In looking at such questions, we begin to open up the complexity of the culture and the politics of biography, and the value of their further exploration.

12

The Biographer as Archaeologist

WILLIAM ST CLAIR

When we examine the numerous literary biographies of famous authors of the Romantic period in Great Britain, the patterns which emerge are, for the most part, as we would expect. As literary compositions, the biographies have normally been shaped by, indeed have often been largely determined by, the quantity and the nature of the surviving primary documentary evidence, especially by diaries, letters, notes of conversations, and descriptions and mentions by contemporaries. The sources have not only shaped the nature of the biographies but the biographical method adopted.

In the case of William Blake, for example, where the primary sources are meagre and impersonal, his biographers have usually attempted to reconstruct the character of the author from indications in the published works. Some have successfully attempted to locate the individual by reconstructing the circumscribing historical and cultural context within which he lived.[1] With a range of other authors of the period, occasional batches of primary materials have survived within a thin archival record, rich and fertile oases in an otherwise barren desert. In the case of Austen, Hazlitt, Peacock, and Wollstonecraft, the biographers have usually devoted a high proportion of their narratives to a discussion of those episodes in the lives, and those aspects of the characters, which are revealed by the easily exploitable resources. Some, in frustration with the intractable gaps, have diverged into family history, where information on births, deaths, marriages, property transactions, appointments, and other such official or quasi-official details can be found, even if it may sometimes reveal little

[1] Notably Michael Phillips, 'Blake and the Terror', in *The Library*, XVI, 4 (1994), 163.

more biographical material than the names and dates of the author's relatives.

With some of the other famous authors of the period, by contrast, including Byron, Coleridge, Keats, Scott, Mary Shelley, Shelley, and Wordsworth, the surviving primary archival material is not only plentiful, but varied, and well spread across the length of the writers' lives. The records contain many full and revealing personal as well as official documents written by a large number of contemporary observers whose closeness to, and knowledge of, the authors differed, who adopted a range of points of view, and wrote with their own purposes in mind. In the case of these authors we not only have their printed works, often in modern editions, but printed collections of their letters, diaries, and notebooks, as well as manuscript drafts of their works which enable biographers to trace the development of their writing. Virtually every scrap of writing which can be attributed to their pens has been published. In the cases of these authors, the scope for biographers to reconstruct the main events in the lives, to detect recurring patterns, and to choose and to shape the writing, has been wider, and the resulting range of biographies, considered both as narratives and as interpretations, is far more varied.

The general observation that the life as biographized is a function of the surviving historical sources, should, however, I suggest, raise a number of questions in our minds. Placed side by side on the shelf, the biographies of the Romantic period authors neatly illustrate the necessary limitations attendant on any kind of writing which is dependent on historical sources, just as a history of ancient Assyria is necessarily more constrained than one of modern France. But why, in the case of biographical writing, should more evidence mean less certainty? With many other areas of study which attempt to recover an understanding of the past, the opposite is more normal. In a court of law, for example, the greater the amount of evidence, the greater confidence we are likely to have that the salient facts have been recovered and that the verdict is a reasonable one. Many disciplines which search for, and make use of, previously unused empirical evidence are cumulative in their conclusions. Archaeology, for example, progresses by adding the results of one detailed study to another so that, gradually, the picture of the past which emerges from on-going research is more secure. The same is true of the social sciences. In economics, the more economic information we can gather, the more confirmation we receive that our explanatory models are reliable.

Of course all historical disciplines experience upsets. Explanations and paradigms have to be shifted as a result of the discovery of new evidence; a new eye can sometimes see patterns which were not previously noticed; and new generations are interested in new questions. Many of the differences to be found among the biographies which faced much the same corpus of primary sources can be explained by the cultural assumptions and aspirations of the time when they were written. Thus, to John Gibson Lockhart, his admiring son-in law, Sir Walter Scott was the real-life embodiment of the chivalric values which the Waverley novels sought to celebrate.[2] To the Pre-Raphaelites who 'rediscovered' the two Romantic poets who they believed had been unjustly neglected in their own time, Blake was a visionary prophet, Keats an apostle of beauty.[3] In recent times, almost all the writers of the Romantic period, even Austen, have been portrayed as participating in the political and cultural movements of their age, if only by their silences, and their lives and their works have been quarried for indications of constructions of national, social, gender, and other identities. The varied record across time confirms that the writing of biography is as much subject to what the Romantics called 'the spirit of the age' as other forms of writing. Regular updatings and reappraisals are, therefore, not only to be expected as more source material is discovered, but can be legitimately regarded as a necessary part of each generation's attempts to reach its own understanding of the past.

But, even after making allowance for the changing cultural presumptions within which literary biography is written, it seems more unstable than its neighbours in adjoining historical disciplines. Although few subjects of study are as complex as an individual human being, what are we to make of a form of historical writing which by its nature is narrowly limited to a specific historical context, where the discovery by the biographer of some previously unnoticed letters is thought to require that the biographical edifice previously constructed by others should have to be redesigned and rebuilt? Where the latest biographer, faced with much the same corpus of primary materials as his or her predecessors, decides that a particular event in the subject's life was far more determinative, more of a turning-point, or more telling as a vignette of the operation of character in action, than had previously been appreciated, and then goes on to construct the whole written life in a different shape? Far from reassuring us that we are approaching a more complete understanding of the individual being biographized, should not the procession of one unstable version after another tend to undermine our confidence in the procedures of the genre? Why read the latest biography if a new one which claims to supersede it is already advertised as forthcoming?

In recent decades we have seen examples of a biographical approach

---

[2] J. G. Lockhart, *Memoirs of the Life of Sir Walter Scott, Bart.* (Edinburgh, 1836–8).
[3] For example in the series of memoirs written by W. M. Rossetti from 1870 to the early twentieth century for Moxon's *Standard Poets* series.

which both welcomes and increases the instability.[4] Although the biographers concerned seldom explicitly abandon the genre's claims to be an investigative historical enterprise founded on evidence, they implicitly accept that biography is mainly a form of storytelling, a literary form which is generically as close to the novel as it is to history. Confident too that it is not just the boundary between fiction and non-fiction which has become less clear as a result of advances in critical understanding of the nature of texts, but the whole notion of a 'biographical fact', some biographers try deliberately to free themselves from the tyranny of the documentary record. It is almost certainly true, such a biographer might say, that Keats lived at 8 Dean Street, and not at 9 Dean Street, but who cares? The house number may be a 'fact' but it is uninteresting, indeed uninformative, in itself, and in any case it is not the kind of information which potential readers of my biography want. If I wish to help my potential readers to understand how Keats lived his life, with some discussion of his childhood emotions, his literary aspirations, his understanding of the world of his day, and all the myriad forces and circumstances which made him a great poet, I cannot allow my narrative to be imprisoned within the confines of so-called biographical facts. These 'primary sources', to which our biographical predecessors accorded such respect, are just a random survival of texts which happen to have been composed and written down by people whose purpose was usually very different from helping me, as a present-day biographer, to offer an account of a life to readers living nearly two centuries later.

Furthermore, the same biographer might continue, as Woolf and the other modernists have shown, few if any biographies which are exclusively founded on recorded 'facts' and which construct strong narratives from these factual records, can by themselves help us to understand the shapelessness of lives, the anarchy of thought, and the unpredictability of the future, as they are actually experienced.[5] Indeed, with their strong narratives which imply a unified self, they may be unfair to other aspects of the life, to other important biographical 'facts' which were not recorded. At best, biographies which stick too closely to the documentary record can therefore never be more than elaborated chronicles which collect the simplest external recorded steps from birth to death. They are documentary lives, such as Samuel Schoenbaum's *William Shakespeare: A Documentary Life* (1975),

---

[4] The most explicit example is Kenneth R. Johnston, *The Hidden Wordsworth: Poet, Lover, Rebel, Spy* (New York and London, 1998), p. 8: 'Wordsworthian biography does not need more facts, though these are always welcome, so much as it needs more speculation.' See also n. 7 below.

[5] Discussed in Virginia Woolf, *Jacob's Room* (1922), *Orlando: A Biography* (1928), and *Flush: A Biography* (1933).

excellent and indispensable scholarly compilations which provide a skeletal framework within which the reader's imagination can either range freely or be kept under tight restraint, depending on the mental disposition of the individual.

The defence of the deliberately speculative approach is, in many ways, a convincing one, and it perhaps represents an advance over the more positivistic and less self-reflective practices of the past, but what are the implications? If we appreciate more fully than our predecessors that the documentary materials which survive about a writer's life are bound to be fragmentary, are probably unrepresentative, were always written with a rhetorical purpose, and that some of the sources which biographers find most seductive such as diaries or autobiographies were often deliberately written, designed, planted, or manipulated to try to influence posterity's view, can we write better biographies than they did? Should the postmodernist insight, coming on top of the modernist, be regarded as a new liberation or as a new constraint? Freed from the biographer's traditional, implicit, and by no means self-evidently true, principle of Ockham's razor, which demands that, other things being equal, the simplest explanation which connects the recorded facts should be preferred, is the way opened to speculation and to invention? Are biographical practitioners now free not only to pick and choose and reinterpret among the recorded evidence, but to offer interpretations and to deliver judgements for which the surviving evidence, taken as a whole, offers scant support? Some biographers evidently think so. In the 1990s, we were given Wordsworth the government spy and Byron the child rapist.[6] As we have seen with Shakespeare, gaps in the archival record both invite, and provide opportunities for, speculation if they are biographically reconceptualized as 'lost years'.

Many biographical narratives which veer towards speculation are provided with plentiful footnotes to source references. The authors thereby claim to be part of a historical discipline with a tradition of careful investigative scholarship and they draw authority from the reputation of the genre which has been built up by predecessors. But is the test by which the more speculative biographers measure their work the extent to which their biographical narratives are more truthful than those of their predecessors? Or is it rather their success as authors in persuading potential readers that their biographies are simply different? The abandonment of Ockham's razor has encouraged a kind of restless biographical consumerism, a constant

---

[6] Johnston, *The Hidden Wordsworth*, pp. 530ff. The claim was exploded in correspondence in the *Times Literary Supplement* in March 2000, which showed conclusively that another man called Wordsworth was referred to in the document upon which Johnston built his speculations. Benita Eisler, *Byron: Child of Passion, Fool of Fame* (London, 1999), pp. 384ff.

repackaging of the same materials in ways which give an appearance of novelty. As Kenneth R. Johnston declared, when he was faced with a choice of possibilities for explaining some question about Wordsworth's life, he chose 'the riskier one'.[7] Despite their detailed bibliographical references, some of these biographies, when seen as examples of a literary genre, have much in common with André Maurois' popular, commercially successful, unfootnoted romances about Shelley and Byron, although with a different agenda.[8] Indeed some historical novels, avowedly fictional works which provide no source references but which are based on the fiction writer's careful prior reading and respect for the primary sources, may be more faithful to the evidence of the record than the biographies, although the main examples are not from the Romantic period.

Questions about the nature of biographical evidence lie at the heart of the whole biographical enterprise. And although we may believe that biography, as a form of writing, flourished in the past without the need for being theorized, or even that biography flourished because it was untheorized, now that the questions are out in the open, they cannot, with good conscience, be ignored. Indeed in our day, no cultural practice can be accorded full respect if it is unaware of its own history or uncritical of its own procedures. Although I have no general answers to offer, I propose to discuss in the rest of this essay one limited aspect of the problem. How, I ask, can those biographers who regard their work primarily as an historical investigation deal with the hard and immovable fact that the sources on which they necessarily rely are normally likely to be an unrepresentative record of the patterns of the lived life?

One approach is to include a critical discussion of the nature of the sources, and of how they have come down to us, within the biography itself, or in the supporting apparatus. The thoughtful biographer, furthermore, is able to shift his or her stance towards the reader across a wide variety of rhetorical positions ranging from confident, well-informed, and summarizing narrator, through undecided expositor, to sceptical and detached interrogator, and he or she may occasionally leave the sources altogether in flights of speculation, carefully signalled as such to the reader. Most genuine biographers, I believe, attempt to help the reader to judge the

---

[7] Johnston, *The Hidden Wordsworth*, p. 9. 'My "method" often consists of no more than raising possibilities. My rule of thumb has been: when there's a choice of possibilities, investigate the riskier one'. As an example, having speculated that Wordsworth made an unrecorded visit to France, Johnston fills in details with further speculation: 'Wild as it seems, it is not wholly outside the realm of possibility that Gorsas and Wordsworth travelled to Paris together' (p. 381).

[8] André Maurois, *Ariel: The Life of Shelley* (English translation, 1924) and *Byron* (1930), both of which were selected for inclusion among Penguin's introductory series of paperbacks.

extent of the biographer's assumed freedom in one way or another, the more skilful by incorporating the degree of uncertainty into the writing itself, the less skilful by relying on 'he must have', 'she probably', and 'I believe'. Some biographers are also able gradually to build up the confidence of the reader in their respect for the sources, their scholarly integrity, and their judgement, to the point where readers are willing to grant their trust without having to be convinced, sentence by sentence, that the biographer has actually done the indispensable preliminary scholarly and critical work. Two of the biographies of Romantic period authors which remain indispensable are Newman Ivey White's *Shelley* (1948) and Leslie A. Marchand's *Byron: A Biography* (1956). Their approach was patiently to search out as many original documents as they could in libraries, record offices, and private collections in many countries, to transcribe and to contextualize them, to reconstruct the historical and biographical surroundings, to arrange their biography mainly in a strict chronological order, and to allow the poets to speak for themselves. Seldom have biographers been more modest, keeping well in the background, avoiding making unnecessary or definitive judgements, offering no overarching psychological or theoretical explanations, while at the same time providing the reader with the materials to form his or her view.

But still the question nags. What degree of credence can we, as readers, give to the biographer's reconstruction of the life? Is he or she not using literary or rhetorical skills to increase the reader's dependence on his or her judgements by offering an illusion of openness and of uncertainty, usually in small matters, within a pattern whose essentials are already fixed either by the sources or by the biographer's pre-decided patterning of the sources? And is the biographer, openly or stealthily, in practice applying a more general view of human nature which is a perception already in the biographer's mind? Is he or she, for example, applying a Freudian approach, or a model of social competition, or simply having recourse to scattered pieces of conventional wisdom, such as childhood rejection, sibling rivalry, personal ambition, or whatever appears to fit? A biographer who resorts to comments such as 'inevitably', 'as we would expect', or 'surprisingly', attempts to co-opt the reader into sharing his or her general opinions and attitudes on these matters. Instead of providing the accumulation of detailed case-studies on which an increasingly more sophisticated view of human nature can be built, is biography at risk of simply providing variations on a predetermined theme? While purporting to be an investigative discipline, proceeding from detailed empirical observation of individuals to more general conclusions, or testing the validity of provisional theories by adducing investigated cases against which they can be compared, is biography not in practice reversing this process, fitting the choice of facts to match ideologies of essential human nature already firmly settled in the biographer's mind?

Furthermore, the readers of biographies are caught in a closed system. Once we go beyond the simplest external matters, all our normal readerly procedures for judging the degree of truthfulness of a biography are based on the extent to which the biographer has been successful in convincing us, that is, on the biographer's literary and rhetorical merit, or on our own skill as readers in applying our critical faculties to the biographical text. We can look up the occasional reference and form our own judgement on whether the source does indeed support the interpretation put on it, and we can often perceive the underlying stance of the biographer. But none of these readerly critical strategies can ever take us, as readers, beyond the texts, either the source texts or the biographical text which is built on them.

Is there any way of breaking out of the closed circle? One potential means, in theory, would be by experiment. In archaeology, to take my chosen parallel, it is possible to gain some understanding of how flint tools were chipped or marble was quarried in Antiquity by attempting to repeat the process in simulated conditions and then comparing the resulting debris with the surviving ancient debris. Archaeologists can determine by scientific experiment the rate of deterioration of materials in different conditions and then apply the knowledge to their understanding of what is found in digs. As far as biography is concerned, the room for experiment is obviously extremely limited. However, I recall that a few years ago, when as part of moving house I was sorting out the accumulations of unsorted papers I had put in boxes over several decades, I decided to ask myself whether any biographer, if presented only with the debris in these boxes, would ever get near to reconstructing the aspects of my life which I considered of most importance. Some episodes, I quickly discovered, had left virtually no trace in the record, while others, to my mind relatively trivial, were disproportionately overweighted.

Of course such an experiment could only, at best, compare my own still unformed and never-to-be-written autobiography with the surviving documentary records available to me at that time. It could only compare one clear but changing text with occasional bundles of muddled but fixed texts. Even although I, as the experimenter, tried to be sincere with myself, in the event I found myself continually refashioning my putative autobiography with every box opened, every old letter read, and every memory rekindled. I found myself reshaping my view of myself to make it consistent with the records instead of, as I had thought I was doing, checking the surviving records of the facts against the real facts. Experiments of this kind usually confirm that the memory is itself a faulty and unstable narrative and that contemporary documents are to be preferred as evidence over the narratives in authors' own autobiographies. At the same time some of the most important events, or circumscribing limitations, of a life may leave few traces in the documentary record, not because they were secret or shameful, but because they were so universal or so ubiquitous as to be taken for granted.

From my experiment I also began to appreciate more fully why it was that many famous literary men and women who knew they were liable to be biographized have actively destroyed their records, or asked their heirs to destroy them, or have hurriedly written their own autobiographies, or commissioned friends to write their lives in predetermined ways. These can be regarded as alternative strategies of trying to forestall, and to mitigate, the errors and misunderstandings which they realize are intrinsic to exclusively document-based biography. Fellows of the British Academy, incidentally, among whose privileges is an expectation that an extended obituary notice will appear in due course in the *Proceedings*, are encouraged to provide their unnamed future obituarists not only with information on dates, appointments, publications, etc., such as appear in reference books, but with advice on how to shape the narrative, including aspirations, turning-points, disappointments (if any), and achievements, in effect invited to have a say in the writing of what will be, for many, the only biographical narrative to be passed on. Contributing to one's own *éloge* was a feature of the French academies of the nineteenth century:[9] those who praised their predecessors were aware that they in their turn would be praised by their successors.

There is another potential approach towards gaining a better understanding of the relationship between the life and the record which is not self-enclosed. This is to try to build a fuller critical understanding of the normal structures of that relationship, so that, in any individual case, we can more confidently appreciate the extent and the likelihood of biases and, if necessary, take steps to offset them. Although this suggestion can, at best, make only a modest contribution, I can offer an actual case, and again I begin with a parallel with archaeology. No archaeologist, looking at the artefacts which are brought to light from digging a site, is liable to conclude that the men and women of the past society concerned spent their whole time making and breaking pottery. Artefacts made from wood, leather, and textiles have perished from decay, those made from metal have been recycled to other uses. The site itself has a history, and in many cases it has been dug before. Unlike the biographer, the archaeologist is always aware that his or her source materials, however plentiful, are not only

---

[9] See Chapter 5 above.

incomplete, randomly surviving, and incomprehensible without careful
interpretation, but that the surviving record is not only biased but systemic-
ally biased. Archaeologists are therefore rightly delighted when a site is
discovered, say in the dry desert or the frozen mountains, in which the
unusual climatic and other conditions have permitted materials to survive
which, in more common circumstances, have perished. For such sites are
not only extremely valuable in themselves but they offer a means of understanding the systemic biases present in the evaluation of more normal sites.
Can we apply this approach to biography?

Although the amount of surviving evidence for some authors is astonishingly plentiful, in the case of William Godwin, whose life spanned the whole
period, and who knew almost all of the authors of the time personally, it
is of an altogether different order of magnitude.[10] Let me summarize. First
his published works:

	works	volumes when published
Biography	4	5
Philosophy	5	6
History	3	6
Novels	9	22
Plays	2	2
Pamphlets and essays	8	8
Children's books	11	13
Sermons	1	1
Satire	1	1
Genealogy	1	3
Translations	1	1
Works by members of his family which Godwin edited for publication	2	7

Plus a large amount of published journalism, articles, reviews, and obituaries, most of which, because of the survival of marked-up copies and other
external evidence, can be confidently attributed. The manuscripts of some
of these published works also survive, from which we can see the process of
initial ideas, authorial revision, and amendment by the publishers. Several
were also substantially revised by the author for later editions which were
published in his lifetime.

Godwin wrote many hundreds of letters, of which the texts exist either

[10] See William St Clair, *The Godwins and the Shelleys: The Biography of a Family* (London, 1989).

in the original manuscripts or in copies. Unusually, in many cases, we also have the letters which formed the other half of the correspondence. Again, most unusually for the time, Godwin also kept drafts and copies of letters which he sent, sometimes using a wax copier to make facsimiles. He wrote passages of autobiography at various times of his life, and composed essays in self-analysis. He kept notes of key episodes in his life, made lists of his literary and other ambitions, and kept many financial documents. All this material can be matched with, and supplemented by, large amounts of contemporary and later material left by family, friends, and acquaintances. Godwin is present in the archival record of virtually all the writers of the time, including (besides those authors already mentioned in this essay) De Quincey, Holcroft, Charles and Mary Lamb, Tom Paine, and Southey, as well as in the voluminous diaries of Henry Crabb Robinson.

Then there is Godwin's diary, thirty-two volumes, which cover most of his adult life with scarcely a day missed. Each day is given only a few lines. Besides noting a few public events, Godwin recorded in detail the writing he accomplished day by day, the books he read, even to the page numbers, and the people he met. Unlike many diaries, this is neither a confessional document nor a narrative written with half an eye on posterity. It is a factual record intended solely for his own use, and he included numerous private abbreviations, sometimes in Latin or French, as a protection against peepers. There are occasional words on which he relied to connect him to the chain of his memory, but which do not necessarily perform the same service for other readers. Thus the syllable 'Panc' for 29 March 1797 notes his visit to St Pancras Parish Church to marry Mary Wollstonecraft.

With primary documentary resources of such extraordinary richness, we have opportunities, as biographers, to know more about Godwin as a writer and as an individual and to understand more about the immediate historical context within which he lived than we can about most persons long dead. Because the diary gives us the names of all the books he read and all the persons he met, we can interrogate the record as well as simply accepting the patterns it immediately offers us when we read. How far, we can ask, for example, were British writers up-to-date with intellectual currents on the Continent? The answer is that we find him reading all the most up to date books and also meeting many visitors from abroad. Was Godwin, we can inquire of the sources, part of a close circle of radical intellectuals as is generally agreed, and we find the answer that he was indeed a member of such a circle, but also of many other circles, some far from radical.

We can also use his case to shine light into areas usually left dark. Take health, for example. Because of the entries in the diary over many decades, we know about Godwin's piles and his constipation, a combination which can shake the equanimity of the most stoical of philosophers, and about the rhubarb which is also noted and which may not have always been efficacious. I found it possible, too, with the help of modern medical knowledge, to diagnose with confidence that Godwin suffered from a long-term degenerative disease of the nervous system now known as catalepsy. Since Godwin knew that the only protection against the onset of fits was to try to remain calm, however stressful the circumstances, we have an explanation for behaviour which those contemporaries who wrote down their impressions of him misinterpreted as a studied coldness of character. Biographers then repeated the unsympathetic comments of contemporaries. Without his diaries, we would not only have been ignorant of the medical factors which affected his life but would have been misled. How many of the authors who have left a thin record had health problems which are unrecorded and have therefore not been fully appreciated in biographies?

Another area where the Godwin archive offers a potential benchmark against which the gaps in others can be compared and offsetting action considered is sex. Biographical information about sexual behaviour is rare for any period, reliable information even more so. But the discovery of a code in Godwin's diary, involving a mixture of punctuation signs (notably a dash followed by a full stop) which can be matched with a series of unself-regarding intimate notes that Godwin and Wollstonecraft exchanged day by day at the beginning of their affair, is more than the higher gossip. It gives not only a record of their sexual behaviour but reveals how they practised a form of contraception, based upon Wollstonecraft's menstrual cycle, which we now know is seriously erroneous. It was this 'chance medley' system, as Wollstonecraft called it, which led to Wollstonecraft becoming pregnant, against her intentions, with the child who was to become Mary Shelley. We may legitimately extrapolate from the Godwin record that other eighteenth- and nineteenth-century couples may have attempted to follow the same flawed advice. We can also generalize to some extent the gynaecological details of Wollstonecraft's illness and death after childbirth, another experience common at the time but seldom recorded frankly.

Some biographers, particularly in the nineteenth and early twentieth centuries, who followed the celebratory tradition of biography, were reticent about such matters, even if they knew about them. As far as Godwin and Wollstonecraft were concerned, the record shows that they would not have regarded my interest as prying or prurient. Both believed from their Enlightenment perspective that the fearless study of the long dead, who are beyond hurt, biography without taboo or self-censorship, is among the best ways by which human beings can advance their understanding of humanity. I, of course, by deciding to reveal the details, showed myself as a biographer caught in my own time when, perhaps untypically in a long historical perspective, sexuality is put centre stage, and is often regarded as being especially useful both as a potential window into the internal self and as a paradigm for explaining the development of individual character.

The most direct biographical corrective which the Godwin archive may provide for biography as a whole is in the matter of friends. We can note from the diary the names of dozens of friends whom he saw more often, and probably knew better, than Coleridge, Hazlitt, or Shelley, but about whom almost nothing is recorded beyond their names. Godwin appears, for example, to have spent more hours with Sarah Elwes than he did with Wollstonecraft. And who was the Thomas Rodd whom he visited twice a week for years on end? Then there are the relatives, the uncles and aunts, nephews and nieces. Since no writer of the time bothered to record them, it is as if they never existed, but there they are in the diary, a glimpse of the domestic sphere, sitting by the Godwin family fireside. Did they take part in the conversations? Did they contribute to the development of the ideas in his work?

Let us take, as an example of this bias, a particular incident, on 2 February 1804, when Godwin and Coleridge dined with Charles and Mary Lamb. Mary Jane Godwin, the second Mrs Godwin, was also present, and so were a couple called Fenwick and four younger women called Duckworth. An argument developed which took in literature, religion, politics, the morality of the war, and much else. We can recover a great deal about what was said that afternoon. Godwin noted the event in his diary and wrote a memorandum of the main points. Coleridge described the discussion in a letter to Godwin, and then in subsequent letters to Sara Coleridge, to Wordsworth, and to Southey, and Southey then described it second hand in one of his letters. We have no less than seven excellent sources for the incident, irresistible riches for any biographer, and biographers are right to exploit them. But the Godwin diary allows us to see the biases in action—since only the contributions of the literary were normally recorded, they alone made their way into the biographies. From some literary biographies it appears that the only people whom their subjects met were other famous people, and that their lives consisted only of dramatic incidents of high human intensity. It is not that the biographers are necessarily literary name-droppers, although some are, but that the whole enterprise, at any rate as far as the authors of the Romantic period are concerned, has a bias towards recording only those lives with entries in the *Dictionary of National Biography*. Unfamiliar figures such as the Fenwicks and the Duckworths are hard to place, troublesome to introduce, not easily summed up in a phrase or two—and there are so many of them.

The archive illustrates how our modern perception of the character of some individuals and of some relationships can become petrified by the accidents of survival of sources. Mary Jane Godwin, for example, when she first arrived in Godwin's life, was the target of several bitchy letters from Charles Lamb, which are almost invariably quoted by biographers, whenever she has to be introduced, as a vivid example of the dislike in which the second Mrs Godwin was held by Godwin's friends in contrast with the first. But we can see from Godwin's diaries that the Godwin and Lamb families were in and out of each others' houses for years with scarcely a week without a meeting. For every tempestuous incident which found its way into a letter, there were dozens of others when they visited, drank tea, and conversed. The quality of their long friendship is distorted by the Lamb letters, even though they are prime sources for a particular moment.

The Godwin archive, furthermore, offers an understanding of the transmission of archives as such. Incomparably full as it is, it was once even fuller. In the nineteenth century the Shelley family weeded it in accordance with the standards of their day and of their social class. They burned letters, tore out pages of journals, and cut out passages of manuscripts with scissors. They engaged Richard Garnett, the Librarian of the British Museum, to advise on which documents should be destroyed and which kept. It seems certain that the family bought and then destroyed Wollstonecraft's letters to Fuseli, noting that they read like a Minerva Press, that is a romantic, novel. The general intention of the family was to enhance the reputation of Shelley and of Mary Shelley, and to suppress knowledge of matters which contradicted the image, or rather the myth, which they wanted to see projected. As an offset, we can read the correspondence of Edward Dowden, W. M. Rossetti, and Garnett, the first biographical scholars to explore the archive, and see how they set about shaping it, including the creating of gaps, by, for example, removing evidence of irreligion, and attempting to raise the reputation of Shelley and Mary Shelley by slurring that of Shelley's first wife, Harriet.[11] Sifting through the debris from earlier digs reveals that the censoring of the archive was only partially effective. Not only did the would-be censors fail to notice Godwin's code, but they allowed several documents to survive, usually unsigned letters in unrecognized handwriting, whose potential significance they did not appreciate. The attempted censoring of the Godwin/Shelley archive is an illuminating example of Victorian values in action, but it can also be read as simply an extreme version of what tends to happen to all collections of papers when the heirs come to sort them out. The letters from the famous are kept,

---

[11] See R. S. Garnett, ed., *Letters about Shelley, Interchanged by Three Friends—Edward Dowden, Richard Garnett and Wm. Michael Rossetti* (London, 1917) and *Letters of Edward Dowden and his Correspondents* (London, 1914).

apparently humdrum documents are thrown away. All biographical archives can be looked upon not only as archaeological sites but as sites which have normally been dug before, their layers disturbed, their previously jumbled artefacts rearranged, and many objects thrown away.[12]

The evidence of the Godwin archive suggests therefore that biographers need to take account of at least three systemic biases in their primary materials. First, the literary men and women of the Romantic period were far more likely than most of their contemporaries to have written down the reminiscences, descriptions, and comments which provide much of our biographical evidence. Secondly, the literary eye was highly selective, highly literary, in what it chose to see and then to record in writing, being often focused on other literary men and women. And thirdly, the letters and other writings of the literary men and women are far more likely to be preserved through to the present day. The fame of the famous, and the canonization of fame as such, was reinforced at every stage from the initial writing of the original primary records, through the processes of selection and survival, to the first biographies and their successors all the way to the latest modern biography.

Godwin was himself, unusually for a Romantic period author, much interested in the nature of biography. His *Memoirs of the Author of a Vindication of the Rights of Woman* (1798), written shortly after Wollstonecraft's death, and based both on his own memories of the months they had been together and on interviews and documents, is a biography of astonishing honesty, volunteering information on matters such as sexual frustration which had previously never been discussed so openly, and defying and reshaping the conventions of the genre. But Godwin also wrote a biography of Chaucer, a figure for whom the sources were meagre, and the documents which he patiently uncovered consisted mainly of official records, the reading and historical contextualization of which were formid-

---

[12] I had my own lesson in censorship many years ago when my mother decided to move to a smaller house in Scotland and gave notice to her three sons that all the papers they had accumulated before they left home had to be removed. In my case there were numerous papers, some, like my school reports, quite pleasing. But when I started to read my teenage diaries I was so embarrassed that I decided that they had to be destroyed at once, preferably that day, before anyone else in the family took an interest. But how? Houses no longer had fires and I did not like to put my diaries in the wastepaper bin. I was going climbing that day, so I took them with me in the car, and sank the whole bundle in a Highland loch under a pile of stones, a suitable permanent burial. Or so I thought. About a month later the postman in London rang the bell to ask me to sign for a registered parcel. It contained a letter and a few sodden but still readable diaries. A kind stranger had found them floating in the loch, collected them, read them, realized that St Clair is an unusual name, and by impressive research found an uncle who gave him my address. The diaries still exist, and I decided that, after such a warning, I would never again try to throw away my past life like an old boomerang.

ably difficult preliminary tasks. 'Antiquities', he wrote, meaning the
recording of historical facts for their own sake, can never be enough, but
must be made alive by 'the workings of fancy and the spirit of philosophy'.
His role as a biographer was 'to rescue for a moment the illustrious dead
from the jaws of the grave, to make them pass in review before me, to
question their spirits and record their answers'.[13] The biographer needs
imagination, I understand him to say, but may only exercise it within
tight, self-imposed, limits which have to be honestly constructed by the
biographer from a critical appreciation of the nature of the evidence. It
was, for its time, an unusually proactive attitude for an author to take
both towards the life and towards the sources, but one which provided a
useful aspiration to the present author to follow in his attempt to write
Godwin's biography, however hard it was to make such judgements in
practice.

[13] William Godwin, *Life of Geoffrey Chaucer* (London, 1803), II, xi.

13

Writing Lives Forwards:
A Case for Strictly
Chronological Biography

MARK KINKEAD-WEEKES

If, as sceptics insist, the truth about the past is not to be had, perhaps the best a biographer can hope to achieve would be a convincing fiction that fits all the facts. That looks ambitious enough to be going on with, needing not only meticulous scholarship in an age of huge archives but also some measure of the novelist's gifts of imagination, narrative, scene, and character. Should such talents and learning coincide, as they blessedly do sometimes, it might seem that no imperative of method need arise. There could (presumably) be as many ways of writing good biography as there are kinds of novel. Modern biographers, sensitive to trends in fiction and criticism, might be keen to avoid a chronological approach as old-fashioned, the equivalent perhaps of Forster's 'and then, and then', prefer-ring some more subtle kind of structuring. Hermione Lee in her justly praised biography of Virginia Woolf suggests several ways a 'Life' might begin; but one she clearly excludes, which indeed 'no longer seems possible', is to start from her subject's birth.[1] Jean-Paul Sartre goes further, asserting the need to regress before progress can be properly grounded. Indeed he inverts chronology, by (in essence) reading the decisive phase of Flaubert's life backwards from the fictions of the sixteen- to thirteen-year-old, where

---

[1] Hermione Lee, *Virginia Woolf* (London, 1996), p. 3.

he first clearly reveals himself to Sartre, into his prehistory, before one can progressively understand the man and writer he became.[2]

I think, however, there may be something to be said for chronological biography even nowadays—perhaps even for *strictly* chronological biography with a self-disciplining ban on all hindsight. If so, subversion of chronology may turn out to have a certain cost, which could be shown by comparing 'Lives' that use different methods—especially if the biographers were so manifestly gifted that any drawbacks must derive from method rather than ability.

There is however a problem for anyone wishing to make such comparisons—even worse than that faced by reviewers of biographies for the newspapers. How are reviewers to judge scholarship, unless they are well acquainted with the sources on which the life-story is based? It is possible to review a biography as though it were a novel; but if one cannot judge the grounding responsibly, or the safeness of the structure built on it, praise of the narrative may be damagingly misdirected. One would not admire a driver careering off the road because it is done with panache, but it is not unknown for a pacy and lively biography, widely publicized (and occasionally also serialized) in the media, to be in fact seriously superficial and inaccurate, or even distorting. It is no wonder that some reviewers devote only a couple of guarded lines to a biography before filling the rest of their space with an essay on its subject, using information the book provides (when that suits their views). Yet I am in a none too different position here, wishing to compare authoritative biographies, when what I know of the relevant English archives is only what might be expected of a teacher of literature with a serious interest in the lives behind the writings, and what I know of the French case is rather less than that. So if I begin from a case of which I have more comprehensive and direct knowledge—the biography of D. H. Lawrence—this is not from a wish to advertise, but because there I feel more sure of my ground.

Why did the authors of the Cambridge biography of Lawrence choose not only an old-fashioned chronological approach but a strict one, following his life forwards, miming the way that it was lived, and banning all hindsight? Of course biographers who have been researching for years do already know the general shape of the story they have to tell and how it will end, before they write the first word; and of course a life could not be written week by week, let alone day by day, even if enough data were

---

[2] Jean-Paul Sartre, *L'Idiot de la famille*, 3 vols (Paris, 1971–2), vol. I: *Gustave Flaubert de 1821 à 1857*, tr. Carol Cosman, *The Family Idiot*, 5 vols, vol. I: *Gustave Flaubert 1821–57* (Chicago, 1981). See my argument below, pp. 241–4 on the structure of Sartre's diagnosis as opposed to the apparent starting-point of his story.

available, without insufferable tedium. What is possible, however, at the crucial first-draft stage when a general sense of things begins to develop into an organized story, is to work on, and then narrate in, time-spans small enough to allow all the evidence to be freshly commanded at once, with nothing but space ahead.

This approach brings immediate advantages. Misconceptions show up, puzzles can be clarified, unexpected connections appear, simply through careful attention to the exact sequence and context of events, as a few brief examples will show. Attention to dates reveals the connection between a sudden downturn in the progress at grammar school of the working-class boy, and the criminal trial and conviction of Lawrence's violent and drunken Uncle Walter, with accounts in the newspapers of how he killed his son by throwing a carving steel at him[3]—bearing later on the creation of Walter Morel in *Sons and Lovers* (which should never have been taken as a 'portrait' of Lawrence's father). Careful dating of the first meeting with Frieda to a Sunday, when her husband would not be at the university, shows that her competitive boasting to Mabel Luhan many years afterwards of how she had got her visitor into bed within twenty minutes is most unlikely to be true, even without its contradiction by another Frieda story. (Greater caution is needed in characterizing Frieda than has often been shown. Attention to the chronology of Lawrence's stay in Metz will again suggest considerable scepticism about the use of *Mr Noon* for biographical evidence. The sexy—and comic—scenes in 'Detsch' are almost certainly fictive.)[4]

Again, Lawrence's notorious denunciation of Katherine Mansfield for 'stewing' in her consumption, which seemed inexplicable to her biographer Antony Alpers, can in fact be explained (if not excused) by paying careful attention to the exact dates and contexts of letters between Lawrence, Murry, and Mansfield in 1919–20, and to their whereabouts, together with the effect of an Italian postal strike which ensured that packets posted at different times should reach Lawrence simultaneously. This made it seem that Katherine had joined Murry in rejecting DHL's peace offerings (after a previous quarrel), and that she was even more treacherous, self-absorbed, and uncaring about him than Murry.[5] The result was the end of her

---

[3] John Worthen, *D. H. Lawrence: The Early Years 1885–1912* (Cambridge, 1991), pp. 86–9.
[4] Worthen, *Early Years*, pp. 372, 380, and n. 5, pp. 562–3; Mark Kinkead-Weekes, *D. H. Lawrence: Triumph to Exile 1912–1922* (Cambridge, 1996), pp. 5–6 and nn. 2–3, pp. 761–2. On Metz and 'Detsch' see *Triumph to Exile*, pp. 9–10 and n. 16, p. 764.
[5] Kinkead-Weekes, 'Rage against the Murrys: "Inexplicable" or "Psychopathic"?', in *D. H. Lawrence in Italy and England*, ed. George Donaldson and Mara Kalnins (London, 1999), pp. 116–34; also *Triumph to Exile*, pp. 499–501, 541–2, 559–63.

friendship with DHL; a sad misunderstanding, but by no means inexplicable.

What had seemed a plausible story of Lawrence's involvement with a quasi-Fascist ex-servicemen's organization, active in Australia during his time there, plausible enough indeed to have been quoted by Australian historians, is discounted by the chronology of the composition of *Kangaroo* and the computation of how long this would have taken at his usual rate—thus how little time he had to become involved in Sydney in any such fashion.[6]

On the other hand biographers following a chronological method, aware of how much of a writer's life is a writing life (while careful to preserve the distinction between biography and literary criticism), can reveal unexpected connections between the life and the manuscript or revision being worked on at the time—going behind the often much later printed versions. Treated carefully enough, for example, the connections between Lawrence's extra-marital affair in Florence with Rosalind Baynes, the poems about tortoises, fruits, and flowers that he wrote at the time and soon afterwards, and the subsequent breaking of the block that had been holding up the progress of *Aaron's Rod*, will be most illuminating for biography and not unuseful (though not at all definitive) to the literary critic.[7]

The main reason for adopting a chronological method however was to resist the urge, so powerful in biographers, to structure a life too early and too simply into some overall pattern and explanation. Such patterning would have been remarkably inappropriate for a writer whose major work began as an attack on 'the old stable ego' of the nineteenth-century novel—the idea that character can be 'fixed' through analysis of behaviour and choice—and sought instead to picture human beings as in constant flux and transformation.[8] It (conversely) did seem appropriate, given that his life fell into three easily defined periods, to subvert overall patterning even more surely by having a different biographer for each period. The three 'Lawrences' would naturally differ because of what happened to him, but enough continuity could be assured if the biographers worked closely together. Another remarkable feature of Lawrence's fictions is how open-

---

[6] David Ellis, 'D. H. Lawrence in Australia: The Darroch Controversy', *D. H. Lawrence Review*, XXI (Summer 1989), 167–74; see also his *Dying Game: D. H. Lawrence 1922–1930* (Cambridge, 1998), p. 45 and nn. 88–9.

[7] Kinkead-Weekes, 'An Affair into Art: A Question of Boundaries', in *Rereading Texts/ Rethinking Critical Presuppositions: Essays in Honour of H. M. Daleski*, ed. Shlomith Rimmon Kenan, Leona Toker, and Shuli Barzilai (Frankfurt, 1996), pp. 275–90; see also *Triumph to Exile*, pp. 601–6, 647–50.

[8] *The Letters of D. H. Lawrence*, vol. II, ed. George J. Zytaruk and James T. Boulton (Cambridge, 1981), p. 183.

ended they are. Appropriately again, two volumes of the Cambridge biography leave us with a man whose life could obviously have gone in very different directions afterwards. Only one is necessarily shadowed towards its close by what Frank Kermode has described as 'kairos' rather than 'chronos' time, the sense of an ending which shapes a life or story not yet ended; but all three try hard not to read the later man back into the earlier, at any stage. If patterns emerge, they should come naturally and gradually from the evidence as it develops. A similar sense of flux, and of how reading-back distorts, should result from chronological treatment of secondary characters—Jessie Chambers and Louie Burrows, Murry, Mansfield, Ottoline Morrell, Mabel Luhan, Dorothy Brett—and of Lawrence's changing relationships with them.

Biographies of Lawrence have suffered more than most from the biographer's urge to find some underlying explanation which can be read backwards and forwards irrespective of chronology—and to which the awareness (or otherwise) of the subject of the biography is irrelevant. The chronological method, insisting as it does on flux, change, development, and experience through time, suggests how much more multi-layered and complex human life and consciousness are when freed from such procrustean distortion.

Was Lawrence, for example, an Oedipal case? He came to know something of Freud himself at third hand through Frieda in 1912, and he met the pioneer English Freudians in 1913–14; but Paul Morel had developed between 1909 and 1912 out of the raw material of his own experience, and though the further growth into *Sons and Lovers* (1912–13) coincided with his taking up with Frieda, he was intensely irritated at a Freudian review of his first major novel. A process of revaluing his mother and father began soon after he finished it, and slowly intensified until his earlier attitude was *reversed*, together with a growing sense of how a wife may become a mother-substitute in ways that must be resisted (1913–20). All this culminated in an attack on Freud and an attempt at a different basis for psychology in *Psychoanalysis and the Unconscious* and *Fantasia of the Unconscious*—not to speak of the 'psychology' of his major fiction over the same period, no less fluctuating and changeful in its emphases. The question remains, but any answer would surely have to take into account his own self-scrutiny over the years.

Can we explain him as a repressed homosexual then? Quite apart from querying the simple dualism of 'hetero' and 'homo', a respectable answer would again have to trace, carefully, his long, remarkably frank, and courageous investigation of his feelings about homosexuality: from the unashamed admission of homoerotic attraction in 1913; through the homophobic nightmares of his encounter with 'Bloomsbuggers' in 1915 and his relation of their sexuality to what he disliked most about the brittle cynicism of 'Cambridge' intellectuals; to the relationship with William Henry Hocking in Cornwall in 1917, which may have involved some homoerotic feeling but is very unlikely to have issued in homosexual acts. One would then have to take into account the complexity of the writing and rewriting of *Women in Love* (1916–19), where the nature of 'love' is from the beginning far more important than the question of gender. Equally relevant would be the insistence in *The Reality of Peace* (1917) on open confrontation of one's own secret or 'shameful' feelings; and finally the concession, in an unpublished essay on Whitman (1918), that in anal sexuality, too, between male opposites who maintain their individuality (unlike Whitman's queenly 'merging'), there might be a mode of mutual transformation analogous to the death and resurrection he found in sexual love between men and women—after which Lawrence loses interest in the question. That he was capable of erotic feelings for both sexes we have his open admission. That he was in any sense determined by a condition he could neither confront nor free himself from, chronological investigation shows to be untrue.

Was consumption responsible for excessive eroticism and rages? Here again a chronological narrative, placing his illnesses in their full context, will show how difficult it is in fact to determine just when he can be said to have 'had tuberculosis'. His health broke down in 1911, but a sputum test proved negative. There were further negative medical examinations in 1916 and 1917 by GPs and probably also a London specialist. He nearly died in 1918, but that was due to the epidemic of Spanish 'flu. There were only minor illnesses when he moved to Italy, and nobody mentions him coughing there. It is in fact not until August 1924, when he first suffered a haemorrhage at the ranch in New Mexico, that it is legitimate to call him consumptive. There followed a collapse in Oaxaca in 1925, after which the diagnosis by American doctors in Mexico City and the increasingly serious haemorrhages of 1927 put the matter out of doubt. The difficulty is partly a matter of the nature of the disease. Like tens of thousands at the time who never developed consumption, Lawrence certainly had the tubercle in his lungs, as Murry did, as well as Mansfield. There is evidence of spells of coughing and even perhaps of spots of blood in 1913–14 (though that could have been bronchial). Yet it was not at all infrequent, even if a lesion developed, for it to heal and leave only a scar, as probably happened to Yeats. Moreover, Lawrence could never have walked much of the way from Austria into Italy and most of the way from Italy back into Switzerland in 1912 and 1914, often managing twenty-five miles a day, if he had been consumptive at the time; and everyone who knew him speaks, at every stage before the collapse in Oaxaca, of his extraordinary physical energy. It is because he is known to have died from the disease later that there is such temptation to read it back into his earlier life. And, even if one granted a dubious derivation of lust and rage (which in his case can easily be explained quite otherwise) from TB, there remains the irony that after 1925 he became impotent, and after 1927 quieter and gentler than before.

It is also likely that chronological narrative, avoiding hindsight, will be the best way of querying the imaginative writer's own essays in autobiography, which—whether in Lawrence, or Yeats, or Virginia Woolf as I hope to suggest—need to be treated with a good deal of caution.

Sartre's Life of Flaubert marks an opposite method. He assumes his reader already knows the external facts: his aim is a 'total' analytical explanation of how the man's consciousness was formed from the pressures put on the boy by his bourgeois family. One cannot but be greatly impressed by the assurance and subtlety with which an enormous first volume—all I can hope even to touch on—seeks to establish the essential structure of that consciousness. Though the foundation in factual evidence may seem distinctly slender, it makes a compelling story: an authoritarian and irritable father, who treats his family like a feudal unit on the socio-economic make; a subservient and melancholy mother, who married for love but cares more for her husband than her children; an eldest son, on whom all the Flaubert ambition and pride are concentrated. This elaborate account of the doom which an ambitious but unloving bourgeois family imposes on the younger sibling reminds one vividly of the Harlowes, and there are signs that Sartre has read Richardson's *Clarissa*. But though the fictive might seem to outweigh the documentary, in which Sartre has little interest, this is no novel but an unusually ambitious attempt to make the essential structure of a life *completely* intelligible, through a fusion of existentialist psychoanalysis with Marxist history.

The story, however, may seem the more fictive (and hence more open to question) the more it is interiorized. Sartre's Mme Flaubert holds herself guilty of the death of her mother in bearing her, and of hastening the death of her father (though in fact this came ten years later). So she marries a father-substitute, gives him the son he craves as heir to himself and the Flauberts, and then seeks to assuage her guilt, compensate for the past, and perpetuate her own image by bearing a daughter. But after having done her duty by her husband, the births (and early deaths) of several more sons come as doubly bitter blows, which the survival of Gustave cannot heal. A surviving girl, at long last, receives the love she cannot feel for her younger son, though she may try to compensate by over-protecting him. Yet this is mostly a 'fabrication', on little or no evidence, as Sartre cheerfully admits after 132 pages of analysis,[9] and as indeed his narrative often concedes—though he will also speak of her quite comfortably later as 'incestuous' and a 'murderer', as if hypothesis had become established fact.

In the case of Flaubert's father Achille-Cléophas, and subsequently of the elder son Achille, the other, Marxist, arm of Sartrean analysis comes into play. The rustic, even peasant, background which the brilliant medical student escapes has ingrained in him a feudal, patriarchal, and authoritarian conception of the family. But the successful doctor's progress through the bourgeoisie produces an economically acquisitive and social-climbing drive which, concentrating itself on his eldest son, is bound to make his younger one feel a failure—though it also ensures that the privileged Achille the younger will become a mere conventional bourgeois, a watered down version of his father. This interpretation is remorselessly elaborated, as no skeletal summary can remotely suggest—but it is also remarkably deterrminist, leaving out all the complicating evidence which suggests a complex, sensitive, and kind, if sometimes nervy, authoritarian and irritable Achille-Cléophas. Why is this? One answer is that, for Sartre, a man's character is 'purely a structural distinction [. . .] a slight gap between the person's modes of behavior and the objective behavior prescribed for him by his milieu'[10]—and therefore, it seems, relatively insignificant. A deeper reason comes into focus when we understand what the prehistory of Flaubert's parents is needed to explain: not only the fact that Flaubert was unable to read at seven whereas his siblings learned easily (hence *L'Idiot de la famille*), but also the psychology revealed in the stories the adolescent wrote between the ages of thirteen and sixteen. These are seen as revelations of a consciousness already unalterable in its essential structure, opening out what has indeed been fixed (in Sartre's view) at the age of seven, by what *must* have been a failure to love him by his mother, and a rejection of him as a dunce by his father. Does one gently demur by suggesting that Yeats also learned to read very late (and never learned to spell), or that the adolescent Joyce also affected a precocious world-weariness, ennui, disgust (and resort to prostitutes), with significantly different prehistories? Ah, but only this kind

---

[9] *The Family Idiot*, I, 132, translating *L'Idiot*, I, 138—'Je l'avoue: c'est une fable'—perhaps a little pungently.

[10] *The Family Idiot*, I, 62, translating *L'Idiot*, I, p. 71: 'En fait, ce qu'on nomme caractère est purement différentiel et se manifeste comme un décalage léger entre les conduites de la personne et les conduites objectives que son milieu lui prescrit'. Sartre might seem to concede some complexity of character to Achille-Cléophas—if only in derogation—when he speaks on the same page of fits of anger which could end in tears, or of nervous instability and mental tension which might suggest immaturity. But Sartre never seriously engages with the more amiable qualities of character shown in the letters (and other biographies) or concedes that complexity of character might in any sense modify, let alone challenge, the socially 'prescribed' role in which Sartre casts him.

of mother and that kind of father could, for Sartre, have produced *these* adolescent stories, the real starting-point of the analysis, from which both a traumatic crisis, at seven, and its prehistory can be *deduced* by a regressive/progressive method. The analysis appears to begin in early childhood and shuttle back and forth, but in fact it essentially reverses chronology into prehistory in order to build, then, towards Flaubert's crisis at Pont l'Evêque and consequent choice of life, from a basis fully established in boyhood.[11] Two further assumptions are also necessary (and equally debatable): that the juvenilia of a writer, even a precocious one, can accurately mirror a permanent structure of consciousness irrespective of questions of stylistic immaturity, adolescent posture and the influence of reading Chateaubriand, Byron, Hugo, etc.; and that they can therefore be taken, further, as accurate indications of what in life 'must' have gone to make Flaubert what he was.

The paradox is that the more 'total' the explanation, and the more removed from chronological development, contingency, and change, the more determinist it seems, although Sartre still insists that we are all free to choose, and do choose our lives, whether authentically or in bad faith. But since the structure of consciousness of the Flaubert who collapsed at Pont L'Evêque is already fixed, and since Sartre's analytic tools permit no purely medical explanation such as epilepsy, the collapse has to be seen as *Flaubert's own choice*, an act of 'hysterical commitment'[12]—a somewhat desperate solution. *At the same time* (Sartre's emphasis) it can be seen as a response to history embodying, as it were in a representative act, the social conflicts which determined the position of the French writer of his time[13]—and which, in a permanent state of alienation at Croisset, he would then explore in his novels. In response to the twin complaints—that Sartre's analytic methods exclude a great deal of evidence (in voluminous correspondence and the research of other biographers) of contingencies and developments which bear on the growth of Flaubert's consciousness; and, conversely, that evidence is lacking for a great deal of Sartre's determinist account—critics have suggested that propositions might be 'considered true to the extent that they agree, not with empirically verifiable data, but with other propositions in the series'. More bluntly, it has been argued that where there are gaps in the data, the biography tells us 'not necessarily what actually happened, merely what Sartre believes *must have*

---

[11] The personality of the adolescent and young man may become more complicated, in the second 'personalizing' section of Sartre's biography; but there can be little doubt that Sartre regards it as having been essentially formed before the age of seven, and become articulate by thirteen—hence his title.

[12] *The Family Idiot*, IV, 83, translating *L'Idiot*, II, 1854: 'L'Engagement Hystérique'.

[13] *The Family Idiot*, V, 31, translating *L'Idiot*, III, 39; 'Et comment une même maladie peut-elle *en même temps* valoir comme solution d'antinomies sociales et comme issue individuelle?', etc.

happened in order to lead to the next stage in the dialectical process'.[14] Whatever one may think of this, it does seem that the ambition to analyse deep-structurally, free from the chronological 'anecdotage' of conventional biography, feeds a strong tendency to determinism even in an apostle of freedom.

In a perhaps less tendentious contrast, the most recent and widely admired biographer of Yeats, Roy Foster, sets out a case for chronology as opposed to the 'dazzling structure' of Richard Ellmann's classic work.

> Faced with the multifarious activities, the feints and turns, the wildly differing worlds which WBY embraced, Ellmann followed his subject's example in dealing with his life thematically. WBY's own *Autobiographies* dictate an arrangement for his life, and it is a thematic one; this is hard not to follow, even if it looks like the way of the chameleon. [. . .] The natural reaction is to shadow him [. . .] to accept his *Autobiographies* as straightforward records rather than to see them in terms of the time they were composed; and to deal with periods of frantic and diverse involvements [. . .] by separating out the strands [. . .] and addressing them individually. The result, in Ellmann's work, was a masterpiece of intellectual analysis and psychological penetration, to which all Yeatsians are for ever indebted. However, we do not alas live our lives in themes, but day by day; and WBY, giant though he was, is no exception.[15]

Foster's first volume, *The Apprentice Mage*, shows just how his chronological method enables him to deepen, complicate, correct, and illuminate our view of Yeats's life to 1914—by which time the major phase of his poetry was beginning, and the political history of Ireland was about to reach a crucial turning-point. The process of Yeats's own image-building is fascinatingly illustrated, and certain Yeatsian myths are undermined, or at least substantially modified, by following him for the most part in periods of no more than two years. We have to substitute for the Irish Patriot a complicated, shifting, and devious process of manoeuvring between factions, in which Yeats presented different faces on different sides of the Channel and in tours of America. We have to understand the steps by which the Founder of the Irish National Theatre exploited his relationships with Augusta Gregory and Annie Horniman, both emotionally and financially, in order to see off challenges and stamp his authority and his agenda on the Abbey, both for good (the championing of Synge and the staging of

---

[14] Douglas Collins, *Sartre as Biographer* (Cambridge, MA, 1980), pp. 107–8; Michael Scriven, *Sartre's Existential Biographies* (London, 1984), p. 107. I owe the Collins reference, and much else, to David Ellis; see his *Literary Lives: Biography and the Search for Understanding* (Edinburgh, 2000), p. 149.

[15] R. F. Foster, *W. B. Yeats: A Life*, I: *The Apprentice Mage: 1865–1914* (Oxford, 1997, reprinted 1998), pp. xxvi–xxvii.

new kinds of play) and ill (the gradual expulsion of the actors and directors who had helped most to build up the Abbey company, and the later minimizing of their contribution). For the Poet we have to take on board not only the process of revision by which each new 'Yeats' reshaped his previous work, but also the manipulation of contacts and reviewers and the constant log-rolling by which his poetic reputation was built. Yet the effect of Foster's meticulous scholarship and the sheer density of his chrono- logical history is not a debunking. Much of Yeats as hero and his retrospective imaging and sculpting of his life has to go or be modified. Yet the man's adaptability and multiplicity (before he found a psychology to explain and justify himself to himself) and his biographer's historical understanding of the shifting Irish and English contexts and the conflicting pressures against which Yeats had to work, give us not only a different but in many ways a more interesting figure than before.

Above all, chronological method alerts us to connections between activi- ties, energies, and interests that might otherwise seem to have nothing to do with one another. Here Foster substantiates his case against Ellmann, for whom 'a strictly chronological account' of Yeats's life from 1889 to 1903, for example, 'would give the impression of a man in a frenzy, beating at every door in the hotel in an attempt to find his own room'. The clue for Ellmann must lie in the poet's 'increasing self-consciousness',[16] and his solution is to sort out the tangle by theme, anticipating the later Yeatsian psychology of his subtitle, *The Man and the Masks*. So (like Sartre with Flaubert) he turns to Yeats's early fictions, and their habit of opposing pairs of characters each embodying part of the writer, for ways of structuring the diversity of life. The chapter headings show the strategy: 'Robartes and Aherne' is followed by 'Michael Robartes and the Golden Dawn' (Yeats's occultism during these years), and then by 'Aherne and the Nationalists' (about Irish politics). But the writer is beyond the masks, using them in an attempt to integrate himself. So the next chapters treat the ways Yeats tried to do so in life: first, the 'Search for Unity' in his creation of 'An Irish Mystical Order' on the one hand and 'An Irish Mystical Theatre' on the other; and then in art, by 'Making a Style' (the poems and plays and their revision); and finally in love, the emotional turmoil of Yeats's love affairs with Maud Gonne and Olivia Shakespear, culminating in the heavy blow of Maud's marriage to MacBride in 1903 and 'A New Division of the Self'.

If one were giving a reading list to an undergraduate with an essay to write, one might still recommend Ellmann. His book is far shorter than Foster's—a major disadvantage of the chronological method being the length that it requires—and admirably lucid, and he has a literary sensitivity

[16] Richard Ellmann, *Yeats: The Man and the Masks* (London, 1949, reprinted 1961), p. 73.

and subtlety that the historian Foster is probably aware that he cannot rival.[17] But there is no doubt that Foster's is the better account of Yeats's life, showing how much is lost and simplified by Ellmann's division into themes. For to follow the life as it was lived shows the vital connection between each and every one of Ellmann's disentangled strands. In dense detail Foster shows the constant yet always shifting connections between the cultural, nationalist, and theatrical politicking, and the making of poems and plays. Irish faery lore and the interest in the occult were inseparably connected too, and both had nationalist aspects. The occult was also a way—indeed the only way—of keeping some hold over Maud Gonne; and their relationship was inseparably linked at every stage with the factional ups and downs of Irish nationalist infighting. Torn between his origins and his aspirations, between Dublin and London, and between the English language and metropolitan literature and the Irish cultural revival, Yeats was the same 'politician', often up against the same opponents, whether in politics proper or the literary, cultural, theatrical, and occult arenas which for him were (equally) politics by other means, and the hinterland of the creative imagination. Finally, even though there is something more dutiful than inspired in Foster's efforts to deal with the manuscript evolution, where we can watch Yeats making himself over and over under all these pressures, the context Foster brings to this is far denser and wider than Ellmann's, better literary critic though the latter may be. To 'live' thus with Yeats month by month, year by year, is to *experience*—only approximately of course, but more richly than ever before—what such a life was 'like'. It makes for less lucid reading, but greater and more complex understanding.

By contrast again, Hermione Lee's solution to the problem of how to begin a life of Virginia Woolf, if a chronological approach is 'no longer possible', is apt to her subject, and challenging. She begins with VW's[18] thoughts on biography and the unsatisfactoriness of this 'bastard' art: the almost unbridgeable gap between the outer and the secret self; the difficulty therefore of knowing anybody; the difference between 'life' in biographies where waxwork figures move in patterns (as VW felt they also did in Edwardian fiction) and life as we ourselves experience it. Moreover VW insists, with

[17] Foster argues crisply, however, for his historian's approach: 'WBY's life has been approached over and over again, for the purposes of relating it to his art. [. . .] What this volume attempts to do is restore the sense of a man involved in life, and in history: notably in the history of his country. [. . . .] His extraordinary life deserves to be studied for its relationship to his work; it also needs to be studied for its influence on his country's biography' (*The Apprentice Mage*, pp. xxvii–xxviii).

[18] 'VW' solves not only the clumsiness of repeating 'Virginia Woolf' and the curtness of 'Woolf', but allows a clear chronological distinction between her single (VS) and her married years (VW).

Lawrence, that to be truly alive is to be constantly changing; hence good biography 'is the record of the things that change rather than of the things that happen'. Facts, however, have their importance, and 'Since life has to begin with birth and to continue through the years these facts must be introduced in order', until biography 'swells into the familiar fungoid growth'.[19] But how much do the facts in their order have to do with the real person? Perhaps the biographer should accurately record all the facts without comment, and then write the life as fiction—especially its epiphanic scenes and moments. Or perhaps the traditional form could be sabotaged by working backwards or by having different writers at each stage, both of which VW considers before falling back on a more conventional method for her life of Roger Fry.

Lee however chooses an Ellmann-like approach in order both to cut across strict chronology (and its mushrooming) and yet show her subject gradually changing. The first section maps Virginia Stephen in her world, up to the age of twenty-two, from a series of angles whose time-scale is not however limited to 1882–1904, but draws heavily on the later Virginia Woolf looking back. We begin with 'Houses', in Kensington and St Ives: at once the settings of the life, a sunny and a sombre landscape of the mind, and the sources of VW's critique of late Victorian society. Then 'Paternal' and 'Maternal' are about the Stephen and the Patten families; 'Childhood' about Virginia and her parents in her earliest years; and 'Siblings' about her relations with her brothers and sister as well as her half-brothers and half-sisters, up to the death of Julia Stephen in 1895 which altered everything. 'Adolescence' shows the effects of that loss and of the tragic death of her half-sister Stella, and how VS educated herself. 'Abuses' angles in on her father's exploitation of his daughters, and on the abuse by her eldest half-brother of his position before and after Leslie Stephen's death. 'First Loves' is an account of Virginia's relationships with a number of older women. Finally 'Madness' deals with her breakdowns in 1895 and 1904, and the question implied by the title. Then Parts II, III, and IV focus, each from a series of thematic angles, on periods of fifteen, ten, and twelve years, to the suicide in 1941. VW is shown in roughly chronological development, but the periods are long enough and the thematic anglings sharp enough to make the book much shorter than a strictly chronological method could have managed. Though hindsight becomes habitual, fixity of pattern is discouraged by the facetings, the shifts in focus, the constant sense of a multi-layered or many-mansioned personality. It is a learned,

---

[19] Lee, *Woolf*, pp. 10–11.

and also an imaginative, subtle, and wise book; and though its author voices a fear of not being worthy of her subject, there is a remarkable inwardness and affinity. I cannot imagine anyone using her method better.

Yet the rejection of strict chronology has a price—all the clearer because it is a matter of method, not of talent. Lee's major strength can also be a worry; for Part I envelops us from the start in a consciousness that tends to collapse the gap between the apparent time and the mature time of the later artist, and also to identify the biographer with her. There is always a danger that the inwardness with one's subject that is needed for good biography may lead to enclosure. One may catch attitudes: there are (for instance) moments when Lee seems oddly infected with the intellectual snobbery which is as problematic as VW's social snobberies. A strictly chronological method might not have tended so to identify biographer with subject. There is also the need to disentangle people from the overwhelming power of a major work of art. It seems as vital to show how different Leslie and Julia Stephen were from the Mr and Mrs Ramsay of *To the Lighthouse* in the years before Julia's death, as it is to disentangle biography from imagination in *Sons and Lovers*. Hermione Lee is not unaware of this. Yet the method which allows the later Woolf to be present and dominant from the start also does not allow time and space to re-create her parents through the flux and change of those thirteen years. The ambivalence of the child who preferred her father to her mother, but who was then all the more disturbed by the bereavement, the failure to grieve, and the radical change in her feelings towards the widower cannot be fully developed. The method foreshortens: we get too rapidly to the dark flowering in life of what became Mr Ramsay, and never quite focus on the triumph of fictive reconciliation later, whereby the mother who had so quickly made Adrian her favourite, and who so often chose to be away nursing other people, was transformed into the wonderfully life-enhancing, if still complex, Mrs Ramsay.

Foreshortening also begs questions about the notorious 'sexual abuse'— in quotation marks only because the words can mean such different things—by her half-brothers. Lee threads her way with balanced tact through much hypothetical, inaccurate, and sometimes silly comment by others. Yet the near juxtaposition of something that happened when VS was six (and was not recalled until she was fifty-seven), with something that happened when she was twenty-one and was soon told to others in outrage, together with the use of VW's own much later accounts (one of these after meeting Freud, another an admitted performance for effect to the Memoir Club), tends to obscure the questions of how far they were the same sort of thing, or whether they were similarly damaging. Push them together and the answer might seem to go one way. Separate them out, years apart and each in its context, and try to establish what actually happened—remembering that VW's later accounts should be seen also in *their* context—and the answer might look rather different. Is there evidence of paedophilia in Gerald? If not, the first looks like curiosity rather than erotic assault,[20] though this does not of course displace the question of its effect on its victim, about which, however, VW herself is far more complex and tentative than others have been.[21] The second was entirely out of order—but George's habits of speech and touch had always seemed excessive to the reserved Stephen girls, and it is doubtful whether he went further than kissing and fondling; and unclear, because of VW's later desire to shock, that the offence was repeated. This is not in the least to minimize or excuse the abuse of the child and the young woman, and of their own position, by the two men: Gerald at eighteen; and George at thirty-five virtually the head of the family in Leslie's last illness. Yet the effect of these experiences on VS—which is what matters—needs to be traced with great care. (Her response to George may also have to do with *her* sexuality.) Lee is not among those who have seen here the determining causes of VW's eating difficulties, 'frigidity', and mental disorders. Yet her method does tempt Lee to echo much of VW's contemptuous and outraged portraying of George afterwards, even though she is half-aware of the outrageousness of the caricature. A chronological method might have ensured a more complex and changing experience of the boy, the man, and the relationship, before imagining the effect of what VS probably felt as betrayal as well as assault.[22]

The question whether foreshortening time may distort a changing experience seems even more pressing in a thematic chapter called 'Madness', about the 'breakdowns' of 1895 and 1904 and the problem of what was wrong not only with Virginia Stephen, but with Virginia Woolf. But weren't the 'breakdowns' of 1895 and 1904 in fact quite different? Must they not

[20] We forget how sexually ignorant young men could be in the 1880s. In 1907, aged twenty-two and at university, Lawrence was deeply shocked to be told that women had pubic hair.
[21] See Virginia Woolf, 'A Sketch of the Past', in her *Moments of Being: Unpublished Autobiographical Writings*, ed. Jeanne Schulkind (Brighton, 1976), pp. 67–9. The Freudian influence—belated, since she had earlier been scornful about him—is very clear in the association with the horrible animal face in the mirror—though the connection with the Gerald episode is made very tentatively, and it may seem doubtful that a six-year-old would have associated the episode with lust, or lust with animality. The effects that wilder commentators have derived from the episode are much better referred to the experience with the horrible man who exposed himself to the adolescent VS in the Park.
[22] There are several indications of feelings for George (see Lee, *Woolf*, pp. 104, 157, 653–4) which were buried beneath VS's resentment and VW's later vengefulness.

have *felt* quite different at the time? In 1895 after her mother's death VS seems to have worried the family enough for them to seek medical advice (as Stella was still doing a year later); but though the racing pulse, red-faced emotionalism, and headaches would be repeated on later occasions, there seems no reliable evidence of mental breakdown. Given the thirteen-year-old's complex distress about her mother, and also the onset of puberty and menstruation, her disturbance was explicable, however distressing. She seems to have coped with Stella's death in 1897. In 1904, however, the breakdown was both mental and physical, with hallucinations, and a leap from a low window. Lee herself is properly cautious about taking VW's much later and rather literary account of the delusions (at a time when she was working on Septimus and *Mrs Dalloway*) as 'exact narratives of raw experience' with coherent biographical meanings.[23] Moreover, if there had been no later attempts at suicide, would this have been regarded as one? It may be that pushing together different experiences of VS seven years apart and using them for an enquiry into whether or not VW was 'mad', involves as problematic a reading-back as the backdating of Lawrence's tuberculosis. And does it not also distort the changing *experience* of VS, and VW? She must have felt more apprehensive about herself in 1904; but she was angry with her family when their fears of a recurrence forced her to take what she thought unnecessary 'rest-cures' in a 'home' in 1910 and 1912. Most of all, a chronological treatment would give fuller weight to the difference, yet again, from the later experience of 1913—an unquestionable attempt at suicide this time—and the question of how this new breakdown (nine years after the last one) related to her sexuality and the experience of marriage, as well as to the stress of finishing and publishing a first novel about a girl who didn't want to get married, and killed herself. Lee's chapter 'Marriage' in Part II begins oddly. She will not discuss 1912–13 until she has shown in a whole series of quotations from 1925 to 1937 that the Woolf marriage became a good one, of its own kind. So it did; but it is the response of VW and LW to the problems of marriage *at the time*, and the effect on their relationship (and the future) of the breakdown that followed, that were important in 1912–13, especially if life-writing is, as VW thought it should be, 'the record of the things that *change*'. The question of what was wrong with VW, and of how her family, Leonard, and she herself came to view it, is a difficult, complex and evolving one. Careful chronology might be not only the best antidote to determinist explanations, which Lee distrusts as much as I do, but also the best way

[23] Lee, *Woolf*, pp. 195–7.

of tracing the no less complex and evolving relation of VW's life to her art, through the stages of the manuscripts.[24]

Above all, strict chronology allows some miming for a reader of how a life may have felt to live, at the time. There will be too many spaces, unknowns, opacities, for this to be more than partial, and frustrating, as biographers know only too well; but the strictly chronological method also tends to show up the gaps in the evidence which confident analysis conceals. It constantly throws the emphasis on the experience of the biographee rather than the commentary of the biographer. It is also a way of inviting the reader in on more equal terms, watching the life unfold rather than having its significance anticipated, or being enclosed in the biographer's analytic structure, or for that matter the subject's own retrospective imaging. In trying to make change and development more manifest, it also affects the treatment of relationships, aiming at greater complexity and changefulness in other characters too. Finally—although an avidity for judgement is one of the less admirable reasons for the fascinations of biography, and no biographer can be wholly free from presupposition and prejudice—the chronological method does tend to delay verdicts until there has been sufficient exploration of process and development.

The price that has to be paid for strict chronology, however, is also huge. Every one of its gains will increase the length, slow the pace, and involve a degree of repetition when the eventual bearing of previous developments becomes clearer. Reviewers are not slow to complain of bagginess and monstrosity (VW's 'fungoid growth') while sometimes praising the very qualities which produce the length and the lack of clear form. The 'general reader' too may feel that a long and complicated book is a great evil. To be able to treat relationships or problems thematically, abstracted from chronology, brings obvious advantages in both clarity and economy, though the example of Sartre shows how aiming at any total explanation may also produce a monster.

Chronological biography may seem to depend ideologically on 'humanistic' assumptions, that the Self *is* ultimately undetermined, contingent, and changeful—assumptions which are open to challenge from various quar-

---

[24] Even if it could be proved that her condition had its determinant cause in the chemistry of the brain, and was only secondarily affected by psychological factors or behaviour, it would remain true, as Lee argues, that 'We can only look at what it did to her, and what she did with it' (p. 199)—and that is a story that evolves differently, through time. I would also endorse the view that it is a story of 'heroism not oppression, a life of writing wrested from illness, fear and pain'.

ters. Conversely it may be that a strictly chronological method shows greater reverence and respect than confident analysis does for the changefulness and mystery of human beings.

14

Shaping the Truth

MIRANDA SEYMOUR

This is Robert Louis Stevenson, writing in 1893 to Edmund Gosse:

> I like biography far better than fiction myself: fiction is too free. In biography you have your little handful of facts, little bits of a puzzle, and you sit and think and fit 'em together this way and that, and get up and throw 'em down, and say damn, and go out for a walk. And it's really soothing; and when done, gives an idea of finish to the writer that is very peaceful. Of course, it's not really so finished as quite a rotten novel; it always has and always must have the incurable illogicalities of life about it. [. . .] Still, that's where the fun comes in.[1]

To Stevenson, writing towards the end of the Victorian era, biography was, despite those 'incurable illogicalities', the work of a craftsman rather than an artist, methodically fitting together the jigsaw pieces of a picture which already had a frame and an image. He lived in an age when, with a few great exceptions—Froude's Carlyle, Lockhart's Scott—public lives, the lives which were written about, were shown as exemplary. The biographer stayed out of sight, crouched under the table where his unblemished puzzle-portrait lay on show.

A century on, biography can seem to have less in common with puzzle-built pictures of heroes than a visit to Frankenstein's laboratory. The monster, we remember, has been assembled from a variety of sources and endowed with the name of his creator. So it often is with modern biography. The subject is fashionably kitted out to fit the latest theories, or to point up a marketable resemblance to some significant media figure, be it a princess or a soap-star. The biographer's name will not be shyly displayed.

---

[1] R. L. Stevenson, letter to Edmund Gosse, 10 June 1893, in *The Letters of Robert Louis Stevenson*, ed. Bradford A. Booth and Ernest Mehew, 8 vols (New Haven, CT, 1994–5), VIII, 104.

Handsomely paid and conscious that a serialization will be looked for to help redeem the publisher's advance, the 'life-writer' will seek out and emphasize any sensational material, claim deep identification with the subject and, of course, defend her (or his) interpretation of the facts as the never-before-told unvarnished truth.

Until, that is, the next biographer offers a fresh slant.

Henry James's horrified perception of Flaubert, 'dragged after death into the middle of the market place, where the electric light beats fiercest [. . .] with every weakness exposed, every mystery dispelled, every secret betrayed', seems sweetly behind the times.[2] What celebrated figure of the past fifty years has not been hauled into that unwelcome circle of light? It comes as rather a shock to find that James himself was referring, not to some work of disgraceful revelation, but to the publication of an edited selection of Flaubert's letters.

Standards have changed since James and Stevenson's day, and so has our attitude to privacy. The tapes of Anne Sexton's private therapy sessions were used by Diane Middlebrook to chart Sexton's process of poetic development (1991); Jane Dunn, in her biography of Antonia White (1998), drew on confidential hospital notes to describe the novelist's breakdowns. Nicholas Shakespeare's life of Bruce Chatwin (1999) raised the possibility that Chatwin might have transmitted AIDS to one of his most famous male attachments; Shakespeare also drew on private hospital records in order to authenticate his account of the writer's final months. At a lecture by Katherine Frank about her research for a forthcoming life of Mrs Gandhi, the biographer told her audience that friends of the former president who had chosen not to disclose information were, in effect, making themselves fair game. If they wouldn't tell, Frank argued, she felt herself entitled to obtain that information elsewhere, by whatever means.

Broadening the circle of inquiry again, ponder the late Sir Ernst Gombrich's memorable account in *Art and Illusion* (1960) of the impossibility of presenting a thing as it is in a variety of ways for simultaneous apprehension. The London Underground logo, in his example, has been incorporated in posters to represent several things, including: a happy grin or a nose in profile on a moon face; the letter 'o' in 'FOR'; one of three buttons on a bridegroom's sleeve.[3] The logo can easily be identified as any of these things on an independent basis. It cannot be identified as all of them at once. We can oscillate between our interpretations of the sign, but we cannot accept, and neither—returning to the arena of biography—can the life-writer hope to impose, conflicting interpretations. This is a point worth remembering,

[2] Henry James, review of *Correspondance* of Gustave Flaubert, *Macmillan's Magazine* (1893).
[3] E. H. Gombrich, *Art and Illusion* (1960, 5th edn Oxford, 1977), pp. 197–8.

for it marks the distinction between a written life, however scholarly, and a known life. We, in our emotional human state, can establish and develop and retain different interpretations of people familiar to us. It is part of the biographer's difficult challenge to examine these untethered interpretations and create from them a portrait which will be identifiable from every angle. A biography cannot present a life in the inchoate, multi-faceted form which is its familiar and daily form. A biography is, in this respect, a work of illusion, a cheat.

Is this a serious flaw in the genre? Is the invasion of privacy justifiable when 'truth' is to be told? Are there standard rules by which we can encode the way a biographer should use confidential information or documents? The roaming subject of this essay is the ethics of biography, the rights and wrongs of representation of those to whom death affords little protection. Roaming, because I do not expect to discover a solution; the subject is one of endless fascination but there are no easy answers. Autobiography, a separate subject, has clearer rules. It can be safely stated that it is unethical to exploit the lives of the living by drawing on their personal correspondence or on their relationship with the autobiographer without consulting the appropriate persons. The use of pseudonyms is an acceptable alternative, but again, the autobiographer is advised to consult the persons being discussed before publishing. This is a point, not of law, but of common decency.

There was a controversy in 1998 over the release of a film (*Hilary and Jackie*) about the cellist Jacqueline du Pré. The film, based on a book by the cellist's sister and brother-in-law, made much of an occasion on which du Pré allegedly demanded (and was granted) sexual relations with her sister's husband. The film-scene was unforgettable; anybody who saw it would now have difficulty in thinking of du Pré without recalling it.

But was the film true to the facts? Faced with this question by an interviewer from *The Times*, the director Anand Tucker gave an evasive response. 'There's no such thing as truth', he was quoted as saying. 'It doesn't exist. What there is is this side of the story and that side and probably 20 more sides. Films are very simple things. Lives are very complicated'.[4] This is not too far from the point Gombrich was making; the story grows more troubling when we learn, from Tucker's interview, that he decided to make the film on the strength of a four-page synopsis for a biography shown to him by du Pré's sister and brother-in-law. Those pages formed the basis for the film.

Here, we have an odd and disturbing situation. The authors were

---

[4] *The Times*, 20 January 1999.

offering a self-confessedly non-musical film-maker something they evidently hoped was sensational enough to interest him. Their sample, as Tucker acknowledged, focused on the story of du Pré's sexual aggressiveness, just the kind of thing to grab a story-loving audience. An incident with the brother-in-law evidently did take place; we and Tucker have the word of only him and his wife that du Pré was the predator. Friends of the cellist who saw the film protested in print that the incident was out of character. 'Anyone else would have made a different film and I'm not going to pretend I've hit upon the absolute truth', Tucker said afterwards with shrewd disingenuousness.[5] The damage done to du Pré's personal reputation by both book and film was considerable.

Condemning du Pré's biographers, I'm not sure how well I emerge myself from the quandaries which present themselves to those writing about the (recently) dead. Lady Ottoline Morrell's niece was still alive and intellectually alert when I began work on my life of her in 1990. So was Lady Ottoline's daughter, Julia Vinogradoff, who diverted herself by claiming to have forgotten where her mother's diaries had been deposited. (She used to invite me to share a bottle of white wine with her across the table under which the diaries lay, tucked away in an iron trunk.)

Mrs Vinogradoff died the following year and her children generously gave me free and unconditional access to the diaries, which they had never been shown. They were more amused than shocked to hear that the journals offered evidence of Ottoline's passionate affair in middle age with a twenty-two-year-old gardener at Garsington who later died in her arms. I doubt if their mother would have consented to such details being revealed; they made no objection.

A bigger shock was in store. I was transcribing the last of the diaries when I came upon a series of entries which showed that, beyond any doubt, Ottoline had allowed herself to be drawn into a sexual relationship with her half-brother, the Duke of Portland. His daughter was still alive. I knew her well. She had adored her father; she believed her parents' marriage to have been happy and faithful. She had already told me she was looking forward to reading my book. To be confronted by this episode would, I thought, be a death-blow. I began to hope that she might die before I got to the last chapter; reaching it, I received a cheerful anticipatory letter from her. What was I to do?

I compromised. John Forster, writing the first biography of Charles Dickens, had found it impossible to mention his friend's relationship with Ellen Ternan. What he did instead was to insert a signal. He printed the will in which Ternan was strikingly bequeathed £1,000, a large enough

---

[5] Ibid.

sum to cause any curious reader to speculate on the nature of her friendship
with Dickens, a married man, and draw the obvious conclusion.

The biography which I eventually published in 1992 contained no
precise details of this bizarre relationship between Lady Ottoline and her
doting half-brother. I offered no incriminating quotations, made no alle-
gation. Just enough of the truth was suggested in a cryptic sentence for a
shrewd reader to guess that this relationship might have gone beyond the
normal boundaries of family affection. Dropping a veiled hint, I hoped to
have preserved one elderly reader from emotional distress. Lady Victoria
Wemyss died a few years later, aged 104. Only then did I feel able to add
a full account of the relationship between Lady Ottoline and the duke
to a new edition of the book (1999).

The argument I made in my defence for having held back this information in the first place was that the relationship did not and does not
alter my general perception of Ottoline Morrell. It occurred in the last
years of her life; it was hard to see how it enhanced my understanding of
her earlier life. And yet, had I written the entire book with the certain
knowledge that this would have been its final episode, it is possible that
the portrait I created of Ottoline would have been in some way different.
I can't let myself off the hook.

One more personal case-study, of which less detail can be given. A
revelation, more troubling than Lady Ottoline's incest, was made to me
some time ago. The person who offered the information explained that it
had been withheld while I was writing *Robert Graves: Life on the Edge*
(1995) because knowing it would have made me reluctant to continue with
the book. The information appeared to be accurate and based on first-hand
evidence; it was true that such knowledge would have made it impossible
for me to continue working in close co-operation with the poet's family.
The discloser asked for this piece of information to be embargoed for fifty
years, in order to limit the hurt that would be caused to the living.

This was and is an uncomfortable situation. My book had already been
published. Here, reposing in a large brown envelope, was material which
would undoubtedly cause an important shift of perspective. But the dis-
closure was made, in the context of a friendship of some years, in confidence
that I would maintain silence. Is the biographer in such a situation under
oath to the subject, now dead, to the living informant, or to the reader
who has been denied a full grasp of the facts? In what circumstances should
such a trust be broken?

Fiona MacCarthy faced this problem when writing the life of Eric Gill
(1989). The sculptor's diaries soon showed her how restrained Robert
Speight's use of them in the 1970s had been; they left no doubt that Gill
had sexually abused two of his three daughters. The surviving daughter

freely acknowledged to MacCarthy that this had been the case, while stressing that the experience had been wholly untraumatic.

MacCarthy was never in any doubt that the abuse had to be mentioned. It was, in her opinion, vital to the understanding of Gill's work, and to his belief in sex as all-embracing. If she had been refused permission to mention it, she said that she would have abandoned the book. I asked her, having myself always shown the families concerned the manuscript prior to publication, if she had shown hers to Gill's daughter. She had not. But neither, as she pointed out, had the daughter asked to see it.[6]

MacCarthy acted with propriety and produced a fine book, but what if the surviving daughter had seen the manuscript and asked for the sensitive material to be omitted? Should MacCarthy's commitment to telling the truth about her subject have overruled the wishes of the living?

The answer, in her own view, is plain. Gill's unconventional sexual behaviour was integral to his artistic beliefs. The information provided by MacCarthy leads the reader to a deeper understanding of the work. To have suppressed it would have been a betrayal of the man and his art. I, on the other hand, would probably accept that Ottoline's disconcerting relationship with her half-brother does not enlarge our understanding of her character, her taste, or her convictions. The family would, in this case, have been justified in asking that I maintain privacy, although I am grateful to them for taking the bolder course.

The battle between discretion and candour has been going on for a long time. Dr Johnson seems to have approved of frankness: 'If a man is to write a Panegyrick he may keep vices out of sight', he commented, 'but if he professes to write a life, he must represent it as it really was'.[7] Carlyle, defending what was regarded by some as a shockingly disloyal life of Sir Walter Scott for a son-in-law (John Gibson Lockhart) to write, launched a furious attack on the Victorian biographers' passion for reticence.

> How delicate, decent, is English biography, bless its mealy mouth! A Damocles sword of *respectability* hangs forever over the poor English life-writer. [. . .] The English biographer has long felt that if in writing his biography he wrote down anything that could [. . .] offend any man, he had written wrong.[8]

The shock of finding himself revealed in his late wife's letters as a monstrous egotist who had not stopped short of physical violence did not shake Carlyle's belief that the truth should be told. He wrote his memoir of their marriage with appropriate candour; he left out only the problem of

---

[6] Fiona MacCarthy, interview with Miranda Seymour, 23 December 1998.
[7] Samuel Johnson, quoted by Ian Hamilton, *Keepers of the Flame* (London, 1992), p. 72.
[8] Thomas Carlyle, *Westminster Review*, XXVIII (1837), 299.

impotence which had, in the opinion of his wife's loquacious friend Geraldine Jewsbury, made him an impossible husband. (Mrs Carlyle was Jewsbury's source and presumably knew what she was talking about.) Carlyle did not publish the memoir; instead, he asked his friend and biographer James Froude to do so after his death, following 'careful examination and revision'. Froude, despite furious opposition from Carlyle's niece, produced one of the most impressive and scrupulously honest biographies of the Victorian age. He was praised for it, but the damage done to his subject's heroic status was considerable: Carlyle's followers had great difficulty in rallying support for their scheme to buy the Scottish author's home in Chelsea as a literary shrine in the years after Froude's book had been published. Nobody, in the 1880s, felt that they were any longer bound to admire Carlyle. The biographer who had unveiled him had the comfort of knowing that he had kept faith with his subject. 'It is a Rembrandt picture', he told Charles Kingsley's widow in 1884, 'but what a picture!'[9]

Candid though he was, even Froude did not feel able to tell all he had discovered; no mention was made of Carlyle's slightly absurd devotion to Lady Ashburton, of the violence he showed to his wife, or of his alleged impotence. Froude's motives for keeping these details back were mixed. They would have inflicted further damage on Carlyle's reputation; they might have done equal injury to his own. The tributes to his frankness could easily have given way to disapproval. Instead, following in Carlyle's footsteps, he set down all he knew and had not revealed, leaving the dilemma of publication to his children. They, as feeling began to harden against Froude for having damaged the reputation of a great man, knew where their duty lay. Sir James Stephen, more leniently disposed towards Froude than his brother Leslie, felt that Carlyle had shirked his.

> He threw upon you [he told Froude in a letter which the biographer gratefully published] the responsibility of a decision which he ought to have taken himself in a plain, unmistakable way. He considered himself bound to expiate the wrongs which he had done to his wife. If he had done this himself it would have been a courageous thing; but he did not do it himself. [. . .] If any courage was shown in the matter, it was shown by you, and not by him [. . .] you were in fact guilty of no other fault than that of practising Mr Carlyle's great doctrine that men ought to tell the truth.[10]

On the other side of the fence from Carlyle and Froude, in the same century, we can identify some staunch defendants of a family's right to deny public access to its secrets. Mary Shelley, writing in 1839, seventeen

---

[9] Waldo Hilary Dunn, *J. A. Froude* (Oxford, 1961), p. 497.
[10] Sir James Stephen, letter to James Anthony Froude, 9 December 1886, quoted in Froude, *My Relations with Carlyle* (London, 1903), p. 62.

years after her husband's death, strongly opposed revelations. 'This is not the time to tell the truth', she wrote, echoing an opinion offered earlier by her friend Leigh Hunt, 'and I should reject any colouring of the truth'.[11] Her daughter-in-law's version of some unsavoury past events showed how skilfully the truth could be managed. A leap from the carefully undated death of Shelley's first wife to his meeting with Mary in 1814 allowed Lady Shelley, writing in 1859, to present her mother-in-law as the sweet consoler of a bereaved man. Nobody reading the *Shelley Memorials* would suspect that Harriet, the first Mrs Shelley, was alive and pregnant with their second child in 1814. (She drowned herself two years later.)

Mary's honest vote for discretion is preferable to such shameless manipulation, but the wish of family members to promote a comforting narrative demands some sympathy, especially if the omissions are frankly acknowledged. 'I have told what I choose to tell', William Michael Rossetti wrote in the Preface to a life of his late brother, Dante Gabriel: 'if you want more, be pleased to consult some other informant'.[12] John Walter Cross, having married George Eliot shortly before her death in 1880, was good enough to own that he had not, in *Her Life as Related in her Letters and Journals* (1885–7), printed a single one of his wife's letters in its entirety. He did readers no favours, however, in concealing the fact that he had revised them wherever Eliot's language seemed inappropriate to her status. Such an eminent author was not expected to declare that it was raining 'blue devils'; out, therefore, went the blue devils and with them, all the vivacity of Eliot's comment. A hundred similar examples of Cross's silent diligence can be cited and regretted. This is a dangerous form of tampering with the truth, leading to the possibility of confusion and misinterpretation.

What of the quarry? What are our rights over our own lives? A celebrated British novelist recently told me that she puts imaginary meetings into her diaries in order to entertain the (slightly bored) archivists who are cataloguing her diaries and letters. Will they guess enough to pass on a tip? Will future biographers be warned that they must unearth every fictional narrative in this story-loving woman's life? And if not, what kind of artificial construct will her biography be? Does she have the right to be so wilfully misleading with material for which she is, after all, being paid so that it can be lodged for public use at a university?

John Updike, while making no such efforts to muddy the water, opposes the right of any biographer to intrude on private life, 'disturbing my children, quizzing my ex-wife, bugging my present wife, seeking for judases

---

[11] Mary Wollstonecraft Shelley, Preface to *Shelley: The Poetical Works* (London, 1839).
[12] William Rossetti, quoted by Hamilton, *Keepers of the Flame*, p. 137.

among my friends, rummaging through yellowing old clippings, quoting in
extenso bad reviews I would rather forget, and getting everything slightly
wrong'.[13]

Tennyson and Henry James would have applauded. Tennyson was
thinking of himself as much as of Keats when he defended a dead poet's
right to be known only through his own works:

> For now the Poet cannot die
> Nor leave his music as of old,
> But round him ere he scarce be cold
> Begins the scandal and the cry:
>
> 'Proclaim the faults he would not show:
> Break lock and seal: betray the trust:
> Keep nothing sacred: 'tis but just
> The many-headed beast should know.'[14]

Henry James did everything he could to make the biographer's task impossible. His story 'Sir Dominic Ferrand', published in 1892, shows how
strongly James shared Tennyson's mistrust for the idea that his readers, the
public, had any right to knowledge of an intimate nature. The situation
James set up here was of a tussle between a newspaper editor and the
young reporter, Peter Baron, who has discovered Ferrand's secrets in a
bundle of papers. The editor, Mr Locket, while freely acknowledging that
'the scandal, the horror, the chatter would be immense' if the papers were
published, makes the familiar argument of journalists that the public has
the right to know. 'Immense', he continues, 'would be also the contribution
to truth, the rectification of history'. Ferrand is dead; where's the problem?
The journalist who has discovered the papers represents James's own view.
Baron, James tells us, 'felt him [Ferrand] sufficiently alive to suffer; he
perceived the rectification of history so conscientiously desired by Mr
Locket to be somehow for himself not an imperative task'.[15]

James had already published *The Aspern Papers* when he wrote this
subtle tale. Richard Salmon, in an essay published in 1998, has suggested
that the earlier story's Shelleyan subject (based on an anecdote about the
acquisition of papers from Mary Shelley's stepsister by an assiduous visitor)
was deliberately picked.[16] In 1886, the year in which the first complete
biography of Shelley was published, its author Edward Dowden published

---

[13] John Updike, *New York Review of Books*, 4 February 1999.
[14] Tennyson, 'To—, After Reading a Life and Letters' (1848).
[15] Henry James, 'Sir Dominic Ferrand', *Collected Stories*, ed. Leon Edel (London, 1963), VI,
397–8.
[16] Richard Salmon, 'The Right to Privacy/The Will to Knowledge: Henry James and the Ethics
of Biographical Enquiry', in *Writing the Lives of Writers*, ed. Warwick F. Gould and Thomas
F. Staley (London, 1998), pp. 135–50.

a remarkable essay, 'The Interpretation of Literature'. Here, Dowden presented the biographer as a ferocious warrior. Referring to Sainte-Beuve, Dowden admiringly called attention to the way in which the French writer 'made his advances; how he invested and beleaguered his author; how he sapped up to him, and drew his parallels and zigzags of approach; how he stormed the breach and made the very citadel his own'. Nothing, in Dowden's view, appeals more to the critical biographer than those with secrets to hide: 'these, perhaps, are the most fascinating of all, endlessly to be pursued'.[17]

Henry James found this attitude repellent. His private answer was to burn his papers; publicly, he seems to have responded directly to Dowden's siege metaphor in his celebrated statement of the subject's right to resist. Faced with such tenacious hounding, James argued, the quarry had only one option: to self-destruct. 'This is the only route by which the pale forewarned victim, with every track covered, every paper burned and every letter unanswered, will, in the tower of art, the invulnerable granite, stand, without a sally, the siege of all the years'.[18]

How then did James think a biographer should behave? His own two-volume life of William Wetmore Story (1903) was discreetly written, as he admitted, with the intention of selling copies and pleasing the family who had asked him to undertake the task. Defending the way in which he had silently rewritten William James's letters for *Notes of a Son and a Brother*, James staked his plea on personal loyalty. William would not have wanted his early writing to be published just as it was, he wrote to William's son: 'It was as if he had said to me on seeing me lay my hands on the weak little relics of our common youth, "Oh, but you're not going to give me away, to hand me over, in my raggedness and my poor accidents, quite unhelped, unfriendly; you're going to do the very best for me you *can*, aren't you?" '[19] Was James merely being protective? He rewrote many of his brother's sentences in his own ornate style. Was William being punished for the dislike he had expressed of that very style? Should James not have alerted the reader to the way he had shaped not only the events of William's life but the very language in which his plainspoken brother had described them? Does a family member have exceptional rights? If so, was James justified in taking them so far?

Lytton Strachey shared Virginia Woolf's belief that the biographer has a

[17] Edward Dowden, 'The Interpretation of Literature', *Contemporary Review*, IV (May 1886).
[18] Henry James, *Selected Literary Criticism*, ed. Morris Shapira (London, 1963), p. 158.
[19] Henry James, letter to Henry (Harry) James, Jr, 15–18 November 1913, in *Collected Letters*, ed. Leon Edel (Cambridge, MA, 1984), IV, 802.

right to be fanciful in order to present the essence of the biographical subject. It was, in Strachey's view, inconsequential that Florence Nightingale did not die in a shaded room (it faced south, and the blinds were up), and that Cardinal Manning and Miss Bevan may not have been loitering in a shrubbery when they discussed spiritual matters. What mattered was that saying so fitted the version of the story that was being presented.

This is very close to saying, 'Well, if it didn't happen, it should have', a view defended by Ira Bruce Nadel in a provocative study of biography published in 1984. Making an argument for what he described as 'authorized fictions', Nadel made the broader and valuable point that 'how a life is written is as important as how that life was lived'.[20] We do not need to share his enthusiasm for the now widely condemned school of psychobiography; we can—cautiously—share his enthusiasm for the idea of the creative fact, first endorsed by Virginia Woolf in her celebrated 'Art of Biography' (1939). She wrote it in defence of Strachey's *Queen Victoria* (1921). Strachey had omitted any mention of the queen's later correspondence because it failed to conform with his image of the monarch: Woolf argued that what mattered was the way her friend had shaped and used the earlier letters to offer a unique image of the queen. Biographers, she correctly predicted, would proliferate; the task, in order to escape the danger of repetitiveness, was to take the facts and mould them in a singular way. The clever biographer was the one who knew the value of 'hanging up looking glasses at odd corners'. Granted a proper respect for the facts, she argued, the ambitious biographer has the right to move beyond them. To what? 'He can give us the creative fact; the fertile fact; the fact that acts and engenders'.[21] Woolf licensed the biographer to be as free as the novelist in order to convey the essence of the subject.

Woolf may have been reacting against the necessary conventionality of her father's approach as editor of the *Dictionary of National Biography* (Sir Leslie Stephen himself contributed some four hundred of the entries). Certainly, her fictionalized life of Vita Sackville-West as Orlando was an elegant example of how the carefully angled looking-glass could provide an unforgettable image. Giving herself the relatively open space of the historical novel, Woolf felt free in *Orlando* to invent, exaggerate, make leaps across centuries. The result was a work of art which escapes categorization. Here, where biography and fantasy live in an open marriage, creative facts earn their place. Imagination creates a fresh, intriguing, and strangely persuasive figure.

[20] Ira Bruce Nadel, *Biography: Fiction, Fact and Form* (London, 1984), pp. 156 and 186.
[21] Virginia Woolf, 'The Art of Biography', in *The Death of the Moth, and other Essays* (London, 1942), pp. 195 and 196–7.

Writing a biography of her friend Roger Fry (1940), however, Woolf felt, for whatever reason, unable to exercise similar freedom. Creative facts here took the form of unacknowledged omissions. No mention was made either of the twenty-five years Fry had spent with Helen Anrep or of his affair with Virginia Woolf's sister. This is a case in which we should ask whether, knowing how much she intended to exclude, Woolf acted properly in becoming Fry's first biographer?

While few biographers would attempt the fantastic form of Woolf's *Orlando*, most submit to the artifice of creating a life in which events proceed more or less chronologically and with a form, however delusive, of explanation. Life in the raw is often shapeless; the biographers must create their persuasive narrative by inserting a connecting thread. Subjectivity inevitably comes into play in this manufactured coherence.

We all have our own hunches and interests; an experiment I performed recently on a month's entries from William Godwin's journals, presented to ten different readers, seemed to prove this point. This was not, in terms of significant events, an important month; it was, however, a characteristic one. Among the responses, one reader noted the diarist's obsession with recording weather details; another thought that his frequent visits to the theatre suggested that he was studying the art of playwriting; one thought the theatre offered the possibility of meeting a wife (this was in the months after Mary Wollstonecraft's death), while yet another speculated on the object of writing a record which contained no form of commentary, and what this might tell us about the subject. Each of the readers would, it was clear, have followed a different track and shaped a slightly different personality.

What we had exemplified here was the process which George Eliot memorably described in *Middlemarch*. Scratched in all directions by cleaning, the tiny random lines on the surface of a steel pier-glass become visible when a light is held near to it. 'It is demonstrable that the scratches are going everywhere impartially', Eliot wrote; 'it is only your candle which produces the flattering illusion of a concentric arrangement, its light falling with an exclusive optical selection'.[22] Thus, Godwin's month of recorded events was used by each of us to reflect an interest which we had independently brought to the text.

Boldly continuing along this path, we could argue that biography is inescapably subjective, that it offers a marriage between the recorded life of the subject and the personality of the biographer. Reading Boswell's life of Johnson, do we see Johnson as he was, or do we see him as Boswell

---

[22] George Eliot, *Middlemarch* (1871–2), ch. 27.

wished him to be? How objective is Mrs Gaskell's extraordinary account of herself watching Charlotte Brontë show off Branwell's portrait of herself and her sisters? Isn't this a sly way of yoking biographer and subject together, placing them above interrogation? Is there a significant difference between Boswell's intrusive presence in Johnson's biography and a curious life of President Reagan (*Dutch: A Memoir of Ronald Reagan*, 1999) into which the biographer Edmund Morris shamelessly inserted a fictionalized version of himself? Can we confidently say that one is wrong and the other right? Given that the biographer is likely to have views and interests which will affect his/her interpretation of the subject, is it not an act of honesty to appear in the book and declare them, even, as in Morris's case, in fictitious form?

There is something, after all, to be said for the old-fashioned 'Life and Letters' approach. This offers interesting modern possibilities for the ethically-minded biographer. The life is written as a subjective narrative; an extended second half of the book contains the unedited letters and documents which have most affected the interpretation and structure. The reader becomes co-interpreter, free to reach a (somewhat) independent judgement.

This approach can be abused. Ulick O'Connor, analysing Richard Ellmann's life of Oscar Wilde in 1991, showed the process at work in an example that may bear repetition.[23] Ellmann, on page 88 of his book, stated that his presentation of Wilde's character had been guided by his belief that Wilde was syphilitic. He had been convinced of this fact by statements made by two of Wilde's friends, by the certificate of the doctor present at his death, and by the 1912 edition of Arthur Ransome's life of Wilde, in which (Ellmann said) Ransome gave syphilis as the cause of death.

No further evidence was given; the reader was simply referred to page 547 of his book. Here, he printed the doctor's death certificate. It contains no mention of syphilis; there is, however, an allusion to 'cerebral disturbances stemming from an old suppuration of the right ear'. Ellmann encourages us to see this as a reference to syphilis; he quotes an account of ottorhea, an aural discharge, from a paper given by Dr Terence Cawthorne in 1958 on Wilde's death in support of his claim. Unmentioned is the fact that Cawthorne was arguing that Wilde did not suffer from syphilis; on the contrary, his unquoted conclusion was that the dramatist 'died of nothing less than an intracranial complication of suppurative otis media'.[24] This is not syphilis.

---

[23] The example cited here was first identified by Ulick O'Connor, *Biographers and the Art of Biography* (Dublin, 1991), pp. 46–7.
[24] Ibid., p. 47.

Ellmann was equally misleading in referring readers to the 1912 edition of Ransome's book. Here, the cause of death was indeed stated to be 'meningitis, the legacy of an attack of tertiary syphilis'.[25] In 1913, however, a further edition of Ransome's book was published. Syphilis no longer featured. Wilde's death, Ransome now wrote, 'was directly due to meningitis'. Ellmann, we must conclude, preferred the earlier edition—he made no mention of a later one—because it confirmed the case he wished to make.

Of course the careful reader should check such facts. But Ellmann was writing for a largely non-academic audience unused to making scrupulous second-checks on the source material provided. No pointers were given to cause them to question his veracity. This was not ethical behaviour.

Subjectivity is hard to avoid. It need not be seen as a bad thing. Biography is, in Britain, at least, a thriving genre; a limited number of marketable subjects means that there will always be alternative versions on offer to the reader. There is no book of rules. No law states that we may not deduce private experience from published works or forbids us to insert ourselves into the text as a companion to or interrogator of our subject. We are not constrained from following our own interests in seeking to enter the mind of the chosen subject. If it is likely that what will emerge is an amalgamation of subject and self, then the best the biographer can do is to be aware of that and to be on guard against it. Biography should be, and rarely is, a selfless art.

Without laws, we must rely on commonsense and police ourselves. We fabricate detail, wilfully mislead, or silently omit significant evidence at our own peril; it will never be long before another biographer is treading the same track and looking with interest and scepticism at the last set of footprints in the dust.

[25] Arthur Ransome, *A Life of Wilde* (London, 1912), p. 99.

15

Sartre's Existentialist Biographies: Search for a Method

CHRISTINA HOWELLS

The first biography to feature in Jean-Paul Sartre's writing exists only to be discarded: in Sartre's first novel, *La Nausée*, published in 1938 when its author was thirty-two, the hero Antoine Roquentin's biography of the Marquis de Rollebon is what led him to Bouville, and its abandonment is what allows him to leave the dreary provinces on an early evening train for Paris. But what Roquentin finds so disturbing in his biographical study is precisely what, for Sartre, gives it its value: it is 'a work of pure imagination'.[1] Roquentin's 'honest hypotheses' account well enough for the facts, he feels, but ultimately they emanate from him, and are no more than a means of unifying and making sense of what he knows. M. de Rollebon may seem to constitute 'the only justification for his existence' (p. 85), but despite this, or perhaps because of it, he bores Roquentin stiff: 'M. de Rollebon m'assomme' (p. 22).

Roquentin's experience with Rollebon is sometimes held up as a puzzle: if Sartre disliked and mistrusted biography, the question goes, then why did he write so many biographical studies? Various answers are proffered: 'Sartre changed his mind' is the easiest and least satisfactory. 'Roquentin is writing the wrong kind of biography' is perhaps a more attractive possibility, and indeed seduced me at one stage.[2] According to this view,

---

[1] Jean-Paul Sartre, *La Nausée*, in *Oeuvres romanesques* (Paris, 1981), p. 19. All translations from French are my own.
[2] See Christina Howells, *Sartre: The Necessity of Freedom* (Cambridge, 1988), p. 166.

Roquentin's biographical project is too empirical and therefore necessarily trivial. In some senses this is probably true. But, on reflection, it is clear that the question of whether Rollebon participated in the assassination of Paul I is considerably less trivial than the question of some of Flaubert's schoolboy pranks, related in detail by Sartre in *L'Idiot de la famille*. No, Roquentin's biography is not so much the wrong kind of biography, rather Roquentin has the wrong attitude to it. It is indeed the product of 'pure imagination' and hypotheses, but this is what all intellectual work necessarily entails. If even the micro-physicist is barred from total 'objectivity' because his experimentation inevitably affects his experiments, *a fortiori* the historian cannot expect to attain an extra-temporal, objective perspective. For, of course, such a perspective could never be human: caught as we are between the *pensée de survol*, or the uninvolved overview which sees the wood but can't understand the trees, still less the leaves, bark, and roots, and the avowedly subjective perspective which acknowledges its own situatedness, the best we can probably do is to embrace the latter. Deprived of a God's eye view which would achieve both immanence and transcendence, 'the intellect of man is forced to choose',[3] and to strive for a form of 'universal singular' in which the individual and singular ultimately rejoins the universal by achieving, in its very specificity, a kind of representative status.

So Roquentin is expecting too much, and also perhaps too little, of his biography. He grows to hate 'the slow, lazy, grumpy facts' (p. 19); he has more documentation than he can cope with ('letters, fragments of memoirs, secret reports, police archives'), but what is lacking is 'firmness and consistency' (p. 18). Other historians work happily with such material, he reflects: are they more intelligent than he is, or just less scrupulous? Whether Sartre himself was less scrupulous is a difficult question, as we have little evidence of Roquentin's working methods, whereas we know that Sartre used increasingly copious documentation from his early *Baudelaire* (1947), through the huge tome on Genet (*Saint Genet, comédien et martyr*, 1951), to the multi-volume study of Gustave Flaubert (*L'Idiot de la famille*, 1971–2). But that Sartre was more intelligent than Roquentin is beyond question. Roquentin is like the natural existentialist described at the end of *L'Etre et le néant*, he is in the halfway house of those I have likened elsewhere[4] to Pascal's *demi-habiles*: he has abandoned the *esprit de sérieux*

---

[3] W. B. Yeats, 'The Choice':

> The intellect of man is forced to choose
> Perfection of the life, or of the work,
> And if it take the second must refuse
> A heavenly mansion, raging in the dark.

[4] Howells, *Sartre*, pp. 25–6.

of the bourgeois who believe values to be inscribed in some absolute or divine realm, but he has not taken the next step of realizing himself to be 'the being through whom values exist'.[5] This is also why Roquentin cannot accept that Adolphe's braces are mauve, or that the tram bench is definitely not a dead donkey, or that his tongue is not liable to turn at any moment into a live centipede. The fact that there are no God-given certainties does not mean that our world is chaotic; on the contrary it is organized by patterns of time and space, utility and purpose, and these patterns are human. For Roquentin they are rather all too human. Similarly, then, Roquentin is dismayed rather than exhilarated by his own implication in the biography he weaves around the 'facts' of Rollebon's life history.

Unlike Roquentin, Sartre as biographer embraces the paradoxes of an attempted yet always impossible totalization of the fragmentary, and acknowledges the extent to which he is implicated in the 'story' he tells. His biographical purpose strikes one by its innovatory nature when set against the norms of French biography in the twentieth century; it is critical, epistemological, and political rather than literary, as in the classic texts by André Maurois, or narrowly academic, as in the series subtitled 'L'Homme et l'œuvre'. The question he asks is overwhelming in both its ambition and its apparent simplicity: 'What can we know of a man today?'.[6] His committed method involves historical and psychological interpretation, not predominantly empirical exposition. It is a hermeneutic quest which can never claim to be complete. If he is happy to call his mammoth study of Flaubert a *fable* (*IF*, I, 139), this is more than a mere provocation of the scholarly establishment, the work is a fable to the extent that all truth, and especially truth about men, is human. But to acknowledge the situated nature of truth is by no means to espouse idealist subjectivism: truth may be historical; this does not mean that all objectivity is impossible. In *Saint Genet*, Sartre is scathingly dismissive of the subjectivism of bourgeois idealism, which he refers to as a vicious circle; he maintains on the contrary that for all the 'deformation', 'relativism' and necessary 'historicism' of criticism, its meaning and significance are none the less objective for our time.[7]

Sartre's biographies are not consistent in format or approach, but they have certain constants in common, not least as examples both of existential psychoanalysis and of the progressive-regressive method outlined first in *L'Etre et le néant* and later elaborated in the *Critique de la raison dialect-*

---

[5] Sartre, *L'Etre et le néant* (Paris, 1943), p. 722. Henceforth *EN*.
[6] Sartre, *L'Idiot de la famille*, 3 vols (Paris, 1971–2), I, 7. Henceforth *IF*.
[7] Sartre, *Saint Genet, comédien et martyr* (Paris, 1951), p. 622, n.l. Henceforth *SG*.

ique. Their major differences lie in the increasing complexity with which they are carried out. In all cases Sartre is concerned to conceive human life as a totality rather than a collection of disparate data, and to interpret events, attitudes, and projects as part of a chosen destiny rather than as contingent or accidental phenomena. In this sense, the biographies all form part of Sartre's epistemological enquiry into the relations between man and the world, as well as of his continuing ethical exploration of the nature of freedom.

There is also a sense in which they participate in his phenomenological method: just as in his descriptions of imagination or emotion, Sartre bases his 'phenomenological psychology' not on an accumulation of empirical data but rather on 'an intuition of essences',[8] so in his existential biographies he moves from an event, action, or choice directly to its meaning without the need to seek corroboration by amassing evidence. The inductive psychologist can only reach probable conclusions since he cannot ever be sure of having sifted all the facts; the phenomenological psychologist seeks the essential conditions of a particular structure through an intuitive examination of a particular example. Intuition here, of course, is used not in the general sense of insight but rather in the philosophical sense of what is apprehended by the mind as immediate evidence. This is not, however, to say that Sartre's intuitions (even in this philosophical sense) go untested: the proof of the pudding is in the eating. It is not so much apparently incompatible facts that would bring down a phenomenological theory as its uselessness as an explanatory model. Hypotheses are tested not so much against further evidence as according to their productivity as interpretative tools. This is the progressive-regressive method as it operates in the biographical domain. An action or event is interpreted as revealing of a particular choice or project, its integration and role within the project thus uncovered is then determined. As Sartre spells it out in *L'Etre et le néant*:

> Any action is comprehensible as a project of oneself towards a possible goal. [. . .] And understanding takes place in two opposed directions: by a regressive psychoanalysis we move up from the act under consideration to my ultimate possibility—by a synthetic progression we come back down from that ultimate possibility to the act being examined and we grasp its integration in the total form. (*EN*, 537)

The apparent circle is benevolent rather than vicious; it is the hermeneutic circle of all interpretation which necessarily starts from a limited, because situated, perspective, but which is not thereby immobilized in its wait for absolute corroboration, because it seeks rather to move ever onwards towards a goal of understanding which is recognized from the outset as

---

[8] Sartre, *L'Imagination* (Paris, 1936, reprinted 1969), p. 140.

inevitably imperfect because incapable of ultimate totalization. And as so often with Sartre, it is this partial failure which guarantees its ultimate success, since it saves it from the sclerotic immobility and 'seriousness' of a final answer.

Baudelaire

It could be argued that Sartre's study of Baudelaire is not a biography at all. Composed as an Introduction to the poet's *Journaux intimes*, the essay draws on the events of Baudelaire's life in order to subject that life to a form of existential psychoanalysis. All Sartre's biographies do this; what varies is rather the elements other than psychoanalysis that contribute to the interpretative process. In the case of Baudelaire, Sartre's account of his insertion within the socio-historical world of his day is relatively sketchy. This has the heuristic advantage of showing most clearly the outline of Sartre's psychoanalytic method. In *L'Etre et le néant* Sartre spells out the aims and principles of existential psychoanalysis and discusses its similarities to and differences from Freudian analysis. These have been discussed elsewhere and this is not the occasion to rehearse them again. However, the aims of Sartre's own procedures certainly need to be explained briefly. Existential analysis is based on the principle that man is a totality and that each of his acts is therefore 'revealing' (*EN*, 656); its aim is to decipher and conceptualize the meaning of his behaviour; and it is supported by man's intuitive understanding of himself:

> The *principle* of this psychoanalysis is that man is a totality and not a collection; that, in consequence, he expresses himself in his entirety in the most insignificant and superficial of his actions.
> The *goal* of this psychoanalysis is to decipher man's empirical behaviour, that is to say, to cast light on the revelations which the behaviour contains and to conceptualize them.
> Its *point of departure is experience*; its *support* is the fundamental pre-ontological understanding which man has of the human person. [. . .]
> Its *method* is comparative [. . .] it is by comparing examples of behaviour that we will bring to light the unique revelation which they all express in different ways. (*EN*, 656)

Like Freud, Sartre envisages man as perpetually developing within his own personal history, and attempts to uncover the meaning, direction, and transformations of this history. And history, however personal, is more than just a matter of psychology; it implies situation within and interaction with the world:

> Psychoanalytic investigations aim to reconstitute the subject's life from his

birth to the moment of his cure: they use all the objective documents they can find: letters, personal accounts, diaries, 'social' information of all sorts. And what they try to restore is not so much a pure psychic event as a pair: the crucial event of childhood and the psychic crystallization around that event. (*EN*, 657)

Sartre's use of the word 'cure' here owes much to the fact that he is trying to construct a description that will work for both existential and Freudian psychoanalysis. His own preferred vocabulary is in terms rather of project, choice, and perhaps in this context, purifying reflection. Certainly Sartre maintains that the 'complex' is the Freudian equivalent of the existential notion of original choice; equivalent not, of course, in the sense of having the same meaning, but rather of having the same role and function, that of influencing and even structuring the subject's life and choices. For Freud, this is a matter of determinism, for Sartre, a matter of fundamental project, envisaged as freely chosen. Similarly, Sartre's conception of the importance of social environment is in terms of the subject's understanding and transformation of it: 'The environment can act on the subject only to the exact extent that he understands it: that is, transforms it into a situation. So no objective description of this environment could be of any use to us'(*EN*, 660).

In his discussion of Baudelaire, one of Sartre's purposes is to show up the fallacy underlying the cliché that the poet did not have the life he deserved: 'What if he did deserve his life? What if, contrary to common opinion, men only ever had the lives they deserved?'[9] This radical notion of total responsibility will be modified in the course of the next two decades[10] to the point where Sartre can say, in 1971: 'In a certain sense, we are all born predestined'.[11] In fact, it was already clear in *L'Etre et le néant* that liberty is not a matter of being or doing whatever we want. Other people and the world itself are always there to intervene. Men are free within their situation and starting from the basis of their facticity. Moreover, freedom is not a matter of achieving one's ends but rather of choosing freely: ' "To be free" does not mean "to get what one wanted" [. . .] The technical, philosophical concept of freedom [. . .] means only: autonomy of choice' (*EN*, 563). In Baudelaire's case, choice seems to have entailed allowing others to choose for him: 'So, as it is true that each of us shapes his destiny in his own image, Baudelaire, who originally chose to live under supervision, had his wish granted in full' (*B*, 79–80). But,

[9] Sartre, *Baudelaire* (Paris, 1947, reprinted 1963), p. 18. Henceforth *B*.
[10] See for example the *Critique de la raison dialectique* (Paris 1960; henceforth *CRD*), where Sartre attempts to reconcile existential freedom and responsibility with a Marxist view of historical conditioning.
[11] Sartre, *Situations*, 10 vols (Paris, 1947–76), X, 98.

Sartre argues, this cannot remove his responsibility for his life: 'The free choice that a man makes of himself is absolutely identifiable with what we call his destiny' (*B*, 245). The relationship between freedom and destiny is complex and ambiguous. Baudelaire's choice is one of dependence and reaction, but he does not want to *know* that this is the path he has chosen; it is easier and more consoling for him to view it as imposed by others and to protest against it:

> The choice he has made of himself is more deeply rooted in him. He is unable to distinguish it because it is one with him. But nor should we assimilate a free choice of this sort to the obscure chemistry that psychoanalysts relegate to the Unconscious. Baudelaire's choice is *his* consciousness, *his* essential project. [. . .] But in this very choice there is an intention not [. . .] to be known [. . .] In a word, his original choice is from the outset in bad faith. (*B*, 100–1)

As Sartre himself is the first to admit, his portrait of Baudelaire may disappoint us if we are hoping for new information or, alternatively, for an explanation of the appeal of the poetry (*B*, 124). Sartre's purpose is other. He is content to take the well-known material surrounding Baudelaire's life and character—his horror of nature, his cult of frigidity, his dandyism— as givens. Because, of course, these traits are his starting-point rather than his conclusion. Indeed, he argues that the 'empirical characteristics' which we notice first in Baudelaire are, in fact, not primary: 'They bear witness to the transformation of a situation by an original choice' (*B*, 125), that is to say, 'They are complications of that choice and [. . .] in each of them coexist all the contradictions which tear him apart, but reinforced, multiplied, by their contact with the diversity of objects in the world' (*B*, 125). In other words, as was argued in *L'Etre et le néant*, Baudelaire expresses himself in his entirety in the most apparently insignificant of his actions; the goal of Sartre's existential analysis is 'to cast light on the revelations which each act contains and to conceptualize them' (*EN*, 656).

Sartre's account of Baudelaire shares many of the characteristics of biography as Roquentin describes it and of psychoanalysis as Sartre describes it, that is to say it draws on documents, letters, diaries, and family archives, and tries to make some overall sense of them. But if the documentation could be criticized from an academic point of view as skimpy and second-hand (Sartre is very dependent on other critics and biographers for his information), Sartre's hypotheses and interpretations are far from being derivative or self-evident. On the contrary, they would amaze Roquentin by the degree to which they espouse the overtly imaginative: 'I'd be prepared to bet [Baudelaire] preferred meat in sauce to grilled meat, and preserved vegetables to fresh' (*B*, 142). Or again, 'Anyway, Baudelaire never met a frigid woman' (*B*, 151). History figures lightly in the reconstruction; there are a few references to 1852, and the way in which the stagnation of the Second Empire suited the poet's own backward-looking, nostalgic mentality (*B*, 213), but no serious historical analysis. Were the essay not so brilliant, it would be tempting to dismiss it as unfounded, as indeed many Baudelaire scholars did at the time, annoyed by its apparent criticism of the poet's character, and its failure to consider such staples of criticism as the theory of *correspondances*. René Laforgue's *L'Echec de Baudelaire* of 1931 had ruffled critical feathers by its Freudian approach; Sartre's existential analysis lacked the credentials even of that half-resented, half-accepted German theorist.

Jean Genet

Baudelaire is dedicated to Jean Genet, and shares the ethical preoccupation with evil and perversity of the twentieth-century novelist and playwright. *Saint Genet, comédien et martyr*, of 1951, takes Sartre a step forward in his biographical project. Already in *Situations, I*, he had argued that 'novelistic technique always reflects the novelist's metaphysics' ('La temporalité chez Faulkner', *Situations*, I, 66), now he elaborates further, and suggests a two-way process of reflection between the writer and his writing. His aim in his study of Genet is to 'discover the choice that a writer makes of himself, his life and the meaning of the universe, right down into the formal characteristics of his style and mode of composition, into the structure of his images' (*SG*, 645). Life does not so much explain art, as art reveals and explains life. Sartre's study of Genet is closely textual, and stunning in its interpretation of the fine detail of Genet's prose style. Genet's life, too, is explored with a seriousness and apparent commitment lacking in the account of Baudelaire. However, *Saint Genet* still concentrates on Genet at the expense of his historical situation, on existential psychoanalysis at the expense of dialectical, Marxist critique. Indeed, its avowed aim is precisely

> To show the limits of psychoanalytic interpretation and of Marxist expla-
> nation, and that only freedom can account for a person in his totality, to
> show this freedom battling with destiny, first crushed by the components of
> its fate, then turning back on them to digest them gradually, to prove that
> genius is not a gift but the solution invented in desperate cases [. . .] to trace
> in detail the history of a self-liberation. (*SG*, 645)

Sartre's intention to show the *limits* of psychoanalysis and Marxism in so far as neither takes account of individual choice and freedom necessarily means that his account of Genet is neither very Freudian nor very Marxist. Although he does give an account of Genet's childhood adoption by a peasant family (who are scandalized to find him stealing from them and who, Sartre claims, return him forthwith to Mettray Reformatory), there is little discussion of the psychological effects of early maternal deprivation, or, indeed, of the aggravation of such effects by a second rejection. Sartre's account is rather in terms of the linguistic alienation experienced by Genet who feels himself external to the society which has labelled him 'thief'. In Sartre's reconstruction, Genet determines to turn the language of the bourgeois against them, by using his writing to draw his readers into a world of perversity, homosexuality, and treachery that they would never enter voluntarily, even in an effort of empathetic imagination, but which is forced on them by the powerful aesthetic effect of Genet's style.

Genet's defiant assumption of the label 'thief', his decision to become precisely the traitor his foster-parents imagine him to be, his homosexuality, which is in part a further defiance of convention, in part a response to being 'surprised from behind' while stealing, all these features are explored at some length. But *caveat lector*: Sartre pulls the carpet out from under his own (trusting) readers' feet, in an act of apparent authorial betrayal somewhat analogous to Genet's own: 'It happened like this, or in some other way' (*SG*, 26). It is not the 'facts' that matter, rather their significance. Sartre does lay more stress on Genet's background and conditioning than he did in the case of Baudelaire, but it is still Genet's choice within his situation that concerns him most, at the expense of a detailed empirical, sociological, or historical account of that situation.

In an interview in the 1960s, Sartre criticizes his account of Genet as poorly grounded: 'It is evident that the study of Genet's conditioning by the events of his objective history is insufficient, very, very insufficient' (*Situations*, IX, 114). What Sartre seems to mean is that it is insufficiently Marxist, for although he was already elaborating his attempt to create an existential Marxism (or a Marxist existentialism) in the 1950s, at the time of composition of *Saint Genet* it was still at an embryonic stage. Even in *Questions de méthode* (1957), Sartre was primarily concerned to show the limitations of a rigid, reductive Marxism, which imagines, for example, that it can explain a writer by correctly defining his social class: 'Valéry is a petty-bourgeois intellectual, there's no doubt about that. But every petty-bourgeois intellectual is not Valéry.'[12] So although the progressive-regressive method which we looked at in the context of *L'Etre et le néant* was formulated a decade before the publication of *Saint Genet*, its historical basis was not fully elaborated until nearly a decade later. In the *Critique de la raison dialectique* we read:

---

[12] *CRD*, p. 44.

We will define the existentialist method as a regressive-progressive, analytic-synthetic method; it is an enriching movement back and forth between the object (which contains the whole epoch in the form of hierarchized meanings) and the epoch (which contains the object in its totalization) [. . .] the simple, inert juxtaposition of the epoch and the object gives way suddenly to a living conflict. (*CRD*, 94)

It is not until Sartre's study of Flaubert in 1971–2 that both poles of the dialectical method will receive equal weight and importance and the 'living conflict' will be allowed to emerge.

Freud

In the meantime, however, Sartre is to be reimmersed not only in Marxist theory in his writing of the *Critique*, but also in Freudian theory for the composition of a film-script. One of the most intriguing of Sartre's biographies is the posthumously published *Le Scénario Freud*,[13] the film scenario of part of Freud's early life, which he wrote as a commission for John Houston in 1958, but which was never filmed in its original version. Sartre's script would have made a film of over five hours. His revised version was even longer, and in the end he was so out of sympathy with what Houston eventually produced that he refused to attach his name to it. However, as well as the film itself, we do have Sartre's scenario, and it holds a triple fascination: as a biography of one of the most significant theorists of human behaviour against whom Sartre repeatedly pitted himself; as a viable if tendentious interpretation of Freudianism; and as evidence of the further development of Sartre's own biographical method. The latter two facets of the text are simultaneously relevant in this context. Sartre reveals Freud as much closer to his own views than one might have expected: in particular he shows him struggling to free himself from the positivist, mechanistic mode of understanding that he inherited from his mentor Dr Meynert, and moving towards a less deterministic interpretation in terms of human intentions and meanings. In his account of Freud, Sartre is as cavalier in his treatment of empirical detail and chronology as he was for Baudelaire and Genet. In the Introduction to the scenario, the psychoanalyst J.-B. Pontalis, a long-term friend of Sartre's, who remembers the film-script being composed, argues that only 'les esprits sérieux' or 'chagrins' (over-serious or quarrelsome critics) will accuse Sartre of consulting insufficient documentation, and that his purpose is not to conform to the facts in their minutiae. His aim is at once more Sartrean and more

---

[13] Sartre, *Le Scénario Freud* (Paris, 1984).

Freudian: to get beyond the strict empirical distinction between true and false, memory and invention, and, in Sartre's terms, 'mentir pour être vrai'. Freud's life is as open to creative interpretation in this respect as those of the poets and novelists whose biographies Sartre imaginatively reconstructs. The *Scénario* spans a twelve-year period, starting in September 1885, when Freud was about to leave the hospital at which he had worked with Meynert to go to Paris to study hypnosis with Charcot, and ending shortly after the death of Freud's father in 1897. In the *Scénario* Freud passes from one father-figure to the next, eventually explaining to Breuer that he has effectively carried out his own self-analysis (an indisputable anachronism) and, now that Meynert and his father are both dead, has come to understand that his aggressivity towards his gentle father was precisely a consequence of that gentleness:

> FREUD: His gentleness disarmed me. I wanted a Moses for a father. The Law!
> BREUER: To revolt against it?
> FREUD: And to obey it. Meynert played that role for a time. (*Scénario*, 402)

Sartre creates dramatic scenes to convey Freud's relations with his colleagues and family, he invents and conflates dream-sequences, he uses existing accounts of Freud's life, in particular the biography by Ernest Jones which appeared in French translation in 1958. Jones shows a Freud with whom Sartre would not have been familiar previously: nonconformist, rebellious, obstinate, the victim of anti-Semitism, and himself quite neurotic. Like Freud, Sartre is fascinated by the relationship between neurosis and artistic creativity, explored in most depth in his study of Flaubert. And like Freud also, Sartre is intrigued by the status of hysteria: dismissed by Meynert in the *Scénario* as mere 'lying', viewed by Freud as a psychosomatic disorder, and by Sartre as a psychosomatic 'choice' which is again given its clearest exploration in the case of Flaubert. A key notion in the understanding of hysteria is *compréhension*, a term already encountered in *L'Etre et le néant*, where it is opposed to *connaissance*, and which involves preconceptual understanding at the level of lived experience rather than analytic or scientific knowledge.[14] *Compréhension* implies a synthetic approach which relies on empathy, intuition, and imaginative reconstruction rather than external understanding in terms of causal, mechanistic, or biological models. This underlies Sartre's own progressive-regressive method which is dialectical and synthetic rather than analytic, and in the *Scénario* he endeav-

---

[14] My understanding of the Freud scenario, especially with respect to the notion of *compréhension*, is greatly indebted to Rhiannon Goldthorpe's account of it in 'Search for a Method: Le Scénario Freud', in *Situating Sartre in Twentieth-Century Thought and Culture*, ed. J.-F. Fourny and C. D. Minahen (New York, 1997), pp. 11–28.

ours to interpret Freud's psychoanalytic method itself as a form of this intuitive mode of understanding.

But as well as the discussion of hysteria, Sartre brings forward chronologically many other of Freud's major theories, including several that were not elaborated until the early years of the twentieth century. In the *Project for a Scientific Psychology* (1895), Freud's model for memory was still clearly neurological, in terms of permeable and impermeable neurons, grids, and resistances; in the essay 'The Mystic Writing Pad' (1896), memory is already envisaged more 'graphically', in terms of 'sign', 'inscription' and 'transcription'. It is thus evident that Sartre has taken a vital turning-point to mark the end of the period under discussion. Indeed, it might be argued that he has taken us right up to the birth of psychoanalysis proper, since *The Interpretation of Dreams* appeared in 1899–1900, but this goes no way towards explaining how Freud's major theories have been projected backwards into the late nineteenth century. In particular the theories involving infantile sexuality, repression, the Oedipus complex, the death-wish, and the interpretation of dreams all feature in this anachronistically condensed psychodrama. 'It happened like this. Or some other way' (*SG*, 26) has a different ring when well-documented theoretical texts are being discussed, rather than the trivia of everyday life or the lost details of childhood events and traumas. In the case of Freud, Sartre's biographical reconstruction is perhaps at its most inventive—but this may well have been, in a sense, part of his remit from Houston, since the film was not conceived as even a semi-scholarly presentation, but rather intended to bring the major aspects of Freud's life and theories to a wide audience. Condensation, displacement, and symbolization are being used by Sartre not to evade the censor as in dreams, but rather to entertain and instruct the audience in the broad lines if not the fine detail of Freud's progressive liberation from the straitjacket of nineteenth-century positivism.

Flaubert

In *Questions de méthode* of 1957, Sartre was already using Flaubert to demonstrate his Marxist/existentialist method. Marxism must deepen our understanding of 'real men' and not dissolve them in a bath of sulphuric acid (*CRD*, 37). Existentialism must revivify Marxism by insisting it attend to individual specificity; it must attempt to account for the mediations that transform general social contradictions into the concrete reality of individual lives and experiences. Contemporary Marxism, Sartre argues, can show Flaubert's realism as related symbolically to the social and political evolution of the Second-Empire *petite bourgeoisie*, it cannot show the genesis of this relationship; neither why Flaubert opted for literature, nor why he lived like a hermit, and least of all, why he wrote *these* particular books rather than others (*CRD*, 45). Nothing is a matter of either chance or determinism in the usual sense of the terms; the child grows up into the adult he eventually becomes because he lives the universal as a particular experience. This is where the role of psychoanalysis is vital: in its attempt to understand childhood, and the role of the family in mediating social structures (*CRD*, 46). Sartre contrasts, as an example of two diametrically opposed contemporary responses to the society of mid-nineteenth-century France, Flaubert, whose childhood was dominated by his father in a hier-archical, outmoded, 'feudal' family, and the fatherless Baudelaire, whose fixation was rather with his mother. These family experiences transform the way in which the two writers respond to the social conditions of their age. But this is not to say that their lives explain their works; on the contrary, for Sartre, the work is, in a sense, more 'complete' than the life, and it is rather the work that illuminates the life. What is more, the two domains are incommensurable: there is an inevitable hiatus between life and work (*CRD*, 91).

These are some of the questions Sartre sets out to explore further and perhaps resolve in his three-volume *L'Idiot de la famille* (1971–2). His aim is methodological as much as biographical: 'My aim is to show a method and to show a man' (*Situations*, X, 93); 'The underlying project in the *Flaubert* is to show that ultimately everything is communicable, and that one can succeed, without being God [. . .] in understanding a man perfectly, if one has the necessary elements' (*Situations*, X, 106). The 'necessary elements' include not only empirical/factual material but also Marxist and psychoanalytic methods. Sartre's bold formulations belie his awareness of the immense complexity of his 'totalizing imperative' (*CRD*, 88):

> Nothing proves at the outset that this totalization is *possible* and that the truth of a person is not plural; the pieces of information are very different *in nature*. [. . .] Do we not risk ending up with layers of heterogeneous and irreducible meanings? This book attempts to prove that the irreducibility is only apparent. (*IF*, I, 7)

Sartre's analysis of Flaubert's writings reveals his narcissism, onanism, idealism, solitude, and dependence (*CRD*, 91). His conflict-ridden, petty-bourgeois background is shown to be both the origin of Flaubert's passive nature *and* what he rejects in his preference for art above utility. In Sartre's terms, Flaubert both preserves and overcomes his 'constitution' in the process of *personnalisation* in which he decides what he will make of what has been made of him. This is in fact Sartre's later definition of responsibility and of project: 'I believe that a man can always make something of what has been made of him' (*Situations*, IX, 101). Moreover:

> Gestures and roles are inseparable from the project that transforms them. [. . .] Overcome and preserved, they constitute what I would call the internal colouring of the project; but its colouring, that is to say subjectively its taste, objectively its style, is nothing other than the overcoming of our original deviations: this overcoming is not a single moment, it is a long endeavour [. . .] for this reason, a life goes by in spirals; it always passes by the same places, but at different levels of integration and complexity. (*CRD*, 71)

Personal characteristics which Sartre would once have described as freely chosen are now interpreted as ineradicable structures of facticity, formed in infancy. Flaubert's apathy is understood in terms which are psycho-somatic rather than part of a willed project: 'Apathy is the family experienced at the most elementary psychosomatic level—that of breathing, sucking, the digestive functions, the sphincters—by a protected organism' (*IF*, I, 54).

Already in *L'Etre et le néant*, situation and facticity constituted the basis from which the world was experienced, 'character' constructed, and choices made. And thirty years later Sartre is still maintaining that these structures and circumstances are not so much limitations to our freedom as the necessary starting-points from which freedom may be developed. The relationship between freedom and conditioning is now described, however, in terms which owe more to Marx and Freud than to phenomenological ontology:

> This dialectic of chance and necessity comes about freely without troubling anyone in the pure existence of each of us. [. . .] What we are seeking here is the child of chance, the meeting of a certain body and a certain mother [. . .] these elementary determinants, far from being added together or affecting each other externally, are immediately inscribed in the synthetic field of a living totalization. (*IF*, I, 60–61)

Sartre's account of Flaubert is always in terms of intentions, not of deter-minism. Even—or perhaps especially—his crisis, his quasi-epileptic fit which 'condemns' him to life as a recluse in the family home at Croisset, is interpreted as part of a project which will free him from his law studies and allow him to stay at home to write. Here Sartre calls on Freud for support in his finalistic interpretation of the gain to be derived from illness. Flaubert's *chute* is both a negative and tactical response to his father, and, more fundamentally, 'a strategic and positive response to the question posed by the necessity and impossibility for Gustave of being an Artist' (*IF*, II, 1920). His illness is precisely, and paradoxically, the expression of his freedom (p. 2136).

But as Sartre is well aware, there is little hard evidence for any of this.

His comment on his own account of Genet 'It happened like this. Or some other way' is repeated for the story he has woven around Flaubert's childhood:

> I admit it: it is a fable. Nothing proves that things were like that. And worse still, the absence of proof—which would necessarily involve specific details— means that, even when constructing the fable, we have to fall back on schemas and generalities. [. . .] I can imagine, without the slightest vexation, that the real explanation is exactly the opposite of the one I am inventing. (*IF*, I, 139)

Like all Sartre's biographical studies, *L'Idiot de la famille* represents a work of imagination: it is 'un roman vrai' (a true story), a hypothetical rather than empirical exploration. And just as Sartre is not hidebound by scruples concerning evidence or documentation, nor is he restricted by purist concerns about orthodox methodology. On the contrary, he is an innovator and synthesizer who sets out precisely to reunite what man has put asunder, in this case the insights of Marx and Freud. Marx and Freud themselves may have been extremely unorthodox, none the less a stagnating orthodoxy has settled around them, creating churches and branches and splinter groups, all of which claim to know the 'truth' of the Masters' words. Sartre, of course, has no time for enshrined dogma and doctrine, and in his study of Flaubert he transgresses the well-established separation of the faculties to construct a radical dialectical interplay between Marxism and psychoanalysis, as bold in its conception as the heterodox study *Capitalisme et schizophrénie*, by Gilles Deleuze and Félix Guattari, the first volume of which was also published in 1972.[15]

Sartre's use of Marx and Freud involves, then, no mere juxtaposition of historical and psychoanalytic analysis, but rather a dynamic dialectic manifest on the simplest level in his description of Flaubert internalizing his historical situation precisely through the mediation of his family. The domestic problems of the Flaubert family are not unique, they are rather endemic to a whole society in transition. What is experienced (subjectively) as singular is revealed (objectively) to be universal. The contradictory demands or 'double-binds' which the young Gustave internalizes from his parents are not merely contingent and random; on the contrary, they arise from social disorder, and reflect what Marx would call introjected conflict. Flaubert internalizes a whole series of conflicts, starting with the contradictions inherent in the position of the *classe moyenne* under Louis XVIII: certain of his father's interests, for example, are served by the very monarchical system which excludes him from participation in the elections.

---

[15] Gilles Deleuze and Félix Guattari, *Capitalisme et schizophrénie*, I: *L'Anti-Oedipe* (Paris, 1972).

Furthermore, Achille-Cléophas Flaubert himself embodies the latent conflict of industrialists and ex-émigrés: he is simultaneously an atheistic doctor and a royalist provincial. This is further complicated, of course, by the split in the family itself, and in particular by the way it has adapted its 'feudal' hierarchy to a more modern form of bourgeois individualism, resulting in what appears to be the worst of all worlds: family members are still judged hierarchically while appearing to be judged on merit. Sartre refers to this as *hystérésis* ('belatedness') and argues that the family is fifty years behind the times. The result is that Gustave Flaubert, as younger son, is devalorized, and simultaneously made to *feel* personally unworthy. This is the historical and sociological correspondence of Flaubert's mother's non-valorization of him in infancy, and Sartre argues that it is precisely what will make of him both a neurotic and a great writer. The 'neurosis' is, of course, not merely personal; it is also historical and artistic, and is the trademark of a whole generation of post-Romantic artists, exemplified to perfection in Flaubert himself. In fact, Sartre argues, it is paradoxically because Flaubert was neurotic and self-hating long before the *débâcle* of the 1848 Revolution aroused shame and self-loathing in the bourgeois who had participated in its suppression, that he could produce novels that were simultaneously so popular and so misunderstood. Sartre's analysis of the Flaubert family's *hystérésis* and of the way it helped to produce *Madame Bovary* is one of the most convincing and fascinating aspects of *L'Idiot de la famille*. It also provides clear evidence that sophisticated methodology need not lead to a dry text dominated by theory, but may rather be the stimulus for the most passionate of epistemological and biographical enquiries: 'What can we know of a man, today?'

16

A Life on Film

IAN CHRISTIE

The cinema gives an illusion not of the stage but of life itself.

T. S. ELIOT[1]

1.7 billion were there for his birth. 220 countries turned on for his first step. The world stood still for that stolen kiss. And as he grew, so did the technology. An entire human life recorded on an intricate network of hidden cameras, broadcast live and unedited twenty-four hours per day, seven days a week, to an audience around the globe.

Coming to you now, live from Seahaven Island, enclosed in the largest studio ever constructed—now in its thirtieth great year, it's *The Truman Show*![2]

If the nineteenth century was haunted by what Noël Burch has termed a 'Frankenstein complex', which centred on hopes and fears of creating a simulacrum of the human, then the twentieth-century equivalent would be the equally ambivalent prospect of 'total' representation.[3] Typically this has taken the form of omnipresent surveillance by an all-powerful system or state in a technological extrapolation of Bentham's panopticon. It has been the premise of dystopias from E. M. Forster's in 'The Machine Stops' to Aldous Huxley's *Brave New World* and Orwell's *1984*, and continued in such films as Terry Gilliam's *Brazil* and *The Truman Show*. But apart from its status as a political metaphor, what of its significance for our changing conception of the relationship between life as lived and represented? The film-maker and essayist Hollis Frampton proposed a cautionary

---

[1] Quoted in *World Film News and Television Progress*, I, 10 (January 1937).
[2] Voice-over in *The Truman Show*, a film written by Andrew Nicol and directed by Peter Weir, Paramount, 1998.
[3] Noël Burch, 'Charles Baudelaire versus Dr Frankenstein', *Afterimage*, VIII–IX (Spring 1981); also ch. 1 of *Life to those Shadows* (London, 1990).

fable in his account of changing attitudes to narrative in the avant-garde.[4] A friend reported two recurrent, consecutive dreams. In the first, he lived a hyperbolically full and successful life as a woman, with every achievement comprehensively filmed for posterity. The second began with his selection at birth as the woman's heir, condemned to spend his entire life as the passive spectator of hers. With its echoes of Plato's cave and Calderón's *Life is a Dream*, this fable speaks eloquently of the growing sense of image satiation that marked the twentieth century.

But a parallel world of increasingly 'total' representation, either through archival accumulation or real-time surveillance, is not at all the same as biography, if by this we understand the practices of documentation, narration, and interpretation that coalesced in the nineteenth century. What is the relationship, if any, between the exponential rise of audiovisual recording and the development of biography? I will argue, in brief, that there were closer links between the early twentieth-century revolution in biography and the rise of cinema than might be supposed; that the meaning of biographical film cannot be reduced to simplistic canons of accuracy since it is more typically allegorical; and that new forms of biographical film have much to contribute to the continuing debate over postmodernity and the contested place of narrative in history.

The early history of cinema resonates with anticipation of a new era in which tokens of the real and the authentic will supersede mere evocation of the past and the dead. Already in 1895, when the Kinetoscope could capture less than a minute of silent action, Thomas Edison confidently predicted that audiences would soon enjoy 'grand opera being given at the Metropolitan Opera House in New York [. . .] with artists and musicians long dead'.[5] Later that same year, the first Paris reviews of the Lumières' Cinématographe spoke of its potential to make the dead appear living— although Maxim Gorky would reverse this in his report of the cinematograph portraying 'not life but the shadow of life [. . .] a life devoid of words and shorn of the living spectrum of colours'.[6] By 1901, film had arguably entered the sphere of at least chronicle, if not biography, through the chance capture of President McKinley's assassination in Buffalo. To be precise, what Edison's cameramen recorded was a crowd waiting for the

---

[4] Hollis Frampton, 'A Pentagram for Conjuring the Narrative', in *Circles of Confusion: Film, Photography, Video Texts 1968–1980* (Rochester, NY, 1983), pp. 59–68.

[5] In his preface to W. K. L. Dickson and Antonia Dickson, *History of the Kinetograph, Kinetoscope and Kineto-Phonograph* (New York, 1895).

[6] Maxim Gorky's pseudonymous newspaper report of July 1896, in Richard Taylor and Ian Christie, ed., *The Film Factory: Russian and Soviet Cinema in Documents 1896–1939* (London, 1988), p. 25.

president to appear, which he failed to do after Czolgosz's shots inside a pavilion.[7] The resulting film, titled in the blunt style of the period *Mob Outside the Temple of Music*, thus became an early example of contextual evidence—the impact of an historic event rather than the event itself—which might be considered emblematic of cinema's subsequent relationship to contemporary history. But even more significant was the decision by Edison's managers to link together a series of pre-assassination films taken at the Buffalo exposition with further coverage of the stages of McKinley's funeral, and to cap these with a cinematic memorial, *The Martyred Presidents*, which embedded photographic portraits of the three presidents killed in office in a commemorative sculpture. Considered as a whole, this hybrid series (which also included a reconstruction of Czolgosz's execution) marked the arrival of a new form of biographical chronicle: one certainly related to the text-and-illustration narratives of later nineteenth-century popular journalism, but also new in offering an immediacy and the sense of witness inherent in the new medium.

The fact that such chronicles could be entirely contrived, as was Georges Méliès's *Dreyfus Affair* (1899) along with many Anglo-Boer War 'reproductions', contributed to an early and persistent scepticism that cinema could ever be considered 'factually' reliable. How could we know that what we are seeing really 'is' what it claims to be? And even when there is no reason to doubt that it is—in the case, for instance, of Emily Davison's death as a suffrage protest, filmed in 1913—what does the filmic record tell us? Can it shed any light on why, or even precisely how, this death took place? Will not whatever words accompany its reshowing—originally written captions; now inevitably a narrating voice—condition how we interpret the event, and effectively create the 'filmic fact'? Viktor Shklovsky raised this issue when writing critically about the pioneer of Soviet 'cinema truth', Dziga Vertov, noting that for newsreel shots to have meaning they require titles giving date and place, otherwise they are 'like a card catalogue in the gutter' and in danger of becoming mere symbols.[8]

Despite such strictures, the rise of film coincided with a wider shift of attitude towards the object and aims of history, and specifically of biography, in the second decade of the twentieth century.[9] After the solemnity of Victorian biography, typified by her own father's monumental *Dictionary of National Biography*, Virginia Woolf welcomed a growing

---

[7] See Ian Christie, *The Last Machine: Early Cinema and the Birth of the Modern World* (London, 1994), pp. 89–90.

[8] Viktor Shklovsky, 'Where is Dziga Vertov Striding?', in Taylor and Christie, ed., *The Film Factory*, p. 150. Vertov's *kino pravda* gave its name to the very different documentary movement of the 1960s known as *cinéma vérité*.

[9] See Chapter 11 above.

emancipation which had three main features. First, biographers were now free to adopt a critical or even satirical attitude towards their subjects, as Lytton Strachey did in his revisionist account of Victorian idols. Implicit in this new freedom was a permissible degree of fiction, or even fantasy, taken to new lengths in Woolf's *Orlando*, a novel inspired by her friend and lover Vita Sackville-West, which was mischievously subtitled a biography. And common to both the new biography and the new fiction is an increased attention to the inner life and apparently trivial details, rather than to the public achievements of great men. Within the Bloomsbury network, such concerns ran parallel to a growing involvement with psychoanalysis, so that Strachey's *Elizabeth and Essex* is widely regarded as the first essay in 'psychobiography', after Freud's own study of Leonardo and his co-authored polemic against Woodrow Wilson.[10]

At first sight, the 'new biography' of Strachey's *Eminent Victorians* and Harold Nicolson's *Some Lives* might appear to have little bearing on contemporary developments in cinema. Yet the still underestimated filmmaking of that decade offers some striking early examples of biography, not only in a new medium but also in a new and often controversial register. Four examples will indicate the extent of this phenomenon. In Russia, where a belated start in domestic film production was fuelled by an ardent assertion of nationalism, the death of Leo Tolstoy inspired a remarkable dramatization of the novelist's last days in *The Departure of a Great Old Man* (1912).[11] The fact that the Tolstoy family took successful legal action to prevent the film being released in Russia should not obscure its qualities. Indeed, given that the film shows the dying writer fleeing his wife to collapse in a railway station, such a reaction was as inevitable as the resulting scandal and marks it as one of the least inhibited of early film biographies. Deprived of a domestic market and thereby freed from Russia's strict code of censorship, the producers added an extraordinary apotheosis of Tolstoy ascending to heaven, a poetically apt irony in view of Tolstoy's contradictory status as both a heretic in the eyes of the church and a spiritual folk hero.

The obstacle that faced Oskar Messter's *Richard Wagner* (1913), an ambitious life of the composer explicitly subtitled 'eine Film-biographie',

---

[10] *Eine Kindheitserinnerung des Leonardo da Vinci* (1910). The notorious study of Woodrow Wilson was largely written by the American William Bullitt and 'approved' by Freud, according to Peter Gay, *Freud for Historians* (New York, 1985), pp. 140–41. See Chapter 10 above.
[11] Subtitled *The Life of Lev Tolstoi (Ukhod velikogo startsa. Zhizn' L. N. Tolstogo)*. For details, see Ian Christie and Julian Graffy, ed., *Protazanov and the Continuity of Russian Cinema* (London, 1993), pp. 10–11, 62.

was also a premonition of copyright and commercial problems that have increasingly dogged modern biography. To 'quote' Wagner's music in the score planned to accompany the film would have cost half a million marks in rights payments. Accordingly, the composer Giuseppe Becce, who was already contracted to portray Wagner, arranged an 'original' score which drew upon such non-copyright composers as Mozart and Beethoven to present Wagner as the climax of a German musical tradition—a solution which no doubt strengthened the film's celebratory premise.[12] An equally direct patriotic motive lay behind the most famous American film of the period, D. W. Griffith's epic *Birth of a Nation* (1915), hailed internationally as a milestone in large-scale spectacle, although based on a scurrilous novel, *The Clansman*, which demonized emancipated Blacks and their Northern supporters while presenting the Ku Klux Klan as heroic defenders of Southern honour. Most of the film's characters are fictional, but Abraham Lincoln appears a number of times, as do some of the Civil War generals. Three of these scenes, including Lincoln's assassination at Ford's Theatre, are introduced by title cards announcing them as 'historical facsimiles' and citing documentary sources. Although this is clearly intended to signal seriousness, as part of cinema's pervasive claim to a new status around 1912–15, the effect is also somewhat archaic, justifying stilted tableau compositions in the style of traditional history painting, in striking contrast to the dynamism of much of the film. Here the biographical element in what is otherwise an historical melodrama plays an ambiguous role, partly anchoring the film to the patriotic-monumental, while also serving to modernize its narrative structure. This innovative aspect of Griffith's imbrication of history and fiction has been well analysed by Miriam Hansen:

> In *Birth of a Nation* the only female character granted narrationally significant looks is Elsie Stoneman. Her status as a virgin and her acquaintance with Lincoln make her a superior historical witness and raise the function of her look above mere erotic interest. Thus when she discovers John Wilkes Booth *before* he fires the fatal shot [. . .] this look functions primarily as a suspense strategy, playing with the competing epistemological registers of narrative and history.[13]

In spite of its clear incitement to racial hatred and the resulting scandal, *Birth of a Nation* achieved the accolade of praise from the then US president, Woodrow Wilson, who famously described it as 'like writing history

---

[12] Ennio Simeon, 'Music in German Film before 1918', in Paolo Cherchi Usai and Lorenzo Codelli, ed., *Before Caligari: German Cinema, 1895–1920* (Pordenone, 1990), pp. 83–4.
[13] Miriam Hansen, *Babel and Babylon: Spectatorship in American Silent Film* (Cambridge, MA, 1991), pp. 150–51.

with Lightning'.[14] The status of film as the new medium of popular history was beginning to be confirmed.

No such recognition greeted another pioneering essay in biographical cinema at this time, although *The Life of David Lloyd George* could have been a landmark in British and world cinema. The film was conceived in the final months of the Great War as a tribute to the prime minister as 'the man who saved the Empire'—which was its working title. Scripted by a leading academic historian and directed by the rising young Maurice Elvey, who had Fabian connections, despite an extensive publicity campaign it was mysteriously withdrawn on the eve of release and its producers were apparently bound to silence after receiving a payment to cover their costs. Having disappeared, it was forgotten until discovered in a barn belonging to Lloyd George's grandson, Lord Tenby, in 1994.[15] One immediate reason for the film's suppression seems to have been an article by the well-known sensational journalist Horatio Bottomley, which drew attention to the producers' German (and Jewish) origin and wove a web of political innuendo around its appearance on the eve of the postwar election. Whatever the reasons for Lloyd George's turning against a project he must have originally supported, the film effectively disappeared, so no assessment can be made of the contemporary impact of what would have been the first biographical film of a serving national leader.

In view of the febrile political atmosphere of the postwar period, Lloyd George's fears were no doubt justified: whatever advantage the inspiring tale of a humble boy's rise to success might have brought when shown in every cinema throughout Britain, it would have offered an equal opportunity to the Welsh Wizard's enemies. Nor can we be sure that the restored version corresponds to what would have been released in 1918. But the film as it exists today offers a tantalizing summary of the potential for explicit 'life picturing', coincidentally in the same year that Woolf wrote about the 'new biography'. As such, two main features deserve comment. One is the hybridity already noted in connection with *Birth of a Nation*, resulting from a concern to stress authenticity—we visit many carefully signposted scenes of Lloyd George's youth—sitting awkwardly alongside such fluent evocations of actuality as mass demonstrations outside Birmingham Town Hall in 1900 and a suffragette riot in London. Indeed this would continue to be a feature of chronicle films, however 'cinematic', well

[14] Like Lenin's celebrated endorsement of Soviet cinema as 'for us the most important art', Wilson's famous praise appears to come only from secondary sources. Richard Schickel, *D. W. Griffith: An American Life* (New York, 1984), p. 270.

[15] For background information and comment on the film, see David Berry and Simon Horrocks, ed., *David Lloyd George: The Movie Mystery* (Cardiff, 1998).

into the 1920s, with even Abel Gance's highly rhetorical *Napoléon* (1927) pausing to draw attention to its use of authentic locations.

More significant is how *Lloyd George* as a silent film tackles the problem of conveying the substance of a life largely devoted to making speeches and writing. In part, this is of course achieved by the standard convention of title cards; but an important aspect of the film's rhetoric consists of visualizing Lloyd George's thought and speech by means of metaphor, anecdote, and a kind of supernaturalism.[16] Thus, in one of the most striking tropes, his early tenacity and immersion in the scriptures are fused in an identification with David and his struggle against Goliath— whereupon the images of the mature politician and the Kaiser are superimposed on these biblical warriors in a figure of foreshadowing. Elsewhere, the impact of Lloyd George's social policies is shown by 'didactic fictions', such as the materialization of a long queue of old people against a previously blank wall to show how 'the workhouse doors opened' after his introduction of old age pensions. Later, Lloyd George is greeted by the shades of past prime ministers when he enters Downing Street, and similarly communes with past American presidents as he works towards US intervention in the war. At times, also, the direction of film history is reversed, as for example when an early form of visual metaphor, waves breaking against rocks, is revived to illustrate an actual phrase used by Lloyd George in his speech commemorating the battle of Verdun—recalling how closely the emergence of film rhetoric was bound up with the poetics of verbal rhetoric at the turn of the century.

There is little point in speculating on what impact *The Life of David Lloyd George* might have had if released. Potentially, it could have put film on the political agenda in Britain in a quite different way from the panic reaction towards Soviet films displayed by politicians in the late 1920s. And although it contains nothing remotely scandalous about Lloyd George's irregular private life (the future wife of Alfred Hitchcock, Alma Reville, played his wife Megan), it is conceivable that the very fact of its easy intimacy would have chimed with the new informality of Lytton Strachey's *Queen Victoria* (1921). But perhaps the most striking parallel between Elvey's film and the 'new biography' that Woolf theorized is their common sense of *interiority*. Because Elvey chose to visualize metaphor and, in effect, to fictionalize the bare historical record, the film achieves an intermittently modernist discourse that anticipates Woolf's call, in 1926, for cinema to discover 'a secret language which we feel and see, but never speak'. The images that show, not exactly Lloyd George's 'thought', but its

---

[16] John O. Thompson and Roberta E. Pearson explore these aspects of the film in their valuable contributions to Berry and Horrocks, *David Lloyd George*.

meaning or metaphoric correlate, seem almost to anticipate, in form if not in modernity, Woolf's vision of a cinema able to show 'thought in its wildness, in its beauty, in its oddity, pouring from men with their elbows on a table; from women with their little handbags slipping to the floor'.[17]

In fact, the language that cinema discovered very soon after Woolf's speculation proved anything but secret: successful synchronized sound meant that by 1930 any film lacking recorded music and speech was considered 'silent'. The fears of many film-makers and theorists of the medium, that recorded sound would overwhelm the visual dimension of cinema and subordinate it to theatrical reproduction, seemed at first to be well founded. The 'talkies' talked, and sang, incessantly in their early years, losing much of that intimacy which had bound films and viewers together during the first quarter of the century, so well evoked by Sartre in his account of childhood film-going:

> [M]y heroes [. . .] were not mute because they knew how to make themselves understood. We communicated through music; it was the sound of what was going on inside them [. . .] *that was not me*, that young widow crying on the screen, and yet she and I had but one soul: Chopin's *Funeral March*; that was all it needed for her tears to moisten my eyes.[18]

But if there was an apparent loss of empathy in sound cinema, there were also opportunities. One of these, linked in some way which has yet to be adequately explored, was a new appetite for film biography. In every national cinema, and especially in the supranational Hollywood cinema, 'life-stories' became a major genre.

Recorded sound of course had long accompanied films, in more or less close synchronization. But it seems likely that the rapid growth of broadcast radio during the late 1920s was decisive in creating a new intimacy between celebrities and their admirers (which television, already present in its limited pre-war experimental mode, would further expand). New styles of illustrated magazine and the use of small-format cameras to take informal photographs, together with the new syntax of the sound newsreel—typically bantering, or hectoring, voice-over accompanying mute images—intensified the texture of celebrity and its mediation. In his biography of one of the earliest global stars, Douglas Fairbanks, subtitled 'the first celebrity', Richard Schickel offers a useful summary of this development:

> Once the star system—and the technologically expanded media system that fed upon it and was fed by it—began to function in something like the

---

[17] Virginia Woolf, 'The Cinema' (1926), reprinted in *The Crowded Dance of Modern Life: Selected Essays*, ed. Rachel Bowlby (Harmondsworth, 1993), II, 58.
[18] Jean-Paul Sartre, *Les Mots* (1964), tr. Irene Clephane as *Words* (Harmondsworth, 1967), p. 78; emphasis in original.

modern manner in the 1920s, our definition of reality began to alter. It is not too much to say that we then had two realities to contend with. Daily life, of course, remained. [. . .] Then, however, there was the reality [. . .] we apprehended through the media and through the employment of one or at most two senses intensively [. . .] the stars and celebrities were as familiar to us, in some ways, as our friends and neighbours. In many respects, we were— and are—more profoundly involved with their fates than we are with those of most of the people we know personally. They command enormous amounts of our psychic time and attention.[19]

By the end of the decade, this would be apparent in such impressive meditations on the nature of power and glamour as Jean Renoir's *La Règle du jeu* (1939) and Orson Welles's *Citizen Kane* (1941). While neither of these is literally biography, both allude to contemporary figures—flyers such as Charles Lindbergh and Saint-Exupéry in Renoir's case, and, notoriously, the media mogul William Randolph Hearst, who tried to suppress *Kane*—as part of their preoccupation with the nature of modern fame and hubris. The apparatus of modern mass communications plays an important part in both films, renegotiating, as Peter Wollen has observed, the relationship between public and private.[20]

If one scans the vast output of 1930s 'biopics', certain patterns and themes can be recognized. In Hollywood, which had suffered a drastic collapse of profitability during the Depression, they expressed a new mood of responsibility that chimed with the New Deal; a commitment to popular education and 'uplift', celebrating the achievements of great figures from the past. Warners became the studio most closely associated with this genre, running a gamut from George Arliss as *Disraeli* (1929), *Voltaire* (1933), and *Cardinal Richelieu* (1935) to Paul Muni in *The Story of Louis Pasteur* (1936) and *The Life of Emile Zola* (1937), followed by Edward G. Robinson in *Dr Ehrlich's Magic Bullet* (about the pioneer of syphilis treatment) and *A Dispatch from Reuters* (both 1940). Such films were relatively economical to produce and had wide appeal, especially among middle-class and 'respectable' audiences. Other genres, such as the musical and the gangster movie, could cater for different tastes—although these cannot be seen as mutually exclusive, since both Muni and Robinson initially made their screen reputations playing psychopathic gangsters in the quasi-biographical *Scarface* (1932) and *Little Caesar* (1931).

Sensational contemporary life-stories such as these films told had an ostensible message—*Scarface* was subtitled *The Shame of the Nation*— even if their appeal was also to baser instincts. But another important theme, and perhaps function, of the 1930s biopic was more overtly ideo-

[19] Richard Schickel, *Douglas Fairbanks: The First Celebrity* (London, 1976), p. 12.
[20] Peter Wollen, '*La Règle du jeu* and Modernity', *Film Studies*, I (Spring 1999), 9.

logical. From America to Russia, across all the national cinemas of Europe now able and required to speak in their own languages, there seemed to be a concerted project of 'national biography' through cinema. In Britain, this was launched by Alexander Korda's popular success with *The Private Life of Henry VIII* (1933), shrewdly adapting the knowing intimacy of Ernst Lubitsch's boudoir history in *Madame DuBarry* (1919) and *Anna Boleyn* (1920), leading through a variety of other biographical subjects to the romantic propaganda of *The Hamilton Woman* (1941), starring Vivien Leigh as Lady Hamilton and Laurence Olivier as Nelson. Well known to have been Winston Churchill's favourite film, this frank bid to equate Britain's situation in 1940 with that during the Napoleonic wars prompted a US Senate investigation of British pro-war influence through film activity. But such propaganda by means of historical parallel was not new, as Gore Vidal recalled in his memoir *Screening History*:

> On our screens, in the thirties, it seemed as if the only country on earth was England and there were no great personages who were not English, or impersonated by English actors. I recall no popular films about Washington or Jefferson or Lincoln the president. [. . .] As a result, England, and to a lesser extent, France, dominated all our dreams.
>
> There were the ubiquitous newsreels of the new king and queen on coronation day, as well as feature films of gallant little England menaced by Spain's Armada and Napoleon's armies. There were also biographical films of Chatham and Pitt, of Clive and Disraeli, of Wellington and Nelson.[21]

Vidal conveys vividly how contemporary news film blended with popular historical fiction and biography in the imagination of a precocious teenager to create, by 1941, a sense of empathy—'with the British totally, with the French somewhat; and with the Germans and the Japanese not at all'.

While the British film industry continued to enjoy a close, if usually client, relationship with Hollywood, the industries of Germany, Italy, and Soviet Russia all began to respond during the 1930s to new domestic political imperatives. In Germany, the Nazis were quick to expand their already wide propaganda operations by taking over institutions previously outside their control. Some of the films produced under Goebbels's supervision were exemplary historical biographies equivalent to the British films already noted: Hans Steinhoff's *The Old and the Young King* (1935) showed a rebellious young prince accepting his destiny to become Frederick the Great of Prussia; Veit Harlan's *Jew Süss* (1940), although set in the eighteenth century, provided a focus for Nazi anti-Semitism; and Steinhoff's *Ohm Krüger* (1941) celebrated Boer resistance to the British in South Africa. But perhaps more influential was a new kind of inspirational biog-

---

[21] Gore Vidal, *Screening History* (London, 1992), p. 39.

raphy. *Hitler Youth Quex* (Steinhoff, 1933) became the first film produced under immediate Nazi auspices, and it announced a new tactic in seeking to dominate the lives of individual Germans. Although based on an actual incident in 1932, when a member of the Hitler Youth had been killed in a street fight with Communists while leafleting, the life and death of Herbert Norkus served as a pretext for the creation of Heini Völker, who would be portrayed as a 'typical' boy needing to be removed from the influence of his ideologically unsound family and initiated into the new fraternity of the Hitler Youth. As a blueprint for the 'fabrication of a new man',[22] the film provided both a clear statement of Nazi aims and a template for later films of exemplary lives. The sophistication of its play of identification, as Heini struggles against his father, was demonstrated in a remarkable psychological analysis by the ethnographer Gregory Bateson in 1942, offered as a running commentary cut into a special version of the film as a series of intertitles.[23] Here, for the first time, prompted by the demands of psychological warfare, was an analysis of how a tendentious 'life on film' works to mould its audience's sympathies.

A similar pattern emerged among the other totalitarian states, although with differing levels of success. Only in Soviet Russia did the new cinema of biography strike a truly popular chord, starting with two films produced in the same year that 'socialist realism' was codified as the regime's official aesthetic. The Vasilievs' *Chapaev* (1934), based loosely on a memoir, established a formula in its treatment of a Civil War episode that would be repeated for over thirty years, finding earthy humour in an essentially didactic study of how the party sought to control military matters through the authority of commissars.[24] By contrast, Grigory Kozintsev's and Leonid Trauberg's *The Youth of Maxim* (1934) drew upon the experience of pre-revolutionary Party members to create a synthetic 'Maxim', who seemed more real than many actual veterans; and it was indeed ironic that a celebration of 'old Bolshevism' should appear just as Stalin was beginning to eliminate its surviving representatives. Both films benefited from central performances of great energy and conviction which, with their vernacular

[22] The phrase comes from Eric Rentschler's valuable account of the film and its reputation, in *The Ministry of Illusion: Nazi Cinema and its Afterlife* (Cambridge, MA, 1996), Ch. XX. The film was based on a novel serialized in the Nazi Youth paper between May and September 1932.
[23] This version is distributed by the Museum of Modern Art, New York, where Bateson was based while conducting the analysis. An abstract of the analysis appears in Margaret Mead and Rhoda Métraux, ed., *The Study of Culture at a Distance* (Chicago, 1953), pp. 302–14.
[24] Dimitry Furmanov had served as the Red Army commander's political commissar and published a memoir as well as sketching a scenario before his death in 1924. The project was revived by his widow and developed by the unrelated Sergey and Georgy Vasiliev at Lenfilm.

speech and traditional songs, made them enduringly popular with Russian audiences, and in the case of *Maxim* led to two sequels.[25]

Building on their clear success, Soviet film-makers won increased patronage for their work in developing a cohesive new ideology as the 1930s progressed, and exemplary lives were central to this. Sergey Eisenstein's 'rehabilitation' film, after his abortive 1931–2 Mexican project and the banning of *Bezhin Meadow* (1935–7), a film about an exemplary young Communist not unlike *Hitler Youth Quex*, was a patriotic epic about the near-mythic saviour of medieval Russia, *Alexander Nevsky* (1938). The modernization of Russia by Tsar Peter provided the subject for Vasily Petrov's two-part *Peter the First* (1937–9), with its clearly drawn parallels between Stalin's frenzy of planning and production and his illustrious precursor's achievements. More controversial was Eisenstein's portrayal of the deranged *Ivan the Terrible* (1944–6), set in a sinister court that legitimately evoked Jacobean tragedy although with clear contemporary relevance, which clearly fascinated as well as repelled Stalin and led to the film's second part remaining banned until after its true subject's death.[26]

Perhaps the strangest of all developments in early Russian sound cinema was the emergence of a dramatized genre of contemporary chronicle. Eisenstein's choice of a non-professional actor to portray Lenin briefly and heroically in *October* (1928) sparked an intense debate about the politics of such representation, incurring severe criticism from his colleagues on the Constructivist left. Now, amid the 'revolutionary romanticism' of the 1930s, Mikhail Romm would embark on the full-scale hagiography of Lenin and, crucially, the 're-visioning' of history as Stalin's closeness to Lenin was exaggerated in *Lenin in October* (1937) and *Lenin in 1918* (1939). Lenin and Stalin also appear together in a cameo scene in *The Vyborg Side*, smiling benevolently at the sleeping Maxim as if in benediction. From the beginning of the 1940s, almost any Soviet film with a contemporary setting was likely to include the visible (or audible: it could be an awestruck telephone call) portrayal of Stalin, usually played by Mikhail Gelovani.[27] This bizarre form of tribute, linked to Stalin's obsessive,

---

[25] *The Return of Maxim* (1937) and *The Vyborg Side* (1939), written and directed by the co-founders of the 'Factory of the Eccentric Actor' in 1922, Grigory Kozintsev and Leonid Trauberg, with Boris Chirkov continuing to play Maxim, as he eventually becomes a functionary in the Soviet government. This *Maxim* trilogy should not be confused with the trio of Gorky autobiography adaptations, directed by Mark Donskoy, and widely praised abroad although little known in the USSR.

[26] On Eisenstein's relationship with Stalin over *Ivan*, see my 'Canons and Careers: The Director in Soviet Cinema', in Richard Taylor and Derek Spring, ed., *Stalinism and Soviet Cinema* (London, 1993).

[27] These portrayals are gathered and analysed in a fascinating compilation film by Enno Patalas and Oksana Bulgakowa, *Stalin: Eine Mosfilmproduktion* (1993).

detailed control of Soviet cinema, culminated in Mikhail Chiaureli's epic *The Fall of Berlin* (1949), which creates a lavish counter-chronicle of the Great Patriotic War's progress, showing Stalin calmly in control when the Nazi invasion strikes, in contrast to his apparently panic-stricken paralysis, and his final (entirely fictitious) descent from the skies to greet Russian prisoners newly released from German camps in a gleaming white-suited apotheosis. The fact that most fictive Stalin appearances, including this one, were carefully deleted after Khrushchev's 'secret speech' of 1956 meant that a generation remained largely unaware of the sheer scale of Stalin's screen presence—and the extent to which cinema was the main vehicle of this monstrous 'cult of personality'.[28]

The cases of Third Reich and Stalinist cinema (and to a lesser extent Mussolinian and Francoist equivalents) are already over-determined by such designations. They are habitually discussed in terms of 'propaganda', in ways that ignore issues of figuration, address, and textual form, and which focus on their instrumentality and assumed crudeness. Yet it should be apparent, even from this brief outline, that they have much in common with other trends, considered more benign, within cinema's golden age of biography during the 1930s and 1940s. Nor is their relation to 'the historical record' a simple matter, as if this could be conceived as a singular text of universal authority. Inevitably they reflect the priorities and historiographies of their time; and the very fact of their undoubted popularity should reveal much about the diverse interests that cinema increasingly stimulated and satisfied. Graham Greene could damn with faint praise Warners' *Story of Louis Pasteur*: 'because [serious popular films] are so rare, one is ready to accept, with exaggerated gratitude, such refined, elegant, dead pieces as *Louis Pasteur*'.[29] But for ordinary film-goers, such as those interviewed in the 1937 Mass Observation survey of cinema-going in Bolton, films like this were a strong attraction. A thirty-year-old male preferred 'Films founded on History or Adventure of Men and Women who will live forever and stars who by playing these parts bring to the screen the people whose lives we would never have known and whose Lives have [. . .] made the World better for mankind'.[30] Another interviewee, female and aged forty-eight, singled out *Victoria the Great* (Herbert Wilcox, 1937) and *Pasteur* as examples of, respectively, '*historical* pictures that are

---

[28] *The Fall of Berlin* was first seen, after its post-1956 withdrawal, in 1990 and a number of archival retrospectives have since made the relevant films available, including the Locarno Festival programme of 2000 curated by Bernard Eisenschitz.

[29] Graham Greene, 'Subjects and Stories', in Charles Davy, ed., *Footnotes to the Film* (London, 1938), p. 66.

[30] Jeffrey Richards and Dorothy Sheridan, ed., *Mass-Observation at the Movies* (London, 1987), p. 94.

as near authentic as possible' and '*biography* touched with romance and drama'.[31] But however much the 1930s biopics appear to recall the nineteenth-century biography of exhortation and example, they are rarely univocal, and there is as much to learn from their allegories, elisions, and absences as from their overt 'factuality'.

To investigate further this largest category of filmic biography, let us consider one of the best documented examples: John Ford's *Young Mr Lincoln*, one of three films the director made in the *annus mirabilis* of 1939.[32] This takes as its narrative a fictionalized episode from Abraham Lincoln's early career as an Illinois country lawyer, when he successfully defended a young man accused of murder as a favour to the man's mother, and is generally assumed to have been inspired by the growing reverence for Lincoln promoted by Carl Sandburg's epic biography.[33] Its main aim, however, is clearly to celebrate Lincoln's homespun character and to foreshadow his later political role by showing such qualities as tenacity, fairness, simple eloquence, and the like. In this, it belongs to the same tradition as Elvey's *Lloyd George*, revealing that the child or youth is father of the famous man in a series of exemplary anecdotes. Does this invalidate it as history, or biography? According to the verdict of one Lincoln specialist, it does: 'In fact, John Ford's film was mostly fiction, and corny fiction at that, and it is redeemed only by the director's eye for landscape, the folk tunes in the musical score, and Henry Fonda's considerable acting ability'.[34] However, such a verdict surely commits what analytic philosophy would call a 'category mistake'. It implies that an acted fictional film might possess a standard of historical accuracy which this example fails to reach. But this is to confuse two modes of discourse, two genres; and it ignores a distinction recalled by the historian Natalie Zemon Davis, but originally articulated by Aristotle: 'the historian relates what happened, the poet what might happen. [. . .] Poetry deals with general truths, history with specific events'.[35] The historian would properly draw attention to what is not known (or knowable), as Neely does in his critique when he notes that

[31] Ibid., p. 131.
[32] The others were the classic *Stagecoach* and Ford's first colour film, *Drums along the Mohawk*, a pioneer tale. Among the many other enduring classics in other genres released in 1939 are *The Wizard of Oz* and *Gone with the Wind*.
[33] Carl Sandburg, *Abraham Lincoln: The Prairie Years*, had appeared in 1926; four volumes covering the Civil War period would follow in 1939, after the film was in production.
[34] Mark E. Neely, Jr, 'The Young Lincoln: Two Films', in Mark C. Carnes, ed., *Past Imperfect: History according to the Movies* (London, 1996), p. 126. Carnes's collection consists of a series of generally dismal indictments of films ranging from *The Ten Commandments* to *All the President's Men* for their supposed historical shortcomings.
[35] Aristotle's *Poetics* (in the translation of G. M. A. Grube), quoted in Natalie Zemon Davis, *Slaves on Screen: Film and Historical Vision* (Cambridge, MA, 2000), p. 3.

nothing verifiable is known about Lincoln's reputed first love, Ann Rutledge, adding that 'this dearth made her the perfect character for Hollywood's imagination to embellish'. Against this conventional scorn for 'Hollywood', it should be noted that the lack of documentation for Rutledge need not erase her from imaginative history—in fact she can stand for that vast array of 'historical' characters about whom little or nothing is known *except that they existed and may, or may not, have been highly influential on those figures and events that we know more securely.* We are, in short, in the realm of the conditional, the speculative and the poetic.

A fellow film-maker was one of the first to acknowledge Ford's achievement. Eisenstein wrote in 1945, midway through his own *Ivan the Terrible*, that 'of all American films made up to now this is the film that I would wish, most of all, to have made'.[36] Conceding that it is not the most obviously brilliant or popular of Ford's films, Eisenstein praised it for its 'classical harmony' and its modest craftsmanship, both inspired by the 'womb of popular and national spirit'. In this, we might suspect he is stressing the *narodnost'* ('popularness') required by Soviet socialist realism; but he locates the film's great achievement in its organic composition: 'Through the very image of his historical protagonist, Ford touches the principles whose bearer was the historical Lincoln, not only through the words spoken by his historical Lincoln, but in the very structure of the film.'[37] Thus such anecdotal incidents as Lincoln's helping a tug-of-war team and judging a pie-baking contest at a country fair take on the quality of quasi-allegory, recalling Lincoln's future role as unifier of the warring factions in the Union.[38] Yet they do so without seeming heavy-handed or didactic—certainly compared with many ponderous Soviet allegories—and, as Eisenstein notes, they miraculously animate such strictly historical sources as daguerreotype images of the period and eye-witness accounts of Lincoln, not that he is unaware of the latter's ambiguous position on many of the ideals with which he is credited.

The particular significance of Ford's *Young Mr Lincoln*, which enables it to stand for a large category of historical-biographical fictions, is that the film was again taken up in the late 1960s as an exemplary case for analysis by the editors of *Cahiers du cinéma*, then strongly influenced by the combination of Lacanian and semiotic theory associated with *Tel Quel*,

[36] Sergei Eisenstein, 'Mr Lincoln by Mr Ford', in J. Leyda, ed., *Film Essays and a Lecture* (Princeton, NJ, 1982), p. 140. Although written in 1945 for a planned anthology, the essay was not published in Russian until 1960, and not translated into English until 1968.
[37] Ibid., p. 141.
[38] A point underlined by Peter Wollen in his 'Afterword' to the collective text from *Cahiers du cinéma* (see following note), *Screen*, XIII, 3 (Autumn 1972), 45.

and in cinema by the work of Christian Metz.[39] Without pursuing in detail what now seems itself an historical text, the *Cahiers*' 'active reading' usefully investigates the 'intertextual space' in which the film is inscribed: a product of the cinematic codes which it uses and inflects, and of the ideologies of its sources and of its moment of production by Hearst's Cosmopolitan Pictures and Darryl Zanuck's Twentieth Century-Fox, both staunchly conservative. For the *Cahiers* critics, there is no question of the film being considered 'inaccurate': history, for these early readers of Althusser and Foucault, is no more than a web of competing discourses within which this rewriting of earlier texts takes its place. And despite its post-1968 attitudinizing, their commentary catches something of what is at stake even in such an apparently reverential work:

> A storm threatens. Lincoln is slowly climbing the hill. A last shot shows him facing the camera, with a vacant look, while threatening clouds cross the background and the 'Battle Hymn of the Republic' begins to be heard. Lincoln leaves the frame. Rain begins to fall violently and continues into the final shot of the film (his statue at the Capitol) while music intensifies.
>
> Here again, it is the excesses of Ford's writing (accumulation of signs of the tragic; of ascent: hill—mythical reference—storm, lightning, rain, wind, thunder etc) which by overlaying all the clichés, underline the monstrous character of the figure of Lincoln: he leaves the frame and the film (like *Nosferatu*) as if it had become impossible for him to be filmed any longer.[40]

If this is a far cry from either simple praise or blame for the film, it also anticipates the poststructural turn in historiography itself, as exemplified by the essays of Hayden White and others, which call into question the nature of narrative and its ideological assumptions. Put simply, if *no* narrative has an unproblematic or transparent relation to its content, then all historical writing is constructed and contestable *as writing*. It is from such premises that White, as well as Natalie Zemon Davis and Robert Rosenstone, have mounted a defence of historical film, not on grounds of empirical veracity, but rather because it challenges the complacency of an untheorized 'craft notion of historical studies'.[41]

Such a debate was provoked by Oliver Stone's *JFK* (1992), largely

---

[39] Editors of *Cahiers du cinéma*, 'John Ford's Young Mr Lincoln' (1970), tr. Helen Lackner and Diana Matias, *Screen*, XIII, 3 (Autumn 1972), pp. 5–44. Christian Metz's *Essais sur la signification au cinéma* (Paris, 1971) was completed in 1968.

[40] Ibid., pp. 38–9.

[41] Hayden White uses this phrase to characterize the anti-theory practitioners of 'empirical inquiry' in his essay 'Narrativity in the Representation of Reality', collected in *The Content of the Form* (Baltimore, 1987), p. 31. Relevant other works include: Robert A. Rosenstone, *Visions of the Past: The Challenge of Film to our Idea of the Past* (Cambridge, MA., 1995); Vivian Sobchack, ed., *The Persistence of History: Cinema, Television and the Modern Event* (London, 1996); and Natalie Zemon Davis, ' "Any Resemblance to Persons Living or Dead": Film and the Challenge of Authenticity', *Yale Review*, LXXVI (1987), 457–82.

because its complex, unsettling form was clearly intended to problematize official accounts of the Kennedy assassination and so resist any notion of a settled body of historical knowledge. The film's underlying structure is in fact biographical, taking as its central figure—and consciousness—the maverick District Attorney Jim Garrison, who mounted a conspiracy case against the mysterious Clay Shaw. In several important respects, as Rosenstone has noted, Stone does fulfil the criteria for historical inquiry:

> Like a good historian, Stone begins *JFK* with a preface that contains a thesis; he uses Dwight Eisenhower's farewell address, with its warning about the possible effect of the military industrial complex on the future of our country, to set the stage for a film that will illustrate the prescience of Ike's words. [...]
> To be considered 'historical', rather than simply a costume drama that uses the past as an exotic setting for romance and adventure, a film must engage the issues, ideas, data and arguments of that ongoing discourse. Whatever else it does or does not do, *JFK* certainly meets these requirements as a work of history.[42]

However, the text, or *texture*, of the film is quite unlike a conventional filmic questioning of the Warren Commission's verdict on the Kennedy assassination, such as Emile de Antonio's *Rush to Judgment*. Using a (literally) bewildering array of forms—documentary, naturalistic and melodramatic drama, rapid montage, 'dream' images, and actual news film; together with an equally wide range of sound forms, often not matching the images—it seeks to plunge the spectator into a maelstrom of uncertainty, contradiction, and paranoia. Who, if anyone, we are encouraged to wonder, is telling the truth? Despite its apparent scepticism, the film manifests a passionate 'need for history'; and as Robert Burgoyne has suggested, it offers two competing paradigms, without finally endorsing either.[43] One of these assumes that 'a unified and fixed historical reality exists and could be recovered, were it not obscured by willfully deceptive stories and by the inaccessibility of the crucial facts'. The other evokes White's 'concept of the "derealization" of the event in the Twentieth century', conceiving 'history as "epistemic murk" ', so that the film tries to undermine the very concept of the unitary historical text.

Although these considerations open out into much wider debates about the conduct of history by any means, as well as the role of the 'unhistorical' filmic text, they are clearly relevant to many of the films we might want to propose as landmarks in reshaping biography as the twenty-first century progresses. Perhaps the prime example of a work that departs radically

---

[42] Rosenstone, '*JFK*: Historical Fact/Historical Film', *Visions of the Past*, pp. 130, 128.
[43] This and subsequent quotations from Robert Burgoyne, 'Modernism and the Narrative of Nation in *JFK*', in Sobchak, *The Persistence of History*, pp. 113–25.

from any biography in written form is Hans Jürgen Syberberg's massive
Hitler: A Film from Germany (1977), a film in four parts lasting just under
seven and a half hours.[44] Unlike the many previous film biographies of
Hitler, Syberberg proposes that only a new and elaborate form is adequate
to charting the immensity of Hitler's impact and legacy. His method is to
employ a variety of narrators—including a circus director, a young girl,
Wagner, Einstein, Chaplin, Hitler's valet, the other Nazi leaders, the Mayor
of Berchtesgaden—to offer a kaleidoscope of views of Hitler, all organized
around the guiding theme that there is something of Hitler in each of us,
which we must face up to. In one sense, the form is Brechtian, a sprawling
epic also owing something to Karl Kraus's panorama of World War I, *The
Last Days of Mankind*.[45] In another it is phantasmagoric, and the theme
of cinema's history is constantly reinscribed, with the young girl becoming
a latter-day equivalent to the mother rocking the cradle in Griffith's *Intoler-
ance*, and the recurrent image of Edison's 'Black Maria', the first film
studio, standing for the twentieth century's dream factory. Susan Sontag
has suggested, in a brilliant essay on the film, that its ambition may be best
understood as Symbolist, since it is also saturated in Wagnerism, seeking
to *internalize* everything that produced Hitler, that he expressed and that
he bequeathed in our continuing fascination with him.[46] The studio within
which sounds and images are replayed, and in which models, puppets, and
actors act out Syberberg's vast compendium of Hitleriana, serves as a kind
of sensorium, a postmodern 'inner stage' of Symbolism's ideal theatre. Here
in all its repellent, fascinating, shaming, and stirring detail is, undeniably,
the 'subject of the century' that we will not let drop.

Syberberg's *Hitler* already seems to belong to an earlier age, as the
climax of a delayed Symbolist aspiration running throughout cinema's
history which, ironically, was finally made possible only by television,
however much this has proved reluctant to acknowledge its monstrous
offspring.[47] Instead, television has embraced with accelerating enthusiasm
the possibilities offered by domestic video and digital technologies to create
an unlimited representation of 'life itself'. From video diaries and web-
cameras to the multi-media surveillance of *Big Brother*, we have witnessed

[44] *Hitler: A Film from Germany* [known as *Our Hitler* in the US] was co-produced by three
European broadcasters: WDR, Cologne; INA, Paris; and BBC, London.
[45] In 1952–3 the young Syberberg filmed sequences of Brecht rehearsing with the Berliner
Ensemble in East Berlin, which were incorporated into his *Brecht Film: After my Last Move*
of 1971.
[46] Susan Sontag, 'Syberberg's Hitler', in *Under the Sign of Saturn* (New York, 1979); also in
Heather Stewart, ed., *Syberberg: A Filmmaker from Germany* (London, 1992).
[47] BBC Television proved reluctant to broadcast *Hitler*, doing so only once, while other large-
scale chronicle films, such as those of Marcel Ophuls, have encountered resistance from
broadcasters.

what seems in many ways a realization of the dreams that accompanied the birth of photography and sound-recording. We can see and hear almost continuously, and record and replay (in theory) indefinitely. We can 'spectate', or interact, in rapidly proliferating modes. The implications of these new modes of intensely mediated engagement with the lives of others are themselves the subjects of a new wave of reflexive fictions, including *The Truman Show, Edtv* (Ron Howard, 1999), and *eXistenZ* (David Cronenberg, 1999), which have their origins in such earlier works as *Peeping Tom* (Michael Powell, 1960), *Chronicle of a Summer* (Jean Rouch and Edgar Morin, 1962), and the morally challenging *Henry: Portrait of a Serial Killer* (John McNaughton, 1986) and *Man Bites Dog (C'est arrivé près de chez vous*, Rémy Belvaux et al., 1992).

From a different standpoint, the long tradition of artists' diary films by such as Jonas Mekas, Andrew Noren, Stan Brakhage, David Larcher, Derek Jarman, and many others could be seen to anticipate a radical expansion of the categories of autobiography, so that 'life-writing' now encompasses an ever-increasing range of texts considered equally worthy of collection and study. With the advent of widely available digital media, hitherto distinct verbal and visual forms are in the process of coalescing into a new regime that combines word and image in all their modes, of which the personal website may be only a harbinger. Whether we will continue to call the processing of such data 'auto/biography' remains to be seen. It may be that Bentley's famous clerihew is reversed, so that biography becomes less about 'chaps' and has more need of geography's 'maps' to chart its vast new cyber-landscape.[48]

[48]   The Art of Biography
        Is different from Geography.
        Geography is about Maps,
        But Biography is about Chaps.
    E. C. Bentley, Introduction to *Biography for Beginners* (London, 1905).

17

Gender, Biography, and the Public Sphere

KAY FERRES

When Carolyn Steedman was working on her biography of Margaret McMillan, she complained that McMillan's reputation rested on a perception of her as a 'saviour of children'. This image of the teacher obscured her first fifty years, including her career in socialist and Independent Labour Party politics.[1] The title of the biography performed a critical inversion. Steedman called her book *Childhood, Culture and Class in Britain: Margaret McMillan 1860–1931*. McMillan's life was recounted succinctly; the book then set about restoring the contexts in which it was lived. In a final chapter, Steedman reiterated her reservations about writing the lives of 'public' women:

> One legacy [of the scholarship in the field of women's history] is an altered sense of the historical meaning and importance of female *insignificance*. The absence of women from conventional historical accounts, discussion of this absence (and of the real archival difficulties that lie in the way of presenting their lives in a historical context) are at the same time a massive assertion of the littleness of what lies hidden.[2]

Despite, or perhaps because of, the successful installation of a feminist version of 'women's narrative'—one that makes identity claims by bringing private life and sexuality into view—it is still very difficult to account for women's influence and reputation in public arenas. Social history does not

---

[1] Carolyn Steedman, 'Forms of History, Histories of Form', *Past Tenses: Essays on Writing, Autobiography and History* (London, 1992), p. 160. This paper was first published in 1989.
[2] Steedman, *Childhood, Culture and Class in Britain: Margaret McMillan 1860–1931* (London, 1990), p. 248.

provide the same context for narratives of gender that class history does for ordinary lives.

The recognition of gender as an inescapable dimension of self has nevertheless had an impact on various genres of life-writing. At first, it entailed an understanding that women's lives were shaped differently from men's, and that biographical narrative needed to represent those differences. Nineteenth-century fiction provides some models of feminine *Bildung*, shaped around life events: marriage and childbirth. The representation of women's lives has required some dexterity with sources, as well as theoretical revisions. The historical conception of the division of public and private life, on which gender arrangements and life narratives depend, has been subject to new scrutiny. The private sphere has a new visibility as the site of women's experience. Attention to private life and family relationships has also come to occupy more space in narratives of the lives of public men. John Rickard's warmly received account of the private life of Australia's second prime minister, Alfred Deakin, *A Family Romance: The Deakins at Home* (1996), includes dramatic scenes scripted from documentary and imagined sources. In the case of Margaret McMillan, who never married, and left no trace of any personal relationships, Steedman resorts to McMillan's biography of her sister, Rachel, which she reads as autobiography.

Yet, there is a pressing need to think again about the public spaces women inhabit, and how they inhabit them. Much of the extant work in cultural history focuses on the nineteenth century. Griselda Pollock has shown how, in the visual arts, Impressionist painting represented the gendered dimensions of public space. Women appeared in parks and loges, and on balconies and promenades, always separated from the world they observed. 'Fallen' women, by contrast, were not so segregated, and appeared in cafés, brothels, and backstage at the theatre.[3] A brief flurry of debate considered whether a female *flâneur* strolled in city streets, observing and jostling with the crowd.[4] Some feminist theorists, notably Carole Pateman, have discussed the meanings of the appearance in public of 'disorderly' women—prostitutes, dancers, political campaigners.[5] But how have public spaces and institutions been transformed by the increasing participation of women in public life, as workers, as citizens, as public

[3] Griselda Pollock, 'Modernity and the Spaces of Femininity', *Vision and Difference: Femininity, Feminism and the Histories of Art* (London, 1988), pp. 73, 80.

[4] See, for example, Janet Wolff, 'The Invisible *Flâneuse*: Women and the Literature of Modernity', in her *Feminine Sentences: Essays on Women and Culture* (Cambridge, 1990), pp. 34–50.

[5] Carole Pateman, *The Disorder of Women: Democracy, Feminism and Political Theory* (Cambridge, 1989).

intellectuals? How has 'biography', a cultural institution that documents public life and reputations, accommodated women? What has been made of the relation between the realm of private morality and the public domain of justice?

This chapter considers some of the ways biography—biographers and the practices which represent gender, as well as the reading and uses of biography—has treated the problem of women's appearances in public life. My focus is on questions of influence and reputation. What I hope to show is that 'including gender' involves not only the transformation of life narratives, but also the constitution of newly emergent publics. Biography can be a catalyst of dispute and disagreement about the public interest, as well as a document of public lives and careers.

Outsiders and Institutions

In 1976, Ellen Moers described the only intellectual field where women have made a sustained contribution: literature. *Literary Women* explores the ways women lived a 'literary life', and at the same time redefines the institutional boundaries of 'literature'. Placing women's work at the centre of her analysis, and describing the conditions in which they wrote, Moers renewed established reputations and assigned new significance to women's cultural contributions as professional writers. Her study gave free rein to her fascination with 'the fact of [women writers'] sex'.[6] It begins with an extract from a letter, in which Harriet Beecher Stowe complained about waiting for her plumber to find the time to install a sink. It concludes with a 'dictionary' of literary women, a list that supplements its discursive account of 'the great writers'.

Like Carolyn Steedman in her reading of Margaret McMillan's *The Life of Rachel McMillan* (1927), I am taking a liberty here. I am reading *Literary Women* as an unconventional kind of collective biography. It does not isolate and privilege individuals. Writers from different continents rub shoulders; the emphasis on careers, influence, and reputation constructs relationships among them. Moers remaps the public sphere as she conducts her reader through histories and traditions, along the way encountering both 'representative' figures and exceptional and notorious ones, who are classified as 'heroines'. One of the 'great' writers discussed is Virginia Woolf, who appears in many of the book's chapters. For the feminist scholars who were part of the project of restoring women to history in the 1970s, Woolf's work inspired many lines of inquiry. Her accounts of

---

[6] Ellen Moers, *Literary Women: The Great Writers* (New York, 1976), p. xi.

the beadle protecting the Oxbridge turf, of the search of the British Museum catalogue to reveal the extent of authoritative knowledge of 'women', and of the constraining influence of the 'Angel in the House' were vivid and witty reminders of the institutional barriers to women's achievement. Moers's book sets out to redress these exclusions. In a riposte to Woolf's dismay at the disappearance of a feminine tradition, Moers invents one, and gives it a shape and a focus that have informed later feminist work, not least life-writing. Like Woolf, Moers and other feminist scholars look to the material conditions in which women wrote, and to the way lines between public and private life are drawn and redefined, to construct a narrative about gender.

Moers takes *A Room of One's Own* as one point of departure for a narrative of public, gendered identity, but her disposition to feminism and institutional politics differs from Woolf's, as it was expressed in 1927. Their differences over *Jane Eyre* make the point. Woolf deplores Brontë's anger about women's subordination as diminishing her art. Moers notes and approves of Brontë's provocation, quoting the response of the *Quarterly Review*: 'We do not hesitate to say that the tone of mind and thought which has overthrown authority and violated every code human and divine abroad, and fostered Chartism and rebellion at home, is the same which has also written *Jane Eyre*.'[7] In 1927, Woolf described women's marginal position in the public spheres of education and the professions, but this 'daughter of an educated man' was still optimistic that a new generation, freed from the constraints of the private house, would make a difference. Moers and her feminist contemporaries, aided by anti-discriminatory public policy, were beginning to make their presence felt in the Academy. In the USA, the careers of these feminist scholars began in the liberal arts colleges, and their work was part of a transformation of the humanities disciplines. In the UK, a tradition of feminist scholarship emerged from the teaching profession and from debates within the social science disciplines. Woolf's work was getting new publicity at this time, as biographies, letters, and diaries were being published. It provided a way of theorizing the relations of culture and politics, and the separation of public and private domains which underpinned historical narratives of gender.

Moers's discussion of literary careers turns on a theme which has been central to feminist work in history, literary studies, and biography: the intersection of life and art. How did women negotiate the demands of private and professional life? Harriet Beecher Stowe's letter to her sister-in-law about waiting for Mr Titcomb (the plumber), states the problem,

---

[7] Moers, *Literary Women*, p. 15.

and suggests how the solution is found in making domestic life the subject
of writing:

> These negotiations extended from the first of June to the first of July, and at
> last my sink was completed. [. . .] Also during this time good Mrs Mitchell
> and myself made two sofas, or lounges, a barrel chair, divers bedspreads,
> pillow cases, bolsters, mattresses; we painted rooms; we revarnished furniture;
> we—what *didn't* we do?
>
> Then on came Mr Stowe; and then came the eighth of July and my little
> Charley. I was really glad for an excuse to be in bed, for I was tired, I can
> assure you.[8]

The insistent demands of domestic life and the obstacles it puts in the way
of creative work have become a standard trope in narratives of women's
careers. Drusilla Modjeska's *Stravinsky's Lunch* (1999) reinvoked the theme
in its title, which refers to an anecdote about the petty tyrannies of the
Stravinsky household. Modjeska tells us that Stravinsky required absolute
silence when he was composing—even at the table. Her study of the
conflicting demands of art and life in the careers of painters Stella Bowen
and Grace Cossington Smith turns on this anecdote, and she also uses it
to reflect on the situation of contemporary women (like herself).

Moers's study tackled the larger question: what has been the impact
of female creativity and professional writing on the literary traditions of
Western culture? Her collective biography takes the notion of 'representation' seriously. It identifies and places a body of women's work in the
terrain of the 'literary'. She shows how, from the eighteenth century, 'literature' became 'increasingly and steadily the work of women', the only
'intellectual field to which women, over a long stretch of time, have made
an indispensable contribution'.[9] This strategy structures the study into three
parts: 'History and Tradition'; 'Female Heroinism', and the 'Notes', which
provide a catalogue of major and minor figures. The entries, 'arranged
dictionary fashion', give a 'rough guide' to the writer's career and significant
relationships. References to men are 'entered under the name of a woman
chosen sometimes arbitrarily, sometimes gleefully'. Defending her practice,
Moers writes:

> The student of women writers, who knows how rudely they have been
> handled by the makers of indexes, directories, library cards, and other such
> implements of research, will share my pleasure at the thought that here is
> one book where Thomas Carlyle is listed under his wife Jane, William Words-
> worth under his sister Dorothy, and Richardson under his disciple Fanny
> Burney.[10]

---

[8] Moers, *Literary Women*, p. 4.
[9] Moers, *Literary Women*, p. xi.
[10] Moers, *Literary Women*, p. 270.

Behind these 'gleeful' decisions about the form of the entries are the standards of the *Dictionary of National Biography*, which institutionalized collective biography and its concern with public life and reputation. Leslie Stephen and Sidney Lee's *DNB* is marked by the general absence of women as subjects and contributors. Women comprise only about 3.5 per cent of its subjects and only 45 of the 653 contributors. Stephen's wife, Julia, who contributed one article, and Lee's sister Alice, who wrote 'at least 81', were among them.[11] The *DNB*'s project, as James Walter has observed, was concerned with the formation of national élites.[12] Colin Matthew, the first editor of the 'new' *DNB*, measured the 'old' *DNB*'s practices against late twentieth-century benchmarks of inclusiveness. Matthew argues that Leslie Stephen's liberal Unionist politics accounted for the inclusion of 'every Irish rebel of 1798', and that the concept of 'public life' was flexible enough to extend to sport, though not business, as a field of endeavour.[13] Its assumed separation of public and private spheres meant that scant regard was paid to the personal lives of its subjects, men who had forged careers in civic and political life. This is hardly surprising, since national élites, especially those based on 'merit', are necessarily exclusive. Those élites, as Virginia Woolf points out in *Three Guineas*, were nurtured in masculinist institutions: the public schools and universities, the bureaucracy and the military. Women's professional lives, as nurses, teachers, and writers, were lived in a public arena that reproduced the constraints and relations of domesticity.

Moers's study turned the *DNB*'s conventions around not only in the 'Notes', but also in her contextualization of individual careers. Her work provided a guide to women's contributions to the literary profession, not merely describing recurrent themes and plots but showing how women's work, thought, and practice redefined the separation of public and private that organized gendered life. Her scholarship forged new connections and mediated relationships among her subjects, women members of the literary profession, separated by time, geography, and national traditions. She was followed by a generation of feminist scholars who began to transform academic institutional culture in the 1970s. Like her, they took up Virginia Woolf's challenge, to recover a feminine tradition, to think back through their mothers. Woolf's work was often the object of their research.

The editors of the influential anthology *Between Women* (1984) came

---

[11] Colin Matthew, 'Dictionaries of National Biography', in *National Biographies and National Identity: A Critical Approach to Theory and Editorial Practice*, ed. I. McCalman et al. (Canberra, 1996), pp. 8–10.

[12] James Walter, 'Seven Questions about National Biography', in McCalman, *National Biographies and National Identity*, p. 20.

[13] Matthew, 'Dictionaries', p. 8.

together to create a new public for Virginia Woolf's work, after the appearance of Quentin Bell's biography and other 'authorized' editions of her published and unpublished writing. Sara Ruddick 'envisioned women telling personal stories about their reading and writing on Virginia Woolf. Collectively, I thought, we could unnerve the critics who doubted our seriousness or Woolf's greatness; at the same time, the multiplicity of our voices would attest to the partiality of any single perspective on her work.'[14] The project evolved to become a collection of essays on the problems of writing women's lives, regarding both subjects and researcher. The 'between' of the title signified the spaces of the relationship of biographer and subject and among women readers and professional critics, relationships conceived of as at once intimate and ethical. The contributors to the volume expanded beyond literary scholars to embrace other disciplines and subjects. All shared an interest in the way reputations are established and the way intellectual authority is claimed. The contributors make their own investments in feminist cultural politics transparent; and also acknowledge a doubt about their motives. Their ambivalence is signalled in the book's epigraphs, including this one from Christa Wolf:

> Left to herself she was gone; that was always the way with her. At the last moment, one has thought of working on her.
> Under a sort of compulsion, to be sure ... the compulsion to make her stand and be recognised.
> Useless to pretend it's for her sake. Once and for all, she doesn't need us. So we should be certain of one thing: that it's for our sake. Because it seems we need her.

What is the nature of this need? Many of the essays in this book chime with Sara Ruddick's influential 'maternal thinking'.[15] They set out to explore and reclaim the relation to the mother, to revalue the feminine and to transfer those values from the private to the public sphere. So Jane Marcus speaks of the practice of life-writing as 'invisible mending'. Louise de Salvo poses her maternal and ethnic identities against her public persona as a scholar, which she names as 'puttana'. Blanche Weisen Cook addresses the question of institutional custodianship of documents and reputations and exposes ethical concerns about intrusion upon her subject's privacy.

The editors and contributors promote an intimacy between women, but they also betray anxieties about public recognition, their subjects' reputations and their own. The narrative of gender identity they reproduce

---

[14] Carol Ascher, Louise de Salvo, and Sara Ruddick, 'Introduction', *Between Women: Biographers, Novelists, Critics, Teachers and Artists Write about their Work on Women* (Boston, 1984), p. xv.
[15] Ruddick was working on *Maternal Thinking: Towards a Politics of Peace* (London, 1990) at this time.

is drawn from object-relations theory: feminine identity depends on the continuity of the mother-daughter relation; but the sense of an independent self requires separation from the mother and identification with the father. According to Nancy Chodorow, whose work on gender identity was widely taken up at this time, the cultural work required to reproduce mothering results in gender identity being stronger in women than men. Masculinity requires separation from the mother, with the result that men acquire a stronger sense of their individuality.[16]

The essays in *Between Women* explore the 'troubling' elements of the biographer's relation to her female subject: 'protectiveness, jealousy, competition, overidentification'.[17] Christa Wolf's caution against the assumption of reciprocity in the mother-daughter relation is also a caution against essentialist understandings of gender identity. The recognition of difference—not just sexual difference, but the differences within femininity itself—reoriented feminist practice in the 1980s and 1990s. The claims about gender identity which shaped life narratives were complicated by this reconceptualization of gender. Sexual difference was just one dimension of a network of intersecting differences: class, ethnicity, race, sexual orientation, and generational difference.

Virginia Woolf: Between the Acts

Three of the contributors to *Between Women* were working on Virginia Woolf. Since the appearance of Quentin Bell's biography in 1972, many versions of her life have been written. As Hermione Lee remarks, like her own *Orlando*, the 'Virginia Woolf' of her biographers will live for centuries.[18] For the editors of *Between Women*, Woolf was a site of memory, a *lieu de mémoire*. Pierre Nora describes such a site as a place of loss, as well as a place where loss can be redeemed and the self reconstituted.[19] Many of the essays in *Between Women* describe life-writing as a reflexive practice, in which the subject emerges from obscurity and the biographer too moves into the public sphere.

Woolf's fascination with subjectivity, with 'moments of being', and with capturing character has been shared by many feminist biographers who have sought to bring the 'invisible presence' of women into public view.

[16] Nancy Chodorow, *The Reproduction of Mothering: Psychoanalysis and the Sociology of Gender* (Berkeley, 1978, 2nd edn 1999).
[17] Ascher et al., *Between Women*, p. xx.
[18] Hermione Lee, *Virginia Woolf* (London, 1996), p. 4.
[19] Pierre Nora, 'Between Memory and History: *Les Lieux de Mémoire*', in *Histories: French Constructions of the Past*, ed. J. Revel and L. Hunt (New York, 1995), pp. 631–42.

Writing about her mother in 'A Sketch of the Past', Woolf commented: 'if we cannot analyse these invisible presences, we know very little of the subject of memoir; and again how futile life-writing becomes'.[20] Her theories of character and her interest in 'interiority' align her with a feminist project, which sought to scrutinize the private domain, and the sexual and familial relations and identities constructed there. The publication of her letters, diaries, and notebooks supported a narrative of gendered identity that appealed to a feminist public interested in psychology, sexual identity, and the construction of the self. Her work can be used to support a thesis about the social construction of gendered identities and the pro-duction of sexual difference through the separation of public and private domains.

'Virginia Woolf' has also been a catalyst of dispute among feminists, and their work has been shaped by investments in the politics of class and sexuality. In keeping with this tradition, Hermione Lee establishes both an intimate and an ethical relation with her subject. Lee tells us about her first encounter with Woolf's writing—it is *The Waves*, and it is 'part of the excitement of being away from home on my own'—and shares the pleasure of her daily walk to school, Queen's College, which in part retraces Clarissa Dalloway's walk.[21] Lee is very much at home in Woolf's cultural and literary territory. But when she goes to St Ives, she stands in the garden of Talland House, feeling like a 'biographer, a tourist and an intruder'.[22] While she distances herself from the overtly political agendas of biographers like Louise de Salvo, Lee positions her work against the backdrop of second-wave feminism. Feminism, by the time Lee comes to write about Woolf, has established a new public for biographies of women. Lee, however, moves away from the recuperation of femininity and the maternal thinking of scholars like Ruddick and de Salvo. Instead, she reorients her inquiry to Woolf's public life and reputation. In the Lee incarnation of 'Virginia Woolf', the relationship with Leslie Stephen is pivotal.

Woolf is not the only figure who has been a catalyst of public dispute among feminist (and other) scholars: Katherine Mansfield and Sylvia Plath especially come to mind. The reputations of all three have been subject to various 'custodial' claims; but the dispute has been more than a family squabble over literary remains. At stake is a much larger question, one that troubled Woolf: what can women make of their freedom? How does their presence in the public domain, their participation in institutional life, stand

---

[20] Virginia Woolf, 'A Sketch of the Past', in *Moments of Being: Unpublished Autobiographical Writings of Virginia Woolf*, ed. Jeanne Schulkind (London, 1976), p. 80.
[21] Lee, *Woolf*, p. 768.
[22] Lee, *Woolf*, p. 771.

to make a difference? Focusing on the tensions in the father-daughter relation allows Lee to address this question.

Woolf, educated in a 'private house', made her reputation as a writer of fiction. But she made forays beyond this, cultivating a wider public. She worked for the suffrage, and attempted to talk across the class divide, in addresses like 'The Leaning Tower' (to the WEA), or the letter which introduces Margaret Llewellyn Davies's collection of memoirs of working women, *Life As We Have Known It* (1931). She addressed a 'common reader' and attempted to occupy a civic domain where culture and politics converged. In the late 1930s, she despaired of finding that public. Even now, the work of that period attracts little attention: *Three Guineas* has not been nearly so well read as *A Room of One's Own*; *Roger Fry* is overlooked in favour of *Flush* and *Orlando*, which are embraced for their playfulness. 'Bloomsbury' values attract American tourists and audiences for chocolate box cinema of the Merchant Ivory kind.

Woolf was not an 'invisible presence', like her mother or Mrs Ramsay. But she did live outside established institutions, even as she became a central figure in the creation of 'Bloomsbury'. As Hermione Lee puts it:

> Virginia Woolf's *curriculum vitae* is, in public terms, full of gaps. She did not go to school. She did not work in an office. She did not belong to any institution. With rare exceptions, she did not give public lectures or join committees or give interviews. And in private terms her life story is sensational only for her breakdowns and suicide attempts.[23]

Yet Woolf was, above all else, a professional writer, who earned her living from writing. 'Even in a year broken by illness (such as 1925) she would finish revising and publish one novel and a collection of essays, write eight or so short stories, start work on another novel, publish thirty-seven review articles, keep a full diary, read a great number of books and write a great number of letters'.[24] What can Virginia Woolf's professional life tell us about the presence of women in the public sphere and about the institutional transformations that presence secured? I want to pursue this question by taking up Woolf's work of the late 1930s, when the Spanish Civil War and the threat of war with Germany dominated public debate, and Woolf wrote and published *Three Guineas* and *Roger Fry*, and as a respite from 'Roger', wrote 'A Sketch of the Past'. Ideas about biography and its public uses figure in all three; and in all of them Woolf considers the workings of influence: how individuals reproduce and transform public culture. *Three Guineas* expresses her frustration at her own lack of influence. *Roger Fry* describes its subject's failure to gain preferment, as well as

[23] Lee, *Woolf*, p. 16.
[24] Lee, *Woolf*, p. 4.

the impact of his Post-Impressionist exhibition. 'A Sketch of the Past' reflects on the influence of women like Julia Stephen, as well as the unfulfilled promise of lives like those of Stella Hills and Thoby Stephen.

In *Three Guineas*, Woolf is troubled by the problem of culture and politics and by the lack of women's 'influence' in the public domain. The essay's premise is an enquiry: 'how in your opinion are we to prevent war?' In this polemic, she is at once the 'daughter of an educated man' and a professional woman, one of those granted the 'right to earn a living' in 1919, a date repeatedly invoked as the moment when women were properly enfranchised. The question to which she returns in the essay is: what have been the gains of that 'freedom'? On what terms have women been admitted to public life, how have they transformed institutions and how has their influence helped to shape public opinion? Women's admission to the universities freed them from 'the private house', but to what purpose?

Woolf, who did not herself benefit directly from these reforms, and whose education cost a fraction of that of her brothers, resorts to biography, history, and the press as sources and demonstrations of an argument that the public sphere has been shaped by men to serve masculine interests. Her text purports to be a letter to a representative public man:

> You [. . .] are a little grey on the temples; the hair is no longer thick on top of your head. You have reached the middle years of your life not without effort, at the Bar; but on the whole your journey has been prosperous. There is nothing parched, mean or dissatisfied in your expression. And without wishing to flatter you, your prosperity—wife, children, has been deserved. You have never sunk into the contented apathy of middle life, for [. . .] you are writing letters, attending meetings, presiding over this and that, asking questions, with the sound of guns in your ears. For the rest, you began your education at one of the great public schools and finished it at university.[25]

Woolf knew such men: Maynard Keynes, Desmond MacCarthy, Clive Bell, and Leonard Woolf were among them; Thoby might have been another. These men 'live stirring and active lives; all constantly brush up against the great; all constantly affect the course of history in one way or another'.[26] Woolf belongs socially in the company of men like this. But not professionally; for she cannot match their influence, or, she claims, their capacity to analyse and make judgements upon public affairs. She has neither the formal education nor the practical political knowledge provided by public service, whether in the bureaucracy or as a member of public committees. Her public reasoning reflects her education in a private house. It draws on

[25] Woolf, *Three Guineas* (Harmondsworth, 1977), p. 6.
[26] Woolf, 'Am I a Snob?', *Moments of Being*, p. 182.

wide but not 'disciplined' reading, curiosity and a class disposition to civility, and uses a 'domestic' genre: the personal letter.

Many of Woolf's contemporaries were angered by *Three Guineas*. Woolf told Nelly Cecil that many people 'have cut up as rusty as [an . . .] old razor blade over' it.[27] Morgan Forster called it 'cantankerous', and said it was the expression of an 'old-fashioned' feminism. 'Improving the world she would not consider, on the ground that the world is man-made, and that she, a woman, had no responsibility for the mess'.[28] This seems a perverse reading of Woolf's argument, which was not about disavowing responsibility, but rather reasoned about what responsibility women owed the nation and how it might be exercised to best effect. If, by 'old-fashioned' feminism, Forster had in mind the 'separate spheres' logic of some suffrage campaigners, then he missed Woolf's point. Woolf wants to influence public decision-making, not by claiming an authority grounded in the values of the private house, but by finding a new common ground, a public space from which to speak of 'we'. She is making an identity claim, but one which also requires a reassessment of class and gender differences and a reordering of the public sphere to accommodate those differences.

She turns to biography to find examples of 'civilized' women and their influence. The few who have the status 'to have had biographies' include Florence Nightingale, Mary Kingsley, Anne Clough, Sophia Jex-Blake, and Barbara Leigh Smith Bodichon. Many of these women had 'unpaid for' educations. Their four great teachers were 'poverty, chastity, derision and freedom from unreal loyalties'. Woolf concludes from their example that it is possible to 'enter the professions and escape the risks that make them undesirable', provided that 'real loyalties' can be known and served.[29] Far from reneging on responsibility, Woolf sets a standard for determining what 'real loyalties' demand. Her analysis of women's position as outsiders concludes that loyalty to those established institutions may be misplaced, if not in outright conflict with higher responsibilities. Citing the story of Antigone, she suggests that women use their new-found freedom to 'find the law', not to break or subvert it.[30]

Was the request for Woolf's opinion about preventing war genuine or merely token? This question occurred to her, as it would to many women who entered the Academy and other public institutions in the late decades of the twentieth century. Forster's failure to hear her out is especially

[27] Nigel Nicolson and Joanne Trautmann, ed., *Leave the Letters Till We're Dead: The Letters of Virginia Woolf, 1936–1941* (London, 1983), p. 242.
[28] E. M. Forster, 'Virginia Woolf', *Two Cheers for Democracy* (Harmondsworth, 1976), p. 255.
[29] Woolf, *Three Guineas*, p. 92.
[30] Woolf, *Three Guineas*, p. 157.

puzzling, given that he came to a similar conclusion: that real loyalty in some circumstances would demand that he betray his country, rather than betray a friend. Reading Woolf as she rehearses the impediments to conversation with public men, and the difficulties of saying 'we', reminds us of how public institutions have resisted change, even as women's equality as individuals has won general acceptance. Woolf wanted to transform public institutions, but even among her friends her polemic was not well received. She engaged a debate that occupied many of her contemporaries, but did not find allies. Reviewing 'The Leaning Tower', Desmond MacCarthy publicly rebuked her use of the pronoun 'we' when she addressed working men. Woolf was moved to protest:

> *I* never sat on top of a tower! Compare my wretched little £150 education with yours, with Lytton's, with Leonard's. Did Eton and Cambridge make no difference to you . . . Would Lytton have written just as well if he'd spent his youth, as I did mine, among books in a library? . . . And when you say 'She herself as a writer owes everything to having seen the world from a tower which did *not* lean' you make me gnash my teeth. . . . Of course I'm not on the ground with the WEA but I'm about four thousand five hundred and fifty pounds nearer them than you are. So I'm right to say 'we' when I talk to them; just as I'm right to say 'they' when I look up, as I do with constant envy and admiration, at you.[31]

After the publication of *Roger Fry*, Woolf was provoked to a similar protest in correspondence with Ben Nicolson. This time the issue was generational. MacCarthy and Forster warmly approved of the book; Forster writing that 'her accurate account of her friend's life, her careful analysis of his opinions, have as their overtone a noble and convincing defence of civilisation'.[32] Nicolson, on the other hand, objected to the overshadowing presence of 'Bloomsbury' values in the biography.

Woolf wrote many letters about 'Roger'. Along with 'A Sketch of the Past', those letters reveal her concern with the obligations of the biographer whose subject is embedded in shared social and familial networks—in this case, Fry was the friend who above all others had made a difference to her life. A number went to women who were intimate with him, and who had their own investments: his sisters, his companion Helen Anrep, and Vanessa Bell. Letters to such friends as Ethel Smyth and Bessie Trevelyan allowed reflection on the 'art' of biography: the constraints imposed by 'facts'; the need for 'self-suppression'; and how the 'mass of detail' was held together by 'abstracting it into themes'.[33]

[31] Nicolson and Trautmann, *Letters*, pp. 467–8.
[32] E. M. Forster, Review of *Roger Fry* by Virginia Woolf, *New Statesman and Nation*, 10 August 1940.
[33] Nicolson and Trautmann, *Letters*, pp. 425–6.

The letters to Ben Nicolson take up another issue: the public responsibility of the writer. The editors of the *Collected Letters* comment on one of these, dated 24 August 1940: 'Virginia worked on this letter more carefully than on any other private letter of which we have a record'.[34] Ben Nicolson represents an emergent public whose recognition is important to Woolf, the young men who were reshaping cultural institutions and opening out public debate about class and politics. She is gratified by his response, and relishes their disagreement. *Roger Fry* becomes a catalyst of the differences between them, but is also potentially the point from which they can find common ground.

Nicolson rejects the 'Bloomsbury' values that supply one of the major themes of Woolf's biography. This theme is concerned with friendship, conversation, and the apprehension of beauty, touchstones of Fry's life given expression through his association with the Cambridge Apostles. The second major theme is 'transformation'. Fry's significance for Woolf stems from the impact of the Post-Impressionist exhibition of 1910, an exhibition that changed public taste. In her debate with Nicolson, Woolf compares his life with Fry's, taking sentences and substituting the younger man's name for Roger's. There is a rebuke implied in this, a reminder that Ben has been shaped by the same privileges of education and gender. And she counters his view that the claims of 'actualities' always override the value of conversation and art by reiterated reference to the circumstances in which their disagreement is taking place. Ben is serving in an anti-aircraft battery in Kent, and Virginia's letter-writing is interrupted by the same sirens:

> Here the raiders came over head. I went and looked at them. Then I returned to your letter. 'I am so struck by the fool's paradise in which he and his friends lived. He shut himself out from all disagreeable actualities and allowed the spirit of Nazism to grow without any steps to check it . . .' Lord, I thought to myself, Roger shut himself out from disagreeable actualities, did he? Roger who faced insanity, death and every sort of disagreeable—what can Ben mean? Are Ben and I facing actualities because we're listening to bombs fall on other people? And I went on with Ben Nicolson's biography. After returning from a delightful tour of Italy, for which his expensive education at Eton and Oxford had well fitted him, he got a job as keeper of the King's pictures.[35]

Roger Fry became Slade Professor at Cambridge in 1933, having been twice denied the appointment. His own paintings failed to sell, and the Omega Workshop closed. Yet he 'changed the taste of his time by his writing, altered the current of English painting by his championship of the Post-

---

[34] Nicolson and Trautmann, *Letters*, p. 419.
[35] Nicolson and Trautmann, *Letters*, p. 413.

Impressionists, and increased immeasurably the love of art by his lectures. He left too upon the minds of those who knew him a very rich, complex and definite impression'.[36]

Despite his advantages of education, Roger Fry, like Virginia Woolf, lived and made a career outside institutions. Her account of his life, according to Leonard, was too analytical. Her analysis turns, I suggest, on the question of influence: how did Fry make a difference? Woolf says of him that he 'lived many lives, the active, the contemplative, the public, the private'.[37] In her exchanges with Ben Nicolson, as in *Three Guineas*, Woolf's argument is about the forms an 'active' life takes, and the way the spheres of 'culture' and 'politics' intersect.

The Biographer in the Public Sphere

I want to draw the threads of this discussion together by returning to the problem of saying 'we'. Virginia Woolf resorted to biography in *Three Guineas* as a means of constituting herself as part of a public, as a representative of a set of interests previously ignored in public debate. But she used 'we' to call attention to a common purpose and to invoke alliances.

The impact of feminist thinking on the practice of life-writing is perhaps most evident in the now conventional appearance of the biographer in the text and in the attention to the relation of the biographer and her subject. This practice underlined identity claims. The recovery of women's lives constituted an emergent public, raised consciousness of women's history, and constructed political interests. Maria Pia Lara sees the identification of women writers and readers with the subjects of women's narratives as facilitating new forms of self-presentation. She has argued that biography and autobiography have been critical to the feminist project of transforming the public sphere because these narratives connect the moral and aesthetic spheres with the spheres of justice and solidarity. The liberal separation of private morality and public justice has been challenged by such narratives. Identity claims have been crucial to feminist politics and women's narratives 'have reordered understandings of what the public sphere is'.[38] This reordered understanding has accommodated a multiplicity of voices, and sponsored the recent flourishing of autobiography and memoir.

In the decades since the 1970s, there have been some shifts in the

---

[36] Woolf, *Roger Fry: A Biography* (Harmondsworth, 1940), p. 256.
[37] Woolf, *Roger Fry*, p. 174.
[38] Maria Pia Lara, *Moral Textures: Feminist Narratives in the Public Sphere* (Cambridge, 1998), p. 3.

way identity claims have been conceptualized and deployed. Ellen Moers announced her 'fascination' with the fact of sex, while 'gleefully' inverting the hierarchy of sexual difference. The contributors to *Between Women* were anxious about 'overidentification', understanding that the dynamics of sexual difference reproduced patriarchal gender arrangements, and ambivalent about their own psychic investments in femininity. Carolyn Steedman discloses a desire for history, because she recognizes that narratives of femininity obscure women's work in the public sphere. By the time Hermione Lee writes about Virginia Woolf, biographical scrutiny has exposed her private life and she has become public property. Lee sets about reconstructing the private and public spaces in which her life was lived.

When Virginia Woolf wrote to Bessie Trevelyan about *Roger Fry*, she said: 'There is always a certain constraint, which one doesn't feel in fiction, a sense of other people looking over one's shoulder. [. . .] But nobody—none of my friends—made such a difference to my life as he did. And yet, writing about him, one had to keep that under.'[39] And she told both Octavia Wilberforce and Ethel Smyth that it was an 'exercise in self-suppression'. What did she mean? I think she meant something more than an attempt to be 'objective'. Properly accounting for her friend's public life and influence involved more than bringing out his 'qualities' to the satisfaction of his family, or giving substance to his 'invisible presence' in the private domain. It involved a recognition of differences of class, gender, and—in Fry's case—religion, such as she describes when she apportions her last guinea to the cause of preventing war. It also involved redefining the public institutional spaces (for example his school, and the art market) in which he shaped his career. She concludes *Three Guineas* by repeating her insistence on difference as the basis for finding common ground:

> The answer to your question must be that we can best help you to prevent war not by repeating your words and following your methods but by finding new words and creating new methods. We can best help you to prevent war not by joining your society but by remaining outside your society but in cooperation with its aim. That aim is the same for us both. It is to assert 'the rights of all—all men and women—to the respect in their persons of the great principles of Justice and Equality and Liberty'.[40]

The public sphere, the sphere of action, is also the realm of contingency. The shift from identification to the recognition of difference—the shift, I would argue, that Woolf's 'experiment in self-suppression' attempts—involves accounting for contingency.

Early feminist recoveries of women's history often set out to redeem

---

[39] Nicolson and Trautmann, *Letters*, pp. 425–6.
[40] Woolf, *Three Guineas*, p. 164.

loss, neglect, or outright rejection. Identification was the means of making good that loss. Identity claims constituted both intimate and ethical relations among women which could advance their campaigns for equality and justice in the public sphere. But 'identity', with its essentialist debt, quickly became a troublesome concept for feminism. It occluded the differences among and within women: differences of class, ethnicity and race, sexuality, and nation. Fascination with sexual difference came to be displaced by attention to the complex web of differences.

Fascination is not only a cure for loss, Adam Phillips argues, but a refusal to take contingency seriously. Phillips discusses Freud's essay on Leonardo, an essay whose subject he defines as 'fascination and biography', to show how in Freud's account 'fascination is part of the child's wistful attempt to restore difference to sameness'. By extension, Phillips claims, men's fascination with women is 'a denial of their actual existence'.[41] Woolf's awareness of this double edge to the adoration of women like her mother is apparent in her representation of women like Mrs Ramsay. Such women, she noted in *A Room of One's Own*, reflect men at twice their natural size. In *Three Guineas*, Woolf's insistence on difference strikes at this defence, which may go some way to explaining why they 'cut up rusty as old razor blades' about it. Freud's concern was with masculine denial of difference, but from the perspective of femininity, recognition of difference is required to separate from the mother and accept contingency. The reduction of gender to sexual difference has by now been recognized as a 'wistful attempt to restore difference to sameness'.

Another way to construe feminism's recent insistence on differences is to think of it as the basis from which desire can become action. Biography's traditional concern with the public life and career of the subject needs to be supplemented by an account of the continuing reorganization of the public sphere to accommodate newly emergent publics. What is still—and always—to be worked out is how to say 'we'.

[41] Adam Phillips, 'Smile', *Promises, Promises: Essays on Literature and Psychoanalysis* (London, 2000), p. 186.

18

'The Solace of Doubt'? Biographical Methodology after the Short Twentieth Century

JAMES WALTER

What of the writing about writing biography? I will explore here some of the trends that have emerged in such publications in the twentieth century, with emphasis on the past twenty years. I suggest that we can understand present debates as the rethinking of (or resistance to) the suppositions of twentieth-century modernist biography, which held sway from the early 1920s to the early 1980s. Since there are significant cultural differences in biographical practice, my focus is on English-language biography only. Such is the volume of commentary about 'life-writing' that a comprehensive bibliographical essay would be difficult. Fortunately, the regular publication of annotated bibliographies on biography makes that exercise redundant.[1]

Twentieth-century biography was shaped by the preoccupations of modernism. It is commonplace to identify Freud's elucidation of the unconscious, and the iconoclasm of Lytton Strachey, as profoundly affecting the questions biographers have asked of themselves, and their materials. Freud's was an argument not only for systematic psychology, but also for interpretation—as behaviour and events were plumbed for motives and

[1] For instance, the journal *biography* annually publishes a useful 'Current Bibliography of Life Writing'; see also Carl Rollyson, *Biography: An Annotated Bibliography* (Pasadena, 1992), and Catherine N. Parke, 'Bibliographic Essay', in her *Biography: Writing Lives* (New York, 1996), pp. 125–34.

meanings beyond their surface manifestations. Strachey's was an argument for selection and discrimination, for brevity, and—above all—for a point of view. Thus were swept aside the memorial hagiographies of 'great men', with their illusions of capturing 'all the facts'.

The 'new biography', with its concessions to interpretation, promoted on-going dialogue about the weight to be accorded to research (or craft) versus art. Virginia Woolf's brilliant fictional meditations on biography—*Orlando* and *Flush*—were a counter to Strachey. Less of an influence on biographical method than Strachey in the short term, she would nonetheless be adopted by feminist biographers sixty years later as the foundational twentieth-century modernist theorist of biography.[2] Arguably, the incorporation of fictive elements in postmodern biography (see below) owes more to Woolf than to Strachey. That said, Virginia Woolf had a more limiting view of biography's claim to the status of art than did Strachey. Yet as Leon Edel, a later analyst of their debate, was to argue: 'A biographer is an artist from the moment he chooses between different sets of facts and explains and justifies what he has chosen'.[3] Another denizen of Bloomsbury, Harold Nicolson, was to draw a further implication from such propositions: 'Biography is the preoccupation and the solace, not of certainty, but of doubt'.[4] Modernist biographers have continually ruminated on the philosophical problem of 'other minds': 'that I can have direct knowledge of my own experiences and that I cannot have direct knowledge of anyone else's'.[5] But psychoanalysis raised questions even about unmediated knowledge of personal experience. Indeterminacy, then, has long been recognized as the characteristic feature of modern biography, and the fact that biographical truth can never finally be settled, that biography is always tendentious, has inflected every other methodological strategy.

Most methodological essays have been preoccupied with one or more of the following elements. First, acknowledging the problem of 'other minds' entails accepting that biography works by analogy and inference rather than empiricism alone, and that methods of persuasive argument are as important as research. Second, that the meaning of facts is not self-evident, and that discrimination in what is discussed is as important as the comprehensive garnering of knowledge, puts a premium on analysis. Third,

[2] See, for instance, Catherine Parke's eulogistic treatment of Virginia Woolf, in *Biography: Writing Lives*, Chapter 3, pp. 67–89.
[3] Leon Edel, 'Manifesto', *biography*, I, 1 (1978), 2. For Edel's view of the debate between Woolf and Strachey, see Leon Edel, *Writing Lives: Principia Biographia* (New York, 1984), pp. 186–96, and Leon Edel, *Bloomsbury: A House of Lions* (New York, 1980), pp. 253–8.
[4] Harold Nicolson, *The Development of English Biography* (London, 1968), p. 65.
[5] A. J. Ayer, 'One's Knowledge of Other Minds', in D. F. Gustafson, ed., *Essays in Philosophical Psychology* (London, 1967), p. 348.

the admission of the centrality of interpretation brings in its wake open resort to various bodies of theory as providing tools for interpretation. Strachey prefigured each of these elements in his description of a book without a point of view 'resembling nothing so much as a very large heap of sawdust';[6] and 'uninterpreted truth [as] like buried gold';[7] his subversive assertion that 'ignorance is the first requisite of the historian—ignorance which simplifies and clarifies', and that the biographer should merely 'row out over that great ocean of material, and lower down into it [. . .] a little bucket, which will bring up [. . .] some characteristic specimen'[8] as a counter to the delusory attempt to tell the 'complete' life; and in his pioneering resort to psychoanalysis in his *Elizabeth and Essex*.[9] Other working biographers were to write essays and books on these matters, but a useful gloss on the trends within Anglo-American modernist biography is to be found in the work of Leon Edel.

Edel, himself a distinguished biographer, set himself the task of annunciating the modern *Principia Biographia* in a series of books and essays between the mid-1950s and the mid-1980s.[10] He spoke, perhaps unwittingly, for the professionalization of the craft. He sought to bring together theory and method, and to show how the 'art' demanded by interpretation could be reinforced by 'the science of man'.[11] When he began, few were publishing in this domain. The precursors (André Maurois, Harold Nicolson) had preceded him by thirty years. Edel built explicitly on the foundations of Bloomsbury, brought to full flower the principles of modernist biography, and for my purposes was expressive of the end point of 'the short twentieth century' in biography.[12]

In articulating critical theory for the working biographer, Edel wrestled with four dilemmas, first voiced in 1957 as the fundamental issues within his *Literary Biography*, but re-emerging in the 1980s in 'Biography and the Science of Man' and in *Writing Lives*.[13] The first dilemma was that of imposing order, bringing logic and shape to the record of 'something that is as mercurial and as flowing, as compact of temperament and emotion,

---

[6] Lytton Strachey, *Portraits in Miniature* (London, 1933), p. 170.
[7] Quoted by Edel, *Writing Lives*, p. 183.
[8] Lytton Strachey, *Eminent Victorians* (London, 1918, reprinted Harmondsworth, 1977), p. 9.
[9] On Freud's view of *Elizabeth and Essex*, and on Strachey as the father of psychobiography, see Edel, *Writing Lives*, pp. 143–4.
[10] Edel's *Writing Lives* is his attempt to draw the threads together.
[11] Leon Edel, 'Biography and the Science of Man', in A. M. Friedson, ed., *New Directions in Biography* (Honolulu, 1981), pp. 1–11.
[12] I refer to Hobsbawm's thesis about the end of the avant-garde in Eric Hobsbawm, *Age of Extremes: The Short Twentieth Century 1914–1991* (London, 1994), pp. 500–22.
[13] Leon Edel, *Literary Biography* (London, 1957) [references below are to the reissue of 1973]; Edel, *Writing Lives*; Edel, 'Biography and the Science of Man'.

as the human spirit itself'.[14] The second was his rendition of the problem of other minds: how to marry 'the truth of life and the truth of experience [. . . when] a biographer [. . .] by force of circumstances is always outside his subject [. . . seeking to] penetrate into the subject's mind, and obtain insights which are not vouchsafed him even in the case of his most intimate friends'.[15] The third dilemma was how to encompass all available data, and yet reduce them to a manageable compass, to dimensions that can be comprehended by a biographer and an audience. The fourth was how to manage both sufficient immersion in the life of another to understand it, and yet enough detachment to analyse and to explain: 'The biographer [. . .] is required to get into the skin of his subject [. . .] yet all the while he retains his own mind, his own sense of balance and his own appraising eye. [. . .] To be cold as ice in appraisal, yet warm and human and understanding, this is the biographer's dilemma'.[16]

Edel argued that these dilemmas could be resolved by the judicious use of psychoanalytic theory, and the acknowledgement that the successful biographer must be an artist. Psychological awareness solved the problem of getting inside another skin: 'A life-myth is hidden within every poet's work, and in the gestures of a politician, the canvases and statues of art and the "life-styles" of charismatic characters'.[17] The life-myths are the story a subject tells him/herself as the means of coping with the psychological tasks which confront us all: theory unlocks the dynamic of the life-myth, and the meaning of a life's work. Theory in turn solved the problems of the relationship between biographer and subject—the self-aware biographer would be able to achieve empathy, without transference—and of the relationship between a biographer and his/her material—directing attention to evidence most germane to the 'life-myth'. Yet in the end, the imperatives of interpretation and of narrative demand that the biographer become an artist:

> [I]n the writing of biography the material is predetermined: the imagination functions only as it plays over this material and shapes it. The art lies in the telling.[18]

> [A] writer of lives must extract individuals from their chaos yet create an illusion that they are in the midst of life [. . .]. The fancy of the biographer— we repeat—resides in the art of narration, not in the substance of the story. The substance exists before the narration begins.[19]

---

[14] Edel, *Writing Lives*, p. 33.
[15] Edel, *Literary Biography*, pp. 2–3.
[16] Edel, *Writing Lives*, p. 41.
[17] Edel, 'Biography and the Science of Man', p. 7.
[18] Edel, *Literary Biography*, p. 5.
[19] Edel, *Writing Lives*, p. 15.

A biographer is an artist from the moment he chooses between different sets of facts.[20]

By the time he wrote this last comment, Edel was far from alone in his efforts to identify the fundamentals of the biographical art. Significantly, this comment appeared in a 'Manifesto' in the first issue of *biography*—a journal of which Edel was clearly the intellectual progenitor. During the 1960s and 1970s, a widening group had taken up and elaborated upon many of the elements that had concerned him. Edel had not been the catalyst for these effusions so much as their harbinger. James Clifford, for instance, dealt with both the practice of biographical research and the recovery of the critical foundations of the genre.[21] Richard Ellmann, in a series of acute essays on George Eliot, Conrad, Wilde, Gide, Joyce, and T. S. Eliot, showed how biographical knowledge and skill could illuminate literary criticism.[22] Teaching texts began to appear.[23] Robert Gittings tried to recapture something of Harold Nicolson's enterprise, drawing on 'beliefs of a working biographer, based on a quarter of a century of such work'.[24] The practice of anthologizing conference contributions, or commissioned essays, by working biographers became widespread.[25] Social scientists turned to mapping biography systematically into their disciplines.[26] Social scientists also demolished the Everest syndrome (Why write about this prominent person? Because s/he's there . . .) by insisting on key governing questions for the biographical project: Kenneth Morgan, for instance, argued: 'I [. . .] use biography to [. . .] answer political questions about public issues'.[27] Psychobiographers explored the uses of theory both as an aid to self-awareness[28] and as a means for reaching the subject's core.[29]

[20] Edel, 'Manifesto', p. 2.
[21] James L. Clifford, *From Puzzles to Portraits* (London, 1970); James L. Clifford, ed., *Biography as an Art: Selected Criticism 1560–1960* (London, 1962).
[22] Richard Ellmann, *Golden Codgers: Biographical Speculation* (London, 1973).
[23] For instance Allan Shelston, *Biography* (London, 1977), in the Critical Idiom series.
[24] Robert Gittings, *The Nature of Biography* (London, 1978), p. 9.
[25] See for instance Daniel Aarons, ed., *Studies in Biography* (Cambridge, MA, 1978); James Walter, ed., *Reading Life Histories* (Canberra, 1981); Jeffery Meyers, ed., *The Craft of Literary Biography* (London, 1985); John Y. Cole, ed., *Biography and Books* (Washington, DC, 1986).
[26] For example, Lewis J. Edinger's essays on 'Political Science and Political Biography', *The Journal of Politics*, XXVI (1964), 423–39 and 648–76.
[27] Kenneth O. Morgan, 'Writing Political Biography', in Eric Homberger and John Charmley, ed., *The Troubled Face of Biography*, (London, 1988), p. 33. And see, especially, Alan Davies, 'The Tasks of Biography', in his *Essays in Political Sociology* (Melbourne, 1972), pp. 109–17.
[28] For example, Samuel H. Baron and Carl Pletsch, ed., *Introspection in Biography: The Biographer's Quest for Self-Awareness* (Hillsdale, NJ, 1985).
[29] For instance, W. McK. Runyan, *Life Histories and Psychobiography: Explorations in Theory and Method* (Oxford, 1982).

And, carried on the tide of these literatures, the typical anthologizer began to discern another renaissance.[30]

For all the proliferation in writing about biography, and its popularity as a genre, it remained a pursuit that worked against the grain of the mainstream disciplines. Historians, reacting against the facile Carlylean proposition of history as the study of great men, had taken more holistic approaches, inflected at this time by movements in social history, Marxist labour history, and the Annales school. Social scientists by and large had heeded Durkheim's dictum that society must be understood at the social level. And literary critics, having adopted the textual primacy of 'new criticism', were now prey to Barthes' proclamation of 'the death of the author'. The proselytes of 'new directions in biography', and the many contributors to the field exemplified above, were clearly working within the twentieth-century modernist biographical movement that extended from Strachey to Edel, from Bloomsbury to Hawaii. But as the literature of commentary and practice burgeoned, the modernist approach to biography began to unravel. One telling manifestation of this was Janet Malcolm's forensic deconstruction of the Plath biographers, as 'a kind of allegory' of the problem of interpretation in modern biography.[31] Edel, then, was the harbinger of a more extensive literature on biographical practice and theory, and also marked the beginning of the end of a particular way of thinking about biography.

Eric Homberger's and John Charmley's edited volume *The Troubled Face of Biography* (1988) can serve to illustrate this transition.[32] This title itself posed a question: troubled by what? Biography, these authors claimed, was anomalous in crossing disciplinary boundaries in an age of academic specialization; the 'commonsensical, empirical and humane' spirit of British biography confronted 'an intellectual *Zeitgeist* hostile to [its] "central" justification'; the uncertain position of biography in academic life demanded reflection; the biographer's 'love affair with narrative' was challenged by theoretical schisms.[33] Among the contributors, Robert Skidelsky pursued most vigorously the source of unease: 'a feeling that [biography] has not yet fully won its intellectual spurs [. . .], is still not taken seriously as literature, as history, or as a cogent intellectual enterprise'.[34] The essayists, however, seemed selected to demonstrate the obverse of Skidelsky's propo-

[30] Friedson, ed., *New Directions in Biography* is an example.
[31] Janet Malcolm, *The Silent Woman: Sylvia Plath and Ted Hughes* (London, 1994).
[32] Homberger and Charmley, ed., *The Troubled Face of Biography*.
[33] These claims appear in Homberger's and Charmley's Introduction to *The Troubled Face of Biography* (Basingstoke, 1988), pp. ix–xv.
[34] Robert Skidelsky, 'Only Connect: Biography and Truth', in Homberger and Charmley, ed., *The Troubled Face of Biography*, p. 2.

sition. They were intellectual heavyweights, whose contributions displayed rigour about methodological issues, an acute sense of the 'provisional' nature of their conclusions, considerable expertise in their fields, and exemplary seriousness.

One anecdote, by Malcolm Bradbury, pointed to a sort of displacement underpinning the unease identified by Skidelsky. Bradbury spoke of visiting a university in Northern Australia 'where in tropical conditions many contemporary theories had reached a state of exotic enrichment'—structuralism, semiotics, hegemonic paradigms, Lacan, Cixous, and Foucault ruled:

> Yet, wandering through the institution one day, I found—like some alternative government, waiting to take over if the prevailing regime was toppled—a major institute of literary biography. People who wrote authors' lives talked to people who wanted to know how to write authors' lives, and strange matters were discussed: how to assess evidence, construct structured narrative, and explore the psychology of creation. Biography was not dead in the academy; it was alive and well but living in a quite different corner of the building.[35]

From this, Bradbury deduced not only division but also 'some intimacy', for 'strange tentacular relations do exist between modern literary theory and modern literary biography [...] biography itself has come under the shadows of the era of suspicion, and indeed has been moving in that direction since Lytton Strachey'.[36] Indeed, what Bradbury's northern-hemisphere readers may not have known was that his lightly fictionalized biographical institute was a hive of contentious debate, whose published critical essays on theory and method[37] had been floridly attacked in the *Sydney Morning Herald* by a distinguished literary biographer largely because they brought to the fore the 'tentacular relations' between theory and biography.[38]

In one sense, this was not new: the outrage of those who saw any resort to theory as an incursion into the 'commonsensical, humane and empirical' domain of biography had been evident since the biographical experiments of Strachey and Freud. Yet by the late 1980s, the displacement, the sense that biography itself was part of 'the era of suspicion', and the admission that the common enterprise of life-writing was fragmenting, marked an ending of the modernist project in biography. Instead of identifying and

---

[35] Malcolm Bradbury, 'The Telling Life: Some Thoughts on Literary Biography', in Homberger and Charmley, ed., *The Troubled Face of Biography*, pp. 131–40, at p. 137.
[36] Bradbury, 'The Telling Life', p. 137.
[37] Walter, ed., *Reading Life Histories*.
[38] Axel Clark, 'Academics lose themselves in foul verbal swamps', *Sydney Morning Herald*, 7 November 1981. More temperate reviews appeared in *Australian Journal of Politics and History*, XXVIII, 1 (1982), 124–5, and *Journal of European Studies*, XIII (1983), 218–19.

describing a unified 'life-myth', a biographer could compile many stories about a subject, cross-cutting between many voices, implying that any construction of a self was a matter of perspective and situation.[39] In the light of 'the tentacular relations' between theory and life-writing, the tasks of biography themselves would be differently conceived.

Aesthetic forms mirror, rather than lead, larger-scale social changes. There have been many attempts to chart what were seen as tectonic shifts in the 1970s and 1980s: the transition from Fordist to Post-Fordist forms of production, the transformation from organized to disorganized capitalism, the challenge to unifying nationalisms of economic globalization and the abandonment of state regulation for the rule of 'market forces'. In the arts, those changes translated as the end of the avant-garde, scepticism about the progressive assumptions of twentieth-century modernism and the demise of 'grand narratives'. Hobsbawm has memorably identified these conjunctions as signifying the end of the short twentieth century.[40] We need here to be alert to the changes in the way biography has been written, and written about. The theoretical questions emerging at this time were themselves part of the shifting ground.

The issue of how to write biography after the short twentieth century has been especially to the fore in women's life-writing. As part of the 'new biography' of the 1970s and 1980s, there were vigorous attempts to recover the stories of women. These were predicated on resistance to the 'masculinist norms [which] supply the backdrop and provide the measure of what women write about themselves'.[41] An admirably clear example was Carolyn Heilbrun's *Writing a Woman's Life* (1989). Stressing that narratives control women's lives by determining what can be said, Heilbrun made the telling point that 'lives do not serve as models; only stories do that'.[42] The stress on model stories and on narrative, however, led to a preoccupation with 'heroines' of the women's movement[43] at just the time that postmodern theory eschewed 'grand narratives'. Feminist life-writers then raised alternative questions, countering modernist individualism by stressing the self as a product of history, class, and gender;[44] making explicit the implicit

---

[39] See, for instance, Peter Manso, *Mailer: His Live and Times* (New York, 1985).

[40] Hobsbawm, *Age of Extremes*, pp. 1–17.

[41] Nell Irwin Painter, 'Writing Biographies of Women', *Journal of Women's History*, IX, 2 (1997), 154–63, at 160.

[42] Carolyn G. Heilbrun, *Writing a Woman's Life* (London, 1989), p. 37.

[43] See, for instance, Carol Ascher, Louise De Salvo, and Sara Ruddick, ed., *Between Women* (Boston, 1984).

[44] For example, Laura Marcus, ' "Enough About You, Let's Talk About Me": Recent Autobiographical Writing', *New Formations*, I (1987), 77–94.

epistemological and ontological assumptions of biography[45] (and contrasting these with women's ways of knowing); putting unusual stress on the empathy between women as the way of the biographer 'knowing' her subject;[46] and focusing on the micropolitics of subjectivity, identity, and the body. As Liz Stanley summarized this:

> Conventional ideas about the self [...] assign selfhood to only a specific kind of person. This traditional grand narrative of the self is [...] an ideology which promotes its supposed coherence and linearity, its temporal development and significance, and [...] must be challenged and replaced by an understanding of the actual fragmentation, polyphony and atemporality of the self. In postmodernist theory the self is instead positioned in relation to situated knowledges and presentations, as contextually and temporally specific rather than as static and unitary.[47]

Stanley's own biographical work (on Hannah Cullwick and Emily Wilding Davison) arguably succeeds because of the strong impress of sociology: it is 'self-consciously ideological. It explains the "labor process" of the biography's epistemology, locates the biographer intellectually, and places the subject within the context that [...] nurtures the active female subject'.[48] More recently, the stresses on fragmentation and polyphony have been accentuated: 'Bearing multiple marks of location, bodies position the [...] subject at the nexus of culturally specific experiences of gender, race, sexual orientation [...] and at the nexus of "micropolitical practices" that derive from the cultural meaning of those points of identification'.[49]

Such considerations appear to have had a greater impact upon women's autobiography than upon biography, yet they have clearly influenced the questions women biographers raise about their work. At one extreme, however, they appear to undermine the tasks Heilbrun, Stanley, and others envisaged for feminist biography by undermining its political impact. Everything becomes a modality of 'situatedness'. As Herman Rapoport, commenting on Gayatri Spivak, remarks:

> [I]f much of what she writes is strategically incoherent, it is also the work of a multiply situated social subject who does not want to collapse that multiplicity into a singular account that would make her life into a coherent

[45] Liz Stanley, 'Process in Feminist Biography and Feminist Epistemology', in Teresa Iles, ed., *All Sides of the Subject: Women and Biography* (New York, 1992), pp. 109–25.

[46] This is argued strongly in Margaret Forster, 'Woman to Woman', in Iles, ed., *All Sides of the Subject*, pp. 126–33.

[47] Liz Stanley, 'The Knowing Because Experiencing Subject: Narratives, Lives and Autobiography', *Women's Studies International Forum*, XVI, 3 (1993), 205–15, at 206.

[48] Painter, 'Writing Biographies of Women', p. 138.

[49] Sidonie Smith, *Subjectivity, Identity and the Body: Women's Autobiographical Practices in the Twentieth Century* (Bloomington, 1993), p. 130.

narrative. [. . .] Life situations are discontinuous, only partially realized, without closure: on this formulation her incoherence rests.[50]

The issue of how to recover a 'public idiom' in the face of postmodern fragmentation has been energetically debated by feminist political theorists,[51] but it is as yet an open question as to whether this will generate a new coherence in life-writing. The questions of theories of knowledge, theories of being, the social construction of the self, the utilities of empathy, and the micropolitics of subjectivity posed by feminism presage more differentiated forms of biography—far removed from Edel's unifying *principia biographia*. Such questions run alongside (and are part of) a much broader vein of experimentation in contemporary biography. They are also part of a self-reflexive tendency that has seen debates about theory and method incorporated within biographical texts themselves. This is where we should now look for new directions in writing about writing biography, rather than just in the published symposia of working biographers (though the latter continue to appear).[52]

In one direction, recent biographers have stressed the public and the social, moving away from the 'inner life', and questioning the value of empathy. Bernard Crick, in his *George Orwell*, launched an early attack on 'the empathetic fallacy' in a lively interpolation within the text that still stands as a challenging critique of 'the fine writing, balanced appraisal and psychological insight that is the hallmark of the English tradition of biography'.[53]

Some of the more recent challengers of the empathetic tradition have been feminist biographers. Carolyn Steedman, biographer of the socialist theorist of early childhood education Margaret McMillan, is a prominent example. Drawing attention to 'the dead weight of interiority that hangs about the neck of women's biography', Steedman focuses on McMillan as 'a public woman who lived in a public space'.[54]

> She seemed [. . .] to be a woman who demanded a public life; in some way she prevented the delineation of an inside that is 'personal' and 'real' [. . .] what might be seen as McMillan's 'insideness', her meaning, which was her

[50] Herman Rapoport, 'The New Personalism', *biography*, XXI, 1 (1988), 46.

[51] See, for instance, Wendy Brown, 'Feminist Hesitations, Postmodern Exposures', *Differences: A Journal of Feminist Cultural Studies*, III, 1 (1991), 63–83; Wendy Brown, *States of Injury: Power and Freedom in Late Modernity* (Princeton, 1995).

[52] For an exemplary recent instance, see Warwick Gould and Thomas Staley, ed., *Writing the Lives of Writers* (London, 1998).

[53] Bernard Crick, *George Orwell: A Life* (London, 1980, reprinted Harmondsworth, 1982), p. 29. And see pp. 15–39.

[54] Carolyn Steedman, 'Forms of History, Histories of Form', in her *Past Tenses: Essays on Writing, Autobiography and History* (London, 1992), p. 166, 164.

remaking and reassertion of childhood, actually spells out the public space of cultural change.[55]

A spirited chapter within Steedman's biography debates the methods of retailing such a 'public life', and her own intent is clear: 'I want to make the implied meaning of McMillan's own life and writing some kind of denial of interiority—which denial may be a pretence or a fiction, but one which might do some political or public good'.[56]

Judith Brett is another who has much to say of how to write biography drawing on the public domain in her innovative political biography of Robert Menzies.[57] Brett's contention is that the man lives on through his language—through that the career is accessible. Linked to this is the proposition that 'the public man is the real man and the task is to read his life and character where we find it—in the shape of the public life'. Brett's tools for this 'reading' derive from contemporary psychoanalysis. She moves from examples of Menzies's public discourse to instances of his private language, and then to the psychological dynamics underpinning the whole (what it meant to the man) and to the messages conveyed (how it appealed to an audience). Throughout, she draws on the history of conservative thought, the social history of Menzies's society, and the cultural context from which Menzies drew his resources and which he in turn shaped.

While experimentation with what we might call 'public domain' biography led away from 'interiority' towards lives as social narratives with a public point,[58] the preoccupation with language and its uses—the stories subjects tell, the narratives biographers adopt—became even more central, as Crick, Steedman, and Brett show. This, however, could also serve as a bridge to another mode of experimentation with interiority. Raymond Williams had identified the underlying issue in arguing that biography's insistence on generic factuality often disguised the biographer's need to invent, concealing the resort to fictive techniques of epic or drama in the text.[59] Crick's scepticism about precisely this drove one approach: another (and Steedman acknowledged this) was to be open about choices of narrative form, and to admit that the biographer is engaged in a 'rhetoric of persuasion'.[60] This in turn has led to what might be called a new romanti-

---

[55] Carolyn Steedman, *Childhood, Culture and Class in Britain: Margaret McMillan 1860–1931* (London, 1990), pp. 250–51.

[56] Steedman, 'Forms of History', p. 170.

[57] Judith Brett, *Robert Menzies' Forgotten People* (Sydney, 1992).

[58] See, for instance, Martha Banta, *Taylored Lives: Narrative Productions in the Age of Taylor, Veblen and Ford* (Chicago, 1993); Richard Sennett, 'Failure', in his *The Corrosion of Character: The Personal Consequences of Work in the New Capitalism* (New York, 1998), pp. 118–35.

[59] Williams is quoted in Steedman, *Childhood, Culture and Class*, p. 244.

[60] Steedman, *Childhood, Culture and Class*, p. 244.

cism, and to the overt incorporation of fictive techniques, in recent biography.

The possibilities of what I call the new romanticism are best captured in the work of Richard Holmes, especially for our purposes in *Footsteps* (1985). Holmes has concentrated on some of the icons of Romanticism (Stevenson, Shelley, Coleridge, de Nerval), finding all too often 'the Romantic Hero lost beneath the freezing moon of his entranced imagination',[61] but always himself in an entranced quest for imaginative engagement with other lives. For him, it is 'the subliminal battle of imagination between subject and biographer upon which all life-writing ultimately rests'.[62] Holmes's Romantic heroes are never settled, and in joining their self-dramatizing travels, learning about himself through the journey as they had done, he explores anew the imperatives of identification and of distance.

> [I]dentification or self-projection [...] is an essential motive [...] for attempting to re-create the pathway, the journey, of someone's life through the physical past. [...] But the true biographic process begins precisely at the moment [...] where this naive form of love and identification breaks down. The moment of disillusion is the moment of impersonal, objective re-creation.[63]

In finding the limits of identification, Holmes neither fully shares the commitment to empathy (*pace* some feminists) nor falls into what Crick so trenchantly criticizes as empathetic fallacy. Instead, Holmes tries, literally, to follow his subjects as the means 'to produce the living effect, while remaining true to the dead fact'.[64] He is aware that 'you would never catch them [...] But maybe [...] you might write about the pursuit of that fleeting figure in such a way as to bring it alive in the present'.[65] Holmes's reflection on biography as both pursuit of what is out there and as exploration of inner truth is itself an enactment of the Romantic quest trope: 'the past is not simply "out there", an objective history to be researched or forgotten, at will, but [...] it lives most vividly in all of us, deep inside, and needs constantly to be given expression and interpretation'.[66] In a provocative essay on the friendship between Johnson and Savage, Holmes argues that Savage's 'ability to exploit or live out the image of the unrecog-

---

[61] Richard Holmes, *Footsteps: Adventures of a Romantic Biographer* (London, 1985, reprinted Harmondsworth, 1986), p. 274.

[62] Richard Holmes, *Coleridge: Early Visions* (London, 1989, reprinted Harmondswoth, 1990), p. xvi.

[63] Holmes, *Footsteps*, p. 67.

[64] Holmes, *Footsteps*, p. 27.

[65] Holmes, *Footsteps*, p. 27.

[66] Holmes, *Footsteps*, p. 208.

nized and persecuted man of genius [. . .] heralds the coming of the Romantic generation' and that Johnson's 'guilty enchantment' with Savage laid the very foundations of the genre: English biography 'is essentially a Romantic form; and [. . .] Johnson's friendship with Savage first crystallized its perils and possibilities'.[67] Holmes, then, encourages open recognition, and exploitation of the possibilities, of the Romantic form, and will draw on the echoes of the Romantic narratives that have shaped the modern imagination (the shadow story behind his *Dr Johnson and Mr Savage* is of course *Dr Jekyll and Mr Hyde*).

What Holmes describes as the 'battle of imaginations' between biographer and subject has been manifest in the resort to fictive practices in contemporary biography. In reviewing the writing about biography, one might profit by reflecting on novels that take dilemmas of biography as their subject—William Golding (*The Paper Men*, 1984) on the irritated retreat from analysis of a creative writer; Bernard Malamud (*Dubin's Lives*, 1979) and Penelope Lively (*According to Mark*, 1984) on the limits of self-knowledge in shaping the biographer's perceptions; Peter Ackroyd (*Chatterton*, 1987) building a fiction on an historical figure, and so on.

More to the purpose here, however, is the way working biographers incorporate the techniques of fiction into their life-writing—often overtly—to highlight and to resolve the familiar methodological dilemmas. Peter Ackroyd's adoption, in his lives of Dickens, Blake, and T. S. Eliot,[68] of the narrative omniscience of the novelist in facing those gaps and silences about which the biographer can never properly know is commonly remarked. More interesting has been the appearance of the biographer as a character within his/her text. Not quite a fiction at first—see, for instance, Andrew Field's insistent interrogation of Nabokov[69]—more recently these alter-ego narrators have taken on more autonomous life. The purpose behind the creation of such fictional alternative 'authors' has been to dramatize the problems of biography within the text, and to highlight the way speaking positions are defined in the act of writing.

Brian Matthews, in his idiosyncratic *Louisa*,[70] creates an alter-ego for 'the biographer', who debates with him the meanings of silences, who invents bridges for the gaps in the evidence, and whose dialogue about the meaning of Louisa Lawson's life foregrounds the hidden question of every biography: who is speaking, and for whom? Drusilla Modjeska's *Poppy*[71]—

[67] Richard Holmes, *Dr Johnson and Mr Savage* (London, 1994), p. 230.

[68] Peter Ackroyd, *Dickens* (London, 1990); *Blake* (London, 1995); *T. S. Eliot* (London, 1984).

[69] Andrew Field, *Nabokov: His Life in Part* (New York, 1977, reprinted Harmondsworth, 1978).

[70] Brian Matthews, *Louisa* (Melbourne, 1987).

[71] Drusilla Modjeska, *Poppy* (Melbourne, 1990).

a book which, by refusing to define itself as biography or fiction, interrogates the limitations of genre—is preoccupied with voices. It deals with the relations between a mother and daughter. The quest of the mother for her own life, her own voice, is in creative interaction (and tension) with the task of the author (daughter) in establishing a speaking position. In the process, family dynamics, the logocentric constraints of the 'masculine' voice of academic analysis, and the imperative of understanding the language of women are illuminated. Matthews and Modjeska are writing not only life-stories, but also challenging methodological essays on biography.

The explicit use of fictional techniques to foreground, and to stimulate debate about, the methodology of contemporary biography, as Matthews and Modjeska have done, leads to difficulty when a fictional conceit becomes a seamless part of the narrative. This was highlighted by the controversy sparked by Edmund Morris's *Dutch: A Memoir of Ronald Reagan*.[72] Morris borrows cinematic technique, creating a montage of fact and fiction, and inventing himself as an ever-present observer within the 'story' of Reagan's achievements: the Boswell to Reagan's Johnson. Critics saw clearly what Matthews and Modjeska were about (and both books won awards): Morris, on the other hand, provoked deep unease:

> Is this some new literary genre with its own intellectual integrity or merely an artful attempt to make duplicity respectable? [. . .] Should *Dutch* even be placed in bookstores without a clear statement within the text itself that identifies the fictional and non-fictional sections and sources? [. . .] *Dutch* will make history by defying the very standards that make history worth knowing.[73]

The point that Holmes, Matthews, and Modjeska make is that we must acknowledge the implication of the biographer in the story: Morris shows what happens when that is taken too far. In modernist biography, interpretation went on behind the scenes: Edel, for instance, whom we've seen to be a vigorous advocate of psychoanalytic theory as a biographical tool, argued that once motivation is understood the biography should be written 'as if psychoanalysis never existed'.[74] Now, however, the acknowledgement of interpretation as part of the story and the implication of the biographer in the text has led to what one commentator called 'biography with the utility services on the outside [. . .] like Richard Rogers's Centre Pompidou'.[75] In consequence, methodological problems are brought to the

---

[72] Edmund Morris, *Dutch: A Memoir of Ronald Reagan* (New York, 1999).

[73] Joseph P. Ellis, 'Playing the Role of a Lifetime', *Guardian Weekly*, 14–20 October, 1999.

[74] Leon Edel, 'The Biographer and Psychoanalysis', *International Journal of Psychoanalysis*, XLVI (1961), 458–66.

[75] Ian McKillop, 'Vignettes: Leavis, Biography and the Body', in Gould and Staley, ed., *Writing the Lives of Writers*, pp. 293–301, at p. 298.

surface, and some of the most fruitful commentaries on life-writing emerge within biographies, rather than (as was common in the modernist period) as separate critical essays. The self-reflexive imperative in current biography underlies both the stream of first-person reflection on what to make of evidence and silence (see, for instance, Modjeska's reflections on understanding the gaps in Grace Cossington Smith's life)[76] and the increasing tendency to include discussion of—and implicit dialogue with the reader about—authorial judgement and intention within a biography (see, for instance, the 'bookend' chapters on biography in Hermione Lee's *Virginia Woolf*).[77] Working biographers continue to provide the best critical commentary on life-writing, and it is no longer in conferences, journal articles, anthologies or essays, but in the self-reflexive prose of contemporary biography that the most interesting writing about writing biography is to be found.

---

[76] Drusilla Modjeska, *Stravinsky's Lunch* (Sydney, 1999), pp. 203–340.
[77] Hermione Lee, *Virginia Woolf* (London, 1996), pp. 3–40 and 768–72.

Index